TEACHER EDITION

ZANER-BLOSER
Spell It–Write!

Karen R. Harris, Ed.D.
Steve Graham, Ed.D.
Jerry Zutell, Ph.D.

J. Richard Gentry, Ph.D.

GRADE **4**

A SPELLING PROCESS FOR WRITERS

WITHDRAWN

If you want to make a difference you need a different kind of program: Spell It–Write!

See the difference: Spell It–Write! versus other spelling programs

Confident, capable writers versus "Friday test spellers"

Real spelling growth shows in students' writing, not just on spelling tests. *Spell It–Write!* encourages kids to write fluently, proofread their own work, and learn how to spell any word that they want or need to write.

Kids who hunt for new words to learn versus kids who study only assigned words

Good spellers don't limit their learning to assigned words—they have a natural desire to learn new words and use them in writing. *Spell It–Write!* helps students become "word hunters" who go beyond the basics and develop the habit of learning to spell new words.

A word list that fits your needs versus the usual textbook word list

Most spelling programs teach pattern words and high-frequency words. However, many teachers believe students need to study words misspelled in their writing and words from their reading and curriculum. *Spell It–Write!* combines the strengths of all these word lists.

Kids who take charge of their own progress versus kids who only complete assigned activities and tests

How can kids become more responsible and motivated spellers? It's easier with *Spell It–Write!* As you page through this book, notice how kids can be actively involved at each step of the learning process, from choosing some of their own spelling words and practice activities, to setting personal learning goals and charting their own success.

Practice that includes games, manipulatives, teamwork, and fun versus practice based on seatwork alone

Spell It–Write! gives kids a chance to get out of their seats and interact with each other. In addition to excellent practice activities in the student book, the program offers games, manipulatives, and discovery learning activities that make spelling fun and keep students coming back for more.

Program components

1 **Student Edition**

Provides core word lists **plus** the encouragement kids need to hunt for new words to learn, practice their spelling, proofread their writing, and become confident, capable spellers and writers.

2 **Teacher Edition**

Makes instruction flexible and easy to manage. Puts more spelling words at your fingertips. Introduces a repertoire of activities that work with **any** word list. Includes quick and easy ways to teach students who have different needs.

3 **Teacher Resource Book**

Offers a wide array of reproducibles, including word lists for different ability levels, content area word lists, home newsletters in both English and Spanish, and more.

4 **Games**

Help students enjoy practice with a spelling buddy. Games have a write-on, wipe-clean surface with simple directions printed on the back. There are four games for each grade. Two copies of each game are included.

Manipulatives

5 **Hands-on Word Sort Card Book**

Helps students discover and use spelling patterns. As students sort the cards into groups with shared patterns, they engage in critical thinking and hands-on learning.

6 **Flip Folders**

Make spelling practice easy and fun. Based on a research-proven study technique. Five folders are included.

See the difference
The student edition

Build a better, stronger word list based on three important sources

1 Pattern Words and Strategy Words

Did you know that 89% of the words students most often write conform to common spelling patterns? The word lists in our student edition make it easy to introduce these patterns in the appropriate grades. Word lists are also included to target important spelling strategies.

2 Teacher Words

Teachers can choose words from their curriculum to add to any unit word list, or they can rely on the extra words in **More Words for Hungry Word Hunters** (in both the teacher and student edition).

3 Student Words

Each student can personalize the unit word list to include words misspelled in writing, words from reading, and words from the curriculum. The program's **Words I Need to Know How to Spell** journal helps students keep track of words that they need and want to learn.

Words I Need to Know How to Spell appears in the back of the softcover student edition. A separate journal is available for users of the hardcover edition.

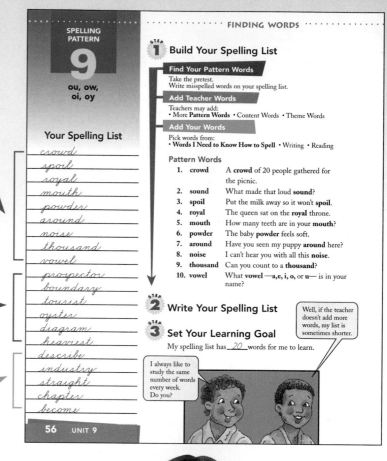

SPELLING PATTERN

9

ou, ow, oi, oy

Your Spelling List

crowd
spoil
royal
mouth
powder
around
noise
thousand
vowel

prospector
boundary
tourist
oyster
diagram
heaviest

describe
industry
straight
chapter
become

56 UNIT 9

FINDING WORDS

STEP 1 Build Your Spelling List

Find Your Pattern Words
Take the pretest.
Write misspelled words on your spelling list.

Add Teacher Words
Teachers may add:
• More **Pattern Words** • Content Words • Theme Words

Add Your Words
Pick words from:
• **Words I Need to Know How to Spell** • Writing • Reading

Pattern Words

1.	crowd	A **crowd** of 20 people gathered for the picnic.
2.	sound	What made that loud **sound**?
3.	spoil	Put the milk away so it won't **spoil**.
4.	royal	The queen sat on the **royal** throne.
5.	mouth	How many teeth are in your **mouth**?
6.	powder	The baby **powder** feels soft.
7.	around	Have you seen my puppy **around** here?
8.	noise	I can't hear you with all this **noise**.
9.	thousand	Can you count to a **thousand**?
10.	vowel	What **vowel** —a,e, i, o, or u— is in your name?

STEP 2 Write Your Spelling List

STEP 3 Set Your Learning Goal

My spelling list has _20_ words for me to learn.

> Well, if the teacher doesn't add more words, my list is sometimes shorter.

> I always like to study the same number of words every week. Do you?

Z4

The inset textbook page (INSPECTING WORDS):

4 Explore the Spelling Pattern
Sorting Words

A. Sort the **Pattern Words** into four groups. Use the vowels in each word and the words below to guide your sort. Make sure you write each **Pattern Word** once.

Try sorting the **Pattern Words** in other ways. How many words are verbs?

1. cr**ow**d	2. s**ou**nd	3. sp**oi**l	4. r**oy**al
crowd	sound	spoil	royal
powder	mouth	noise	
vowel	around		
	thousand		

B. With a partner, do a word hunt. Look for other words that have the vowel sound you hear in **crowd**, spelled **ow** or **ou**, and words that have the vowel sound you hear in **spoil**, spelled **oi** or **oy**. Sort the words you find and add them to your lists.

5 Focus on Word Study
Changes in Spelling

The word **royal** comes from the ancient Latin word **rex**, meaning "king." The word changed as it passed from one language to another. In Old French, **royal** was spelled **roial** because the French word for king is **roi**.

1. Read these names: **Roy, Regina, Rex, Jeffrey, Rebecca.** Write the three names that are related to the word **royal**.

   Roy
   Regina
   Rex

2. Now write a last name that you think is related to a job, such as **Baker**.

   Smith

Spelling Pattern

· Listen to **crowd** and **sound**. The vowel sound you hear in these words is spelled in different ways: **ow**, as in **crowd**, and **ou**, as in **sound**.

· Listen to **spoil** and **royal**. The vowel sound you hear in **spoil** and the first vowel sound you hear in **royal** are the same, but they are spelled in different ways: **oi**, as in **spoil**, and **oy**, as in **royal**.

UNIT 9 57

Deepen kids' understandings of important spelling patterns and strategies

● Explore the patterns and strategies that make spelling work

Help kids see how spelling works. Sort words to discover word patterns. Explore how words that kids know can help them spell new words. Watch for the "aha!" as kids understand spelling better.

● Extend knowledge with word study

Word study helps students learn how features such as the meaning and history of words affect their spelling. It's also interesting and fun!

See the difference

The student edition

Give students the practice options they need to master their word lists

Help students develop a repertoire of practice options

Games, manipulatives, partner activities—this program offers lots of ways to give kids the practice they really need. All these activities work with **any** word list.

Practice important patterns and strategies

The student edition also includes an activity to reinforce the pattern or strategy taught in each unit. This activity helps you make sure students learn important spelling concepts as well as words.

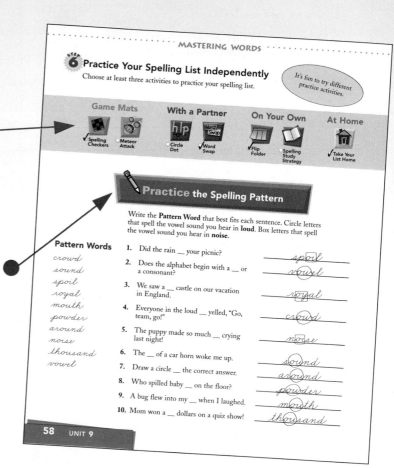

MASTERING WORDS

6 Practice Your Spelling List Independently

Choose at least three activities to practice your spelling list.

It's fun to try different practice activities.

Game Mats
- Spelling Checkers
- Meteor Attack

With a Partner
- Circle Dot
- Word Swap

On Your Own
- Flip Folder
- Spelling Study Strategy

At Home
- Take Your List Home

Practice the Spelling Pattern

Write the **Pattern Word** that best fits each sentence. Circle letters that spell the vowel sound you hear in **loud**. Box letters that spell the vowel sound you hear in **noise**.

Pattern Words

crowd
sound
spoil
royal
mouth
powder
around
noise
thousand
vowel

1. Did the rain __ your picnic? — *spoil*
2. Does the alphabet begin with a __ or a consonant? — *vowel*
3. We saw a __ castle on our vacation in England. — *royal*
4. Everyone in the loud __ yelled, "Go, team, go!" — *crowd*
5. The puppy made so much __ crying last night! — *noise*
6. The __ of a car horn woke me up. — *sound*
7. Draw a circle __ the correct answer. — *around*
8. Who spilled baby __ on the floor? — *powder*
9. A bug flew into my __ when I laughed. — *mouth*
10. Mom won a __ dollars on a quiz show! — *thousand*

58 UNIT 9

Go beyond the Friday test with proofreading, writing, and goal setting

Encourage students to proofread and transfer spelling skills to their writing

Spell It–Write! offers two types of proofreading practice: (1) kids proofread a controlled sample in the student book, and (2) kids proofread their own writing for similar errors. The result? Students are better able to transfer their proofreading skills and spelling knowledge to their writing because they have more help with this important, final step.

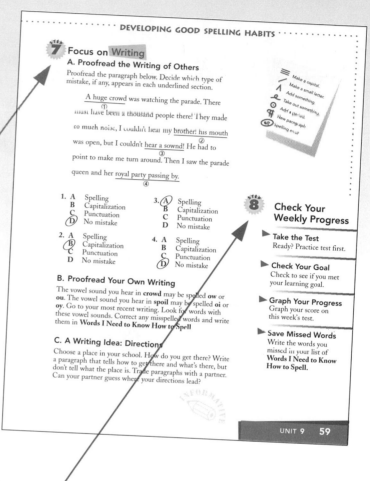

STEP 7 Focus on Writing

A. Proofread the Writing of Others
Proofread the paragraph below. Decide which type of mistake, if any, appears in each underlined section.

A huge crowd was watching the parade. There must have been a thousand people there! They made so much noise, I couldn't hear my brother! his mouth was open, but I couldn't hear a sownd! He had to point to make me turn around. Then I saw the parade queen and her royal party passing by.

1. A Spelling
   B Capitalization
   C Punctuation
   D No mistake

2. A Spelling
   B Capitalization
   C Punctuation
   D No mistake

3. A Spelling
   B Capitalization
   C Punctuation
   D No mistake

4. A Spelling
   B Capitalization
   C Punctuation
   D No mistake

B. Proofread Your Own Writing
The vowel sound you hear in **crowd** may be spelled **ow** or **ou**. The vowel sound you hear in **spoil** may be spelled **oi** or **oy**. Go to your most recent writing. Look for words with these vowel sounds. Correct any misspelled words and write them in **Words I Need to Know How to Spell**

C. A Writing Idea: Directions
Choose a place in your school. How do you get there? Write a paragraph that tells how to get there and what's there, but don't tell what the place is. Trade paragraphs with a partner. Can your partner guess where your directions lead?

STEP 8 Check Your Weekly Progress

▶ **Take the Test**
Ready? Practice test first.

▶ **Check Your Goal**
Check to see if you met your learning goal.

▶ **Graph Your Progress**
Graph your score on this week's test.

▶ **Save Missed Words**
Write the words you missed in your list of **Words I Need to Know How to Spell.**

UNIT 9 59

Help students take charge of their own development as spellers and writers

Learning to spell is an ongoing process that doesn't stop with the Friday test. Each week *Spell It–Write!* helps students set long-term goals and take positive steps to achieve them.

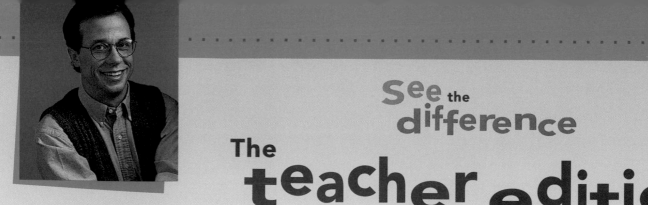

See the difference

The teacher edition

The unit opener offers options that make your program easier to manage and more responsive to students' needs

Management options streamline instruction
Notes help you individualize word lists, activities, and assessment.

Language differences get extra attention
Expert help shows how you can meet the needs of Spanish speakers and other students acquiring English.

A wide range of spelling needs are met
Spell–It Write! makes it easy to work with all the spellers in every class.

SPELLING STRATEGY **20** **Using a Dictionary**

ENGAGING IN THE PROCESS — MATERIALS

Student Edition: Pages 102–105   Teacher Edition: Pages T102A–T105

Materials to help students practice their spelling lists:
- Flip Folders
- Copies of **Flip Folder Practice Sheet** (**Teacher Resource Book**, page 51)
- Take Your List Home (in *Spell It–Write!*)
- Home News, **Teacher Resource Book**, pages 93 in English and 94 in Spanish
- Games Mats Featured in This Unit: **Spelling Checkers, Spelling Soccer**

ENGAGING IN THE PROCESS — GOALS

SPELLING GOALS

Students will
- understand that a dictionary is a valuable spelling tool.
- use a dictionary to find other forms of base words.
- explore similar spellings and meanings of words in English and other languages.
- use the spelling process of finding words, inspecting words, and mastering words as they develop good spelling habits to become better writers.

WRITING GOALS

Students will
- proofread a writing sample.
- proofread a piece of their own writing for misspelled words that are different forms of other words.
- write expressive dialogue for a cartoon.

ENGAGING IN THE PROCESS — MANAGEMENT

Pacing	Notes	Quick Pick Management Option
Period 1 Finding Words (Steps 1–3)	If you wish to add **Teacher Words**, write them on the chalkboard. Sources for more words include: **More Words for Hungry Word Hunters** (page T102), content and theme-related words, or words of your choice.	Assign the list of **Strategy Words** to the whole class. Add the Red List (**More Words for Hungry Word Hunters**, student page 168) for a longer list. Add the Blue List (**More Words for Hungry Word Hunters**) for a more challenging list.
Period 2 Inspecting Words (Steps 4 and 5)	Students write the **Strategy Words** to complete **Explore the Spelling Strategy**.	Assign **Explore the Spelling Strategy** and **Focus on Word Study**.
Period 3 Mastering Words (Step 6) **Period 4** Developing Good Spelling Habits (Step 7)	These two periods can be allocated between selected **Mastering Words** activities and proofreading and writing activities in **Focus on Writing**.	Assign two or three activities to the whole class. Familiarize students with choosing their own activities at their own pace.
Period 5 Assessment (Step 8)	Gradually try different peer-testing options to find the style that best fits your class.	Test the class on the same, whole-class list.

T102A UNIT 20

ENGAGING IN THE PROCESS — INDIVIDUAL NEEDS

Understanding Language Differences

Spanish Speakers

Students from Spanish-speaking backgrounds who are familiar with Spanish dictionaries may encounter some initial confusion when they pick up an English dictionary. Although Spanish and English dictionaries are basically similar, there are some differences. Most Spanish dictionaries treat **ch** as a separate letter—the fourth letter of the alphabet (between **c** and **d**). Similarly, the combination **ll** is treated as a separate letter falling between **l** and **m**. This means that **champú** ("shampoo") comes after **curso** ("course") and that **llama** follows **luz** ("light"). If your students are already literate in Spanish, ask them to look up in an English dictionary words beginning with **ch** (**chair, child,** and so on) to be sure they understand how an English dictionary is organized.

Helping Students Acquiring English

Display a dictionary, and discuss its organization and features with students. Pair less fluent speakers with more fluent partners. Give each pair a dictionary, and ask them to look up each **Strategy Word** and discuss its meaning. Refer students to **Strategies for Checking Your Spelling** in the back of the student edition for a sample dictionary entry.

Meeting Diverse Needs

Less Able Spellers

An effective technique in teaching students with special needs is called "reinforcement, contingent upon performance." For example, providing incentives, such as stickers, may result in improvement on weekly spelling tests. Similarly, awarding points for using cooperative learning activities as intended may also lead to better scores on weekly spelling quizzes.

Children can also be encouraged to develop their own system of self-reinforcement and determine for themselves how they will reward themselves for meeting their weekly spelling goal.

More Able Spellers

Challenge students to use the **Strategy Words** to build a crossword puzzle. Encourage students to include other forms of the words they find in the dictionary. For clues, students should use the dictionary definitions of the words they include. (**Teacher Resource Book** page 54 provides a crossword puzzle grid.)

ENGAGING IN THE PROCESS — INVOLVING FAMILIES

Ask students to copy their lists in the **Take Your List Home** section of the *Spell It–Write!* Home News page for this lesson. Not only does this page provide a convenient way for families to share a student's spelling list, but it also provides a number of opportunities for families to be involved in students' spelling growth. It has a statement of the week's spelling pattern or strategy, a valuable spelling study strategy, and a suggested home spelling practice activity.

Teacher Resource Book, page 93

Teacher Resource Book, page 94

UNIT 20 **T102B**

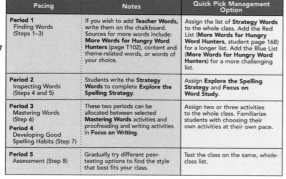

Word lists and lessons expand to fit your needs

More words give you more options
- The **Red List** offers words below grade level.
- The **Blue List** offers words above grade level.
- **Content-Area Words** and **Other Words** reinforce the unit pattern or strategy.

Mini-lessons work with your schedule
Students can complete **Explore the Spelling Strategy** on their own, or you can introduce the strategy with a mini-lesson.

FINDING WORDS

 STEP 1 Build Your Spelling List

Students will build their spelling lists with **Strategy Words, Teacher Words,** and **Your Words.** Students should study a minimum of twelve new words each week.

Find Your Strategy Words
- Pretest the students on these words.
- Tell students to write each misspelled pretest word on their spelling lists.

Add Teacher Words
- Select words for students to add to their spelling lists. Choose words from **More Words for Hungry Word Hunters** (on this page and on student page 168), words related to a theme or content area, or words students often misspell.

Add Your Words
- Ask students to pick words from their list of **Words I Need to Know How to Spell** and their writing.
- Tell students to write these words on their spelling lists.

 STEP 2 Write Your Spelling List

Remind students to verify all spellings. (Ask students to see **Strategies for Checking Your Spelling** in the back of the student edition.)

STEP 3 Set Your Learning Goal

Tell students to count the words on their spelling lists. This total is their learning goal. It may vary depending on ability, individual goals, and the difficulty of spelling words.

MORE WORDS FOR HUNGRY WORD HUNTERS

RED LIST Strategy Words Below Level	BLUE LIST Strategy Words Above Level	Science Strategy Words
begin	argue	behavior
brave	buffalo	digestion
busy	describe	hardness
carry	foggy	prospector
lady	freeze	
lie	industry	**Social Studies Strategy Words**
pretty	marry	boundary
think	panel	crafts
tooth	plod	tourist
write	straight	

These lists also appear on page 168 in the student edition and page 26 in the Teacher Resource Book.

STRATEGY MINI-LESSON

NOTE: The **Explore the Spelling Strategy** activity on page 103 is a self-directed mini-lesson. If you wish to supplement that activity with direct instruction, use the following mini-lesson. Dictionaries, as available, should be distributed for use with the mini-lesson.

* **Help** students brainstorm what uses a dictionary may have. (Possible responses: *to find the meaning of a word; to check spelling*)

* **Tell** students they can also use a dictionary to spell other forms of words. Explain that another form of **country** is **countries.** Provide dictionaries and ask students to look up **countries.** Ask several volunteers to explain how and where they found the word countries. (Possible response: *The word **countries** can be found by looking up **country;** **countries** is found within the entry for **country.**)* If no one can find **countries,** model the procedure to follow.

INSPECTING WORDS

* **Divide** the class into groups. Assign each group one of the remaining **Strategy Words** on page 102. Challenge students to see how many other forms they can find in the dictionary for the assigned word. Make a list on the chalkboard of the words they find. Emphasize that to find these words in a dictionary, they must look up the simplest form of the word.

* **Use** students' responses to discuss the types of words that might be found under a given entry word. These might include some kinds of plurals, some words with **-ed** and **-ing** endings, and other parts of speech.

* **Ask** students to read the **Spelling Strategy** on page 103 with you. Call on several volunteers to summarize the **Spelling Strategy** in their own words.

(Student page reproduction — left)

FINDING WORDS

SPELLING STRATEGY 20 Using a Dictionary

Your Spelling List

STEP 1 Build Your Spelling List

Find Your Strategy Words
Take the pretest.
Write misspelled words on your spelling list.

Add Teacher Words
Teachers may add:
• More Strategy Words • Content Words • Theme Words

Add Your Words
Pick words from:
• Words I Need to Know How to Spell • Writing • Reading

Strategy Words
1. country   My cousin lives out in the **country,** far away from any city.
2. zero   One minus one equals **zero.**
3. scare   Loud thunder will **scare** our dog.
4. speak   Did you **speak** to the new girl today?
5. rough   Sara hurt her knee on the **rough** rocks.
6. picnic   Who invited ants to our **picnic?**
7. company   My bird keeps me **company** at home.
8. scar   Shawn has a **scar** on his chin.
9. gentle   Please be **gentle** with the baby.
10. reply   Send a **reply** to the invitation soon.

STEP 2 Write Your Spelling List

I always go through stuff I've written, especially in language arts and science, for words I need to know how to spell.

STEP 3 Set Your Learning Goal
My spelling list has _____ words for me to learn.

What's a good way to find words for your spelling list?

(Student page reproduction — right)

INSPECTING WORDS

STEP 4 Explore the Spelling Strategy
Looking Up Words

A. A dictionary lists entry words alphabetically. Looking up a word in the dictionary can help you spell other forms of the word. The words in each item below are other forms of a **Strategy Word.** Write the **Strategy Word** you would look up in the dictionary to find these other forms.

1. roughly, roughness	rough
2. picnicking, picnicker	picnic
3. replies, replying	reply
4. scarred, scarring	scar
5. gentler, gentlest	gentle
6. zeros or zeroes	zero
7. companies	company
8. scared, scares	scare
9. countries, countryish	country
10. speaking, spoke	speak

B. Use a dictionary to find other words that have different forms. Write each word you find and its different forms.

Spelling Strategy
You can use the dictionary to find the spelling of another form of a word. You can find the spelling of **countries** by looking up **country.**

STEP 5 Focus on Word Study
Words From Other Languages

If you can spell **zero,** you are writing in three languages! In English, French, and Italian, **zero** has the same spelling and the same meaning.

Compare the spellings of these number words. Which letters are the same in all three languages?

English	French	Spanish	
1. one	un	uno	n
2. three	trois	tres	t and r
3. six	six	seis	s and i

STEP 4 Explore the Spelling Strategy

Looking Up Words
This activity is a self-directed mini-lesson on this week's **Spelling Strategy.**

STEP 5 Focus on Word Study

Words From Other Languages
This activity is intended to stimulate students' interest in words and help them become more enthusiastic word hunters.

Spelling Process Handbook
Students who need to review any part of the spelling process, including practice options, should refer to the Spelling Process Handbook (pages 7–21).

Spell It—Write!
A spelling Process for writers

Each unit involves kids in a four-part spelling process

1 **Finding Words** (first unit page)
Students find words they do not know how to spell in their reading and writing, in their curriculum (words suggested by their teachers), and in *Spell It–Write!*

2 **Inspecting Words** (second unit page)
Students inspect words to learn important spelling patterns and strategies that make it easier to spell the words they use in their writing.

3 **Mastering Words** (third unit page)
A wide array of spelling activities and games help students practice and remember new words.

4 **Developing Good Spelling Habits** (last unit page)
Students use strategies for proofreading and word hunting. In this way, they make direct connections to their writing and develop good spelling habits.

Managing the Spelling Process Through the Week

Period 1 **Finding Words** Steps 1-3 in each unit	If you wish to add **Teacher Words**, write them on the chalkboard. Sources for more words include **More Words for Hungry Word Hunters** (in the teacher and student edition), content or theme-related words, or words of your choice.
Period 2 **Inspecting Words** Steps 4 and 5 in each unit	Students complete **Explore the Spelling Pattern** or **Explore the Spelling Strategy** and **Focus on Word Study**.
Period 3 **Mastering Words** Step 6 in each unit	These two periods may be allocated between selected **Mastering Words** activities and the proofreading and writing activities in **Focus on Writing**.
Period 4 **Developing Good Spelling Habits** Step 7 in each unit	
Period 5 **Assessment** Step 8 in each unit	Select and manage the testing option (page Z12) that best fits your class.

Quick Pick

Management Option

The Quick Pick Management Option streamlines instruction

The **Quick Pick Management Option** streamlines the three basic operations of the spelling process:

1. Building the spelling list (Steps 1-3 in each unit)

2. Creating a plan for independent spelling practice (Step 6 in each unit)

3. Peer testing or other alternative assessment formats (Step 8 in each unit)

You can activate these three operations when you think your class is ready.

When you are ready to take those steps with your class, the authors recommend you first concentrate on

constructing a spelling list, and then develop a comfortable system for assessing a classroom of individual lists. Developing a repertoire of activities and games to practice any spelling list should be a consistent goal for your students to build toward from the very first day.

The **Quick Pick Management Option** allows you to implement *Spell It–Write!* at your own pace. With the **Quick Pick**, you will manage the program easily from the first day of school. And you can integrate parts of the spelling process when you feel the time is right.

Quick Pick Management Option	
Period 1 **Finding Words** Steps 1-3 in each unit	Introduce the list of **Pattern** or **Strategy Words** to the whole class. Add the Red List for a longer list. Add the Blue List for a more challenging list. (See **More Words for Hungry Word Hunters** in the teacher edition or student edition.)
Period 2 **Inspecting Words** Steps 4 and 5 in each unit	Assign **Explore the Spelling Pattern** or **Explore the Spelling Strategy**. Assign **Focus on Word Study**.
Period 3 **Mastering Words** Step 6 in each unit	Choose and assign two or three activities to the whole class. Familiarize students with choosing their own activities at their pace.
Period 4 **Developing Good Spelling Habits** Step 7 in each unit	
Period 5 **Assessment** Step 8 in each unit	Test the class on the same, whole-class list.

Spell It–Write!
and assessment

One measure of the success of a spelling process program is the number of different spelling lists in your class at the end of a spelling lesson. Your students are likely then to be truly engaged in building their own lists and compiling a powerful reservoir of words and strategies for their writing. Monitoring these individual spelling lists is best done by **Peer Testing** (Option 1 below).

The **Quick Pick** (Option 2 below) offers a familiar streamlined approach to assessment. It allows you to get used to *Spell It–Write!* before fully implementing all aspects of the process. **Alternative Assessment** (Option 3 below) provides a broader view. It combines weekly informal assessment with periodic assessment of students' ability to use the spelling patterns they have studied after every eight units.

Assessment Options			
	Attributes	**Frequency**	**How**
Option 1: Peer Testing	author recommended; manages individualized spelling lists	every week	final testing done by pairs of students; can be modified for various levels of teacher control
Option 2: Quick Pick	easy to manage; familiar	every week	teacher-directed; traditional testing and grading
Option 3: Alternative Assessment	assesses global success in the spelling process, not just with weekly lists	every eight weeks	**Check Your Progress** to assess understanding of patterns; **Strategy Assessment** to assess understanding and use of strategies

Option 1: Peer Testing

There are many variations on the theme of peer testing. It is important that you select the one that is comfortable for you.

Buddy Testing

At the beginning of a spelling process unit, assign spelling buddies to work with each other on building, practicing, and assessing their spelling lists. Familiarity with each other's lists increases word knowledge and makes pronunciation of the words at test-taking time more proficient and reliable.

Combining Whole Class and Peer Testing

This is a modified peer-testing technique. Assign the **Strategy Words** or **Pattern Words** as a whole-class exercise that will be tested in common at the end of the unit. After testing these words, ask partners to peer test each other on the self-selected words or **Teacher Words** on their lists that are not in common.

Peer Testing Ground Rules

- Students should refer to their **Spelling Process Handbook** when they have a question about giving a test to a partner, taking a test with a partner, or correcting a test.

- Partners should be at similar reading levels so they can fluently read each other's lists.

- Partners should be compatible and work well without supervision.

- Partners should take turns testing first.

- Students should be told it's okay to ask for help if needed.

- Parent concerns should be addressed honestly if they arise.

Option 2: Quick Pick

The easiest way to create a class spelling list is to add Blue List and/or Red List Words to the unit's **Pattern** or **Strategy Words**. (See **More Words for Hungry Word Hunters** for each unit, either in your teacher edition or at the back of the student edition.) Students then practice the assigned list for the remainder of the unit and are tested as a whole class on those words.

Option 3: Alternative Assessment

Formal Assessment

Check Your Progress and **Strategy Assessment** provide a useful snapshot of how well your students are incorporating these essential attitudes and skills for developing good spelling and writing consciousness.

- **Check Your Progress** is an excellent way to assess students' progress in using essential spelling patterns. It occurs after every eight units.

- **Strategy Assessment** helps you assess how students are progressing in their use and awareness of the strategies they have learned. (The **Strategy Assessment** pages are in the **Teacher Resource Book.** See pages 120 and 121.)

  Make one copy of the **Strategy Assessment** pages for each student. These checklists will help you evaluate individual student progress in specific areas. The completed pages provide information to help individualize instruction and to guide parent and student conferences.

Informal Assessment

For suggestions on ongoing informal assessment, see teacher edition pages Z14-Z15.

assessing
spelling
growth
in student writing

Assessing Growth in Spelling Conferences

Individual conferences don't need to be lengthy, but results will be better if conferences are held regularly with a specific purpose in mind.

Focus on a recent piece of a student's writing.

- Ask the student to identify one word he/she thinks may be misspelled.

- Ask what he/she was thinking when he/she wrote the word. (Children's misspellings often have an underlying logic.)

- Write the correct spelling above the student's misspelling. Compare the spellings.

- Focus on what is correct about the misspelling and help the student understand how he/she can remember to spell the word correctly in the future. You may be able to relate the word to a spelling generalization or suggest that the student practice the word with the **Flip Folder**.

- Suggest that the student write the word correctly in **Words I Need to Know How to Spell**.

Assessing Misspellings

You may be surprised to discover that a student has spelled the same word differently in the same writing sample. Reasons for this phenomenon include

- The student may still be learning the word and not have it fluently under control.

- The student may have used different information and/or strategies to generate each spelling.

- The student's attention may have been on other aspects of the writing process when he/she generated the different spellings.

Bringing such examples to students' attention can help them address the problem.

- Focus on recent pieces of writing. Ask the students to check first drafts for misspelled words.

- Ask them to check the same writing samples for other occurrences of the same words.

- Discuss why they might have spelled these words in different ways.

- Suggest using **Flip Folders** to practice the targeted words.

Assessing Growth Through Word Sorting

Word sorting is a powerful way to assess whether students have fully understood and internalized the patterns they have studied. (See the **Hands-on Word Sort Book** for more information on word sorting.)

- Use the **Hands-on Word Sort Cards** from a unit already studied to work with students individually.

- Lay out the Master Words and briefly review the patterns and categories. Give the student the cards and ask him/her to do the sort independently. (To make the task more demanding, you may wish to do a **blind sort,** i.e., say the word without showing it to the student until he/she has chosen where to place the word.)

- Note both how **accurately** and how **easily** the student is able to do the sort. If the student misplaces several words or works very slowly, demonstrate the sort and ask the student to try again. Observe to decide whether to continue working with the student or to plan for small group or individual review of the spelling pattern.

Note: Blank cards are provided in each **Hands-on Word Sort Card Book.** Use these blanks to create word sort cards to assess students' retention of a variety of contrasting spelling patterns (e.g., different spellings of long vowel sounds, unexpected spellings, etc.).

Assessing Growth Through Words I Need to Know How to Spell

Students' lists of **Words I Need to Know How to Spell** are an excellent resource for words to be added to weekly lists. It is also important to monitor that students are choosing words wisely, adding them to their weekly lists, and successfully learning them.

- Check **Graph Your Progress** to decide if a student has been learning a reasonable number of words each week.

- Together with the student, look over the words the student has entered in **Words I Need to Know How to Spell.** Look for very easy words and for words that are well beyond the student's developmental level.

- Check to see how many words—and which words— are marked as studied and learned. Discuss with the student why he/she chose some of the words and where he/she found them.

- If you determine that the student has had some difficulty in making appropriate choices, review the reasons and procedures for selecting words and provide advice for choosing words in the future.

The authors and research
behind the program

Karen R. Harris, Ed.D.
Steve Graham, Ed.D.

Dr. Karen R. Harris and Dr. Steve Graham are professors in the College of Education at the University of Maryland. In addition to being coauthors of **Spell It–Write!**, *they have written many books and articles, including* **Making the Writing Process Work: Strategies for Composition and Self-Regulation**, *a textbook used by university Education Departments nationwide.*

Self-Regulated Learning

The same kinds of self-regulation strategies that put children in control of their writing can help them take ownership of the process of learning to spell. For example, students can be actively engaged in choosing the words that they need and want to learn to spell. They can write those words in a personal word journal, choosing a few words from their journals to study and learn every week.

Developing the ability to understand and regulate their own behavior is an important undertaking for children, and it is a key ingredient in effective writing and spelling. Without fluent spelling skills, students continue to struggle with the mechanics of the writing process and cannot focus attention and energy on what and why they are writing.

Jerry Zutell, Ph.D.

Dr. Jerry Zutell is a professor in the College of Education at The Ohio State University. A speaker at national and international conferences, he is best known for his research on word sorts and word webs. In addition to being a coauthor of **Spell It–Write!**, *Dr. Zutell has published his work in many well-known journals and books, such as* **Reading Teacher**, **Reading and Writing Quarterly**, **Language Arts**, *and* **NCTE's Encyclopedia of English Studies and Language Arts**.

Word Sorts

Patterns help all of us make sense of our world. They are a source of enjoyment and satisfaction, like the rhythm and rhyme in song and poetry. Teachers can use word sorts to help students see and construct the patterns in English spelling. Here's how:

1. Begin with words students know. Encourage students to find words in their own reading and writing.

2. Encourage discovery. See if students can find the pattern.

3. Use word cards. Active manipulation of the cards makes it easier for students to notice important details.

4. Work with more than one spelling pattern at a time so that students must decide how the patterns work.

5. Encourage flexibility. There may be more than one pattern associated with a particular pronunciation (e.g., *long a* in *lane* versus *long a* in *rain*).

J. Richard Gentry, Ph.D.

In addition to being a co-author of **Spell It–Write!**, *Dr. Gentry is author of the celebrated book,* **Spel...Is a Four-Letter Word**. *That book, and his recent books,* **Teaching Kids to Spell** *and* **My Kid Can't Spell**, *are widely read by teachers, parents, and others interested in spelling today. In the past two years, Dr. Gentry has worked with teachers in twenty-six states to help promote better instructional practices for spelling and literacy.*

Spelling and Literacy

Spelling plays a vital role throughout students' literacy development. What's more, research shows that for most students spelling cannot be "caught" through wide reading or simply correcting misspellings in their own writing. Spelling must be taught.

Spelling and Emergent Literacy

Recently researchers discovered the importance of spelling in emergent literacy. We now know that two kinds of knowledge can predict a child's success in reading: (1) knowledge of the alphabet and (2) phonemic awareness. These are the same two areas that are focused on in kindergarten and first grade spelling.

Spelling and Later Literacy

Spelling and word study improve reading and writing fluency, correct pronunciation, and develop vocabulary. Students are better able to understand concepts in the content areas, to clarify their own thinking, and to communicate clearly and with confidence.

ZANER-BLOSER
Spell It–Write!

A SPELLING
PROCESS
FOR WRITERS

Karen R. Harris, Ed.D.   Steve Graham, Ed.D.   Jerry Zutell, Ph.D.

J. Richard Gentry, Ph.D.

Zaner-Bloser, Inc.
Columbus, Ohio

Contributing Author

Richard Lutz, Ph.D.
Adjunct Professor,
Applied Linguistics
Georgetown University
Washington, D.C.

Program Consultants

Delores Block
Language Arts Supervisor
Round Rock, Texas

Allen Cox
Language Arts Supervisor
Fort Worth, Texas

A. John Dalmolin II
Elementary Principal
Phoenix, Arizona

Graciela Farias
Language Arts Supervisor
McAllen, Texas

Gladys Hillman-Jones
Educational Consultant
South Orange, New Jersey

Jean S. Mann
Educational Consultant
Sharon, New Hampshire

Robert McGrattan
Elementary Principal
Asheville, North Carolina

George Mundine
Elementary Principal
Houston, Texas

Fran Norris
Language Arts Director
Conroe, Texas

Patti Pace
Assistant Elementary Principal
Houston, Texas

Loretta Parker
Language Arts Supervisor
Corpus Christi, Texas

Terry Ross
Language Arts Supervisor
Round Rock, Texas

Grade Level Consultants

María A. Alanis
Chapter I Coordinator
Austin, Texas

Ella Bell
Sixth Grade Teacher
Shenandoah Junction, West Virginia

Patricia Boyd
Seventh Grade Teacher
Cheektowaga, New York

Claudia Cornett, Ph.D.
Professor, Education
Wittenberg University
Springfield, Ohio

Deborah S. Daniels
Fifth Grade Teacher
Portsmouth, Virginia

Michele Gagen
Kindergarten Teacher
Columbus, Ohio

Marlene Goodman
Second Grade Teacher
St. John, Indiana

Dominic F. Gullo, Ph.D.
Professor, Early Childhood Education
University of Wisconsin–Milwaukee
Milwaukee, Wisconsin

Nancy Hamlet
Reading Specialist
Glendale, Arizona

Beverly Hill
Fourth Grade Teacher
Booneville, Mississippi

Janice T. Jones
Prekindergarten Facilitator
Chicago, Illinois

Denise Larson
Third Grade Teacher
Portland, Oregon

Debra M. Leatherwood
Third Grade Teacher
Candler, North Carolina

Cathy Maloney
Fifth Grade Teacher
Boise, Idaho

Peter Monether
Middle School Teacher
Fitzwilliam, New Hampshire

Cheryl Prescott
First Grade Teacher
Brandon, Florida

Anita Ross
Kindergarten Teacher
Detroit, Michigan

Janet Strong
Eighth Grade Teacher
West Point, Mississippi

Mary Thomas Vallens
Fourth Grade Teacher
Irvine, California

Spanish Language Consultants

Maria M. Corsino Bolander
Houston, Texas

Amalia Hermandez
San Antonio, Texas

Lucy Herrera
Weslaco, Texas

Joan Nieto
Columbus, Ohio

Sources for word histories and etymologies include:

Ayto, John. *Dictionary of Word Origins.* New York: Arcade Publishing, 1990.
Barnhart, Robert K., ed. *The Barnhart Dictionary of Etymology.* New York: The H.W. Wilson Company, 1988.
Claiborne, Robert. *The Roots of English.* New York: Anchor Books, Doubleday, 1989.

Spell It—Write! referred to *Webster's Ninth New Collegiate Dictionary* in the development of these materials. *Webster's Ninth New Collegiate Dictionary.* Springfield, MA: Merriam-Webster Inc., 1988.

Editorial and Production Development: Brown Publishing Network

Illustrations:

Cover: Theo Rudnak
Student Edition: Ben Mahan
Game Mats: Ron Leiser

ISBN: 0-88085-387-5

Copyright © 1998 Zaner-Bloser, Inc.

Zaner-Bloser, Inc., P.O. Box 16764, Columbus, Ohio 43216-6764 (1-800-421-3018)

Printed in the United States of America

TABLE OF CONTENTS

TABLE OF CONTENTS *continued*

Welcome to *Spell It–Write!*—a new and different spelling program! You'll learn the important spelling patterns and strategies you need to know.

Learning to spell is a process. First you'll learn to find words to make a list. Then you'll inspect and master them to develop good spelling habits.

The **Spelling Process Handbook** is an important tool for making students independent *Spell It–Write!* users— and independent spellers. Within the **Handbook,** students will find valuable information on the four key parts of the spelling process:

1. **Finding Words** Includes word hunting tips and strategies to build their spelling lists.

2. **Inspecting Words**

3. **Mastering Words** Includes activities and strategies for practicing spelling words effectively on their own and with a partner.

4. **Developing Good Spelling Habits**

At the beginning of the school year, you may wish to ask students to do a "treasure hunt" in the **Spelling Process Handbook**. Distribute these questions (or questions like these) to the students and ask them to work in pairs or individually to find the answers as quickly as possible:

- Look at the **Handbook's** table of contents on page 7. What are the four main categories within the **Spelling Process Handbook**? (Response: *Finding Words, Inspecting Words, Mastering Words, and Developing Good Spelling Habits*)

- Under which of these categories would you find information on sorting words? (*under* **Inspecting Words**)

- On what pages can you find information about word hunting? (*pages 8-9*)

- How many game mats are there in this grade level? (*four*)

- Explain how to play **Circle Dot**. (*Answers will vary. The directions for this practice activity appear on page 17.*)

- On what page can you find information about taking a test with a partner? (*pages 20-21*)

Challenge students to develop other questions relating to the **Handbook** that they can share with a partner.

Spelling Process Handbook

Word Hunting

"Finding words" begins with word hunting. Word hunting will make students hungry word hunters! Students should be encouraged to hunt words—in both their writing and reading—that they want to learn how to spell.

At the beginning of the school year, you may wish to:

- Read the word hunting tips on page 9 with the students. (Consider posting these tips on a bulletin board. Students can write the words they have hunted on index cards and pin them to the bulletin board.)

- Model each word hunting tip for your students.

- Duplicate the Hungry Word Hunters bookmark in the **Teacher Resource Book** (page 5). Provide one page of bookmarks for each student to use as he/she hunts words in his/her reading. Keep remaining copies in reserve.

- Explain that students should write the words they have hunted under the first letter of the word in **Words I Need to Know How to Spell** (student pages 180-192 for softbound users; copies of **Teacher Resource Book** page 6 for hardbound users).

- Emphasize that these words are being saved in **Words I Need to Know How to Spell** so they can be put on weekly spelling lists, studied, and learned.

Review the word hunting tips regularly as needed.

Words I Need to Know How to Spell

In order to be proficient word hunters, students always need to have a handy repository for the words they find. Every directive to **Words I Need to Know How to Spell** in the student edition is meant to direct students to this repository and to make its use habitual.

Words I Need to Know How to Spell is located in the back of the softbound student book (pages 180-192). It is also available as a separate booklet, or can be made by duplicating page 6 in the **Teacher Resource Book**. You may also ask students to make their own **Words I Need to Know How to Spell** from a three-hole punched or spiral-bound notebook.

The point is for students to have a convenient, usable place to store the words they identify as those words they need to learn how to spell. Keeping a list of **Words I Need to Know How to Spell** is an important element in becoming a thoughtful, independent speller.

FINDING WORDS

Word hunting is simple—you hunt for words you need to know how to spell. You hunt words in your writing, words in your reading, and words that interest you. Good word hunters find words or spelling patterns they use often but cannot spell.

Ask yourself:

- "Do I already know how to spell this word?"
  If you can spell a word easily, hunt another word instead.
- "Do I know what this word means?"
  It's best to know what a word means before you try to learn the spelling. If a word catches your interest and you're not sure what it means, find the meaning first.

Collect the word.

Write the word in your list of **Words I Need to Know How to Spell**. Each week you will choose some of these words to learn to spell.

Check the spelling.

When you write a word in **Words I Need to Know How to Spell**, make sure you check the spelling carefully. If you copied the word from a sign or a book, compare the way you wrote the word with the sign or the book. Or use a dictionary or ask someone who knows the correct spelling.

WORD Hunting Tips

Your Writing

- As you work on a piece of writing, circle words you could not write quickly and words you think you may have misspelled.

- Ask a partner to check your writing for spelling mistakes.

- Tape an index card to your desk. Write words you are unsure of on the card.

Your Reading

- Fold a piece of notebook paper in half. Use the paper as a bookmark when you read. Write words you would like to learn how to spell on the bookmark.

- Write interesting words on self-sticking notes and stick them to the pages in your book.

Other Words

- Carry a little notebook. Write words from signs, billboards, ads, newspapers, and magazines.

Share Your Words

- Ask your teacher if you can write words you have hunted on index cards and post them in your classroom.

- Talk about words you have hunted—and why you hunted them—with a partner. Ask about the words your partner has hunted.

Save Your Words

- Remember to save words in your **Words I Need to Know How to Spell**.

Building Your Spelling List

Each week students will build a spelling list with the words they missed on their pretest (**Pattern Words** or **Strategy Words**), words teachers add to their lists from classroom study (**Teacher Words**), and words they have chosen from their lists of **Words I Need to Know How to Spell** (**Your Words**).

Emphasize these points to students about building their spelling lists:

• It is important to check the spelling of the words carefully as they record them on their spelling lists to be certain they study the correct spellings during the week. (More information on checking spelling is provided in **Strategies for Checking Your Spelling** at the back of the student edition.)

• Each type of word is important:

   Pattern and **Strategy Words** help students build knowledge about important spelling patterns and strategies. This knowledge will help them understand the English spelling system.

   Teacher Words will help them integrate spelling into other content areas.

   Your Words will help make them more effective writers as they study the words they misspell most often in their writing. The flexibility to study words students themselves find interesting and important will heighten motivation.

• It is important to keep recycling any word missed on a unit test into future spelling lists until the word is mastered.

NOTE: The **Quick Pick** management option at the start of each unit in the teacher edition (and on page Z11) provides information on managing list construction easily.

FINDING WORDS

Building Your Spelling List

> Each week, you build your spelling list. These are the words **you** will be responsible for learning that week. Your spelling list will be made up of three different kinds of words.

Pattern Words or Strategy Words

Every *Spell It—Write!* unit helps you understand an important spelling pattern or spelling strategy. At the start of each unit, you will take a pretest on **Pattern Words** or **Strategy Words**.

Write words you misspell on the pretest on your spelling list.

Teacher Words

Your teacher may give you more words to learn to spell. These could be other words that match the spelling pattern or spelling strategy, words from other subjects, or themes, or words your teacher knows you have trouble spelling.

Write words from your teacher on your spelling list.

Your Words

Pick words from your list of **Words I Need to Know How to Spell**. These are words you have hunted in your writing and your reading.

Write these words on your spelling list.

Setting Your Learning Goal

After each student has built his/her spelling list, he/she will set a learning goal for the week. That goal is simply the number of words on the individual's spelling list. This goal may vary depending on ability, individual goals, and the difficulty of the spelling words. Students should study a minimum of twelve new words each week. Each student should record his/her goal for later reference.

Setting Your Learning Goal

Each week you set a learning goal to spell all the words on your spelling list. Try to learn at least twelve words that you do not already know how to spell. Some weeks you may choose to set a higher goal.

To set your goal:

Count your words.
Count the number of words on your spelling list.

Write the number.
Record the number of words that is your goal. At the end of the unit, you will compare what you wrote to your score on your spelling test.

Sorting Words

Word sorting is an extremely effective technique for focusing students' attention on the spelling patterns—and variations among those spelling patterns—within the English spelling system. Understanding the similarities and differences among words will help students inspect words successfully, internalize the spelling system, and develop into independent spellers.

The student edition will suggest specific word sorts, but students should also be encouraged to experiment with sorting the words in other ways. While word sorts may be done by individual students, the authors suggest that students work in pairs as much as possible to discuss word placement. (The **Hands-on Word Sort Cards** from two or more units can also be combined to create multi-unit word sorts.) Other types of word sorts you may wish to try with your students include:

- **a blind word sort** One student calls a word to a partner, and the partner is asked to place the word within a defined spelling pattern category without seeing the word.

- **an open word sort** Individuals secretly decide on the criteria for the word sort and sort the words according to that criteria. Then other students are asked to define the criteria after examining the completed word sort.

Hands-on Word Sort Cards

Hands-on Word Sort Cards, both preprinted and blank, are provided for specific *Spell It–Write!* units at Grades 2 through 6. (Corresponding **Hands-on Word Sort Sheets** can be found in each grade-level **Teacher Resource Book**.) Blank word sort cards are also provided in the **Hands-on Word Sort Card Book,** and students should also be encouraged to make their own word sort cards. For more information on **Hands-on Word Sort Cards** see the **Hands-on Word Sort Card Book** for this grade level.

• INSPECTING WORDS •

Sorting WORDS

Sorting words is fun—and it helps you discover how the **Spelling Pattern** or the **Spelling Strategy** works.

Sorting words also helps you see how the words are alike—and how they are different!

You can sort words in lots of different ways.

• Sort words by comparing how they sound.

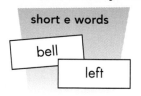

short e words
bell
left

long e words
eat
eel

• Sort words by comparing spelling patterns.

long a spelled ay
may
hay
pay

long a spelled ai
hail
pail

long a spelled a-consonant-e
tale
whale

INSPECTING WORDS

• **Sort words by comparing what they mean.**

words that name things

car
table
computer

words that name people

boy
girl
teacher
doctor

No matter how you sort words, you may have a word that doesn't fit. You can put that word under a question mark.

long a spelled ay

may
hay
pay

long a spelled ai

hail
pail

long a spelled a-consonant-e

tale
whale

?

eight

Ask your teacher about **Hands-on Word Sort Cards** and a **Hands-on Word Sort Sheet.** They are available for certain units.

What new ways can you think of to sort words?

Practicing Your Spelling List Independently

Each student will have the opportunity to choose specific activities to practice and gain mastery over his/her spelling list.

NOTE: Each practice activity has a strong, and hopefully carry-over, effect. It is important to note that these activities can be used to practice any spelling list. Both cooperative and independent activities are featured.

Activities vary from unit-to-unit to provide students with the opportunity to try different practice activities. This variety makes spelling practice more motivating, can increase actual time-on-task, and maximizes student attention to help students better retain spelling knowledge.

At the start of the school year:

• Emphasize that students should choose at least three different activities each week. These choices should be recorded in the student edition (softbound users) or on copies of **Teacher Resource Book** page 50 (hardbound users).

• Introduce and model each activity. (Directions for the four game mats featured at this grade level are provided on the game mats. Fine-point dry erase markers work best on the game mats. Directions for other practice activities appear on pages 16-18 in the student's **Spelling Process Handbook**. **Take Your List Home** is a feature of the Home News page for each unit. Home News pages in English and in Spanish can be found in the **Teacher Resource Book,** starting on page 55.)

MASTERING WORDS

Practicing Your Spelling List Independently

Each week you should choose activities to help you master your words. These activities make up your learning plan. This plan will help you keep track of what you plan to do. Here are some tips on making your plan.

• **Pick more than one activity.**

Spell It—Write! gives you lots of choices. Don't try to do everything on the plan every week. Just try to pick at least three different activities that you enjoy.

• **Try every activity at least once.**

You'll like some activities better than others. But at the start of the year, you should try every activity a few times to see how it works for you.

• **Stick with your learning plan.**

Once you make your plan, stick with it. If your plan doesn't work, you can make a new plan with different choices next week.

Read the next few pages to find the directions to lots of fun practice activities. **Try them all!**

NOTE: Directions for the game mats are provided on each game mat. Fine point dry-erase markers work best on the game mats.

Game Mats

1. Find the game mat for the game you want in the *Spell It—Write!* classroom package.
2. Find a partner.
3. Use directions—and your spelling list—to play the game.

Spelling Checkers

Meteor Attack

Rockets

Spelling Soccer

NOTE: Be sure to model each activity for your students before they attempt the activity on their own.

With a Partner

 Spelling Tic-Tac-Toe

1. Find a partner. Draw a tic-tac-toe grid on a piece of paper.

2. Trade spelling lists. Make sure you can read all the words on each other's lists.

3. Decide who will go first. (It's best to take turns going first.) Decide who will use **X** and who will use **O**.

4. Say the first word on your partner's list out loud. Your partner should spell the word out loud while you use his list to check the spelling. If your partner is correct, he should write either **X** or **O** (whichever he is using) on the tic-tac-toe grid. If your partner is not right, spell the word correctly—out loud and one letter at a time—for your partner.

5. Trade jobs. Your partner will say a word from your spelling list and you will try to spell it. If you are right, make an **X** or **O** (whichever you are using) on the board. If you are not correct, your partner will spell your word out loud.

6. Keep taking turns until you or your partner makes three **X**'s or three **O**'s in a line on the board. If you fill up the board before either of you makes a line, start again.

NOTE: The teacher edition high-lights a different practice activity each week in **A Practice Option**.

MASTERING WORDS

Circle Dot

1. Find a partner.

2. Trade spelling lists. Ask your partner to read your list and tell you if there are any words he doesn't know how to say. Say those words for your partner.

3. Ask your partner to read the first word on your list. Write the word on a piece of scrap paper.

4. Now ask your partner to spell that word out loud—one letter at a time.

5. As your partner says each letter, draw a dot under every correct letter. If you wrote a letter that is not correct, or if you left out a letter, draw a little circle.

6. Use the circles to see the parts of the word that gave you trouble.

7. Write the word again. Check your spelling with your partner.

8. Keep going until you have tried every word on your list.

Word Swap

1. Find a partner.

2. Swap spelling lists. Ask your partner to read your list and tell you if there are any words she doesn't know how to say. Say those words for your partner.

3. Ask your partner to read the first word on your list.

4. Write the word on a piece of scrap paper.

5. Ask your partner to use your spelling list to check your spelling. If you spelled the word correctly, your partner should say the next word on your list.

6. If you did not spell the word correctly, ask your partner to spell the word out loud for you. Write the correct spelling.

7. Keep going until you have practiced five words. Then trade jobs. You will say the first word on your partner's list, and she will try to write the word correctly.

8. Keep going until you and your partner have practiced all the words on your lists.

NOTE: Directions for using the **Flip Folder** also appear on the actual **Flip Folder**. Duplicate the **Flip Folder Practice Sheet** (page 51 in the **Teacher Resource Book**) for your students' use with the **Flip Folder**.

MASTERING WORDS

On Your Own

Spelling Study Strategy

Look, Say, Cover, See, Write, Check, Rewrite

1. Look at the word you want to learn.

2. Say the word.

3. Cover the word. See the word in your mind. (You may want to close your eyes.)

4. Write the word.

5. Check your spelling.

6. Rewrite the word correctly.

Flip Folder

1. Get a **Flip Folder** and **Flip Folder** Practice Sheet.

2. Print your spelling list in the first column. Check to see that you spelled each word correctly.

3. Slide your Practice Sheet into the **Flip Folder**.

4. Open Flap 1.
• Look at the first word.
• Say the word.

5. Close Flap 1.
• See the word in your mind. (You may want to close your eyes.)

6. Open Flap 2.
• Write the word on the first line.

7. Open Flap 1 and Flap 2 at the same time.
• Check your spelling.

8. Open Flap 3.
• Write the word again.

9. Open Flaps 1 and 3 at the same time.
• Check your spelling.

NOTE: **Take Your List Home** is a feature of the Home News page for each unit. Home News pages in English and Spanish can be found in the **Teacher Resource Book**, beginning on page 55.

MASTERING WORDS

Take Your Spelling List Home

Spell It—Write! provides lots of fun ways to learn more about spelling at home. Word play can be fun for the whole family, so don't forget to do spelling activities at home, too.

Taking Spelling Tests

Students should be encouraged to take self-tests and/or practice spelling tests with a partner before each unit test.

> **NOTE:** Pretest and posttest sheets can be found in the **Teacher Resource Book.**

At the start of the school year:

• Read the directions on pages 20 and 21 with your students. Work with a student partner to model the procedures described on these pages. (Softbound users can graph their scores on pages 175–176. Hardbound users can use copies of **Teacher Resource Book** page 123.)

• If you intend to use peer-testing in your classroom, place the students in teams who will work successfully together. For more information on testing options, including buddy testing and combining whole-class and peer-testing, see pages Z12 and Z13.

DEVELOPING GOOD SPELLING HABITS

Developing good spelling habits means knowing that correct spelling is important.

Correct spelling makes it easier for others to read your writing and understand what you are saying. Correct spelling also means that you care about your work. Your written work represents you!

Taking Spelling Tests

Taking a Self-Test

1. Look quickly at the first word on your spelling list. Cover the word. Write the word on a piece of paper.

2. Do this for each word on your list.

3. Use your spelling list to check your test.

4. Write the correct spelling next to any word you did not spell correctly.

Taking a Test (or a Practice Test) With a Partner

1. Find a partner.

2. Give your partner your spelling list. Ask your partner to tell you if he cannot read a word on your list.

3. Write your test in pencil. (You should use a pen to correct your test.)

4. Ask your partner to read all the words on your list out loud, one at a time.

5. Listen carefully. Ask your partner to repeat any word you don't understand.

6. Write the words on a piece of paper.

7. Use your spelling list to correct your own test. Write the correct spelling next to any word you did not spell correctly.

NOTE: Remind students to recycle the words they miss on spelling tests into future spelling lists.

DEVELOPING GOOD SPELLING HABITS

Giving a Test to a Partner

1. Read your partner's spelling list to yourself before the test. If you don't know how to say a word, ask your partner or your teacher to help you.
2. Say each word clearly. Make sure your partner heard the word. Repeat it if you need to.
3. Give your partner time to write that word before you say the next word.

Checking a Spelling Test Letter-by-Letter

1. Get out your pen, your spelling list, and the test you want to check.
2. Put the first word on the test paper next to the first word on the spelling list. Check the spelling one letter at a time. (You may want to point to each letter as you check. You can say each letter in the correct spelling out loud as you check, too.)
3. If the word is spelled wrong, circle it and write the correct spelling next to the mistake.
4. Keep going until you have checked every word on the test.

Graphing Your Progress

Each week you should color the number of words you spelled correctly on your spelling test at the end of the week. Use the progress graph in the back of your book or a graph from your teacher.

Writing Missed Words

It's important to keep track of the words you misspelled on your spelling test at the end of the week. After you correct your test, write the words you misspelled in your list of **Words I Need to Know How to Spell**. Check the spelling of each word carefully to make sure you wrote each word correctly.

Spelling Is Important

ENGAGING IN THE PROCESS — MATERIALS

Student Edition: Pages 22–25   **Teacher Edition:** Pages T22A–T25

Materials to help students practice their spelling lists:

- **Flip Folders**
- Copies of **Flip Folder Practice Sheet** (**Teacher Resource Book,** page 51)
- **Take Your List Home** (in *Spell It–Write!*)

Home News, **Teacher Resource Book,** pages 55 in English and 56 in Spanish)
- Game Mats Featured in This Unit: **Meteor Attack, Spelling Checkers**

ENGAGING IN THE PROCESS — GOALS

SPELLING GOALS

Students will

- understand the importance of spelling in writing.
- learn how to be a word hunter.
- use the spelling process of finding words, inspecting words, and mastering words as they develop good spelling habits to become better writers.

WRITING GOALS

Students will

- proofread a writing sample.
- proofread a piece of their own writing for misspelled words.
- write an expressive story.

ENGAGING IN THE PROCESS — MANAGEMENT

Pacing	Notes	Quick Pick Management Option
Period 1 Finding Words (Steps 1–3)	If you wish to add **Teacher Words,** write them on the chalkboard. Sources for more words include: **More Words for Hungry Word Hunters** (page T22), content and theme-related words, or words of your choice.	Assign the list of **Strategy Words** to the whole class. Add the Red List (**More Words for Hungry Word Hunters,** student page 159) for a longer list. Add the Blue List (**More Words for Hungry Word Hunters**) for a more challenging list.
Period 2 Inspecting Words (Steps 4 and 5)	Students write the **Strategy Words** to complete **Explore the Spelling Strategy.**	Assign **Explore the Spelling Strategy** and **Focus on Word Study.**
Period 3 Mastering Words (Step 6) **Period 4** Developing Good Spelling Habits (Step 7)	These two periods can be allocated between selected **Mastering Words** activities and proofreading and writing activities in **Focus on Writing.**	Assign two or three activities to the whole class. Familiarize students with choosing their own activities at their own pace.
Period 5 Assessment (Step 8)	Gradually try different peer-testing options to find the style that best fits your class.	Test the class on the same, whole-class list.

Understanding Language Differences

A number of words on this week's lists are pronounced in different ways by American English speakers. If the following pronunciations are common in your area, suggest that students pay special attention to the spellings of these words.

The word **toward** is pronounced in various ways throughout the United States. Some speakers say **tord**\, while others say **too-ward**\.

Variations also exist in the American pronunciations of several other words on this week's lists, including **police, couldn't, interest,** and **route**.

Some speakers accent the first syllable in police and pronounce the first vowel as a **long o**.

In casual speech, some speakers leave out the **d** in **couldn't**. Be careful to include the **d** in your pronunciation of this word as you say it for the students.

The word **interest** can be pronounced with two or three syllables: **in-trust**\ or **in-tuh-rest**\. (The adjective form, **interesting,** is often pronounced without the first **t**: **in-uh-rest-ing**\.)

The vowel sound in **route** is often pronounced **oo**\, especially in the eastern United States: **root**\. In the Midwest and other regions, the **ow**\ diphthong is used: **rowt**\.

Helping Students Acquiring English

Write each **Strategy Word** on a separate card and display one card at a time. Pronounce the word and use an appropriate strategy to convey the word's meaning, e.g., pantomime, gestures, illustrations. After you have introduced all the **Strategy Words,** place all the cards along the chalk rail. Name a word, and have a volunteer select the correct card and say and spell the word aloud.

Meeting Diverse Needs

Less Able Spellers

Students who have difficulty learning to spell may benefit from the use of a spell checker in a word processing computer program. Note that some spelling miscues may not be identified if:

- they involve the correct spelling of other real words, such as homophones.

- the spell checker cannot recognize the word.

- the child fails to pick the correct spelling from the list of options.

- the word is not in the spell checker's "dictionary."

Periodically check to see that the spell checker is used correctly.

More Able Spellers

Challenge students to develop as many new words as they can by adding prefixes and suffixes to a spelling word.

Ask students to copy their lists in the **Take Your List Home** section of the *Spell It–Write!* Home News page for this lesson. Not only does this page provide a convenient way for families to share a student's spelling list, but it also provides a number of opportunities for families to be involved in students' spelling growth. It has a statement of the week's spelling pattern or strategy, a valuable spelling study strategy, and a suggested home spelling practice activity.

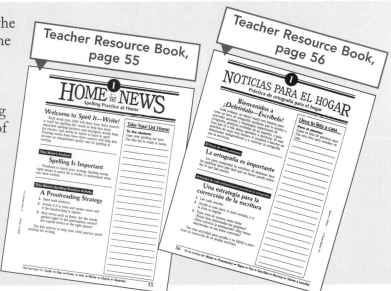

FINDING WORDS

STEP 1 Build Your Spelling List

Students will build their spelling lists with **Strategy Words, Teacher Words,** and **Your Words.** Students should study a minimum of twelve new words each week.

Find Your Strategy Words

• Pretest the students on these words.

• Tell students to write each misspelled pretest word on their spelling lists.

Add Teacher Words

• Select words for students to add to their spelling lists. Choose words from **More Words for Hungry Word Hunters** (on this page and on student page 159), words related to a theme or content area, or words students often misspell.

Add Your Words

• Ask students to pick words from their lists of **Words I Need to Know How to Spell** and their writing.

• Tell students to write these words on their spelling lists.

STEP 2 Write Your Spelling List

Remind students to verify all spellings. (Ask students to see **Strategies for Checking Your Spelling** in the back of the student edition.)

STEP 3 Set Your Learning Goal

Tell students to count the words on their spelling lists. This total is their learning goal. It may vary depending on ability, individual goals, and the difficulty of spelling words.

MORE WORDS FOR HUNGRY WORD HUNTERS

RED LIST — Strategy Words Below Level	BLUE LIST — Strategy Words Above Level	Other Strategy Words	Math Strategy Words
alone	among	annual	array
dinner	interest	beauty	factor
done	language	biscuit	problem
fourth	practice	exact	
half	prepare	honest	**Science Strategy Words**
letter	route	million	fault
real	sentence	neither	orbit
sometime	special	scarce	polar
winter	usually	scary	
world	vacation	touch	**Social Studies Strategy Words**

Social Studies Strategy Words	
canal	ocean
dune	swamp
mesa	

These lists also appear on page 159 in the student edition and page 7 in the **Teacher Resource Book**.

SPELLING STRATEGY

1

Spelling Is Important

Your Spelling List

_____
_____
_____
_____
_____
_____
_____
_____
_____
_____
_____
_____
_____
_____
_____
_____

STEP 1 Build Your Spelling List

Find Your Strategy Words
Take the pretest.
Write misspelled words on your spelling list.

Add Teacher Words
Teachers may add:
• More **Strategy Words** • Content Words • Theme Words

Add Your Words
Pick words from:
• **Words I Need to Know How to Spell** • Writing • Reading

Strategy Words

1. prize	My pig won first **prize** at the fair.
2. toward	Go **toward** your left for ten steps.
3. ninth	This is the **ninth** inning of the baseball game.
4. office	Mom's **office** is on the sixth floor.
5. police	The officer works at the **police** station.
6. build	Did you **build** this model car?
7. carried	The wave **carried** me to the shore.
8. mountain	Let's climb to the top of the **mountain**.
9. since	It's been four years **since** I saw you.
10. couldn't	John **couldn't** get his coat off.

STEP 2 Write Your Spelling List

STEP 3 Set Your Learning Goal

My spelling list has _____ words for me to learn.

> Look at the word list. Is it only ten words?

> No. That's just the **Strategy Word** list. You get to build your own word list every week.

STRATEGY MINI-LESSON

NOTE: The **Explore the Spelling Strategy** activity on page 23 is a self-directed mini-lesson. If you wish to supplement this activity with direct instruction, use the following mini-lesson.

* Review this proofreading process with students, after writing the following steps on the chalkboard:

1. Read each sentence.
2. Is it clear?
   * Does the sentence make sense?
   * Can others read your handwriting?
3. Note errors.
   * Are the words spelled right?
   * Is the punctuation correct?
   * Did you use capital letters in the right places?

* Discuss with students, "When might you use the steps in this process?" (Possible response: *when getting ready to share a piece of writing*)

* Guide students to answer the question, "Why is it important to correct your writing?" (Response: *It makes writing easier to understand.*)

* Ask students to look at the newspaper headlines on page 23 under **Proofread It!** (You may also wish to write the headlines on the chalkboard or on an overhead transparency.) Read the directions together.

* Help students decide how to correct each underlined misspelled word. Make the corrections on the chalkboard or transparency.

* Point out that editing marks used for proofreading are featured on the last page of each student edition unit. Go over these marks with students, but caution them that a final draft should always be rewritten correctly.

* Ask students to read the **Spelling Strategy** on page 23.

· · · · · · · · · · · INSPECTING WORDS · · · · · · · · · · ·

STEP 4 Explore the Spelling Strategy
Proofread It!

A. Read each newspaper headline. Notice each underlined spelling mistake. Then write the correct spelling.

1. Climbers Conquer World's Highest <u>Mountin</u> — **Mountain**
2. <u>Polees</u> Nab Robbery Suspects — **Police**
3. Firefighter <u>Carryed</u> Child to Safety — **Carried**
4. Goldman Seeks <u>Offis</u> of Mayor — **Office**
5. Senate Moves <u>Tooward</u> Budget Plan — **Toward**
6. Ten-Year-Old Wins Science <u>Pryze</u> — **Prize**
7. <u>Couldent</u> Stop in Time, Driver Says — **Couldn't**
8. U.S. Trying to <u>Bild</u> Peace Agreement — **Build**
9. Sox Scoreless Until <u>Nineth</u> Inning — **Ninth**
10. No Rain <u>Sence</u> April Worries Farmers — **Since**

B. At home, work with a family member to proofread a piece of writing. Write the words you want to learn in **Words I Need to Know How to Spell**.

STEP 5 Focus on Word Study
Be a Word Hunter!

It's fun to hunt and collect interesting words that you want to know how to spell. Hunt in a piece of your writing for two words that you think you have misspelled.

1. Write the words you find.

   Answers will vary.
   _____

2. Check the spelling carefully.
3. Now copy the words under the first letter in each word in **Words I Need to Know How to Spell**.

▼▼▼▼▼▼▼▼▼▼▼▼▼
Spelling Strategy
Proofread to check your writing. Spelling words right is important because it makes it easier for a reader to understand what you have written.
■ ■ ■ ■ ■ ■ ■ ■ ■ ■

Hunt words in your reading, too. Use a piece of paper as a bookmark. Write words you want to use in your writing. Add them to **Words I Need to Know How to Spell**.

STEP 4 Explore the Spelling Strategy

Proofread It!
This activity is a self-directed mini-lesson on this week's **Spelling Strategy**.

STEP 5 Focus on Word Study

Be a Word Hunter!
This activity is intended to stimulate students' interest in words and to help them become more enthusiastic word hunters.

Spelling Process Handbook

Students who need to review any part of the spelling process, including practice options, should refer to the **Spelling Process Handbook** (pages 7–21).

MASTERING WORDS

STEP 6 Practice Your Spelling List Independently

Ask the students to choose activities to practice their spelling words and to master this week's **Spelling Strategy**. Students should complete at least three activities each week. You may wish to:

- assign **Practice the Spelling Strategy** to all students to reinforce this week's **Spelling Strategy**.

- involve students' families by assigning **Take Your List Home** for this lesson (**Teacher Resource Book**, pages 55 in English and 56 in Spanish).

- encourage students to use partner activities without game mats (**Word Swap, Spelling Tic-Tac-Toe, Circle Dot**) and activities with game mats (**Meteor Attack, Rockets, Spelling Checkers, Spelling Soccer**). Directions for game-mat activities appear on each game mat. Directions for all other activities are found in the **Spelling Process Handbook** (pages 7–21).

NOTE: These activities and games can be used to practice any spelling list.

A Practice Option

METEOR ATTACK

Students will attack spelling words with enthusiasm as they pair up to play **Meteor Attack**. Partners take turns spelling and writing their spelling words as they "destroy" meteors and collect points. The more words they spell correctly, the more points they collect. It's great fun, and great spelling practice, especially for auditory and visual learners. (Directions appear on the **Meteor Attack** game mat. This activity is appropriate for practicing any spelling list.)

MASTERING WORDS

STEP 6 Practice Your Spelling List Independently
Choose at least three activities to practice your spelling list.

Need Help? Read the Spelling Process Handbook (pages 7–21).

Game Mats	With a Partner	On Your Own	At Home
○ Spelling Checkers ○ Meteor Attack	○ Circle Dot ○ Spelling Tic-Tac-Toe	○ Flip Folder ○ Spelling Study Strategy	○ Take Your List Home

Practice the Spelling Strategy

Read the story that Joe wrote about his sister. Help Joe proofread his story. Find the ten misspelled **Strategy Words** and rewrite them correctly.

Strategy Words

prize
toward
ninth
office
police
build
carried
mountain
since
couldn't

My sister Kim is in the nineth grade. She works in the school ofice. The principal is friendly tord her.

She wants to join the polise force when she is older. She has been planning to do that sinse she was a little girl.

Kim is always busy. Once she had to billed a mounten for a science project. It was very heavy, so she koodn't carry it. We carride it to school together. She won a priz for it! Isn't she great?

1. ___ninth___   6. ___build___
2. ___office___   7. ___mountain___
3. ___toward___   8. ___couldn't___
4. ___police___   9. ___carried___
5. ___since___   10. ___prize___

DEVELOPING GOOD SPELLING HABITS

STEP 7 Focus on Writing

A. Proofread the Writing of Others

This activity provides proofreading practice in a variety of formats, including popular standardized test formats.

B. Proofread Your Own Writing

Students return to their own writing, armed with strategies to identify and collect words they need to know how to spell, and make an authentic link between spelling and writing.

C. A Writing Idea: A Story

This suggestion for a more extended writing activity provides opportunities for students to write in different genres for a variety of purposes and modes.

STEP 8 Check Your Weekly Progress

▶ Take the Test

Remind students that they can take a practice test before the final test on their spelling lists. To find the testing procedure that is right for you, refer to page Z12.

▶ Check Your Goal

Have students compare their tests to their spelling lists. Did they spell all the **Strategy Words** on their spelling lists correctly?

▶ Graph Your Progress

Ask students to graph the number correct (student page 175 for softbound users; **Teacher Resource Book** page 123 for hardbound users).

▶ Save Missed Words

Tell students to write misspelled words on their lists of **Words I Need to Know How to Spell**. Remind students to verify spellings and to recycle these words on future weekly spelling lists.

NOTE: **Words I Need to Know How to Spell** is located in the back of the softbound student edition. If your students are using a hardbound edition, or if they need additional space, you may wish to:

- duplicate the **Words I Need to Know How to Spell** page in the **Teacher Resource Book**;
- obtain copies of the softbound, separate **Words I Need to Know How to Spell**;
- ask students to use a spiral notebook for this purpose.

· · · · · · · · DEVELOPING GOOD SPELLING HABITS · · · · · · · ·

STEP 7 Focus on Writing

A. Proofread the Writing of Others

Proofread the message below. Decide which type of mistake, if any, appears in each underlined section.

Dear Mom,

Mr. Lester called from your offise. He said he
①
coodn't find the news story you wrote. since you may
② ③
know where the story is, please call him
④

Love,
Sarah

≡ Make a capital.
/ Make a small letter.
⅄ Add something.
⌒ Take out something.
⊙ Add a period.
¶ New paragraph
SP Spelling error

1. A Spelling
   B Capitalization
   C Punctuation
   D No mistake

2. A Spelling
   B Capitalization
   C Punctuation
   D No mistake

3. A Spelling
   B Capitalization
   C Punctuation
   D No mistake

4. A Spelling
   B Capitalization
   C Punctuation
   D No mistake

B. Proofread Your Own Writing

It is important to spell words correctly. Go to your most recent writing. Look for misspelled words. Draw a line through the misspelled word. Write the correct spelling above the word. Copy the word in **Words I Need to Know How to Spell**.

C. A Writing Idea: A Story

Write a story like the one Joe wrote about his sister. Tell about a person who is important to you. After you finish your story, check to be sure all the words are spelled correctly.

STEP 8 Check Your Weekly Progress

▶ Take the Test
Ready? Practice test first.

▶ Check Your Goal
Check to see if you met your learning goal.

▶ Graph Your Progress
Graph your score for this week's test.

▶ Save Missed Words
Write the words you missed in your list of **Words I Need to Know How to Spell**.

Contractions

ENGAGING IN THE PROCESS — MATERIALS

Student Edition: Pages 26–29   **Teacher Edition:** Pages T26A–T29

Materials to help students practice their spelling lists:
- **Flip Folders**
- Copies of **Flip Folder Practice Sheet** (**Teacher Resource Book,** page 51)
- **Take Your List Home** (in *Spell It–Write!*

Home News, **Teacher Resource Book,** pages 57 in English and 58 in Spanish)
- Game Mats Featured in This Unit: **Meteor Attack, Rockets**

ENGAGING IN THE PROCESS — GOALS

SPELLING GOALS

Students will

- understand that two or more words can be combined to form a contraction.

- recognize that homophones are words that sound alike but are spelled differently and have different meanings.

- use the spelling process of finding words, inspecting words, and mastering words as they develop good spelling habits to become better writers.

WRITING GOALS

Students will

- proofread a writing sample.

- proofread a piece of their own writing for misspelled contractions.

- write two informative paragraphs.

ENGAGING IN THE PROCESS — MANAGEMENT

Pacing	Notes	Quick Pick Management Option
Period 1 Finding Words (Steps 1–3)	If you wish to add **Teacher Words,** write them on the chalkboard. Sources for more words include: **More Words for Hungry Word Hunters** (page T26), content and theme-related words, or words of your choice.	Assign the list of **Pattern Words** to the whole class. Add the Red List (**More Words for Hungry Word Hunters,** student page 159) for a longer list. Add the Blue List (**More Words for Hungry Word Hunters**) for a more challenging list.
Period 2 Inspecting Words (Steps 4 and 5)	Students write the **Pattern Words** to complete **Explore the Spelling Pattern.**	Assign **Explore the Spelling Pattern** and **Focus on Word Study.**
Period 3 Mastering Words (Step 6) **Period 4** Developing Good Spelling Habits (Step 7)	These two periods can be allocated between selected **Mastering Words** activities and proofreading and writing activities in **Focus on Writing.**	Assign two or three activities to the whole class. Familiarize students with choosing their own activities at their own pace.
Period 5 Assessment (Step 8)	Gradually try different peer-testing options to find the style that best fits your class.	Test the class on the same, whole-class list.

Understanding Language Differences

Spanish Speakers

Many people, including Spanish speakers, tend to omit the **t** in **ts** combinations in such words as **let's** and **that's**. Students may pronounce only the **s**. As a result, **that's** can become **thas**\ and **let's** can become **less**\.

Informal speech is not a dialect, but our audience and the rate at which we are speaking can make a difference in the way we pronounce words. In casual speech, we are more likely to give up clear articulation in favor of speaking quickly.

In careful speech, most people pronounce all the letter sounds in **didn't**. In casual speech, the second **d** often disappears: **didn't** becomes **dint**\. Another example is **we'll**. We expect this word to have a **long e** sound, as in **wheel**. However, in casual speech we often pronounce **we'll** as **will**\.

A contraction that has annoyed English teachers for years is **ain't**. This word is actually an old contraction and was originally used for **am not**. Many Americans use this form, even though it is considered nonstandard. You may wish to model **I'm not** when you teach contractions. To provide opportunities for students to practice the correct model in a gamelike atmosphere, model a sentence such as *"I'm not a bird,"* and ask each student in turn to say a sentence in the *"I'm not . . ."* pattern.

Helping Students Acquiring English

Since contractions are peculiar to English, students may have difficulty understanding the concept. Begin by writing the full form of a contraction, such as **you are,** on a strip of paper. Then cut the letters apart, remove the **a,** and insert an apostrophe to form **you're,** enabling students to see how the change occurs.

Meeting Diverse Needs

Less Able Spellers

Students who have difficulty learning to spell may set goals that are either too hard or too easy. For that reason, it is important to monitor how many new words the child is working on each week. If too many or too few new words are selected, help the child moderate or increase his or her goal. The methods the student uses to study new words should also be examined.

More Able Spellers

Ask stronger spellers to select one word from their weekly spelling lists and locate as many synonyms and antonyms for that word as they can. Ask them to examine the word pairs for similarities in spelling. If students have used prefixes to generate their synonyms and antonyms, encourage them to discuss the meaning of each prefix and use the prefixes to generate other words.

Ask students to copy their lists in the **Take Your List Home** section of the *Spell It–Write!* Home News page for this lesson. Not only does this page provide a convenient way for families to share a student's spelling list, but it also provides a number of opportunities for families to be involved in students' spelling growth. It has a statement of the week's spelling pattern or strategy, a valuable spelling study strategy, and a suggested home spelling practice activity.

Teacher Resource Book, page 57

Teacher Resource Book, page 58

FINDING WORDS

STEP 1 Build Your Spelling List

Students will build their spelling lists with **Pattern Words, Teacher Words,** and **Your Words.** Students should study a minimum of twelve new words each week.

Find Your Pattern Words

- Pretest the students on these words.
- Tell students to write each misspelled pretest word on their spelling lists.

Add Teacher Words

- Select words for students to add to their spelling lists. Choose words from **More Words for Hungry Word Hunters** (on this page and on student page 159), words related to a theme or content area, or words students often misspell.

Add Your Words

- Ask students to pick words from their lists of **Words I Need to Know How to Spell** and their writing.
- Tell students to write these words on their spelling lists.

STEP 2 Write Your Spelling List

Remind students to verify all spellings. (Ask students to see **Strategies for Checking Your Spelling** in the back of the student edition.)

STEP 3 Set Your Learning Goal

Tell students to count the words on their spelling lists. This total is their learning goal. It may vary depending on ability, individual goals, and the difficulty of spelling words.

MORE WORDS FOR HUNGRY WORD HUNTERS

RED LIST — Pattern Words Below Level	BLUE LIST — Pattern Words Above Level	Other Pattern Words
can't	aren't	he'd
didn't	hasn't	he'll
don't	hadn't	it'll
I'll	here's	needn't
I'm	she's	she'd
isn't	there's	she'll
it's	we've	they'd
I've	what's	who'll
weren't	you'd	
won't	you've	

These lists also appear on page 159 in the student edition and page 8 in the **Teacher Resource Book.**

SPELLING PATTERN

2

Contractions

Your Spelling List

_____
_____
_____
_____
_____
_____
_____
_____
_____
_____
_____
_____
_____
_____
_____
_____
_____
_____
_____
_____

FINDING WORDS

STEP 1 Build Your Spelling List

Find Your Pattern Words
Take the pretest.
Write misspelled words on your spelling list.

Add Teacher Words
Teachers may add:
- More **Pattern Words** • Content Words • Theme Words

Add Your Words
Pick words from:
- **Words I Need to Know How to Spell** • Writing • Reading

Pattern Words

1.	you're	When **you're** ready, we can begin.
2.	we're	We can leave when **we're** finished.
3.	we'll	After lunch, **we'll** play outdoors.
4.	he's	**He's** moving to Japan next month.
5.	doesn't	Amy **doesn't** like pizza, but she loves hot dogs.
6.	wasn't	Jeff **wasn't** on the bus today.
7.	haven't	I **haven't** had time to look yet.
8.	let's	**Let's** ride our bikes to the park.
9.	that's	**That's** not my raincoat.
10.	o'clock	Is it ten **o'clock** yet?

STEP 2 Write Your Spelling List

STEP 3 Set Your Learning Goal

My spelling list has _____ words for me to learn.

I'm putting all the **Pattern Words** in my spelling list.

You can do that, but I put down only the words I missed in my pretest. But I'll add other spelling words, too.

PATTERN MINI-LESSON

NOTE: The **Explore the Spelling Pattern** activity on page 27 is a self-directed mini-lesson. If you wish to supplement that activity with direct instruction, use the following mini-lesson.

* **Write** an apostrophe and these letters on index cards (one per card): **a, c, c, d, d, e, e, f, h, h, i, i, k, l, l, m, n, n, o, o, r, s, t, t, u, v, w, w, y.**

* **Write** the **Pattern Words** from page 26 on the chalkboard. Ask volunteers to read the words aloud.

* **Tell** students that **contract** means "to get smaller." Ask students to explain why these words are called contractions. (Possible responses: *They are shortened; the words have been "contracted."*)

* **Ask** students what words each contraction represents. Use the cards to spell out the complete words for one contraction. For example, spell out **you are**. Then take out the **a** and add **'** to spell **you're**. Explain that the apostrophe replaces a letter or letters.

* **Encourage** volunteers to use the cards to spell the words in each contraction and the contraction.

NOTE: The word **o'clock** means "of the clock." Point out that in **he's, that's** and **it's, 's** may stand for **is** or **has**. Explain that **will not** becomes **won't** (Red List). Also point out that **its** means "belonging to it" and may not be used in place of **it's**.

* **Ask** students to state what they know about contractions. Then have them read the **Spelling Pattern** on page 27 with you and compare their ideas to the information presented.

STEP 4 Explore the Spelling Pattern
Contraction Action!

A. It's time for some spelling math. Write a **Pattern Word** to solve each spelling problem. Remember, you subtract letters and add apostrophes to form contractions.

1. he is − i + ' = **he's**
2. was not − o + ' = **wasn't**
3. let us − u + ' = **let's**
4. we will − wi + ' = **we'll**
5. of the clock − f the + ' = **o'clock**

6. we are − a + ' = **we're**
7. that is − i + ' = **that's**
8. you are − a + ' = **you're**
9. have not − o + ' = **haven't**
10. does not − o in not + ' = **doesn't**

B. Work with a partner to find other contractions. Take turns using this strategy to practice spelling each word you find:

1. **Look** at the word.
2. **Say** the word.
3. **Cover** the word and see it in your mind.
4. **Write** the word.
5. **Check** your spelling.

Spelling Pattern

A contraction shortens two or more words into one word. In a contraction, an apostrophe (') takes the place of the letters that are left out. The contraction of **you are** is **you're**.

STEP 5 Focus on Word Study
Homophones

Homophones are words that sound alike but are spelled differently and have different meanings. The words **you're** and **your** sound alike, but their meanings are very different. **You're** is the contraction of **you are**, and **your** means "belonging to you."

Write two homophones for each of the words below.

1. they're **their** **there**
2. too **to** **two**

STEP 4 Explore the Spelling Pattern
Contraction Action!

This activity is a self-directed mini-lesson on this week's **Spelling Pattern**.

STEP 5 Focus on Word Study
Homophones

This activity is intended to stimulate students' interest in words and to help them become more enthusiastic word hunters.

Spelling Process Handbook

Students who need to review any part of the spelling process, including practice options, should refer to the **Spelling Process Handbook** (pages 7–21).

A Practice Option

WORD SWAP

Word Swap is an extremely simple but effective partner spelling study strategy. Students simply swap spelling lists and quiz each other. (This activity is also an effective way to introduce students to key aspects of peer testing.) And as in all partnered practice activities, students reap the benefits of exposure to two spelling lists—their own and their partner's. It's a painless spelling bonus! (Directions appear in the **Spelling Process Handbook,** student pages 7–21. This activity is appropriate for practicing any spelling list.)

 Practice Your Spelling List Independently

6 Ask the students to choose activities to practice their spelling words and to master this week's **Spelling Pattern**. Students should complete at least three activities each week. You may wish to:

- assign **Practice the Spelling Pattern** to all students to reinforce this week's **Spelling Pattern**.

- involve students' families by assigning **Take Your List Home** for this lesson (**Teacher Resource Book,** pages 57 in English and 58 in Spanish).

- encourage students to use partner activities without game mats (**Word Swap, Spelling Tic-Tac-Toe, Circle Dot**) and activities with game mats (**Meteor Attack, Rockets, Spelling Checkers, Spelling Soccer**). Directions for game-mat activities appear on each game mat. Directions for all other activities are found in the **Spelling Process Handbook** (pages 7–21).

NOTE: These activities and games can be used to practice any spelling list.

---

6 **Practice Your Spelling List Independently**
Choose at least three activities to practice your spelling list.

You can practice any spelling list with these activities.

Game Mats		With a Partner		On Your Own		At Home
○ Meteor Attack	○ Rockets	○ Spelling Tic-Tac-Toe	○ Word Swap	○ Flip Folder	○ Spelling Study Strategy	○ Take Your List Home

Practice the Spelling Pattern

Match one **Pattern Word** to the underlined words in each sentence. Write the contraction for the underlined words. Don't forget to put the apostrophe in the right place! Use the **Pattern Words** to check your spelling.

Pattern Words

you're
we're
we'll
he's
doesn't
wasn't
haven't
let's
that's
o'clock

1. This <u>does not</u> look like pepperoni to me.   doesn't

2. I <u>was not</u> ready for the test.   wasn't

3. Please wake me at seven <u>of the clock</u>.   o'clock

4. If <u>you are</u> happy, sing a song.   you're

5. <u>Let us</u> race to the corner!   Let's

6. I <u>have not</u> seen Amelia today.   haven't

7. <u>We are</u> ready when you are.   We're

8. <u>That is</u> your new shirt.   That's

9. Miguel says <u>he is</u> not going to watch TV.   he's

10. <u>We will</u> call you later.   We'll

DEVELOPING GOOD SPELLING HABITS

STEP 7 Focus on Writing

A. Proofread the Writing of Others

This activity provides proofreading practice in a variety of formats, including popular standardized test formats.

B. Proofread Your Own Writing

Students return to their own writing, armed with strategies to identify and collect words they need to know how to spell, and make an authentic link between spelling and writing.

C. A Writing Idea: Classificatory Paragraphs

This suggestion for a more extended writing activity provides opportunities for students to write in different genres for a variety of purposes and modes.

STEP 8 Check Your Weekly Progress

▶ Take the Test

Remind students that they can take a practice test before the final test on their spelling lists. To find the testing procedure that is right for you, refer to page Z12.

▶ Check Your Goal

Have students compare their tests to their spelling lists. Did they spell all the **Pattern Words** on their spelling lists correctly?

▶ Graph Your Progress

Ask students to graph the number correct (student page 175 for softbound users; **Teacher Resource Book** page 123 for hardbound users).

▶ Save Missed Words

Tell students to write misspelled words on their lists of **Words I Need to Know How to Spell**. Remind students to verify spellings and to recycle these words on future weekly spelling lists.

DEVELOPING GOOD SPELLING HABITS

STEP 7 Focus on Writing

A. Proofread the Writing of Others

Proofread the paragraphs below. Find the seven misspelled contractions. Write each contraction correctly.

My friends and I went out for pizza at five oclock yesterday. It wasno't easy choosing what kind to have! José doesint like mushrooms. I hav'nt ever liked pepperoni. Lisa and Fred said, "We'ill eat anything but peppers."

Finally, we agreed and said, "Lets' have a plain cheese pizza!" And thats exactly what we had.

≡ Make a capital.
/ Make a small letter.
ᘯ Add something.
⊙ Take out something.
⊙ Add a period.
ᑊᖴ New paragraph
ⓢᑭ Spelling error

1.	o'clock	5.	We'll
2.	wasn't	6.	Let's
3.	doesn't	7.	that's
4.	haven't		

B. Proofread Your Own Writing

An apostrophe takes the place of letters that have been left out when two or more words are combined to form a contraction. Go to your most recent writing. Look for contractions. Check to see that they have been formed correctly.

C. A Writing Idea: Classificatory Paragraphs

Ideas for writing are all around you! Make two lists—one list of things you like to do and another list of things you don't like to do. Pick one of the things on each list and write one paragraph to explain why you like to do one thing and another paragraph about why you don't like to do the other. When you are finished writing, check to see if you've spelled all the words correctly.

STEP 8 Check Your Weekly Progress

▶ Take the Test
Ready? Practice test first.

▶ Check Your Goal
Check to see if you met your learning goal.

▶ Graph Your Progress
Graph your score for this week's test.

▶ Save Missed Words
Write the words you missed in your list of **Words I Need to Know How to Spell**.

Hunt Words

Remind students to continuously hunt words that they wish to learn how to spell and to write these words in **Words I Need to Know How to Spell**.

Long Vowels: V-C-e

ENGAGING IN THE PROCESS — MATERIALS

Student Edition: Pages 30–33 **Teacher Edition:** Pages T30–T33

Materials to help students practice their spelling lists:

- **Flip Folders**
- Copies of **Flip Folder Practice Sheet** (**Teacher Resource Book,** page 51)
- **Take Your List Home** (in *Spell It–Write!*

Home News, **Teacher Resource Book,** pages 59 in English and 60 in Spanish)
- Game Mats Featured in This Unit: **Rockets, Spelling Soccer**

ENGAGING IN THE PROCESS — GOALS

SPELLING GOALS

Students will

- transfer knowledge of the vowel-consonant-**silent e** pattern to spell multisyllable words.
- sort words according to the vowel sound in the last syllable.
- develop an understanding of how the meanings of words can change over time.
- use the spelling process of finding words, inspecting words, and mastering words as they develop good spelling habits to become better writers.

WRITING GOALS

Students will

- hunt for words with the vowel-consonant-**silent e** pattern in a piece of their writing.
- write an informative letter.

ENGAGING IN THE PROCESS — MANAGEMENT

Pacing	Notes	Quick Pick Management Option
Period 1 Finding Words (Steps 1–3)	If you wish to add **Teacher Words,** write them on the chalkboard. Sources for more words include: **More Words for Hungry Word Hunters** (page T30), content and theme-related words, or words of your choice.	Assign the list of **Pattern Words** to the whole class. Add the Red List (**More Words for Hungry Word Hunters,** student page 160) for a longer list. Add the Blue List (**More Words for Hungry Word Hunters**) for a more challenging list.
Period 2 Inspecting Words (Steps 4 and 5)	Students write the **Pattern Words** to complete **Explore the Spelling Pattern.**	Assign **Explore the Spelling Pattern** and **Focus on Word Study.**
Period 3 Mastering Words (Step 6) **Period 4** Developing Good Spelling Habits (Step 7)	These two periods can be allocated between selected **Mastering Words** activities and proofreading and writing activities in **Focus on Writing.**	Assign two or three activities to the whole class. Familiarize students with choosing their own activities at their own pace.
Period 5 Assessment (Step 8)	Gradually try different peer-testing options to find the style that best fits your class.	Test the class on the same, whole-class list.

Understanding Language Differences

Spanish Speakers

The notion of a **silent e** pattern may be difficult for many non-native English speakers. Spanish, for example, often pronounces a final **e** with the **short e** sound, as in **let**. As a result, students from Spanish-speaking backgrounds may need special help in learning to spell English words that end in **silent e**.

In casual speech, American English speakers sometimes omit sounds. For example, **surprise** is often pronounced \suh-prize\. (The sound represented by the first **r** is omitted.) Because of this, some students may forget to include the first **r** when they write **surprise**.

The **h** in **awhile** may present a similar spelling problem because most Americans do not pronounce it.

Helping Students Acquiring English

Write each **Pattern Word** on a 3"x 5" card. Give each student an equal number of cards. Pronounce a **Pattern Word**. Ask the student who has that word to hold up the card. Then pronounce the word and ask the students to repeat it in unison. Remind students that the final **e** is not pronounced. Continue until all the words have been pronounced.

Meeting Diverse Needs

Less Able Spellers

Students who have difficulty remembering the correct spelling of the words on their spelling lists may benefit from tracing each word when learning to spell it. Demonstrate the following study strategy:

1. **Look** at the word you want to learn.
2. **Say** the word.
3. **Trace** the word with your index finger.
   Say the word as you trace it.
4. **Cover** the word.
   See the word in your mind.
5. **Write** the word.
6. **Check** your spelling.

Emphasize that tracing helps you remember the word because you "feel" how it is made. Ask students to practice the study strategy until they can do it quickly, easily, and independently. Periodically check to see that they are using the strategy correctly.

More Able Spellers

Encourage strong spellers to locate multisyllable words with a long vowel sound in the last syllable that is not spelled with the vowel-consonant-**silent e** pattern (e.g., **delight**).

Also encourage them to look for multisyllable words with a vowel-consonant-**silent e** in the last syllable in which the vowel does not make a long vowel sound (e.g., **relive**).

Ask students to copy their lists in the **Take Your List Home** section of the *Spell It–Write!* Home News page for this lesson. Not only does this page provide a convenient way for families to share a student's spelling list, but it also provides a number of opportunities for families to be involved in students' spelling growth. It has a statement of the week's spelling pattern or strategy, a valuable spelling study strategy, and a suggested home spelling practice activity.

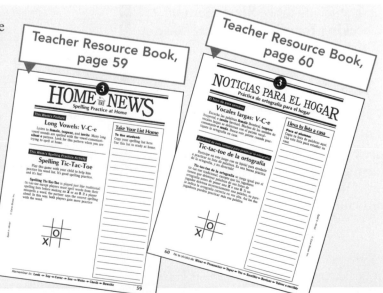

Teacher Resource Book, page 59

Teacher Resource Book, page 60

FINDING WORDS

STEP 1 — Build Your Spelling List

Students will build their spelling lists with **Pattern Words, Teacher Words,** and **Your Words.** Students should study a minimum of twelve new words each week.

Find Your Pattern Words

- Pretest the students on these words.
- Tell students to write each misspelled pretest word on their spelling lists.

Add Teacher Words

- Select words for students to add to their spelling lists. Choose words from **More Words for Hungry Word Hunters** (on this page and on student page 160), words related to a theme or content area, or words students often misspell.

Add Your Words

- Ask students to pick words from their lists of **Words I Need to Know How to Spell** and their writing.
- Tell students to write these words on their spelling lists.

STEP 2 — Write Your Spelling List

Remind students to verify all spellings. (Ask students to see **Strategies for Checking Your Spelling** in the back of the student edition.)

STEP 3 — Set Your Learning Goal

Tell students to count the words on their spelling lists. This total is their learning goal. It may vary depending on ability, individual goals, and the difficulty of spelling words.

MORE WORDS FOR HUNGRY WORD HUNTERS

RED LIST — Pattern Words Below Level	BLUE LIST — Pattern Words Above Level	Other Pattern Words	Math Pattern Word
alike	arrive	celebrate	decade
alive	compose	cooperate	
aside	decide	fertilize	**Science Pattern Words**
awake	desire	generalize	earthquake reptile
became	entire	include	explode
divide	excite	operate	
erase	locate	polite	**Social Studies Pattern Words**
parade	oriole	populate	bauxite sugarcane
	reduce	recite	interstate timberline
	suppose	require	landscape vibrate
			skyline

These lists also appear on page 160 in the student edition and page 9 in the **Teacher Resource Book.**

SPELLING PATTERN

3

Long Vowels: V-C-e

Your Spelling List

FINDING WORDS

STEP 1 — Build Your Spelling List

Find Your Pattern Words

Take the pretest.
Write misspelled words on your spelling list.

Add Teacher Words

Teachers may add:
- More **Pattern Words** • Content Words • Theme Words

Add Your Words

Pick words from:
- **Words I Need to Know How to Spell** • Writing • Reading

Pattern Words

1. **female** — A **female** whale is called a cow.
2. **complete** — Her dress, shoes, and hat made a **complete** outfit.
3. **invite** — You may **invite** ten people to the party.
4. **define** — We will **define** these words later.
5. **explode** — That water balloon is going to **explode**!
6. **awhile** — We walked **awhile** along the lake.
7. **surprise** — I can't wait to show you the **surprise**!
8. **antelope** — The **antelope** has long horns on its head.
9. **altitude** — The plane flew at an **altitude** of 30,000 feet.
10. **umpire** — The **umpire** said the runner was safe at home plate.

STEP 2 — Write Your Spelling List

STEP 3 — Set Your Learning Goal

My spelling list has _____ words for me to learn.

Maybe. But I think we'll get a few science words, too. That'll help us write our lab reports.

Do you think our teacher will give us more **Pattern Words** to study?

INSPECTING WORDS

PATTERN MINI-LESSON

NOTE: The **Explore the Spelling Pattern** activity on page 31 is a self-directed mini-lesson. If you wish to supplement that activity with direct instruction, use the following mini-lesson.

* **Guide** students to understand that a syllable is a word part in which one vowel sound is heard. Ask students to open their books to page 30. Ask a volunteer to read each **Pattern Word** aloud while the class listens for the number of syllables. Encourage volunteers to identify the number of syllables in each word by clapping or tapping their feet.

* **Draw** attention to the last syllable in each word and ask what these syllables have in common. (Possible responses: *Each has a long vowel sound; each has the vowel-consonant-silent e spelling pattern*) Provide prompts and give as much time as needed.

* **Ask** students to read the **Spelling Pattern** on page 31 with you. Summarize by saying that when a long vowel sound is heard in a final syllable it may be spelled vowel-consonant-**silent e**.

* **Encourage** the students to hunt other multisyllabic words in which they hear a long vowel sound in the final syllable. Write these words on the chalkboard, listing words with the vowel-consonant-**silent e** pattern in one column and all the other words in another column. You may wish to include examples from **More Words for Hungry Word Hunters** (on student page 160 and page T30). Remind students that they may add any of these words to **Words I Need to Know How to Spell**.

INSPECTING WORDS

STEP 4 Explore the Spelling Pattern
Sorting Words

Try sorting the **Pattern Words** in other ways. How many words begin with a vowel?

A. Sort the **Pattern Words** into five groups. Use the vowel sound in the last syllable and the words below to guide your sort. Make sure you write each **Pattern Word** once.

1. female	3. invite	4. complete
female	invite	complete
	define	
2. explode	awhile	5. altitude
explode	surprise	altitude
antelope	umpire	

B. You can sort the **Pattern Words** according to how many syllables there are in each word. Write the **Pattern Words** that have three syllables.

6. antelope
7. altitude

C. Do a word hunt to find other words that have more than one syllable and end in one of the five vowel-consonant-**silent e** patterns. Look in your writing and in **Words I Need to Know How to Spell**. Add them to the word sort.

STEP 5 Focus on Word Study
Meaning Changes

Long ago, people gave the name **antelope** to an imaginary animal. They told tales of a savage beast with long horns like saws that could cut down trees! Today we use **antelope** to name a real animal with long horns.

Other animal names have interesting histories. Match each animal name with the name's history.

1. meant "lizard" __b__   a. hippopotamus
2. meant "spiny pig" __d__   b. alligator
3. meant "pig fish" __c__   c. porpoise
4. meant "horse of the river" __a__   d. porcupine

Spelling Pattern
Listen to **female, complete,** and **invite**. In words with more than one syllable, the long vowel sound in the last syllable is often spelled with the vowel-consonant-**silent e** pattern.

STEP 4 Explore the Spelling Pattern
Sorting Words
This activity is a self-directed mini-lesson on this week's **Spelling Pattern**.

STEP 5 Focus on Word Study
Meaning Changes
This activity is intended to stimulate students' interest in words and to help them become more enthusiastic word hunters.

Spelling Process Handbook
Students who need to review any part of the spelling process, including practice options, should refer to the **Spelling Process Handbook** (pages 7–21).

Practice Your Spelling List Independently

STEP 6

Ask the students to choose activities to practice their spelling words and to master this week's **Spelling Pattern**. Students should complete at least three activities each week. You may wish to:

- assign **Practice the Spelling Pattern** to all students to reinforce this week's **Spelling Pattern**.

- involve students' families by assigning **Take Your List Home** for this lesson (**Teacher Resource Book**, pages 59 in English and 60 in Spanish).

- encourage students to use partner activities without game mats (**Word Swap, Spelling Tic-Tac-Toe, Circle Dot**) and activities with game mats (**Spelling Checkers, Meteor Attack, Rockets, Spelling Soccer**). Directions for game-mat activities appear on each game mat. Directions for all other activities are found in the **Spelling Process Handbook** (pages 7–21).

NOTE: These activities and games can be used to practice any spelling list.

A Practice Option

FLIP FOLDER

Flip Folder is a fun practice activity that is especially effective for kinesthetic learners. While **Flip Folder** is similar to the Have-A-Go strategy, the two techniques differ in that the first step in **Flip Folder** is to look at the correct spelling. Students then cover that spelling, visualize it, and attempt to recreate it. When they lift the flap and compare their attempt to the correct spelling, they receive immediate feedback—vital for correcting mistakes and retaining correct spellings. (Directions appear in the **Spelling Process Handbook**, pages 7–21, and on the **Flip Folder** itself. This activity is appropriate for practicing any spelling list.)

· · · · · · · MASTERING WORDS · · · · · · ·

STEP 6 Practice Your Spelling List Independently
Choose at least three activities to practice your spelling list.

Copy your words carefully when you take your list home.

Game Mats		With a Partner		On Your Own		At Home

| Rockets | Spelling Soccer | Circle Dot | Word Swap | Flip Folder | Spelling Study Strategy | Take Your List Home |

Practice **the Spelling Pattern**

Use the clues to unscramble each **Pattern Word**. Write each word and circle the vowel-consonant-**silent e** pattern in each one.

Pattern Words

female
complete
invite
define
explode
awhile
surprise
antelope
altitude
umpire

1. **Clue:** woman
   l e m f a e
   f e m **a l e**

2. **Clue:** give the meaning of
   n e f i d e
   d e f **i n e**

3. **Clue:** something unexpected
   s s r r u i e p
   s u r p r **i s e**

4. **Clue:** blow up
   p l e d o x e
   e x p l **o d e**

5. **Clue:** animal like a deer
   e a t n o l p e
   a n t e l **o p e**

6. **Clue:** ask to come
   t i n e v i
   i n v **i t e**

7. **Clue:** baseball official
   m e i u p r
   u m p **i r e**

8. **Clue:** nothing's missing
   m o t c e p l e
   c o m p l **e t e**

9. **Clue:** for a time
   e h a l w i
   a w h **i l e**

10. **Clue:** height above sea level
    d a t e i t l u
    a l t i t **u d e**

DEVELOPING GOOD SPELLING HABITS

STEP 7 Focus on Writing

A. Hunt Spelling Words in Your Writing

This activity equips students with a specific strategy for increasing students' consciousness of targeted spelling patterns and strategies in their own writing. It also enables them to collect words for spelling study.

B. A Writing Idea: A Letter

This suggestion for a more extended writing activity provides opportunities for students to write in different genres for a variety of purposes and modes.

STEP 8 Check Your Weekly Progress

▶ Take the Test

Remind students that they can take a practice test before the final test on their spelling lists. To find the testing procedure that is right for you, refer to page Z12.

▶ Check Your Goal

Have students compare their tests to their spelling lists. Did they spell all the **Pattern Words** on their spelling lists correctly?

▶ Graph Your Progress

Ask students to graph the number correct (student page 175 for softbound users; **Teacher Resource Book** page 123 for hardbound users).

▶ Save Missed Words

Tell students to write misspelled words on their lists of **Words I Need to Know How to Spell**. Remind students to verify spellings and to recycle these words on future weekly spelling lists.

· · · · · · · · · DEVELOPING GOOD SPELLING HABITS · · · · · · · · ·

STEP 7 Focus on Writing

A. Hunt Spelling Words in Your Writing

Choose one piece of your writing that you have completed recently. Work with a spelling partner to look for words with the vowel-consonant-**silent e** spelling pattern. Write the words you find in two columns like these.

Column 1	Column 2
I spelled these **V-C-e** words correctly.	I misspelled these **V-C-e** words.
Answers will vary.	Answers will vary.

If you can't find any **V-C-e** words, choose a different piece of your writing.

Add the words you wrote in Column 2 to **Words I Need to Know How to Spell**.

B. A Writing Idea: A Letter

Write a letter to your favorite friend. Describe what you did today and what you plan to do this weekend. Before you send the letter, check to see if you've spelled words with the vowel-consonant-**silent e** pattern correctly.

≡ Make a capital.
/ Make a small letter.
∧ Add something.
ℰ Take out something.
⊙ Add a period.
¶ New paragraph
SP Spelling error

STEP 8 Check Your Weekly Progress

▶ Take the Test
Ready? Practice test first.

▶ Check Your Goal
Check to see if you met your learning goal.

▶ Graph Your Progress
Graph your score for this week's test.

▶ Save Missed Words
Write the words you missed in your list of **Words I Need to Know How to Spell**.

Hunt Words

Remind students to continuously hunt words that they wish to learn how to spell and to write these words in **Words I Need to Know How to Spell**.

ENGAGING IN THE PROCESS

MATERIALS

Student Edition: Pages 34–37   **Teacher Edition:** Pages T34A–T37

Materials to help students practice their spelling lists:

• **Flip Folders**
• Copies of **Flip Folder Practice Sheet** (**Teacher Resource Book,** page 51)
• **Take Your List Home** (in *Spell It–Write!*)

Home News, **Teacher Resource Book,** pages 61 in English and 62 in Spanish)
• Game Mats Featured in This Unit: **Spelling Checkers, Spelling Soccer**

ENGAGING IN THE PROCESS

GOALS

SPELLING GOALS

Students will

• transfer knowledge of vowel digraphs to spell multisyllabic words.

• sort words according to long vowel pairs.

• develop an understanding of how the meanings of words can change over time.

• use the spelling process of finding words, inspecting words, and mastering words as they develop good spelling habits to become better writers.

WRITING GOALS

Students will

• proofread a writing sample.

• proofread a piece of their own writing for misspelled words with long vowel pairs.

• write an expressive poem.

ENGAGING IN THE PROCESS

MANAGEMENT

Pacing	Notes	Quick Pick Management Option
Period 1 Finding Words (Steps 1–3)	If you wish to add **Teacher Words,** write them on the chalkboard. Sources for more words include: **More Words for Hungry Word Hunters** (page T34), content and theme-related words, or words of your choice.	Assign the list of **Pattern Words** to the whole class. Add the Red List (**More Words for Hungry Word Hunters,** student page 160) for a longer list. Add the Blue List (**More Words for Hungry Word Hunters**) for a more challenging list.
Period 2 Inspecting Words (Steps 4 and 5)	Students write the **Pattern Words** to complete **Explore the Spelling Pattern.**	Assign **Explore the Spelling Pattern** and **Focus on Word Study**.
Period 3 Mastering Words (Step 6) **Period 4** Developing Good Spelling Habits (Step 7)	These two periods can be allocated between selected **Mastering Words** activities and proofreading and writing activities in **Focus on Writing.**	Assign two or three activities to the whole class. Familiarize students with choosing their own activities at their own pace.
Period 5 Assessment (Step 8)	Gradually try different peer-testing options to find the style that best fits your class.	Test the class on the same, whole-class list.

ENGAGING
IN THE
PROCESS

INDIVIDUAL NEEDS

Understanding Language Differences

Spanish Speakers

Vowels in Spanish differ in pronunciation from vowels in English. The two-vowel combinations in some words on this week's lists may cause some confusion for native Spanish speakers. For example, **ai** in Spanish is pronounced a bit like the English **long i** sound. The Spanish word **traigo** ("I bring") rhymes with the English "I go." The **ea** combination, as in **reason,** may also present a challenge for Spanish speakers.

American English speakers can choose to pronounce the final syllable in the days of the week as **dee**\ or **day**\. For instance, **Tuesday** (Red List) may be pronounced **tooz-dee**\ or **tooz-day**\.

Helping Students Acquiring English

Write **Pattern Words** on separate cards, and give the cards to heterogeneous groups of students so that fluent English speakers can provide peer support to less fluent speakers. Ask students to sort the words into two groups, words with the **long a** vowel sound and words with the **long e** vowel sound and to read aloud the words in each group to confirm their choices. Next, have students sort the words in the **long a** group into two groups, **ai** words and **ay** words. Repeat the procedure for **long e** words spelled **ee** and **ea**.

Meeting Diverse Needs

Less Able Spellers

Students who have difficulty learning to spell, including students with special needs, may benefit from additional practice in learning spelling patterns.

Ask children to search for words in their writing and reading that conform to the spelling patterns they are learning. Write the words students locate on a wall chart. Encourage the children to add other words to the chart that conform to the pattern.

More Able Spellers

Challenge students who are strong spellers to locate five to ten words that they do not know the spelling and/or meaning of and to add these words to their weekly spelling lists. Students should also be asked to find the meanings they do not know and to use each word in an appropriate way orally.

ENGAGING
IN THE
PROCESS

INVOLVING FAMILIES

Ask students to copy their lists in the **Take Your List Home** section of the *Spell It–Write!* Home News page for this lesson. Not only does this page provide a convenient way for families to share a student's spelling list, but it also provides a number of opportunities for families to be involved in students' spelling growth. It has a statement of the week's spelling pattern or strategy, a valuable spelling study strategy, and a suggested home spelling practice activity.

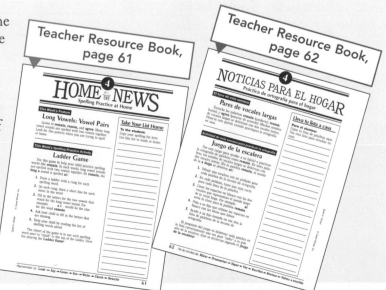

FINDING WORDS

STEP 1 Build Your Spelling List

Students will build their spelling lists with **Pattern Words, Teacher Words,** and **Your Words.** Students should study a minimum of twelve new words each week.

Find Your Pattern Words

- Pretest the students on these words.

- Tell students to write each misspelled pretest word on their spelling lists.

Add Teacher Words

- Select words for students to add to their spelling lists. Choose words from **More Words for Hungry Word Hunters** (on this page and on student page 160), words related to a theme or content area, or words students often misspell.

Add Your Words

- Ask students to pick words from their lists of **Words I Need to Know How to Spell** and their writing.

- Tell students to write these words on their spelling lists.

STEP 2 Write Your Spelling List

Remind students to verify all spellings. (Ask students to see **Strategies for Checking Your Spelling** in the back of the student edition.)

STEP 3 Set Your Learning Goal

Tell students to count the words on their spelling lists. This total is their learning goal. It may vary depending on ability, individual goals, and the difficulty of spelling words.

MORE WORDS FOR HUNGRY WORD HUNTERS

RED LIST
Pattern Words Below Level

afraid
asleep
beaver
delay
feeling
kangaroo
raccoon
Tuesday

BLUE LIST
Pattern Words Above Level

beneath
coffee
contain
continue
decay
explain
feature
freedom
shampoo
statue

Other Pattern Words

charcoal
decrease
detain
disagree
eastern
increase
loosen
obtain
reclaim
release

Math Pattern Word

remainder

Science Pattern Words

beetle
disease
measles

Social Studies Pattern Words

freeway
sailboat

These lists also appear on page 160 in the student edition and page 10 in the **Teacher Resource Book.**

SPELLING PATTERN

4

Long Vowels: Vowel Pairs

Your Spelling List

_____
_____
_____
_____
_____
_____
_____
_____
_____
_____
_____
_____
_____
_____
_____
_____
_____
_____
_____
_____

············· FINDING WORDS ·············

STEP 1 Build Your Spelling List

Find Your Pattern Words
Take the pretest.
Write misspelled words on your spelling list.

Add Teacher Words
Teachers may add:
- More **Pattern Words** • Content Words • Theme Words

Add Your Words
Pick words from:
- **Words I Need to Know How to Spell** • Writing • Reading

Pattern Words

1.	remain	**Remain** seated until the bell rings.
2.	reason	What is your **reason** for being late?
3.	agree	We must **agree** on a place to meet.
4.	anyway	Mom can't go, but we will go to the museum **anyway.**
5.	degree	My fever is up one **degree** today.
6.	season	My favorite **season** is fall.
7.	daily	The **daily** newspaper comes every day.
8.	repeat	I will **repeat** the sentence again.
9.	eager	I was **eager** to meet my new teacher.
10.	between	Stand **between** Sue and Kim.

STEP 2 Write Your Spelling List

STEP 3 Set Your Learning Goal

My spelling list has _____ words for me to learn.

I looked in **Words I Need to Know How to Spell** for words I missed on last week's test. I'll add them to my spelling list.

I got all the words right last week. So I'll look in **More Words for Hungry Word Hunters** for more **Pattern Words.**

INSPECTING WORDS

PATTERN MINI-LESSON

NOTE: The **Explore the Spelling Pattern** activity on page 35 is a self-directed mini-lesson. If you wish to supplement that activity with direct instruction, use the following mini-lesson.

* **Write** the **Pattern Words** from page 34 on the chalkboard. Say each word; ask students to repeat it.

* **Ask** students to identify the vowel pairs that spell the long vowel sound in each word. Underline these letters as students respond: **remain, reason, agree, anyway, degree, season, daily, repeat, eager, between**.

* **Point out** to students that each of these long vowel sounds is spelled with two vowel letters.

* **Remind** students that they already know how to spell many one-syllable words with these patterns. Explain that these patterns also appear in words with more than one syllable.

* **Ask** students to categorize these spelling patterns by sound (**long a—ai** and **ay; long e—ea** and **ee**).

* **Read** the **Spelling Pattern** on page 35 with students.

* **Encourage** students to give other examples of words with a long vowel sound and more than one syllable. List responses on the chalkboard.

* **Ask** students to identify the words with a long vowel sound spelled with two vowels together. Call on volunteers to underline the vowel pair in each word and to erase words that do not fit this pattern. You may wish to include examples from **More Words for Hungry Word Hunters** (on student page 160 and page T34). Remind students that they may add any of these words to **Words I Need to Know How to Spell**.

· · · · · · · · · · INSPECTING WORDS · · · · · · · · · ·

 Explore the Spelling Pattern
Sorting Words

A. One way to sort the **Pattern Words** is by the sound spelled by two vowels together. Say each **Pattern Word**. Which words have two vowels together that spell the **long e** sound? The **long a** sound? Sort the **Pattern Words** according to the long vowel pairs. Make sure you write each **Pattern Word** once.

Try sorting the **Pattern Words** in other ways. How many words have three syllables?

Long Vowel Pairs

Long e | Long a

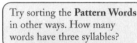

1. agr<u>ee</u>	2. r<u>ea</u>son	3. rem<u>ai</u>n	4. anyw<u>ay</u>
degree	season	daily	anyway
between	repeat	remain	
agree	eager		
	reason		

B. With a partner, hunt for other words that have long vowel pairs. You might look through **Words I Need to Know How to Spell**, in books, or around the room. Write the words you find.

5. Answers will vary.   7. _____

6. _____   8. _____

▼▼▼▼▼▼▼▼▼▼▼▼
Spelling Pattern
Listen to **remain, anyway, reason,** and **agree**. Many long vowel sounds are spelled with two vowels together.
· · · · · · · · · ·

 Focus on Word Study
Word History

Over 700 years ago, a French farmer used the word **season** to mean the time he planted seeds in the ground. One hundred years later, an English farmer used the word **season** to mean spring, summer, winter, fall.

1. Write the word we use today to mean the season plants begin to spring from the ground. _____ spring

2. Write the word we use today to mean the season leaves fall from trees. _____ fall

 Explore the Spelling Pattern
Sorting Words

This activity is a self-directed mini-lesson on this week's **Spelling Pattern**.

Focus on Word Study
Word History

This activity is intended to stimulate students' interest in words and to help them become more enthusiastic word hunters.

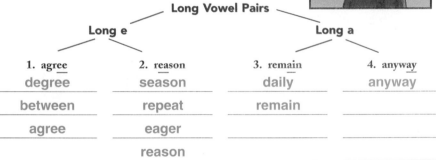
Spelling Process Handbook
Students who need to review any part of the spelling process, including practice options, should refer to the **Spelling Process Handbook** (pages 7–21).

MASTERING WORDS

A Practice Option

STEP 6 Practice Your Spelling List Independently

Ask the students to choose activities to practice their spelling words and to master this week's **Spelling Pattern**. Students should complete at least three activities each week. You may wish to:

- assign **Practice the Spelling Pattern** to all students to reinforce this week's **Spelling Pattern**.

- involve students' families by assigning **Take Your List Home** for this lesson (**Teacher Resource Book,** pages 61 in English and 62 in Spanish).

- encourage students to use partner activities without game mats (**Word Swap, Spelling Tic-Tac-Toe, Circle Dot**) and activities with game mats (**Meteor Attack, Rockets, Spelling Checkers, Spelling Soccer**). Directions for game-mat activities appear on each game mat. Directions for all other activities are found in the **Spelling Process Handbook** (pages 7–21).

NOTE: These activities and games can be used to practice any spelling list.

SPELLING CHECKERS

Students will "jump" at the chance to play **Spelling Checkers,** a game mat that combines spelling practice with the popular board game. And because students write on the board with dry-erase markers to record their progress, game pieces are not needed. This game is especially appropriate spelling practice for auditory and visual learners. (Directions appear on the **Spelling Checkers** game mat. This activity is appropriate for practicing any spelling list.)

MASTERING WORDS

STEP 6 Practice Your Spelling List Independently
Choose at least three activities to practice your spelling list.

It's fun to try different practice activities.

Game Mats		With a Partner		On Your Own		At Home
○ Spelling Soccer	○ Spelling Checkers	○ Circle Dot	○ Spelling Tic-Tac-Toe	○ Flip Folder	○ Spelling Study Strategy	○ Take Your List Home

✏ Practice the Spelling Pattern

Read the sentences. Decide what letters are missing from each **Pattern Word**. Write the whole word and circle the letters that were missing. Use the **Pattern Words** to check your spelling.

Pattern Words

remain
reason
agree
anyway
degree
season
daily
repeat
eager
between

1. Rob was __ger to eat the Swiss cheese.   e(a)ger
2. What s__son comes after summer?   s(ea)son
3. I will rem__n until all the parents leave.   rem(ai)n
4. I agr__ with your answer.   agr(ee)
5. Ed swims d__ly to stay healthy.   d(ai)ly
6. Would you please rep__t your question?   rep(ea)t
7. I didn't want to go anyw__.   anyw(ay)
8. Just betw__n you and me, I can't sing.   betw(ee)n
9. Just one more degr__, and it will be 90.   degr(ee)
10. Give me one r__son to tell you my secret.   r(ea)son

DEVELOPING GOOD SPELLING HABITS

STEP 7 Focus on Writing

A. Proofread the Writing of Others

This activity provides proofreading practice in a variety of formats, including popular standardized test formats.

B. Proofread Your Own Writing

Students return to their own writing, armed with strategies to identify and collect words they need to know how to spell, and make an authentic link between spelling and writing.

C. A Writing Idea: A Poem

This suggestion for a more extended writing activity provides opportunities for students to write in different genres for a variety of purposes and modes.

STEP 8 Check Your Weekly Progress

▶ Take the Test

Remind students that they can take a practice test before the final test on their spelling lists. To find the testing procedure that is right for you, refer to page Z12.

▶ Check Your Goal

Have students compare their tests to their spelling lists. Did they spell all the **Pattern Words** on their spelling lists correctly?

▶ Graph Your Progress

Ask students to graph the number correct (student page 175 for softbound users; **Teacher Resource Book** page 123 for hardbound users).

▶ Save Missed Words

Tell students to write misspelled words on their lists of **Words I Need to Know How to Spell**. Remind students to verify spellings and to recycle these words on future weekly spelling lists.

· · · · · DEVELOPING GOOD SPELLING HABITS · · · · ·

STEP 7 Focus on Writing

A. Proofread the Writing of Others

Proofread the school announcement below. Decide which type of mistake, if any, appears in each underlined section.

> Basketball seeson begins next Monday. so sign up ①   ② today! We're eager to begin! Practice will be held daley ③ in the gym from two to three o'clock. Even if you don't want to play, come anyway and cheer! ④

≡ Make a capital.
/ Make a small letter.
∧ Add something.
ℓ Take out something.
⊙ Add a period.
¶ New paragraph
SP Spelling error

1. (A) Spelling
   B Capitalization
   C Punctuation
   D No mistake

2. A Spelling
   (B) Capitalization
   C Punctuation
   D No mistake

3. (A) Spelling
   B Capitalization
   C Punctuation
   D No mistake

4. A Spelling
   B Capitalization
   C Punctuation
   (D) No mistake

B. Proofread Your Own Writing

Two vowels together often spell a long vowel sound. Proofread your latest piece of writing. Did you spell the words with vowel pairs correctly? Write misspelled words in **Words I Need to Know How to Spell**.

C. A Writing Idea: A Poem

Write a poem about your favorite season. Use words that describe the sights, sounds, and smells of this time of year. Check your finished poem to see if you've spelled all the words correctly. Then trade poems with a friend.

STEP 8 Check Your Weekly Progress

▶ **Take the Test**
Ready? Practice test first.

▶ **Check Your Goal**
Check to see if you met your learning goal.

▶ **Graph Your Progress**
Graph your score for this week's test.

▶ **Save Missed Words**
Write the words you missed in your list of **Words I Need to Know How to Spell**.

Hunt Words

Remind students to continuously hunt words that they wish to learn how to spell and to write these words in **Words I Need to Know How to Spell**.

Endings: -ed, -ing

ENGAGING IN THE PROCESS — MATERIALS

Student Edition: Pages 38–41   **Teacher Edition**: Pages T38A–T41

Materials to help students practice their spelling lists:

- **Flip Folders**
- Copies of **Flip Folder Practice Sheet** (**Teacher Resource Book,** page 51)
- **Take Your List Home** (in *Spell It–Write!* Home News, **Teacher Resource Book,** pages 63 in English and 64 in Spanish)

- Game Mats Featured in This Unit: **Meteor Attack, Spelling Checkers**
- Unit 5 **Hands-on Word Sort Cards** (Grade 4 **Hands-on Word Sort Card Book**) and Unit 5 **Hands-on Word Sort Sheet** (**Teacher Resource Book,** page 40)

ENGAGING IN THE PROCESS — GOALS

SPELLING GOALS

Students will

- demonstrate their ability to spell words in which -**ed** and -**ing** are added to base words.
- sort words by base word changes.
- understand that the original meaning of a word can still be recognized in a word whose meaning has changed over time.
- use the spelling process to become better writers.

WRITING GOALS

Students will

- hunt for words with the endings -**ed** and -**ing** in a piece of their own writing.
- write an expressive journal entry.

ENGAGING IN THE PROCESS — MANAGEMENT

Pacing	Notes	Quick Pick Management Option
Period 1 Finding Words (Steps 1–3)	If you wish to add **Teacher Words,** write them on the chalkboard. Sources for more words include: **More Words for Hungry Word Hunters** (page T38), content and theme-related words, or words of your choice.	Assign the list of **Pattern Words** to the whole class. Add the Red List (**More Words for Hungry Word Hunters,** student page 161) for a longer list. Add the Blue List (**More Words for Hungry Word Hunters**) for a more challenging list.
Period 2 Inspecting Words (Steps 4 and 5)	Students write the **Pattern Words** to complete **Explore the Spelling Pattern.**	Assign **Explore the Spelling Pattern** and **Focus on Word Study**.
Period 3 Mastering Words (Step 6) **Period 4** Developing Good Spelling Habits (Step 7)	These two periods can be allocated between selected **Mastering Words** activities and proofreading and writing activities in **Focus on Writing**.	Assign two or three activities to the whole class. Familiarize students with choosing their own activities at their own pace.
Period 5 Assessment (Step 8)	Gradually try different peer-testing options to find the style that best fits your class.	Test the class on the same, whole-class list.

Understanding Language Differences

Spanish Speakers

The Spanish writing system is a bit easier than the English system. For example, the Spanish letter **e** is predictable: it is pronounced like **short e** when the syllable ends in a consonant and like **long a** when the syllable ends in a vowel. As a result of this predictability, the notion of the English **silent e** may not make sense to some native Spanish speakers. Some students may need additional help in understanding the function of the final **silent e** in English spelling.

For similar reasons, students whose first language is Spanish may become confused by the idea that a vowel is pronounced differently depending on whether the consonant following the vowel is single, double, or part of a blend. For example the **o** in **stopped** is pronounced differently from the **o** in **moved.** (In Spanish, the letter **o** is always pronounced like the **long o** in the English word **go.**) Native Spanish speakers may need help with this concept.

Oral modeling, games, and other activities may be used to reinforce these concepts. Literature models can also be useful. Cooperative learning techniques in which native and non-native English speakers are grouped together can benefit all learners.

Helping Students Acquiring English

On the chalkboard, write the **Pattern Word planned,** using three different colors of chalk for the base word **plan,** the second **n,** and the **-ed** ending. Point to and pronounce the base word **plan,** and have students identify the **short a** vowel sound. Follow a similar procedure to demonstrate dropping a final **silent e** when adding **-ed** or **-ing.** Call on volunteers to add **-ed** and **-ing** to each base word.

Meeting Diverse Needs

Less Able Spellers

Some students who have difficulty learning to spell, including students with special needs, may benefit from the presentation and practice of just a few words each day instead of the traditional practice of presenting the full spelling list at the beginning of the week. This limited presentation allows the child to practice the new words and review the words already presented that week. This may help make the task of learning a longer list of spelling words more manageable for children who struggle with the learning process.

More Able Spellers

Challenge students to "find" as many words within another word as they can by rearranging letters. For example, **architect** contains **arch, cat, rat, teach,** and **tear.**

Ask students to copy their lists in the **Take Your List Home** section of the *Spell It–Write!* Home News page for this lesson. Not only does this page provide a convenient way for families to share a student's spelling list, but it also provides a number of opportunities for families to be involved in students' spelling growth. It has a statement of the week's spelling pattern or strategy, a valuable spelling study strategy, and a suggested home spelling practice activity.

FINDING WORDS

STEP 1 — Build Your Spelling List

Students will build their spelling lists with **Pattern Words, Teacher Words,** and **Your Words**. Students should study a minimum of twelve new words each week.

Find Your Pattern Words

• Pretest the students on these words.

• Tell students to write each misspelled pretest word on their spelling lists.

Add Teacher Words

• Select words for students to add to their spelling lists. Choose words from **More Words for Hungry Word Hunters** (on this page and on student page 161), words related to a theme or content area, or words students often misspell.

Add Your Words

• Ask students to pick words from their lists of **Words I Need to Know How to Spell** and their writing.

• Tell students to write these words on their spelling lists.

STEP 2 — Write Your Spelling List

Remind students to verify all spellings. (Ask students to see **Strategies for Checking Your Spelling** in the back of the student edition.)

STEP 3 — Set Your Learning Goal

Tell students to count the words on their spelling lists. This total is their learning goal. It may vary depending on ability, individual goals, and the difficulty of spelling words.

MORE WORDS FOR HUNGRY WORD HUNTERS

RED LIST — Pattern Words Below Level	BLUE LIST — Pattern Words Above Level	Other Pattern Words	Math Pattern Words
closed	admitted	continued	divided
closing	arriving	hiccupped	rating
flying	beginning	hiccupping	
getting	carrying	laughed	**Social Studies Pattern Words**
having	decided	laughing	climbing
living	deciding	removed	farming
moved	enjoyed	trimmed	jogging
rubbed	finished	trimming	marched
sleeping	proved		sowing
snowed	quitting		
stopped	wrapped		
stopping	wrapping		

These lists also appear on page 161 in the student edition and page 11 in the **Teacher Resource Book**.

SPELLING PATTERN 5

Endings: -ed, -ing

Your Spelling List

_____
_____
_____
_____
_____
_____
_____
_____
_____
_____
_____
_____
_____
_____
_____
_____
_____
_____
_____
_____
_____
_____
_____
_____

STEP 1 — Build Your Spelling List

Find Your Pattern Words
Take the pretest.
Write misspelled words on your spelling list.

Add Teacher Words
Teachers may add:
• More **Pattern Words** • Content Words • Theme Words

Add Your Words
Pick words from:
• **Words I Need to Know How to Spell** • Writing • Reading

Pattern Words

1. **planned**   We had **planned** to leave today.
2. **planning** Judy is **planning** her birthday party.
3. **used**   Dee **used** all the purple yarn to knit the hat.
4. **using**   Ben is **using** the markers.
5. **happened** The fire **happened** last Friday.
6. **tired**   The hard work **tired** the men quickly.
7. **writing**   I am **writing** my shopping list.
8. **grabbed**   Dana **grabbed** his books and ran.
9. **smiling**   Mrs. Morris is **smiling** at me.
10. **shoving** Stop **shoving** things into the closet.
11. **swimming** We are **swimming** over to the island.
12. **following** A puppy is **following** us.

STEP 2 — Write Your Spelling List

STEP 3 — Set Your Learning Goal

My spelling list has _____ words for me to learn.

The first thing I do after our spelling test is write the words I missed in **Words I Need to Know How to Spell**.

I write words I misspelled in my writing. I also add any interesting words I find.

PATTERN MINI-LESSON

NOTE: ▶ The **Explore the Spelling Pattern** activity on page 39 is a self-directed mini-lesson. If you wish to supplement that activity with direct instruction, use the following mini-lesson.

* **Read** the **Spelling Pattern** on page 39.

* **Display** the **Hands-on Word Sort Cards** for Unit 5. Keep blank cards and a marker handy to make new cards.

* **Say** each guide word and point to the underlined part. (Guide words are labeled "Master Word" on the **Word Sort Card**.) Ask students to explain how each base word changed when **-ed** or **-ing** was added. Establish that when a one-syllable word ends in one vowel and one consonant, the consonant is doubled before **-ed** or **-ing** is added, and that a final **silent e** is dropped when **-ed** or **-ing** is added.

* **Sort** the words on this principle. Model your decision making: "In **planning**, a final consonant was doubled when **-ing** was added, so I'll put **planning** under **planned**." For the completed word sort, see the **Answer Card** for this unit in the **Hands-on Word Sort Card Book**.

NOTE: ▶ **Happened** is an example of a word in which the base word is not changed when the ending is added. However, more complex rules for doubling the final consonant apply to base words of two or more syllables. For further information, see *Spell It–Write!*, Grade 5, Unit 12.

* **Duplicate** the **Hands-on Word Sort Sheet** for Unit 5 (**Teacher Resource Book,** page 40). Ask students to cut the words on the sheet apart and practice sorting the words with a partner or independently.

· · · · · · · · · · · INSPECTING WORDS · · · · · · · · · · · ·

4 Explore the Spelling Pattern
Sorting Words

A. Each **Pattern Word** was made by adding **-ed** or **-ing** to a base word. Sort the **Pattern Words** into three groups. Use the underlined spelling patterns in the words below to guide your sort. (The base word is in parentheses.)

1. planned (plan)	3. using (use)
planned	using
planning	used
grabbed	tired
swimming	writing
	smiling
	shoving
2. happened (happen)	
happened	
following	

B. Work with a partner to add other words to each list and to sort the words in other ways.

5 Focus on Word Study
Word Origins

The base word for **writing** is **write**. **Write** comes from **writan**, an Old Saxon word that meant "to scratch." Listen to your pencil as it scratches across the page.

Write the **Pattern Word** whose base word came from these old words.

1. grabben   grabbed
2. smilen   smiling
3. shufen   shoving
4. follewen   following

> You may wish to use **Hands-on Word Sort Cards** and the **Hands-on Word Sort Sheet** for this unit.

Spelling Pattern

• When you add **-ed** or **-ing** to most words, there is no spelling change in the base word.

• When you add **-ed** or **-ing** to a one-syllable word that ends with one vowel and one consonant, double the consonant and add the ending: **plan, planned, planning**.

• When you add **-ed** or **-ing** to a word that ends in **silent e**, drop the **e** and add the ending: **use, used, using**.

4 Explore the Spelling Pattern
Sorting Words

This activity is a self-directed mini-lesson on this week's **Spelling Pattern**.

5 Focus on Word Study

Word Origins

This activity is intended to stimulate students' interest in words and to help them become more enthusiastic word hunters.

Spelling Process Handbook

Students who need to review any part of the spelling process, including practice options, should refer to the **Spelling Process Handbook** (pages 7–21).

STEP 6 Practice Your Spelling List Independently

Ask the students to choose activities to practice their spelling words and to master this week's **Spelling Pattern**. Students should complete at least three activities each week. You may wish to:

- assign **Practice the Spelling Pattern** to all students to reinforce this week's **Spelling Pattern**.

- involve students' families by assigning **Take Your List Home** for this lesson (**Teacher Resource Book**, pages 63 in English and 64 in Spanish).

- encourage students to use partner activities without game mats (**Word Swap, Spelling Tic-Tac-Toe, Circle Dot**) and activities with game mats (**Meteor Attack, Rockets, Spelling Checkers, Spelling Soccer**). Directions for game-mat activities appear on each game mat. Directions for all other activities are found in the **Spelling Process Handbook** (pages 7–21).

NOTE: These activities and games can be used to practice any spelling list.

SPELLING TIC-TAC-TOE

Just about anyone knows how to play tic-tac-toe. And now this strategic game of **X**'s and **O**'s teams up with spelling words to make spelling practice fun! Partners can practice spelling words with **Spelling Tic-Tac-Toe** on any scrap of paper. And because partners spell words aloud and visually check errors against correct spellings, **Spelling Tic-Tac-Toe** appeals to both visual and auditory learners. (Directions appear in the **Spelling Process Handbook**, student pages 7–21. This activity is appropriate for practicing any spelling list.)

STEP 6 Practice Your Spelling List Independently

Choose at least three activities to practice your spelling list.

Hunt words in your writing and reading! Add words you want to learn to **Words I Need to Know How to Spell***.*

Game Mats	With a Partner	On Your Own	At Home
Spelling Checkers / Meteor Attack	Spelling Tic-Tac-Toe / Word Swap	Flip Folder / Spelling Study Strategy	Take Your List Home

Practice the Spelling Pattern

Write a **Pattern Word** to solve each spelling problem. Remember that the spelling of some base words will change when you add **-ed** or **-ing**.

Pattern Words

planned
planning
used
using
happened
tired
writing
grabbed
smiling
shoving
swimming
following

1. swim + ing = __ _____ swimming
2. tire + ed = __ _____ tired
3. shove + ing = __ _____ shoving
4. follow + ing = __ _____ following
5. plan + ed = __ _____ planned
6. happen + ed = __ _____ happened
7. smile + ing = __ _____ smiling
8. plan + ing = __ _____ planning
9. use + ed = __ _____ used
10. write + ing = __ _____ writing
11. grab + ed = __ _____ grabbed
12. use + ing = __ _____ using

DEVELOPING GOOD SPELLING HABITS

STEP 7 Focus on Writing

A. Hunt Spelling Words in Your Writing

This activity equips students with a specific strategy for increasing students' consciousness of targeted spelling patterns and strategies in their own writing. It also enables them to collect words for spelling study.

B. A Writing Idea: A Journal Entry

This suggestion for a more extended writing activity provides opportunities for students to write in different genres for a variety of purposes and modes.

STEP 8 Check Your Weekly Progress

▶ Take the Test

Remind students that they can take a practice test before the final test on their spelling lists. To find the testing procedure that is right for you, refer to page Z12.

▶ Check Your Goal

Have students compare their tests to their spelling lists. Did they spell all the **Pattern Words** on their spelling lists correctly?

▶ Graph Your Progress

Ask students to graph the number correct (student page 175 for softbound users; **Teacher Resource Book** page 123 for hardbound users).

▶ Save Missed Words

Tell students to write misspelled words on their lists of **Words I Need to Know How to Spell**. Remind students to verify spellings and to recycle these words on future weekly spelling lists.

· · · · · DEVELOPING GOOD SPELLING HABITS · · · · ·

STEP 7 Focus on Writing

A. Hunt Spelling Words in Your Writing

Look over your recent pieces of writing. Choose one in which you used words with **-ed** and **-ing** endings. With a partner, hunt for all the words ending in **-ed** or **-ing**. Write the words you find in two columns like these.

Column 1	Column 2
I spelled these **-ed** and **-ing** words correctly.	I misspelled these **-ed** and **-ing** words.
Answers will vary.	Answers will vary.

Add the words you wrote in Column 2 to **Words I Need to Know How to Spell**.

B. A Writing Idea: A Journal Entry

Write a journal entry that tells about your day or your week. What happened? What were you doing or thinking about? When you are finished writing, circle each word that ends in **-ed** or **-ing**. Did you spell these words correctly?

≡ Make a capital.
/ Make a small letter.
∧ Add something.
ℯ Take out something.
⊙ Add a period.
¶ New paragraph
(SP) Spelling error

STEP 8 Check Your Weekly Progress

▶ Take the Test
Ready? Practice test first.

▶ Check Your Goal
Check to see if you met your learning goal.

▶ Graph Your Progress
Graph your score for this week's test.

▶ Save Missed Words
Write the words you missed in your list of **Words I Need to Know How to Spell**.

Hunt Words

Remind students to continuously hunt words that they wish to learn how to spell and to write these words in **Words I Need to Know How to Spell**.

Words Writers Use

ENGAGING IN THE **PROCESS** : **MATERIALS**

Student Edition: Pages 42–45   **Teacher Edition**: Pages T42A–T45

Materials to help students practice their spelling lists:

- Flip Folders
- Copies of **Flip Folder Practice Sheet** (**Teacher Resource Book**, page 51)
- **Take Your List Home** (in *Spell It–Write!*)

Home News, **Teacher Resource Book**, pages 65 in English and 66 in Spanish)
- Game Mats Featured in This Unit: **Meteor Attack, Rockets**

ENGAGING IN THE **PROCESS** : **GOALS**

SPELLING GOALS

Students will

- recognize words that are commonly used and frequently misspelled.
- learn to recognize that unexpected spellings of words may be due to changes in pronunciation over time.
- use the spelling process of finding words, inspecting words, and mastering words as they develop good spelling habits to become better writers.

WRITING GOALS

Students will

- proofread a writing sample.
- proofread a piece of their own writing for misspelled words.
- write an informative e-mail message.

ENGAGING IN THE **PROCESS** : **MANAGEMENT**

Pacing	Notes	Quick Pick Management Option
Period 1 Finding Words (Steps 1–3)	If you wish to add **Teacher Words**, write them on the chalkboard. Sources for more words include: **More Words for Hungry Word Hunters** (page T42), content and theme-related words, or words of your choice.	Assign the list of **Strategy Words** to the whole class. Add the Red List (**More Words for Hungry Word Hunters,** student page 161) for a longer list. Add the Blue List (**More Words for Hungry Word Hunters**) for a more challenging list.
Period 2 Inspecting Words (Steps 4 and 5)	Students write the **Strategy Words** to complete **Explore the Spelling Strategy**.	Assign **Explore the Spelling Strategy** and **Focus on Word Study**.
Period 3 Mastering Words (Step 6) **Period 4** Developing Good Spelling Habits (Step 7)	These two periods can be allocated between selected **Mastering Words** activities and proofreading and writing activities in **Focus on Writing**.	Assign two or three activities to the whole class. Familiarize students with choosing their own activities at their own pace.
Period 5 Assessment (Step 8)	Gradually try different peer-testing options to find the style that best fits your class.	Test the class on the same, whole-class list.

ENGAGING

IN THE

PROCESS

INDIVIDUAL NEEDS

Understanding Language Differences

Spanish Speakers

In this unit, there are several potential sources of errors for students who are learning English as a second language.

One source is what the learner already knows about spelling or writing in another language, especially if the other language uses the same or a similar alphabet. (Spanish is one example of such a language.) These are called interlingual or transfer errors.

The other potential source is English itself, which often seems to break its own rules or use unexpected spellings for individual words. These kinds of errors are intralingual or developmental errors. In this unit, you might anticipate some of the following problems from both transfer and developmental sources.

Spanish speakers may substitute vowels. They may spell **always** (Red List) as **alweys** or substitute **lezy** for **lazy,** since the \ay\ sound is always spelled with **e** in Spanish when a syllable ends in a vowel.

Silent letters are less common in some other writing systems, such as Spanish, than in English, so expect **els** for **else, bilt** for **built,** and **hevy** for **heavy. Silent k,** in **known,** is a peculiarly English spelling phenomenon.

English often uses **gh** for \f\, as in laugh, but speakers of other languages may find this odd.

Helping Students Acquiring English

Write each **Strategy Word** on a 3" x 5" card. Give each student an equal number of cards. Pronounce a word, spell it, and ask the student who has that word to hold up the card. Repeat the word, and ask students to say the word and spell it along with you. When all the words have been presented, place the cards face down. Call on students to take turns drawing a word and spelling it aloud.

Meeting Diverse Needs

Less Able Spellers

Spelling is one area in which families often help their children. This is especially true for families whose children have difficulty learning to spell.

You can help families work with their children more effectively by encouraging the adults to call you with questions and by inviting families to a meeting to learn about the spelling program. It is a good idea to check periodically to see whether families need additional advice.

More Able Spellers

Challenge students to rearrange the letters in a single word or saying to create another word or saying. For example, the letters in **tear** can be rearranged to make **rate.** Explain that in order to be successful in this activity, students must not have any letters left over when they create the new word.

ENGAGING

IN THE

PROCESS

INVOLVING FAMILIES

Ask students to copy their lists in the **Take Your List Home** section of the *Spell It–Write!* Home News page for this lesson. Not only does this page provide a convenient way for families to share a student's spelling list, but it also provides a number of opportunities for families to be involved in students' spelling growth. It has a statement of the week's spelling pattern or strategy, a valuable spelling study strategy, and a suggested home spelling practice activity.

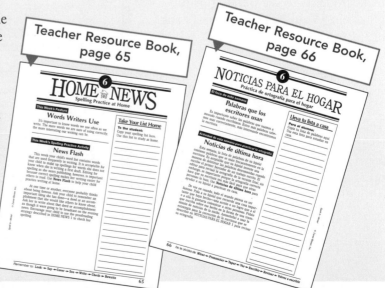

Teacher Resource Book, page 65

Teacher Resource Book, page 66

FINDING WORDS

MORE WORDS FOR HUNGRY WORD HUNTERS

RED LIST Strategy Words Below Level	BLUE LIST Strategy Words Above Level	Other Strategy Words	Science Strategy Word
also	complete	article	stomach
always	dangerous	author	**Social Studies Strategy Words**
everyone	energy	create	blizzard
everything	famous	either	cactus
family	forgotten	inform	tropics
kids	frighten	listen	
never	neighbor	make-believe	
where	promise	movies	
would	themselves	rather	
year	weight	serious	

These lists also appear on page 161 in the student edition and page 12 in the **Teacher Resource Book.**

STEP 1 Build Your Spelling List

Students will build their spelling lists with **Strategy Words, Teacher Words,** and **Your Words**. Students should study a minimum of twelve new words each week.

Find Your Strategy Words

• Pretest the students on these words.

• Tell students to write each misspelled pretest word on their spelling lists.

Add Teacher Words

• Select words for students to add to their spelling lists. Choose words from **More Words for Hungry Word Hunters** (on this page and on student page 161), words related to a theme or content area, or words students often misspell.

Add Your Words

• Ask students to pick words from their lists of **Words I Need to Know How to Spell** and their writing.

• Tell students to write these words on their spelling lists.

STEP 2 Write Your Spelling List

Remind students to verify all spellings. (Ask students to see **Strategies for Checking Your Spelling** in the back of the student edition.)

STEP 3 Set Your Learning Goal

Tell students to count the words on their spelling lists. This total is their learning goal. It may vary depending on ability, individual goals, and the difficulty of spelling words.

SPELLING STRATEGY

6

Words Writers Use

Your Spelling List

_____
_____
_____
_____
_____
_____
_____
_____
_____
_____
_____
_____
_____
_____
_____
_____
_____
_____

· · · · · · FINDING WORDS · · · · · · ·

STEP 1 Build Your Spelling List

Find Your Strategy Words

Take the pretest.
Write misspelled words on your spelling list.

Add Teacher Words

Teachers may add:
• More **Strategy Words** • Content Words • Theme Words

Add Your Words

Pick words from:
• **Words I Need to Know How to Spell** • Writing • Reading

Strategy Words

1. **else** — Would you like something **else** to eat besides your sandwich?
2. **answer** — You knew the right **answer** to the question.
3. **visit** — I would like to **visit** my cousin soon.
4. **built** — We **built** a castle in the sand.
5. **driven** — How often has Dad **driven** his new car?
6. **known** — I have **known** Erin for three years.
7. **lazy** — I do homework on Saturday because I often feel **lazy** on Sunday.
8. **heavy** — That box is too **heavy** for me to lift.
9. **laugh** — Tell me a joke that will make me **laugh**.
10. **moment** — I want to stop and rest for a **moment**.

STEP 2 Write Your Spelling List

STEP 3 Set Your Learning Goal

My spelling list has _____ words for me to learn.

I like the different ways I can practice my spelling words. I practice with a partner or by myself.

I really like doing activities outside the book. It makes it fun to keep practicing until I really know all my words.

INSPECTING WORDS

STRATEGY MINI-LESSON

NOTE: The **Explore the Spelling Strategy** activity on page 43 is a self-directed mini-lesson. If you wish to supplement that activity with direct instruction, use the following mini-lesson.

* **Ask** a volunteer to read aloud the **Spelling Strategy** on page 43.

* **Write** the **Strategy Words** from page 42 on the chalkboard. Say each word and ask students to repeat it.

* **Tell** students that these are words commonly used by many people in their writing, so it is important to be able to spell them correctly.

* **Ask** students to work individually or in pairs to write sentences containing these words. (You may wish to ask students to expand one or two of their sentences into longer pieces of writing.) You may also wish to write on the chalkboard examples from **More Words for Hungry Word Hunters** (on student page 161 and page T42). Remind students that they can add any words they cannot spell to **Words I Need to Know How to Spell**.

· · · · · · · · · · · · · · INSPECTING WORDS · · · · · · · · · · · · ·

Explore the Spelling Strategy
Completing Words

A. Inspect each incomplete **Strategy Word** in the expressions below. Decide which letters are missing. Write the whole word and circle the letters that were missing.

1. We don't have a mo__nt to lose.   mo(me)nt
2. What el__ is new?   el(se)
3. That problem has driv__ us crazy!   driv(en)
4. Rome wasn't b__lt in a day.   bu(il)t
5. He's a la__h a minute!   la(ug)h
6. It's a secret __own only to me.   (kn)own
7. This is as h__vy as lead!   h(ea)vy
8. Let's cut our vi__t short.   vi(si)t
9. Who came up with the an__er?   an(sw)er
10. Don't be a la__ bones.   la(zy)

B. On your own, hunt through your writing. Choose three or four words that are important to you as a writer. Check the spelling. Write them in **Words I Need to Know How to Spell** if you need to study them.

Focus on Word Study
Unexpected Spellings

The word **laugh** contains a **gh** that is pronounced as an **f**. That's not as crazy as it sounds. Long ago, **gh** was pronounced very differently. Although the pronunciation has changed, the spelling has remained.

For each set below, write the word that has the same spelling pattern and pronunciation as the **gh** in **laugh**.

1. cough, daughter   cough
2. night, laughter   laughter
3. tough, height   tough
4. sigh, roughly   roughly

▼▼▼▼▼▼▼▼▼▼▼▼
Spelling Strategy
It's important to know words we use often as we write.

Explore the Spelling Strategy
Completing Words

This activity is a self-directed mini-lesson on this week's **Spelling Strategy**.

Focus on Word Study
Unexpected Spellings

This activity is intended to stimulate students' interest in words and to help them become more enthusiastic word hunters.

Spelling Process Handbook

Students who need to review any part of the spelling process, including practice options, should refer to the **Spelling Process Handbook** (pages 7–21).

MASTERING WORDS

STEP 6 Practice Your Spelling List Independently

Ask the students to choose activities to practice their spelling words and to master this week's **Spelling Strategy**. Students should complete at least three activities each week. You may wish to:

- assign **Practice the Spelling Strategy** to all students to reinforce this week's **Spelling Strategy**.

- involve students' families by assigning **Take Your List Home** for this lesson (**Teacher Resource Book**, pages 65 in English and 66 in Spanish).

- encourage students to use partner activities without game mats (**Word Swap, Spelling Tic-Tac-Toe, Circle Dot**) and activities with game mats (**Meteor Attack, Rockets, Spelling Checkers, Spelling Soccer**). Directions for game-mat activities appear on each game mat. Directions for all other activities are found in the **Spelling Process Handbook** (pages 7–21).

NOTE: These activities and games can be used to practice any spelling list.

A Practice Option

CIRCLE DOT

Circles and dots become powerful learning tools in this simple, effective activity. Each student works with a partner to attempt —and then correct—the spelling of each word on his or her list. As the student corrects, he or she marks a dot for each correct letter and a circle for each error. Because **Circle Dot** makes discrete errors visible, students can practice their spelling words strategically by focusing on the part(s) of the spelling that most challenges them. (Directions appear in the **Spelling Process Handbook**, student pages 7–21. This activity is appropriate for practicing any spelling list.)

· · · · · · · · · · · **MASTERING WORDS** · · · · · · · · · · ·

STEP 6 Practice Your Spelling List Independently

Choose at least three activities to practice your spelling list.

Need Help? Read the **Spelling Process Handbook** (pages 7–21).

Game Mats		With a Partner		On Your Own		At Home
○ Meteor Attack	○ Rockets	○ Circle Dot	○ Word Swap	○ Flip Folder	○ Spelling Study Strategy	○ Take Your List Home

Practice the Spelling Strategy

In Column 1, write a **Strategy Word** that means the same as each word shown. In Column 2, write a **Strategy Word** from the word list that means the opposite of the word shown.

Strategy Words

else
answer
visit
built
driven
known
lazy
heavy
laugh
moment

Column 1: Same

1. giggle
   laugh

2. minute
   moment

3. meet with
   visit

4. other
   else

5. steered
   driven

Column 2: Opposite

6. unknown
   known

7. active
   lazy

8. question
   answer

9. light
   heavy

10. destroyed
    built

DEVELOPING GOOD SPELLING HABITS

STEP 7 Focus on Writing

A. Proofread the Writing of Others

This activity provides proofreading practice in a variety of formats, including popular standardized test formats.

B. Proofread Your Own Writing

Students return to their own writing, armed with strategies to identify and collect words they need to know how to spell, and make an authentic link between spelling and writing.

C. A Writing Idea: An E-mail Message

This suggestion for a more extended writing activity provides opportunities for students to write in different genres for a variety of purposes and modes.

STEP 8 Check Your Weekly Progress

▶ Take the Test

Remind students that they can take a practice test before the final test on their spelling lists. To find the testing procedure that is right for you, refer to page Z12.

▶ Check Your Goal

Have students compare their tests to their spelling lists. Did they spell all the **Strategy Words** on their spelling lists correctly?

▶ Graph Your Progress

Ask students to graph the number correct (student page 175 for softbound users; **Teacher Resource Book** page 123 for hardbound users).

▶ Save Missed Words

Tell students to write misspelled words on their lists of **Words I Need to Know How to Spell**. Remind students to verify spellings and to recycle these words on future weekly spelling lists.

· · · · · DEVELOPING GOOD SPELLING HABITS · · · · ·

STEP 7 Focus on Writing

A. Proofread the Writing of Others

Proofread the writing below. Find the six misspelled words. Rewrite each word correctly.

> To avoid hevy traffic, my mom drove down an unknoan street. Was I surprised to see my friend Jade standing in front of one of the houses there!
>
> Jade waved. "Hey!" she called. "How about stopping a momint? Do you have time for a vizit?"
>
> "Sure," I called back with a lagh. I thought about how lucky I was that we had drivin down her street.

≡ Make a capital.
/ Make a small letter.
∧ Add something.
𝘦 Take out something.
⊙ Add a period.
¶ New paragraph
SP Spelling error

1. _____heavy_____
2. _____unknown_____
3. _____moment_____
4. _____visit_____
5. _____laugh_____
6. _____driven_____

B. Proofread Your Own Writing

You use some words over and over when you write, so it's important to spell them right. Look for words from this unit in your own writing. Also look for other words you use often. Check to see whether you have spelled them right. If you haven't, find out the correct spelling and copy them correctly in **Words I Need to Know How to Spell**.

C. A Writing Idea: An E-mail Message

Write an e-mail message to a friend. Invite your friend to visit, or talk about a visit you just had. After you have proofread your message for the correct spelling of words you use often, send your e-mail on-line, or mail it.

STEP 8 Check Your Weekly Progress

▶ Take the Test
Ready? Practice test first.

▶ Check Your Goal
Check to see if you met your learning goal.

▶ Graph Your Progress
Graph your score for this week's test.

▶ Save Missed Words
Write the words you missed in your list of **Words I Need to Know How to Spell**.

Hunt Words

Remind students to continuously hunt words that they wish to learn how to spell and to write these words in **Words I Need to Know How to Spell**.

Homophones

ENGAGING IN THE P·R·O·C·E·S·S

MATERIALS

Student Edition: Pages 46–49   **Teacher Edition:** Pages T46A–T49

Materials to help students practice their spelling lists:
- **Flip Folders**
- Copies of **Flip Folder Practice Sheet** (**Teacher Resource Book,** page 51)
- **Take Your List Home** (in *Spell It–Write!*)

Home News, **Teacher Resource Book,** pages 67 in English and 68 in Spanish)
- Game Mats Featured in This Unit: **Rockets, Spelling Soccer**

ENGAGING IN THE P·R·O·C·E·S·S

GOALS

SPELLING GOALS

Students will

- transfer knowledge of homophones to spell homophones in context.
- develop an understanding of how the meanings of words can change over time.
- use the spelling process of finding words, inspecting words, and mastering words as they develop good spelling habits to become better writers.

WRITING GOALS

Students will

- proofread a writing sample.
- proofread a piece of their own writing for misspelled homophones.
- write an informative how-to list.

ENGAGING IN THE P·R·O·C·E·S·S

MANAGEMENT

Pacing	Notes	Quick Pick Management Option
Period 1 Finding Words (Steps 1–3)	If you wish to add **Teacher Words,** write them on the chalkboard. Sources for more words include: **More Words for Hungry Word Hunters** (page T46), content and theme-related words, or words of your choice.	Assign the list of **Pattern Words** to the whole class. Add the Red List (**More Words for Hungry Word Hunters,** student page 162) for a longer list. Add the Blue List (**More Words for Hungry Word Hunters**) for a more challenging list.
Period 2 Inspecting Words (Steps 4 and 5)	Students write the **Pattern Words** to complete **Explore the Spelling Pattern.**	Assign **Explore the Spelling Pattern** and **Focus on Word Study.**
Period 3 Mastering Words (Step 6) **Period 4** Developing Good Spelling Habits (Step 7)	These two periods can be allocated between selected **Mastering Words** activities and proofreading and writing activities in **Focus on Writing.**	Assign two or three activities to the whole class. Familiarize students with choosing their own activities at their own pace.
Period 5 Assessment (Step 8)	Gradually try different peer-testing options to find the style that best fits your class.	Test the class on the same, whole-class list.

ENGAGING
IN THE
PROCESS

INDIVIDUAL
NEEDS

Understanding Language Differences

Spanish Speakers

In Spanish, an accent mark may be the only difference in the spelling of two homophones. For example, **si** means "if," while **sí** means "yes." Make sure students from non-English-speaking backgrounds understand the distinct meanings of English homophone pairs. The sentences in the student edition can help you provide context. You can supplement these with sentences of your own, or ask native English speakers to compose sentences to use in cooperative learning groups composed of a mix of native and non-native English speakers. (If students compose sentences, check them for correct spelling and meaning.)

Because pronunciations vary from region to region, words that are homophones in one region may not be in another. For example, in some southern and midwestern regions, **pin** and **pen** are homophones. Both words are pronounced **pin**\\.

Homophones are common in languages around the world. In Chinese, words that sound the same are written with entirely different characters. The word **bóo** can mean "no," "cloth," "walk," "afraid," or "notebook"! Although the pronunciation is the same, each meaning is represented with a different Chinese character.

Helping Students Acquiring English

Write the **Pattern Words** on separate 3" x 5" cards. Show the cards for a pair of homophones, such as **steel** and **steal,** and read the words aloud, calling attention to the different spellings. Sort the cards into two packets, with **steel, break, whose, board,** and **role** in one packet, and the remaining words in the second packet. Divide the class into two groups. Give each group one packet of cards. Ask one member of a group to hold up a card while another group member reads the word aloud. The other group is to find the word that sounds the same, hold up the card, and read and spell the word aloud.

Meeting Diverse Needs

Less Able Spellers

Students who have difficulty learning to spell may select spelling words that are either too hard or too easy. It is important to monitor children's word selection each week to ensure that the words they choose are at—or near—each child's level of spelling competence.

More Able Spellers

Encourage students to look for words that also spell a recognizable word when the letters are arranged backward. For example, **rat** spells **tar** backward. Students will delight in finding words that are real words when turned about in this way.

ENGAGING
IN THE
PROCESS

INVOLVING
FAMILIES

Ask students to copy their lists in the **Take Your List Home** section of the *Spell It–Write!* Home News page for this lesson. Not only does this page provide a convenient way for families to share a student's spelling list, but it also provides a number of opportunities for families to be involved in students' spelling growth. It has a statement of the week's spelling pattern or strategy, a valuable spelling study strategy, and a suggested home spelling practice activity.

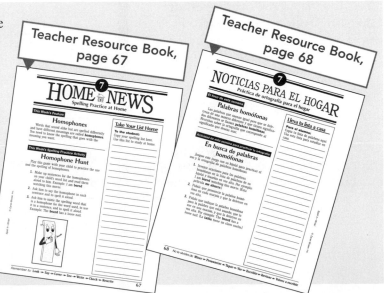

FINDING WORDS

STEP 1 Build Your Spelling List

Students will build their spelling lists with **Pattern Words, Teacher Words,** and **Your Words.** Students should study a minimum of twelve new words each week.

Find Your Pattern Words

• Pretest the students on these words.

• Tell students to write each misspelled pretest word on their spelling lists.

Add Teacher Words

• Select words for students to add to their spelling lists. Choose words from **More Words for Hungry Word Hunters** (on this page and on student page 162), words related to a theme or content area, or words students often misspell.

Add Your Words

• Ask students to pick words from their lists of **Words I Need to Know How to Spell** and their writing.

• Tell students to write these words on their spelling lists.

STEP 2 Write Your Spelling List

Remind students to verify all spellings. (Ask students to see **Strategies for Checking Your Spelling** in the back of the student edition.)

STEP 3 Set Your Learning Goal

Tell students to count the words on their spelling lists. This total is their learning goal. It may vary depending on ability, individual goals, and the difficulty of spelling words.

MORE WORDS FOR HUNGRY WORD HUNTERS

RED LIST Pattern Words Below Level	BLUE LIST Pattern Words Above Level	Other Pattern Words	Math Pattern Word
cent	allowed	guessed	sum (some)
knew	aloud	guest	**Science Pattern Words**
new	coarse	missed	bass (base)
plain	course	mist	flu (flew)
plane	loan	passed	
sent	lone	past	**Social Studies Pattern Words**
tail	mare	vain	ore (or)
tale	mayor	vane	seas (sees)
weak	waist	vein	sowing (sewing)
week	waste		steppe (step)

These lists also appear on page 162 in the student edition and page 13 in the **Teacher Resource Book.**

SPELLING PATTERN 7

Homophones

Your Spelling List

_____
_____
_____
_____
_____
_____
_____
_____
_____
_____
_____
_____
_____
_____
_____
_____
_____
_____
_____

FINDING WORDS

STEP 1 Build Your Spelling List

Find Your Pattern Words

Take the pretest.
Write misspelled words on your spelling list.

Add Teacher Words

Teachers may add:
• More **Pattern Words** • Content Words • Theme Words

Add Your Words

Pick words from:
• **Words I Need to Know How to Spell** • Writing • Reading

Pattern Words

1. **steel** — That sword is made of **steel**.
2. **break** — How did you **break** your leg?
3. **whose** — I don't know **whose** pencil this is.
4. **board** — Angie will saw that wooden **board** in half.
5. **role** — What **role** do you have in the play?
6. **steal** — If the car is not locked, someone might **steal** it.
7. **roll** — Please **roll** the ball to the baby.
8. **bored** — I never get **bored** when I'm reading because my book is so interesting.
9. **who's** — **Who's** going to the football game?
10. **brake** — A **brake** on my bike is broken, so I can't stop.

STEP 2 Write Your Spelling List

STEP 3 Set Your Learning Goal

My spelling list has _____ words for me to learn.

> Me, too. And if I forget how to do an activity, I just check my **Spelling Process Handbook** for the directions.

> Do you think the practice activities are fun to do? I sure do!

PATTERN MINI-LESSON

NOTE: The **Explore the Spelling Pattern** activity on page 47 is a self-directed mini-lesson. If you wish to supplement that activity with direct instruction, use the following mini-lesson.

* **Write** the **Pattern Words** from page 46 on the chalkboard. Say each word and ask students to repeat it.

* **Ask** students if they notice anything unusual about the words on the chalkboard. (Response: *There are pairs of words that sound the same, but they're spelled differently and have different meanings.*)

* **Tell** students that such words are called homophones. Write **homophone** on the chalkboard, and explain that **homo-** means "same" and **phone** means "sound": homophones are words that sound the same.

* **Ask** individual students to define the words on the chalkboard and to use them in sentences.

* **Call** on a volunteer to read the **Spelling Pattern** on page 47. Ask several students to explain it in their own words.

* **Encourage** students to offer other examples of homophones. Write these on the chalkboard along with a sentence to illustrate the meaning. You may also wish to write on the chalkboard examples from **More Words for Hungry Word Hunters** (on student page 162 and page T46). Remind students that they may add any of these words to **Words I Need to Know How to Spell**.

STEP 4 — Explore the Spelling Pattern
Thinking About Meaning

A. Write the **Pattern Word** that has a similar meaning to the words in each group.

1. wood, lumber

   board

2. rest, time-out

   break

3. part, play assignment

   role

4. rob, take without permission

   steal

5. metal, building material

   steel

6. belonging to, of whom

   whose

7. who is, who has

   who's

8. uninterested

   bored

9. turn over and over, twirl

   roll

10. stopper, slowing device

    brake

B. With a partner, do a word hunt to find other words that are part of a homophone pair. Write the pair you find.

Answers will vary. _____

STEP 5 — Focus on Word Study
Word History

More than 300 years ago, an actor's role in a play would be written on a roll of paper. The words **role** and **roll** sound the same for a very good reason. They both come from a Latin word meaning "a small wheel." Remember, though, that not all homophones are related in meaning.

For each pair of homophones below, write the letters that are pronounced alike in both words but are spelled differently.

1. steel, steal _____**ee, ea**_____

2. break, brake _____**eak, ake**_____

3. whose, who's _____**ose, o's**_____

4. role, roll _____**ole, oll**_____

> ▼▼▼▼▼▼▼▼▼▼▼▼
> **Spelling Pattern**
> Words that sound alike but are spelled differently and have different meanings are called **homophones**. It's important to know the spelling that goes with the meaning you want.
> • • • • • • • • • • • •

STEP 4 — Explore the Spelling Pattern

Thinking About Meaning
This activity is a self-directed mini-lesson on this week's **Spelling Pattern**.

STEP 5 — Focus on Word Study

Word History
This activity is intended to stimulate students' interest in words and to help them become more enthusiastic word hunters.

> ## Spelling Process Handbook
> Students who need to review any part of the spelling process, including practice options, should refer to the **Spelling Process Handbook** (pages 7–21).

A Practice Option

STEP 6 Practice Your Spelling List Independently

Ask the students to choose activities to practice their spelling words and to master this week's **Spelling Pattern**. Students should complete at least three activities each week. You may wish to:

- assign **Practice the Spelling Pattern** to all students to reinforce this week's **Spelling Pattern**.

- involve students' families by assigning **Take Your List Home** for this lesson (**Teacher Resource Book**, pages 67 in English and 68 in Spanish).

- encourage students to use partner activities without game mats (**Word Swap, Spelling Tic-Tac-Toe, Circle Dot**) and activities with game mats (**Meteor Attack, Rockets, Spelling Checkers, Spelling Soccer**). Directions for game-mat activities appear on each game mat. Directions for all other activities are found in the **Spelling Process Handbook** (pages 7–21).

NOTE: These activities and games can be used to practice any spelling list.

SPELLING SOCCER

Partners or teams can practice their spelling words as they compete in **Spelling Soccer**. Modeled after the game that is gaining popularity in the United States for both boys and girls, **Spelling Soccer** takes spelling practice to the soccer field. It'll be "hands off" poor spelling scores after students, especially auditory and visual learners, discover **Spelling Soccer**. (Directions appear on the **Spelling Soccer** game mat. This activity is appropriate for practicing any spelling list.)

- - - - - - - - MASTERING WORDS - - - - - - - -

STEP 6 Practice Your Spelling List Independently
Choose at least three activities to practice your spelling list.

You can practice any spelling list with these activities.

Game Mats	With a Partner	On Your Own	At Home
○ Rockets ○ Spelling Soccer	○ Circle Dot ○ Spelling Tic-Tac-Toe	○ Flip Folder ○ Spelling Study Strategy	○ Take Your List Home

✏ Practice the Spelling Pattern

A hink pink is two rhyming words that name something. For example, a **fat cat** is an "overstuffed kitty." Write a pair of **Pattern Words** to make a hink pink that fits each clue. Remember, each pair has to be homophones!

Pattern Words

steel
break
whose
board
role
steal
roll
bored
who's
brake

1–2. wood with nothing to do

bored _____ board

3–4. lost contraction

whose _____ who's

5–6. to take metal

steal _____ steel

7–8. acting part for a bun

roll _____ role

9–10. rest period for a stopping device

brake _____ break

DEVELOPING GOOD SPELLING HABITS

STEP 7 Focus on Writing

A. Proofread the Writing of Others

This activity provides proofreading practice in a variety of formats, including popular standardized test formats.

B. Proofread Your Own Writing

Students return to their own writing, armed with strategies to identify and collect words they need to know how to spell, and make an authentic link between spelling and writing.

C. A Writing Idea: A How-to

This suggestion for a more extended writing activity provides opportunities for students to write in different genres for a variety of purposes and modes.

STEP 8 Check Your Weekly Progress

▶ Take the Test

Remind students that they can take a practice test before the final test on their spelling lists. To find the testing procedure that is right for you, refer to page Z12.

▶ Check Your Goal

Have students compare their tests to their spelling lists. Did they spell all the **Pattern Words** on their spelling lists correctly?

▶ Graph Your Progress

Ask students to graph the number correct (student page 175 for softbound users; **Teacher Resource Book** page 123 for hardbound users).

▶ Save Missed Words

Tell students to write misspelled words on their lists of **Words I Need to Know How to Spell**. Remind students to verify spellings and to recycle these words on future weekly spelling lists.

DEVELOPING GOOD SPELLING HABITS

STEP 7 Focus on Writing

A. Proofread the Writing of Others

Proofread the paragraph below. Decide which type of mistake, if any, appears in each underlined section.

Mrs. Wu's class was happy to put on a play, but they argued over <u>who's turn it was</u> to be the director. The
①
director would give out the <u>rolls and help</u> with every act.
②
Other students would have lots of breaks and might
feel bored. Finally, <u>Mrs. wu listed</u> the names of students
③   ④
who wanted the job, and the class voted.

≡ Make a capital.
/ Make a small letter.
∧ Add something.
⌒ Take out something.
⊙ Add a period.
¶ New paragraph
(SP) Spelling error

1. (A) Spelling
   B Capitalization
   C Punctuation
   D No mistake

2. (A) Spelling
   B Capitalization
   C Punctuation
   D No mistake

3. A Spelling
   B Capitalization
   C Punctuation
   (D) No mistake

4. A Spelling
   (B) Capitalization
   C Punctuation
   D No mistake

B. Proofread Your Own Writing

Look through your recent writing for homophones. Check with your teacher or a partner, or use a dictionary, to find out whether you spelled them correctly. Add misspelled homophones to **Words I Need to Know How to Spell**.

C. A Writing Idea: A How-to

Can you pitch a baseball or draw a map? Choose something you know how to do well. List the steps that explain how to do it, and be sure the steps are in order. Before you publish your list, check for spelling errors.

STEP 8 Check Your Weekly Progress

▶ Take the Test
Ready? Practice test first.

▶ Check Your Goal
Check to see if you met your learning goal.

▶ Graph Your Progress
Graph your score for this week's test.

▶ Save Missed Words
Write the words you missed in your list of **Words I Need to Know How to Spell**.

Hunt Words

Remind students to continuously hunt words that they wish to learn how to spell and to write these words in **Words I Need to Know How to Spell**.

SPELLING STRATEGY 8 — Using a Dictionary

ENGAGING IN THE PROCESS — MATERIALS

Student Edition: Pages 50–53 **Teacher Edition:** Pages T50A–T53

Materials to help students practice their spelling lists:
- **Flip Folders**
- Copies of **Flip Folder Practice Sheet** (**Teacher Resource Book,** page 51)
- **Take Your List Home** (in *Spell It–Write!*)

Home News, **Teacher Resource Book,** pages 69 in English and 70 in Spanish)
- Game Mats Featured in This Unit: **Spelling Checkers, Spelling Soccer**

ENGAGING IN THE PROCESS — GOALS

SPELLING GOALS

Students will

- use a dictionary to check spelling and meaning.
- develop an understanding of how the meanings of words can change over time.
- use the spelling process of finding words, inspecting words, and mastering words as they develop good spelling habits to become better writers.

WRITING GOALS

Students will

- proofread a writing sample.
- proofread a piece of their own writing for misspelled words.
- write an expressive description.

ENGAGING IN THE PROCESS — MANAGEMENT

Pacing	Notes	Quick Pick Management Option
Period 1 Finding Words (Steps 1–3)	If you wish to add **Teacher Words,** write them on the chalkboard. Sources for more words include: **More Words for Hungry Word Hunters** (page T50), content and theme-related words, or words of your choice.	Assign the list of **Strategy Words** to the whole class. Add the Red List (**More Words for Hungry Word Hunters,** student page 162) for a longer list. Add the Blue List (**More Words for Hungry Word Hunters**) for a more challenging list.
Period 2 Inspecting Words (Steps 4 and 5)	Students write the **Strategy Words** to complete **Explore the Spelling Strategy.**	Assign **Explore the Spelling Strategy** and **Focus on Word Study.**
Period 3 Mastering Words (Step 6) **Period 4** Developing Good Spelling Habits (Step 7)	These two periods can be allocated between selected **Mastering Words** activities and proofreading and writing activities in **Focus on Writing.**	Assign two or three activities to the whole class. Familiarize students with choosing their own activities at their own pace.
Period 5 Assessment (Step 8)	Gradually try different peer-testing options to find the style that best fits your class.	Test the class on the same, whole-class list.

T50A UNIT 8

Understanding Language Differences

Spanish Speakers

Native Spanish speakers and other students from foreign backgrounds may not be able to hear or pronounce the subtle differences in some of these words and may even confuse other words that native English speakers would not. Because Spanish never ends with \z\, native Spanish speakers may need special help with words such as the Red List word **lose** (as opposed to **loose**) or the Blue List word **seize** (as opposed to **cease**). Students from Spanish-speaking backgrounds will tend to end these words with \s\.

Casual pronunciations can be a source of confusion with several words on this week's lists. Casual speech can erase some of the distinctions that show up in writing or in formal speech to help clarify meaning. For example, **than** (Red List) is pronounced \then\ when we speak casually, and **accept** often sounds the same as **except** when we speak quickly.

The trouble with **ladder** and **latter** is that American English (but not British English) speakers have a tendency to pronounce a **t** more like a **d** when it occurs between vowels.

Helping Students Acquiring English

On the chalkboard, write one pair of **Strategy Words,** such as **ladder** and **latter**. Pronounce each word and call attention to the differences in both pronunciation and spelling. Using pantomime, gestures, illustrations, and context sentences, demonstrate the meaning of each word in the pair. Then call on volunteers to read each word aloud and use it in a sentence. Follow a similar procedure for the remaining **Strategy Words**.

Meeting Diverse Needs

Less Able Spellers

Students who have difficulty learning to spell, including students with special needs, are often challenged by many of the words writers commonly use. One way to help such students spell these words correctly is to develop classroom wall charts that list words these students are likely to use—and misspell—in their writing. Commonly used words that are spelling demons—for example, **their** and **they're**—may be included on the chart.

More Able Spellers

Challenge students to use their spelling list to build a compact crossword puzzle. A compact crossword puzzle takes as few spaces horizontally and vertically as possible.(Note that there is a crossword puzzle grid on page 54 of the **Teacher Resource Book**.)

Ask students to copy their lists in the **Take Your List Home** section of the *Spell It–Write!* Home News page for this lesson. Not only does this page provide a convenient way for families to share a student's spelling list, but it also provides a number of opportunities for families to be involved in students' spelling growth. It has a statement of the week's spelling pattern or strategy, a valuable spelling study strategy, and a suggested home spelling practice activity.

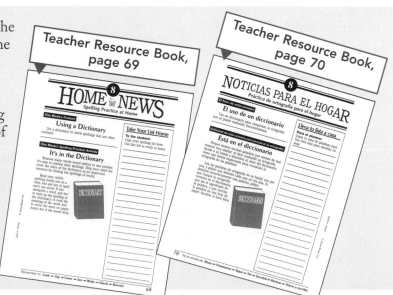

FINDING WORDS

STEP 1 Build Your Spelling List

Students will build their spelling lists with **Strategy Words, Teacher Words,** and **Your Words**. Students should study a minimum of twelve new words each week.

Find Your Strategy Words

• Pretest the students on these words.

• Tell students to write each misspelled pretest word on their spelling lists.

Add Teacher Words

• Select words for students to add to their spelling lists. Choose words from **More Words for Hungry Word Hunters** (on this page and on student page 162), words related to a theme or content area, or words students often misspell.

Add Your Words

• Ask students to pick words from their lists of **Words I Need to Know How to Spell** and their writing.

• Tell students to write these words on their spelling lists.

STEP 2 Write Your Spelling List

Remind students to verify all spellings. (Ask students to see **Strategies for Checking Your Spelling** in the back of the student edition.)

STEP 3 Set Your Learning Goal

Tell students to count the words on their spelling lists. This total is their learning goal. It may vary depending on ability, individual goals, and the difficulty of spelling words.

MORE WORDS FOR HUNGRY WORD HUNTERS

RED LIST Strategy Words Below Level	BLUE LIST Strategy Words Above Level	Other Strategy Words	Math Strategy Words
all ready	angel	borough	liter
already	angle	bridal	quartet
ant	cease	bridle	sentence
aunt	cereal	burrow	
loose	formal	colonel	**Science Strategy Words**
lose	former	country	blizzard
than	receipt	county	digest
their	recipe	kernel	socket
then	seize	naval	
there	serial	navel	**Social Studies Strategy Word** station

These lists also appear on page 162 in the student edition and page 14 in the **Teacher Resource Book**.

FINDING WORDS

SPELLING STRATEGY

8

Using a Dictionary

Your Spelling List

_____
_____
_____
_____
_____
_____
_____
_____
_____
_____
_____
_____
_____
_____
_____
_____
_____
_____
_____

STEP 1 Build Your Spelling List

Find Your Strategy Words
Take the pretest.
Write misspelled words on your spelling list.

Add Teacher Words
Teachers may add:
• More **Strategy Words** • Content Words • Theme Words

Add Your Words
Pick words from:
• **Words I Need to Know How to Spell** • Writing • Reading

Strategy Words

1.	**ladder**	Use a **ladder** to reach the cat on the roof.
2.	**latter**	We left in the **latter** half of the show, just before the end.
3.	**certain**	Are you **certain** your bike was here?
4.	**curtain**	The rain came through the open window and ruined the **curtain**.
5.	**except**	Everyone was there **except** Philip.
6.	**accept**	Maria cannot **accept** the gift.
7.	**diary**	Tai writes in his **diary** every day.
8.	**dairy**	My class visited a **dairy** and saw a cow.
9.	**finally**	Erin **finally** got to meet her pen pal.
10.	**finely**	We need a **finely** chopped onion.

STEP 2 Write Your Spelling List

STEP 3 Set Your Learning Goal

My spelling list has _____ words for me to learn.

I always get all my words right on the test. Maybe I should make a longer list next week.

Well, I'd rather stay with the number of words I have and work to get them all right.

STRATEGY MINI-LESSON

NOTE: The **Explore the Spelling Strategy** activity on page 51 is a self-directed mini-lesson. If you wish to supplement that activity with direct instruction, use the following mini-lesson.

* **Write accept** and **except** on the chalkboard. Ask volunteers to use each word in a sentence. Write the sentences on the chalkboard. Ask other volunteers to look up each word in a dictionary to see whether it is used correctly. Make any necessary changes in the sentences.

* **Ask** the class whether they detect a difference in the pronunciation of these words. Explain that because the difference in pronunciation is slight, it is important to know the meanings of the words in order to use the correct spelling.

* **Follow** the same procedure with the other pairs of words on this week's list.

* **Remind** students that they would not use this strategy for every word they encounter, but that it is helpful with homophones or other words that sound very much alike.

* **Encourage** students to provide examples of other words that sound almost alike. You may also wish to give examples from **More Words for Hungry Word Hunters** (on student page 162 and page T50).

* **Ask** a volunteer to read aloud the **Spelling Strategy** on page 51. Ask several students to comment on the value of using a dictionary. (*Responses should include the idea that a dictionary is valuable for finding meanings and spellings.*)

··········· INSPECTING WORDS ···········

STEP 4 Explore the Spelling Strategy
Word Check

A. Write the **Strategy Word** that goes with the meaning.

1. sure; positive — (cer)tain
2. a piece of cloth that hangs in a window — (cur)tain
3. something used for climbing up — la(dd)er
4. the second of two parts — la(tt)er
5. in small pieces; in a careful way — fin(ely)
6. at last — fin(ally)
7. leaving out — (ex)cept
8. to take something that is given — (ac)cept
9. a place where milk and cheese are made — d(ai)ry
10. a daily journal of one's experiences — d(ia)ry

B. Now go back to the words you wrote. In each pair of words, circle the parts that are easily confused.

▼▼▼▼▼▼▼▼▼▼▼▼▼
Spelling Strategy
Use a dictionary to check spellings that are often confused.
▪ ▪ ▪ ▪ ▪ ▪ ▪ ▪ ▪ ▪

STEP 5 Focus on Word Study
Meaning Changes

The word **dairy** grew out of an Old English word meaning "a place where a woman makes bread." Then the word came to mean "a farm woman who makes butter and cheese." Today, a dairy is a place where milk products are made or stored.

Write the dairy word that came from each Old English word:

1. cu, "animal that gives milk" — cow
2. meolc, "a white drink that comes from cows" — milk
3. cese, "a food made from milk" — cheese
4. butere, "a yellow fat used as a spread on bread" — butter

STEP 4 Explore the Spelling Strategy

Word Check

This activity is a self-directed mini-lesson on this week's **Spelling Strategy**.

STEP 5 Focus on Word Study

Meaning Changes

This activity is intended to stimulate students' interest in words and to help them become more enthusiastic word hunters.

Spelling Process Handbook

Students who need to review any part of the spelling process, including practice options, should refer to the **Spelling Process Handbook** (pages 7–21).

MASTERING WORDS

A Practice Option

STEP 6 Practice Your Spelling List Independently

Ask the students to choose activities to practice their spelling words and to master this week's **Spelling Strategy**. Students should complete at least three activities each week. You may wish to:

- assign **Practice the Spelling Strategy** to all students to reinforce this week's **Spelling Strategy**.

- involve students' families by assigning **Take Your List Home** for this lesson (**Teacher Resource Book,** pages 69 in English and 70 in Spanish).

- encourage students to use partner activities without game mats (**Word Swap, Spelling Tic-Tac-Toe, Circle Dot**) and activities with game mats (**Meteor Attack, Rockets, Spelling Checkers, Spelling Soccer**). Directions for game-mat activities appear on each game mat. Directions for all other activities are found in the **Spelling Process Handbook** (pages 7–21).

> NOTE: These activities and games can be used to practice any spelling list.

TAKE YOUR LIST HOME

Maintaining the home-school connection is important to educational success. One way to involve families in students' spelling growth is to duplicate and send the *Spell It–Write!* Home News to families every week. First, each student copies his or her spelling list in the **Take Your List Home** section of the Home News page. Then students take the page home to share the list and to use the suggested home spelling practice activity. This page also includes a statement of the week's spelling strategy or pattern and a spelling study strategy. (A different Home News page—in both Spanish and English—is available for each *Spell It–Write!* unit in the **Teacher Resource Book.**)

MASTERING WORDS

STEP 6 Practice Your Spelling List Independently
Choose at least three activities to practice your spelling list.

> *Copy your words carefully when you take your list home.*

Game Mats	With a Partner	On Your Own	At Home
○ Spelling Checkers ○ Spelling Soccer	○ Spelling Tic-Tac-Toe ○ Word Swap	○ Flip Folder ○ Spelling Study Strategy	○ Take Your List Home

Practice the Spelling Strategy

Write the **Strategy Word** that best fits each sentence.

Strategy Words

ladder
latter
certain
curtain
except
accept
diary
dairy
finally
finely

1. We reached the window with a (ladder/latter). _____ **ladder**

2. The cat tore the (certain/curtain). _____ **curtain**

3. Jamal writes in his (dairy/diary) daily. _____ **diary**

4. Sarah was happy to (accept/except) the reward. _____ **accept**

5. We (finally/finely) found the hidden cave. _____ **finally**

6. My parents own a (dairy/diary) farm. _____ **dairy**

7. Are you (certain/curtain) you can come? _____ **certain**

8. The (finally/finely) drawn map helped us. _____ **finely**

9. School starts the (ladder/latter) part of August. _____ **latter**

10. Tom likes all the shirts (accept/except) this one. _____ **except**

STEP 7 Focus on Writing

A. Proofread the Writing of Others

This activity provides proofreading practice in a variety of formats, including popular standardized test formats.

B. Proofread Your Own Writing

Students return to their own writing, armed with strategies to identify and collect words they need to know how to spell, and make an authentic link between spelling and writing.

C. A Writing Idea: A Description

This suggestion for a more extended writing activity provides opportunities for students to write in different genres for a variety of purposes and modes.

STEP 8 Check Your Weekly Progress

▶ Take the Test

Remind students that they can take a practice test before the final test on their spelling lists. To find the testing procedure that is right for you, refer to page Z12.

▶ Check Your Goal

Have students compare their tests to their spelling lists. Did they spell all the **Strategy Words** on their spelling lists correctly?

▶ Graph Your Progress

Ask students to graph the number correct (student page 175 for softbound users; **Teacher Resource Book** page 123 for hardbound users).

▶ Save Missed Words

Tell students to write misspelled words on their lists of **Words I Need to Know How to Spell**. Remind students to verify spellings and to recycle these words on future weekly spelling lists.

· · · · · · · DEVELOPING GOOD SPELLING HABITS · · · · · · ·

STEP 7 Focus on Writing

A. Proofread the Writing of Others

Proofread the paragraph below. Find the four misspelled words. Write the correct spelling.

> Today at the store, I looked in the diary case for yogurt. I saw milk, cream, butter, cheese, and everything else accept yogurt. I was curtain it was there, so I looked again. Finely, I found it behind the milk!

1. _____ **dairy** _____
2. _____ **except** _____
3. _____ **certain** _____
4. _____ **finally** _____

≡ Make a capital.
∕ Make a small letter.
⌃ Add something.
℘ Take out something.
⊙ Add a period.
¶ New paragraph
(SP) Spelling error

B. Proofread Your Own Writing

Some words are easily confused. Go to your most recent writing. Look for any word you may have misspelled because it looks or sounds like another word. Write misspelled words correctly in **Words I Need to Know How to Spell**.

C. A Writing Idea: A Description

Describe how to make something. It could be a food or a kite or anything else. Tell your description from the point of view of the thing you are making. What might a kite "say" if it could tell about being made? Use lots of details, too! Proofread your writing before sharing it with others.

STEP 8 Check Your Weekly Progress

▶ Take the Test
Ready? Practice test first.

▶ Check Your Goal
Check to see if you met your learning goal.

▶ Graph Your Progress
Graph your score for this week's test.

▶ Save Missed Words
Write the words you missed in your list of **Words I Need to Know How to Spell**.

Hunt Words

Remind students to continuously hunt words that they wish to learn how to spell and to write these words in **Words I Need to Know How to Spell**.

NOTE: Check Your Progress is not a spelling unit, but some teachers prefer to spend a week on these activities.

Day One: Administer **Review Test**.

Day Two: Check **Review Test**. Use **Spelling Pattern Mastery Chart** to find each student's mastery level.

Day Three: Reteach as needed.

Day Four: Complete **Check Your Writing**.

Day Five: Complete **Check Your Strategies**.

Check Your Spelling

1. Administer the **Review Test** to all students. Dictation sentences appear on page T55. (The words in italics are also from the previous eight units.) Administer the words **in the order** in which they are presented here.

2. Ask students to check their tests as you spell each word and/or write the correct spelling on the board.

3. Ask students to circle the number of each correctly spelled word.

4. Review the categories on the **Spelling Pattern Mastery Chart** (page 54). As you review each pattern, ask students to find the corresponding items on their tests. Based on the number of words correct for each pattern, ask the students to determine their level of mastery for that pattern.

Reteaching Strategies

- Reteach the **Pattern Mini-Lesson** on the patterns students have not mastered.

- Ask students to record the words they missed in **Words I Need to Know How to Spell** for recycling into future spelling lists.

- Record the patterns students have not mastered. Include words with these patterns on future spelling lists.

Check Your Writing

1. Consider teaching the **Proofreading Strategy Mini-Lesson** (page T55).

2. Ask students to choose several pieces of their writing.

3. Ask students to work with a partner to proofread their writing and hunt words with each spelling pattern. They should record misspelled words in **Words I Need to Know How to Spell**.

Check Your Strategies

1. Read each question aloud. Remind the students that they should think about their use of each strategy in the past eight weeks and answer "Yes," "No," or "Sometimes."

2. Use these questions as the focus of a student-teacher conference. You may also wish to use **Strategy Assessment** (pages 120 and 121 in the **Teacher Resource Book**).

Check Your Spelling

Check Your

Here is a fun way to review your progress on spelling patterns. First, take the review test your teacher will give you. Then, check your test.

Review Test

1	o'clock
2	daily
3	used
4	smiling
5	doesn't
6	brake
7	writing
8	role
9	altitude
10	haven't
11	swimming
12	who's
13	invite
14	remain
15	you're
16	repeat
17	surprise
18	complete
19	between
20	whose

Spelling Pattern Mastery Chart

Which words did you spell correctly? Use this chart to find your mastery level for each spelling pattern.

Pattern	All Correct	Most Correct	None Correct
Contractions 1 5 10 15			
Long Vowels: V-C-e 9 13 17 18			
Long Vowels: Vowel Pairs 2 14 16 19			
Endings: -ed, -ing 3 4 7 11			
Homophones 6 8 12 20			

All Correct: Pattern Mastered
Most Correct: Pattern Partly Mastered
None Correct: Keep Working on the Pattern

PROOFREADING STRATEGY MINI-LESSON

* **Write** the title **Read for Errors** on the chalkboard.

* **Explain** that students should proofread their papers for spelling and other errors before they write a copy to share with others. They can do this by reading their paper thoughtfully and carefully.

* **Model** this procedure by putting a piece of your writing, including a capitalization error and a simple spelling error, on the overhead transparency. Read the piece aloud thoughtfully.

Encourage students to read it with you. When you reach the spelling error, circle the error and explain that, "I'll have to find the correct way to spell that word." If appropriate, review **Strategies for Checking Your Spelling** (in the back of the student edition) with the students at this time.

* **Write** the correct spelling above the misspelled word.

Progress

Choose three recent samples of your writing. Use a grid that looks like this. Work with a partner to check your writing for words that match each pattern.

✓ Check Your Writing

Spelling Pattern Writing Chart	Column 1 I spelled these Pattern Words correctly.	Column 2 I misspelled these Pattern Words.
Contractions		
Long Vowels: V-C-e		
Long Vowels: Vowel Pairs		
Endings: -ed, -ing		
Homophones		

Write the words in Column 2 in your **Words I Need to Know How to Spell**.

✓ Check Your Strategies

Self-regulation

Ask yourself each of these questions. Do you answer "Yes," "No," or "Sometimes" to each question?

• Do I add words from **Words I Need to Know How to Spell** to my spelling list each week?
• Is the number of words I add right for me?
• When I practice my words, do I choose activities that help me learn my words?
• Do I take self-tests and practice tests to see if I know my words?

Dictation Sentences

1. **o'clock** – *We'll* meet at the *office* at nine **o'clock**.
2. **daily** – She *planned* to work in the *dairy* **daily** for the *season*.
3. **used** – Sam **used** a *ladder* and a *board* when he *built* his tree house.
4. **smiling** – I *wasn't* **smiling** as I watched them *shoving* the *heavy steel* boxes.
5. **doesn't** – Kim **doesn't** seem *eager* to *visit* at the *moment*.
6. **brake** – He got a ticket from the *police* for not *using* his **brake**.
7. **writing** – Are you *tired* of **writing** in your *diary*?
8. **role** – I *agree* that Amy is *certain* to win the **role**.
9. **altitude** – *We're* careful of the **altitude** when we hike on that *mountain*.
10. **haven't** – *Since* I **haven't** *carried* any water, I will be thirsty.
11. **swimming** – I was *bored*, so I decided to go **swimming** *awhile*.
12. **who's** – **Who's** *planning* to win the *prize* for *following* directions?
13. **invite** – We *couldn't* **invite** everyone *anyway*.
14. **remain** – Please **remain** *toward* the back near the *curtain*.
15. **you're** – **You're** sure you *grabbed* the *finely* chopped peanuts?
16. **repeat** – The *female* was *known* to **repeat** her questions.
17. **surprise** – *Wasn't* it a **surprise** when the *umpire* saw the cake *explode*?
18. **complete** – To **complete** the test you must *define* the *ninth* word.
19. **between** – Just **between** you and me, I *accept* John's *reason*.
20. **whose** – *Let's* see **whose** *answer* is *finally* correct.

ou, ow, oi, oy

ENGAGING IN THE **PROCESS** **MATERIALS**

Student Edition: Pages 56–59   **Teacher Edition:** Pages T56A–T59

Materials to help students practice their spelling lists:

- **Flip Folders**
- Copies of **Flip Folder Practice Sheet** (**Teacher Resource Book,** page 51)
- **Take Your List Home** (in *Spell It–Write!*

Home News, **Teacher Resource Book,** pages 71 in English and 72 in Spanish)
- Game Mats Featured in This Unit: **Meteor Attack, Spelling Checkers**

ENGAGING IN THE **PROCESS** **GOALS**

SPELLING GOALS

Students will

- transfer knowledge of the spelling patterns \ow\ spelled **ou, ow** and \oi\ spelled **oi, oy** to spell one- and two-syllable words.

- sort words according to vowel sound and spelling pattern.

- develop an understanding of how the spelling of words can change as words move from one language to another over time.

- use the spelling process to become better writers.

WRITING GOALS

Students will

- proofread a writing sample.

- proofread a piece of their own writing for misspelled words with the vowel sound \ow\ spelled **ou, ow** and the vowel sound \oi\ spelled **oi, oy**.

- write an informative paragraph.

ENGAGING IN THE **PROCESS** **MANAGEMENT**

Pacing	Notes	Quick Pick Management Option
Period 1 Finding Words (Steps 1–3)	If you wish to add **Teacher Words,** write them on the chalkboard. Sources for more words include: **More Words for Hungry Word Hunters** (page T56), content and theme-related words, or words of your choice.	Assign the list of **Pattern Words** to the whole class. Add the Red List (**More Words for Hungry Word Hunters,** student page 163) for a longer list. Add the Blue List (**More Words for Hungry Word Hunters**) for a more challenging list.
Period 2 Inspecting Words (Steps 4 and 5)	Students write the **Pattern Words** to complete **Explore the Spelling Pattern.**	Assign **Explore the Spelling Pattern** and **Focus on Word Study.**
Period 3 Mastering Words (Step 6) **Period 4** Developing Good Spelling Habits (Step 7)	These two periods can be allocated between selected **Mastering Words** activities and proofreading and writing activities in **Focus on Writing.**	Assign two or three activities to the whole class. Familiarize students with choosing their own activities at their own pace.
Period 5 Assessment (Step 8)	Gradually try different peer-testing options to find the style that best fits your class.	Test the class on the same, whole-class list.

ENGAGING
IN THE
PROCESS

INDIVIDUAL NEEDS

Understanding Language Differences

The pronunciation of the \ow\ diphthong varies from place to place in North America. For some speakers, not all the vowel sounds spelled **ou** and **ow** in the words on this week's lists will sound the same. Most people pronounce the \ow\ diphthong by gliding from \ah\ to \oo\. However, some speakers on the East Coast, in the Middle Atlantic region, and especially in parts of Canada glide from \eh\ to \oo\, resulting in the word **about** being pronounced \uh-beh-oot\ or even \uh-boot\. For many of these speakers, **about** and **mouth** will have a vowel sound different from the vowel sound in **crowd** and **sound**.

Helping Students Acquiring English

Write the word **crowd** on the chalkboard, and introduce its meaning, perhaps with a picture of a crowd scene. Give each student the correct magnetic letters (or letter tiles), and ask them to make the word **crowd**. Have them construct the word and break it apart several times to reinforce the spelling for the vowel sound. Follow a similar procedure to present the remaining **Pattern Words**.

Meeting Diverse Needs

Less Able Spellers

Students with special needs may benefit from additional advice and help in managing their spelling study behavior. For example:

• Check to see if the child is scheduling time to study spelling words at home.

• Encourage the student to pick a quiet place where he or she can study.

• Periodically review with the student the activities he or she chose to practice the spelling words. Work with the child to evaluate the success of specific study activities.

More Able Spellers

Challenge students to play with words by spelling them with more elaborate and less common spelling patterns. For example, the dog's name **Fido** might be spelled **Phydeaux**. Discuss the reasons for variations among the spelling of names. Point out, for example, that ethnic heritage may influence particular spellings.

ENGAGING
IN THE
PROCESS

INVOLVING FAMILIES

Ask students to copy their lists in the **Take Your List Home** section of the *Spell It–Write!* Home News page for this lesson. Not only does this page provide a convenient way for families to share a student's spelling list, but it also provides a number of opportunities for families to be involved in students' spelling growth. It has a statement of the week's spelling pattern or strategy, a valuable spelling study strategy, and a suggested home spelling practice activity.

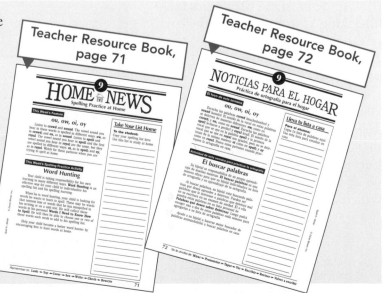

FINDING WORDS

1 Build Your Spelling List

Students will build their spelling lists with **Pattern Words, Teacher Words,** and **Your Words.** Students should study a minimum of twelve new words each week.

Find Your Pattern Words

- Pretest the students on these words.
- Tell students to write each misspelled pretest word on their spelling lists.

Add Teacher Words

- Select words for students to add to their spelling lists. Choose words from **More Words for Hungry Word Hunters** (on this page and on student page 163), words related to a theme or content area, or words students often misspell.

Add Your Words

- Ask students to pick words from their lists of **Words I Need to Know How to Spell** and their writing.
- Tell students to write these words on their spelling lists.

2 Write Your Spelling List

Remind students to verify all spellings. (Ask students to see **Strategies for Checking Your Spelling** in the back of the student edition.)

3 Set Your Learning Goal

Tell students to count the words on their spelling lists. This total is their learning goal. It may vary depending on ability, individual goals, and the difficulty of spelling words.

MORE WORDS FOR HUNGRY WORD HUNTERS

RED LIST Pattern Words Below Level	BLUE LIST Pattern Words Above Level	Other Pattern Words	Math Pattern Words
about	allow	annoy	ounce
clown	avoid	blouse	pound
enjoy	couch	drown	thousand
found	coward	however	
frown	destroy	loiter	**Science Pattern Words**
ground	fountain	oyster	asteroid
joy	noisy	poise	compound
oil	noun	power	noise
point	tower	sour	
town	voyage	trousers	**Social Studies Pattern Words**

boundary	mouth
flounder	oil
mountain	pronoun

These lists also appear on page 163 in the student edition and page 15 in the **Teacher Resource Book.**

SPELLING
PATTERN

9

**ou, ow,
oi, oy**

Your Spelling List

········ FINDING WORDS ········

1 Build Your Spelling List

Find Your Pattern Words
Take the pretest.
Write misspelled words on your spelling list.

Add Teacher Words
Teachers may add:
• More **Pattern Words** • Content Words • Theme Words

Add Your Words
Pick words from:
• **Words I Need to Know How to Spell** • Writing • Reading

Pattern Words

1.	crowd	A **crowd** of 20 people gathered for the picnic.
2.	sound	What made that loud **sound**?
3.	spoil	Put the milk away so it won't **spoil**.
4.	royal	The queen sat on the **royal** throne.
5.	mouth	How many teeth are in your **mouth**?
6.	powder	The baby **powder** feels soft.
7.	around	Have you seen my puppy **around** here?
8.	noise	I can't hear you with all this **noise**.
9.	thousand	Can you count to a **thousand**?
10.	vowel	What **vowel** —a,e, i, o, or **u**— is in your name?

2 Write Your Spelling List

3 Set Your Learning Goal

My spelling list has _____ words for me to learn.

I always like to study the same number of words every week. Do you?

Well, if the teacher doesn't add more words, my list is sometimes shorter.

PATTERN MINI-LESSON

NOTE: The **Explore the Spelling Pattern** activity on page 57 is a self-directed mini-lesson. If you wish to supplement that activity with direct instruction, use the following mini-lesson.

* **Draw** on the chalkboard pictures of an adhesive bandage and a pig. Tell students the bandage will be called "ow" (for "ouch") and the pig "oi" (for "oink").

* **Read** each spelling word aloud, and ask students whether you should write it under the bandage (for "ow") or the pig (for "oi"). Write each word in the appropriate column.

* **Invite** a volunteer to read the words in the bandage column. Ask how the words are the same. (Response: *They have the same vowel sound.*) Then ask whether this vowel sound is spelled the same in all the words. (Response: *In some words it is spelled* ow, *and in others it is spelled* ou.)

Ask two students working together to sort the words in the bandage column according to spelling pattern.

* **Repeat** for words in the pig column.

* **Encourage** students to give other examples of words with these sound-spelling patterns. Allow students to write the words in the appropriate columns on the chalkboard. You may wish to include examples from **More Words for Hungry Word Hunters** (on student page 163 and page T56). Remind students that they may add any of these words to **Words I Need to Know How to Spell.**

* **Ask** students to read the **Spelling Pattern** on page 57 with you. Have pairs of students write the **Spelling Pattern** in their own words.

- - - - - - - - - - - - - **INSPECTING WORDS** - - - - - - - - - - - - -

STEP 4 Explore the Spelling Pattern
Sorting Words

Try sorting the **Pattern Words** in other ways. How many words are verbs?

A. Sort the **Pattern Words** into four groups. Use the vowels in each word and the words below to guide your sort. Make sure you write each **Pattern Word** once.

1. cr<u>ow</u>d	2. s<u>ou</u>nd	3. sp<u>oi</u>l	4. r<u>oy</u>al
crowd	sound	spoil	royal
powder	mouth	noise	
vowel	around		
	thousand		

B. With a partner, do a word hunt. Look for other words that have the vowel sound you hear in **crowd**, spelled **ow** or **ou,** and words that have the vowel sound you hear in **spoil,** spelled **oi** or **oy.** Sort the words you find and add them to your lists.

STEP 5 Focus on Word Study
Changes in Spelling

The word **royal** comes from the ancient Latin word **rex,** meaning "king." The word changed as it passed from one language to another. In Old French, **royal** was spelled **roial** because the French word for king is **roi.**

1. Read these names: **Roy, Regina, Rex, Jeffrey, Rebecca.** Write the three names that are related to the word **royal.**

Roy
Regina
Rex

2. Now write a last name that you think is related to a job, such as **Baker.**

   Answers will vary.

▼▼▼▼▼▼▼▼▼▼▼▼▼
Spelling Pattern

- Listen to **crowd** and **sound**. The vowel sound you hear in these words is spelled in different ways: **ow,** as in **crowd,** and **ou,** as in **sound.**

- Listen to **spoil** and **royal**. The vowel sound you hear in **spoil** and the first vowel sound you hear in **royal** are the same, but they are spelled in different ways: **oi,** as in **spoil,** and **oy,** as in **royal.**

· · · · · · · · · · · · · · ·

STEP 4 Explore the Spelling Pattern
Sorting Words

This activity is a self-directed mini-lesson on this week's **Spelling Pattern**.

STEP 5 Focus on Word Study
Changes in Spelling

This activity is intended to stimulate students' interest in words and to help them become more enthusiastic word hunters.

Spelling Process Handbook

Students who need to review any part of the spelling process, including practice options, should refer to the **Spelling Process Handbook** (pages 7–21).

MASTERING WORDS

STEP 6 Practice Your Spelling List Independently

Ask the students to choose activities to practice their spelling words and to master this week's **Spelling Pattern**. Students should complete at least three activities each week. You may wish to:

• assign **Practice the Spelling Pattern** to all students to reinforce this week's **Spelling Pattern**.

• involve students' families by assigning **Take Your List Home** for this lesson (**Teacher Resource Book,** pages 71 in English and 72 in Spanish).

• encourage students to use partner activities without game mats (**Word Swap, Spelling Tic-Tac-Toe, Circle Dot**) and activities with game mats (**Meteor Attack, Rockets, Spelling Checkers, Spelling Soccer**). Directions for game-mat activities appear on each game mat. Directions for all other activities are found in the **Spelling Process Handbook** (pages 7–21).

NOTE: These activities and games can be used to practice any spelling list.

A Practice Option

WORD SWAP

Word Swap is an extremely simple but effective partner spelling study strategy. Students simply swap spelling lists and quiz each other. (This activity is also an effective way to introduce students to key aspects of peer testing.) And as in all partnered practice activities, students reap the benefits of exposure to two spelling lists—their own and their partner's. It's a painless spelling bonus! (Directions appear in the **Spelling Process Handbook,** student pages 7–21. This activity is appropriate for practicing any spelling list.)

· · · · · · · · · · · · MASTERING WORDS · · · · · · · · · · · ·

STEP 6 Practice Your Spelling List Independently
Choose at least three activities to practice your spelling list.

It's fun to try different practice activities.

Game Mats	With a Partner	On Your Own	At Home
○ Spelling Checkers ○ Meteor Attack	○ Circle Dot ○ Word Swap	○ Flip Folder ○ Spelling Study Strategy	○ Take Your List Home

Practice the Spelling Pattern

Write the **Pattern Word** that best fits each sentence. Circle letters that spell the vowel sound you hear in **loud**. Box letters that spell the vowel sound you hear in **noise**.

Pattern Words

crowd
sound
spoil
royal
mouth
powder
around
noise
thousand
vowel

1. Did the rain __ your picnic? spo[i]l

2. Does the alphabet begin with a __ or a consonant? v(ow)el

3. We saw a __ castle on our vacation in England. r[oy]al

4. Everyone in the loud __ yelled, "Go, team, go!" cr(ow)d

5. The puppy made so much __ crying last night! n[oi]se

6. The __ of a car horn woke me up. s(ou)nd

7. Draw a circle __ the correct answer. ar(ou)nd

8. Who spilled baby __ on the floor? p(ow)der

9. A bug flew into my __ when I laughed. m(ou)th

10. Mom won a __ dollars on a quiz show! th(ou)sand

STEP 7 Focus on Writing

A. Proofread the Writing of Others

This activity provides proofreading practice in a variety of formats, including popular standardized test formats.

B. Proofread Your Own Writing

Students return to their own writing, armed with strategies to identify and collect words they need to know how to spell, and make an authentic link between spelling and writing.

C. A Writing Idea: Directions

This suggestion for a more extended writing activity provides opportunities for students to write in different genres for a variety of purposes and modes.

STEP 8 Check Your Weekly Progress

▶ ### Take the Test

Remind students that they can take a practice test before the final test on their spelling lists. To find the testing procedure that is right for you, refer to page Z12.

▶ ### Check Your Goal

Have students compare their tests to their spelling lists. Did they spell all the **Pattern Words** on their spelling lists correctly?

▶ ### Graph Your Progress

Ask students to graph the number correct (student page 175 for softbound users; **Teacher Resource Book** page 123 for hardbound users).

▶ ### Save Missed Words

Tell students to write misspelled words on their lists of **Words I Need to Know How to Spell**. Remind students to verify spellings and to recycle these words on future weekly spelling lists.

DEVELOPING GOOD SPELLING HABITS

STEP 7 Focus on Writing

A. Proofread the Writing of Others

Proofread the paragraph below. Decide which type of mistake, if any, appears in each underlined section.

A huge <u>croud</u> was watching the parade. There must
①
have been a thousand people there! They made so
much noise, I couldn't hear my <u>brother! his mouth was</u>
②
open, but I couldn't <u>hear a sownd!</u> He had to point to
③
make me turn around. Then I saw the parade queen
and her <u>royal party passing by.</u>
④

≡ Make a capital.
/ Make a small letter.
∧ Add something.
⌒ Take out something.
⊙ Add a period.
¶ New paragraph
SP Spelling error

1. Ⓐ Spelling
   B Capitalization
   C Punctuation
   D No mistake

2. A Spelling
   Ⓑ Capitalization
   C Punctuation
   D No mistake

3. Ⓐ Spelling
   B Capitalization
   C Punctuation
   D No mistake

4. A Spelling
   B Capitalization
   C Punctuation
   Ⓓ No mistake

B. Proofread Your Own Writing

The vowel sound you hear in **crowd** may be spelled **ow** or **ou**. The vowel sound you hear in **spoil** may be spelled **oi** or **oy**. Go to your most recent writing. Look for words with these vowel sounds. Correct any misspelled words and write them in **Words I Need to Know How to Spell**.

C. A Writing Idea: Directions

Choose a place in your school. How do you get there? Write a paragraph that tells how to get there and what's there, but don't tell what the place is. Trade paragraphs with a partner. Can your partner guess where your directions lead?

STEP 8 Check Your Weekly Progress

▶ **Take the Test**
Ready? Practice test first.

▶ **Check Your Goal**
Check to see if you met your learning goal.

▶ **Graph Your Progress**
Graph your score for this week's test.

▶ **Save Missed Words**
Write the words you missed in your list of **Words I Need to Know How to Spell**.

Hunt Words
Remind students to continuously hunt words that they wish to learn how to spell and to write these words in **Words I Need to Know How to Spell**.

Long u: u-C-e, ue, oo, ew

ENGAGING IN THE PROCESS — MATERIALS

Student Edition: Pages 60–63   **Teacher Edition:** Pages T60A–T63

Materials to help students practice their spelling lists:

- **Flip Folders**
- Copies of **Flip Folder Practice Sheet** (**Teacher Resource Book,** page 51)
- **Take Your List Home** (in *Spell It–Write!* Home News, **Teacher Resource Book,** pages 73 in English and 74 in Spanish)

- Game Mats Featured in This Unit: **Meteor Attack, Rockets**
- Unit 10 **Hands-on Word Sort Cards** (Grade 4 **Hands-on Word Sort Card Book**) and Unit 10 **Hands-on Word Sort Sheet** (**Teacher Resource Book,** page 41)

ENGAGING IN THE PROCESS — GOALS

SPELLING GOALS

Students will

- understand that the **long u** sound may be spelled in different ways to spell words with the **long u** sound.
- sort words according to the spelling of the **long u** vowel sound.
- recognize that many words have more than one meaning.
- use the spelling process to become better writers.

WRITING GOALS

Students will

- hunt for words with the **long u** vowel sound in a piece of their own writing.
- write an expressive paragraph.

ENGAGING IN THE PROCESS — MANAGEMENT

Pacing	Notes	Quick Pick Management Option
Period 1 Finding Words (Steps 1–3)	If you wish to add **Teacher Words,** write them on the chalkboard. Sources for more words include: **More Words for Hungry Word Hunters** (page T60), content and theme-related words, or words of your choice.	Assign the list of **Pattern Words** to the whole class. Add the Red List (**More Words for Hungry Word Hunters,** student page 163) for a longer list. Add the Blue List (**More Words for Hungry Word Hunters**) for a more challenging list.
Period 2 Inspecting Words (Steps 4 and 5)	Students write the **Pattern Words** to complete **Explore the Spelling Pattern.**	Assign **Explore the Spelling Pattern** and **Focus on Word Study.**
Period 3 Mastering Words (Step 6) **Period 4** Developing Good Spelling Habits (Step 7)	These two periods can be allocated between selected **Mastering Words** activities and proofreading and writing activities in **Focus on Writing.**	Assign two or three activities to the whole class. Familiarize students with choosing their own activities at their own pace.
Period 5 Assessment (Step 8)	Gradually try different peer-testing options to find the style that best fits your class.	Test the class on the same, whole-class list.

ENGAGING
IN THE
PROCESS

INDIVIDUAL
NEEDS

Understanding Language Differences

Sometimes English inserts a \y\ sound before a **u**, even though the spelling does not reflect this sound. For example, **cute** is pronounced **kyoot**\ and **huge** is pronounced **hyooj**\. Students from both English-speaking backgrounds and non-English-speaking backgrounds may be tempted to include this \y\ sound in their spelling.

Some speakers of American English, especially in the southern part of the United States, may also include this \y\ sound in other words. For example, for these speakers **tune** is pronounced **tyoon**\ and **due** is pronounced **dyoo**\.

Helping Students Acquiring English

Say the words **tune, due, cool,** and **drew,** asking students to listen for the vowel sound. Guide students to recognize that all four words have the **long u** vowel sound. Display the **Hands-on Word Sort Cards** for the words and read them aloud, pointing to the underlined part of each word. Help students understand that these four spellings stand for the same **long u** sound. Ask volunteers to pick out **Word Sort Cards** for words with like spellings to create "**long u** word families."

Meeting Diverse Needs

Less Able Spellers

Students who have difficulty learning to spell, including students with special needs, may benefit from daily testing of the new words they are learning to spell.

- If the daily test is given prior to study, it focuses the child's attention on which words should be studied.

- If the daily test is given at the end of the spelling period, it allows the child to gauge his or her progress. It also provides information on which words will require additional study.

More Able Spellers

Challenge students to collect words based on their origins. Students' collections might include the following:

- words that were borrowed from another language, e.g., **restaurant** from French, **patio** from Italian;

- words that evolved from Greek and Latin roots;

- words that were coined as the need for the word arose, e.g., **skyscraper;**

- words that came from a person's name, e.g., **sandwich** after the Earl of Sandwich, who supposedly invented the sandwich.

ENGAGING
IN THE
PROCESS

INVOLVING
FAMILIES

Ask students to copy their lists in the **Take Your List Home** section of the *Spell It–Write!* Home News page for this lesson. Not only does this page provide a convenient way for families to share a student's spelling list, but it also provides a number of opportunities for families to be involved in students' spelling growth. It has a statement of the week's spelling pattern or strategy, a valuable spelling study strategy, and a suggested home spelling practice activity.

Teacher Resource Book, page 73

Teacher Resource Book, page 74

FINDING WORDS

Step 1 Build Your Spelling List

Students will build their spelling lists with **Pattern Words, Teacher Words,** and **Your Words**. Students should study a minimum of twelve new words each week.

Find Your Pattern Words

• Pretest the students on these words.

• Tell students to write each misspelled pretest word on their spelling lists.

Add Teacher Words

• Select words for students to add to their spelling lists. Choose words from **More Words for Hungry Word Hunters** (on this page and on student page 163), words related to a theme or content area, or words students often misspell.

Add Your Words

• Ask students to pick words from their lists of **Words I Need to Know How to Spell** and their writing.

• Tell students to write these words on their spelling lists.

Step 2 Write Your Spelling List

Remind students to verify all spellings. (Ask students to see **Strategies for Checking Your Spelling** in the back of the student edition.)

Step 3 Set Your Learning Goal

Tell students to count the words on their spelling lists. This total is their learning goal. It may vary depending on ability, individual goals, and the difficulty of spelling words.

MORE WORDS FOR HUNGRY WORD HUNTERS

RED LIST — Pattern Words Below Level	BLUE LIST — Pattern Words Above Level	Other Pattern Words	Math Pattern Words
blue	amuse	blueberry	acute angle
cute	avenue	contribute	obtuse angle
few	costume	cue	
food	dew	gloomy	**Science Pattern Words**
grew	flute	intrude	food web
rule	foolish	nephew	nodule
school	mood	pollute	
soup	rescue	proof	**Social Studies Pattern Words**
too	scoop	prune	fuel
true	value	rude	monsoon
you	view		
zoo	youth		

These lists also appear on page 163 in the student edition and page 16 in the **Teacher Resource Book.**

SPELLING PATTERN

10

Long u: u-C-e, ue, oo, ew

Your Spelling List

_____
_____
_____
_____
_____
_____
_____
_____
_____
_____
_____
_____
_____
_____
_____
_____
_____
_____
_____
_____

FINDING WORDS

Step 1 Build Your Spelling List

Find Your Pattern Words
Take the pretest.
Write misspelled words on your spelling list.

Add Teacher Words
Teachers may add:
• More **Pattern Words** • Content Words • Theme Words

Add Your Words
Pick words from:
• **Words I Need to Know How to Spell** • Writing • Reading

Pattern Words

1.	**tune**	When I'm happy, I whistle a happy **tune.**
2.	**due**	These library books are **due** today.
3.	**cool**	This **cool** weather is a sign of fall.
4.	**drew**	Who **drew** this picture of a horse?
5.	**group**	Kurt is in my swimming **group.**
6.	**pool**	We go to the **pool** on sunny summer days.
7.	**clue**	This map is a **clue** to the treasure.
8.	**news**	Lori heard about the fair on the TV **news.**
9.	**choose**	Anna and Eric will **choose** sides.
10.	**huge**	The **huge** dog broke the chain and ran away.
11.	**balloon**	The clown gave me a red **balloon.**
12.	**smooth**	I like **smooth** peanut butter.

Step 2 Write Your Spelling List

Step 3 Set Your Learning Goal

My spelling list has _____ words for me to learn.

I always look for words that match this week's pattern in my **Words I Need to Know How to Spell**.

That's a good idea!

PATTERN MINI-LESSON

NOTE: The **Explore the Spelling Pattern** activity on page 61 is a self-directed mini-lesson. If you wish to supplement that activity with direct instruction, use the following mini-lesson.

* **Read** aloud the **Spelling Pattern** on page 61. Explain that it will guide the **Hands-on Word Sort**.

* **Display** the **?** card and the **Hands-on Word Sort Cards** for Unit 10. Keep blank cards and a marker handy to make new cards.

* **Say** each guide word, pointing to the underlined letters. (Guide words are labeled "Master Word" on the **Word Sort Card**.) Ask how the spelling patterns vary. (Possible response: *Each word has a* **long u** *sound, but the sound is spelled in different ways.*)

* **Sort** the words based on their spelling patterns. Model your decision making: "The **long u** sound in **pool** is spelled **oo**, so I'll put **pool** under **cool.** "

* **Tell** students that words that do not fit any of these patterns should be placed under the question mark. Challenge students to explain why **group** does not fit under any guide word. (Response: *The* **long u** *sound in* **group** *is spelled* **ou**. *This doesn't match any of the other patterns.*) For the completed word sort, see the **Answer Card** for this unit in the **Hands-on Word Sort Card Book**.

* **Duplicate** the **Hands-on Word Sort Sheet** for Unit 10 (**Teacher Resource Book,** page 41). Ask students to cut the words on the sheet apart and practice sorting the words with a partner or independently.

· · · · · · INSPECTING WORDS · · · · · ·

STEP 4 Explore the Spelling Pattern
Sorting Words

A. Find a partner. Take turns reading the **Pattern Words** out loud. Write each word with the word that has the same **long u** spelling pattern. If a word doesn't fit, put it with the question mark. Make sure you write each **Pattern Word** once.

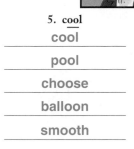

You may wish to use **Hands-on Word Sort Cards** and the **Hands-on Word Sort Sheet** for this unit

1. <u>tu</u>ne	3. d<u>ue</u>	5. c<u>oo</u>l
tune	due	cool
huge	clue	pool
		choose
2. dr<u>ew</u>	4. **?**	balloon
drew	group	smooth
news		

B. Do a word hunt to find other words that have the **long u** sound. Look in your writing, in your reading, and in **Words I Need to Know How to Spell**. Add these words to your word sort.

STEP 5 Focus on Word Study
Multiple Meanings

Many words have more than one meaning. The word **pool** can mean "tank of water to swim in," "small pond," "game played with 16 balls and a long stick on a special table," and "put things or money together."

Write the one **Pattern Word** that best completes all three sentences below.

1. Two horses __ the wagon.
2. The movie star __ a large crowd.
3. An artist __ a picture of me.

drew

▼▼▼▼▼▼▼▼▼▼▼▼▼
Spelling Pattern
Listen to **tune, due, cool,** and **drew**. The vowel sound in these words is spelled in different ways: **u**-consonant-**silent e**, as in **tune; ue**, as in **due; oo**, as in **cool;** and **ew**, as in **drew**.
· · · · · · · · · · · · · · ·

STEP 4 Explore the Spelling Pattern

Sorting Words

This activity is a self-directed mini-lesson on this week's **Spelling Pattern**.

STEP 5 Focus on Word Study

Multiple Meanings

This activity is intended to stimulate students' interest in words and to help them become more enthusiastic word hunters.

Spelling Process Handbook

Students who need to review any part of the spelling process, including practice options, should refer to the **Spelling Process Handbook** (pages 7–21).

MASTERING WORDS

A Practice Option

Practice Your Spelling List Independently

STEP 6

Ask the students to choose activities to practice their spelling words and to master this week's **Spelling Pattern**. Students should complete at least three activities each week. You may wish to:

- assign **Practice the Spelling Pattern** to all students to reinforce this week's **Spelling Pattern**.

- involve students' families by assigning **Take Your List Home** for this lesson (**Teacher Resource Book,** pages 73 in English and 74 in Spanish).

- encourage students to use partner activities without game mats (**Word Swap, Spelling Tic-Tac-Toe, Circle Dot**) and activities with game mats (**Meteor Attack, Rockets, Spelling Checkers, Spelling Soccer**). Directions for game-mat activities appear on each game mat. Directions for all other activities are found in the **Spelling Process Handbook** (pages 7–21).

NOTE: These activities and games can be used to practice any spelling list.

ROCKETS

Can you figure out the spelling word before your partner "blasts off"? That's the challenge for students as they play **Rockets**. Students will develop their knowledge of common spelling patterns as they make strategic guesses to visualize spellings and complete words. It's a countdown to spelling success with **Rockets**. (Directions appear on the **Rockets** game mat. This activity is appropriate for practicing any spelling list.)

· · · · · · · **MASTERING WORDS** · · · · · · ·

STEP 6 Practice Your Spelling List Independently
Choose at least three activities to practice your spelling list.

Hunt words in your writing and reading! Add words you want to learn to **Words I Need to Know How to Spell**.

Game Mats	With a Partner	On Your Own	At Home
Meteor Attack Rockets	Circle Dot Spelling Tic-Tac-Toe	Flip Folder Spelling Study Strategy	Take Your List Home

 Practice the Spelling Pattern

In each sentence below, a **Pattern Word** is spelled wrong. Write the correct spelling. Then in each word you wrote, circle the letters that spell the **long u** sound.

Pattern Words

tune
due
cool
drew
group
pool
clue
news
choose
huge
balloon
smooth

1. The detective looked for a clew.   cl(ue)
2. What show did you chewz to watch?   ch(oo)se
3. I dove into the poole.   p(oo)l
4. Do you know this toon?   t(une)
5. A grupe of children played catch.   gr(ou)p
6. An artist droo Pam's picture.   dr(ew)
7. The grass was soft and smuthe.   sm(oo)th
8. The movie is dew to start at six.   d(ue)
9. A hewge wave knocked me down!   h(uge)
10. Have you heard the latest nooz?   ne(ws)
11. Everyone kept coul in the lake.   c(oo)l
12. My ballune popped!   ball(oo)n

STEP 7 Focus on Writing

A. Hunt Spelling Words in Your Writing

This activity equips students with a specific strategy for increasing students' consciousness of targeted spelling patterns and strategies in their own writing. It also enables them to collect words for spelling study.

B. A Writing Idea: A Paragraph

This suggestion for a more extended writing activity provides opportunities for students to write in different genres for a variety of purposes and modes.

STEP 8 Check Your Weekly Progress

▶ Take the Test

Remind students that they can take a practice test before the final test on their spelling lists. To find the testing procedure that is right for you, refer to page Z12.

▶ Check Your Goal

Have students compare their tests to their spelling lists. Did they spell all the **Pattern Words** on their spelling lists correctly?

▶ Graph Your Progress

Ask students to graph the number correct (student page 175 for softbound users; **Teacher Resource Book** page 123 for hardbound users).

▶ Save Missed Words

Tell students to write misspelled words on their lists of **Words I Need to Know How to Spell**. Remind students to verify spellings and to recycle these words on future weekly spelling lists.

DEVELOPING GOOD SPELLING HABITS

STEP 7 Focus on Writing

A. Hunt Spelling Words in Your Writing

Choose one piece of your latest writing. Work with a spelling partner to look for words with the **long u** sound spelled u-consonant-**silent e**, **ue**, **oo**, or **ew**. Write the words you find in two columns like these.

Column 1	Column 2
I spelled these **long u** words correctly.	I misspelled these **long u** words.
Answers will vary.	Answers will vary.

If you can't find any **long u** words, choose a different piece of your writing.

Add the words you wrote in Column 2 to **Words I Need to Know How to Spell**.

B. A Writing Idea: A Paragraph

How do you keep cool in the summer? How many new and different ways can you imagine for keeping cool? Write a paragraph to describe some of these ways. Circle each word you write that contains a **long u** spelling pattern.

≡ Make a capital.
／ Make a small letter.
∧ Add something.
ℰ Take out something.
⊙ Add a period.
¶ New paragraph
(SP) Spelling error

STEP 8 Check Your Weekly Progress

▶ **Take the Test**
Ready? Practice test first.

▶ **Check Your Goal**
Check to see if you met your learning goal.

▶ **Graph Your Progress**
Graph your score for this week's test.

▶ **Save Missed Words**
Write the words you missed in your list of **Words I Need to Know How to Spell**.

Hunt Words

Remind students to continuously hunt words that they wish to learn how to spell and to write these words in **Words I Need to Know How to Spell**.

ENGAGING IN THE **PROCESS**

MATERIALS

Student Edition: Pages 64–67   **Teacher Edition:** Pages T64A–T67

Materials to help students practice their spelling lists:

- **Flip Folders**
- Copies of **Flip Folder Practice Sheet** (**Teacher Resource Book,** page 51)
- **Take Your List Home** (in *Spell It–Write!*

Home News, **Teacher Resource Book,** pages 75 in English and 76 in Spanish)
- Game Mats Featured in This Unit: **Rockets, Spelling Soccer**

ENGAGING IN THE **PROCESS**

GOALS

SPELLING GOALS

Students will

- develop a spelling strategy to help them spell new words.
- develop an understanding of how the meanings and spellings of words can change over time.
- use the spelling process of finding words, inspecting words, and mastering words as they develop good spelling habits to become better writers.

WRITING GOALS

Students will

- proofread a writing sample.
- proofread a piece of their own writing for misspelled words.
- write a persuasive ad.

ENGAGING IN THE **PROCESS**

MANAGEMENT

Pacing	Notes	Quick Pick Management Option
Period 1 Finding Words (Steps 1–3)	If you wish to add **Teacher Words,** write them on the chalkboard. Sources for more words include: **More Words for Hungry Word Hunters** (page T64), content and theme-related words, or words of your choice.	Assign the list of **Strategy Words** to the whole class. Add the Red List (**More Words for Hungry Word Hunters,** student page 164) for a longer list. Add the Blue List (**More Words for Hungry Word Hunters**) for a more challenging list.
Period 2 Inspecting Words (Steps 4 and 5)	Students write the **Strategy Words** to complete **Explore the Spelling Strategy.**	Assign **Explore the Spelling Strategy** and **Focus on Word Study.**
Period 3 Mastering Words (Step 6) **Period 4** Developing Good Spelling Habits (Step 7)	These two periods can be allocated between selected **Mastering Words** activities and proofreading and writing activities in **Focus on Writing.**	Assign two or three activities to the whole class. Familiarize students with choosing their own activities at their own pace.
Period 5 Assessment (Step 8)	Gradually try different peer-testing options to find the style that best fits your class.	Test the class on the same, whole-class list.

Understanding Language Differences

Spanish Speakers

As this unit points out, students can use meaning relationships to figure out how to spell new words. For students from non-English-speaking backgrounds, this strategy can involve using what they already know about their first language.

Of course, using another language, such as Spanish, to learn English can be a mixed blessing. Because English vocabulary has borrowed heavily from Latin and the Romance languages (such as Spanish, French, and Italian) that developed from Latin, it often helps to compare the two languages.

Students who are learning English as a second language will develop strategies of their own. Yet at the same time they are learning that English words such as **student** and **sport** are related in meaning to Spanish words such as **estudiante** (**student**) and **deporte** (**sport; pastime**), they also must learn that the spellings and pronunciations differ. As you encourage students from other language backgrounds to guess at the meanings of such words, remind them that they cannot rely entirely on these relationships to help directly with English spellings.

Helping Students Acquiring English

Write each **Strategy Word** on a separate 3" x 5" card. Display one card at a time. Pronounce the word and use a variety of means to convey the word's meaning. For **wouldn't,** review contractions and the use of an apostrophe to take the place of omitted letters. After you have introduced all the **Strategy Words,** let pairs of students use the cards as flash cards for practice.

Meeting Diverse Needs

Less Able Spellers

Students who have difficulty learning to spell may need additional help in mastering specific spelling strategies. It is important that they understand the purpose of the strategy as well as when, where, and how to use it.

When presenting a new spelling strategy, be sure to model how to use it and provide guided practice in applying it. Make sure that students understand how using the strategy will help them do better work.

More Able Spellers

Challenge students to find as many words that are related to a targeted word as they can. Words may be related in any number of ways. For example, **student, studious,** and **study** are related in meaning, while **threw, new, drew,** and **flew** are related by rhyme and spelling pattern.

Ask students to copy their lists in the **Take Your List Home** section of the *Spell It–Write!* Home News page for this lesson. Not only does this page provide a convenient way for families to share a student's spelling list, but it also provides a number of opportunities for families to be involved in students' spelling growth. It has a statement of the week's spelling pattern or strategy, a valuable spelling study strategy, and a suggested home spelling practice activity.

Teacher Resource Book, page 75

Teacher Resource Book, page 76

FINDING WORDS

STEP 1 — Build Your Spelling List

Students will build their spelling lists with **Strategy Words, Teacher Words,** and **Your Words.** Students should study a minimum of twelve new words each week.

Find Your Strategy Words

- Pretest the students on these words.
- Tell students to write each misspelled pretest word on their spelling lists.

Add Teacher Words

- Select words for students to add to their spelling lists. Choose words from **More Words for Hungry Word Hunters** (on this page and on student page 164), words related to a theme or content area, or words students often misspell.

Add Your Words

- Ask students to pick words from their lists of **Words I Need to Know How to Spell** and their writing.
- Tell students to write these words on their spelling lists.

STEP 2 — Write Your Spelling List

Remind students to verify all spellings. (Ask students to see **Strategies for Checking Your Spelling** in the back of the student edition.)

STEP 3 — Set Your Learning Goal

Tell students to count the words on their spelling lists. This total is their learning goal. It may vary depending on ability, individual goals, and the difficulty of spelling words.

MORE WORDS FOR HUNGRY WORD HUNTERS

RED LIST — Strategy Words Below Level	BLUE LIST — Strategy Words Above Level	Other Strategy Words
anything	different	ancient
better	evening	aware
cattle	favorite	champion
early	furniture	forever
himself	guard	imagine
lovely	interesting	jacket
rocket	lying	market
south	pleasant	repair
sport	sense	secretary
thought	shoulder	spoken

Math Strategy Words

facts	groups	risk
fraction	loop	stock
graph	measure	

Science Strategy Words

airy	dense	lungs
cause	gas	mood
core	host	polar
crust	itch	

Social Studies Strategy Words

barn	mind	station
dam	pelt	surf
ferry	print	trap
map	resource	

These lists also appear on page 164 in the student edition and page 17 in the **Teacher Resource Book.**

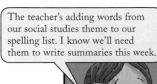

SPELLING STRATEGY

11

Think of a Rhyming Word

Your Spelling List

· · · · · · · FINDING WORDS · · · · · · ·

STEP 1 — Build Your Spelling List

Find Your Strategy Words
Take the pretest.
Write misspelled words on your spelling list.

Add Teacher Words
Teachers may add:
- More **Strategy Words** • Content Words • Theme Words

Add Your Words
Pick words from:
- **Words I Need to Know How to Spell** • Writing • Reading

Strategy Words

1. **fifth**	George was **fifth** in line to buy tickets.
2. **tomorrow**	What day will it be **tomorrow**?
3. **instead**	Buy wheat bread **instead** of white bread.
4. **clothing**	We gave the old shirt to the **clothing** drive.
5. **carpet**	We took the old **carpet** off the floor.
6. **wouldn't**	Our cat **wouldn't** get into the car.
7. **suit**	My dad doesn't like to wear that **suit**.
8. **threw**	Julia **threw** the ball over the fence.
9. **student**	Shawn is a straight-A **student** in math.
10. **raise**	**Raise** your hand to answer a question.

STEP 2 — Write Your Spelling List

STEP 3 — Set Your Learning Goal

My spelling list has _____ words for me to learn.

The teacher's adding words from our social studies theme to our spelling list. I know we'll need them to write summaries this week.

Adding science words to our list last week really helped me write in science class.

INSPECTING WORDS

STRATEGY MINI-LESSON

NOTE: The **Explore the Spelling Strategy** activity on page 65 is a self-directed mini-lesson. If you wish to supplement that activity with direct instruction, use the following mini-lesson.

* **Write** suit on the chalkboard. Explain to the students that **suit** can actually help them spell **fruit** because the words rhyme. Rhyming words are often spelled the same. Write **fruit** on the chalkboard and compare the spellings.

* **Write** student and study. Explain that these words have a meaning relationship. A student is a person who might study. Guide students to understand the relationship between the two words.

* **Ask** students to open their books to page 64.

* **Divide** the class into groups. Give each group a word on the list of **Strategy Words**. (Do not include **suit** or **student**.)

Tell students to think of other words or word parts that can help them spell the word. Tell them they can use a rhyming relationship, as in **suit** and **fruit,** or a meaning relationship, as in **student** and **study**. Provide time for students to share their clues. (Accept any reasonable responses.)

* **Read** the Spelling Strategy on page 65 with students.

* **Ask** students whether they already use any of these methods to remember how to spell certain words. You may also wish to write words from **More Words for Hungry Word Hunters** (on student page 164 and page T64) on the chalkboard and allow the class to think of relationships to help with spelling these words. Remind students that they may add any of these words to **Words I Need to Know How to Spell**.

INSPECTING WORDS

STEP 4 Explore the Spelling Strategy
Match-up

A. For each clue word below, write a **Strategy Word** that is similar to it in some way. The clue word and **Strategy Word** may rhyme, be connected by meaning, or share a similar spelling pattern.

1. juice — suit
2. sorrow — tomorrow
3. cloth — clothing
4. couldn't — wouldn't
5. study — student

6. drew — threw
7. rain — raise
8. if — fifth
9. car — carpet
10. steady — instead

Now circle the letters in each **Strategy Word** that match the spelling pattern in the clue word.

B. At home, work with a family member to find other words that are similar in some way to each **Strategy Word**. Talk about how noticing ways that words are similar can help you remember how to spell a word.

STEP 5 Focus on Word Study
Changes in Meaning and Spelling

The word **carpet** changed in meaning as it traveled through time. In ancient Latin and Italian, a **carpita** was a heavy cloth. Old French used **carpite** to mean "a covering for a table or a bed." About 400 years ago, the English word **karpete** came to mean "a cloth to cover a floor."

Write the **Strategy Word** that came from these earlier spellings.

1. sout, sitew — suit
2. studere, estudient — student

Spelling Strategy
If you're not sure how to spell a word, think of a word you know that is similar. This word may give you a clue about spelling the unknown word.

STEP 4 Explore the Spelling Strategy
Match-up
This activity is a self-directed mini-lesson on this week's **Spelling Strategy**.

STEP 5 Focus on Word Study
Changes in Meaning and Spelling
This activity is intended to stimulate students' interest in words and to help them become more enthusiastic word hunters.

Spelling Process Handbook
Students who need to review any part of the spelling process, including practice options, should refer to the Spelling Process Handbook (pages 7–21).

UNIT 11 T65

MASTERING WORDS

STEP 6 Practice Your Spelling List Independently

Ask the students to choose activities to practice their spelling words and to master this week's **Spelling Strategy**. Students should complete at least three activities each week. You may wish to:

- assign **Practice the Spelling Strategy** to all students to reinforce this week's **Spelling Strategy**.

- involve students' families by assigning **Take Your List Home** for this lesson (**Teacher Resource Book,** pages 75 in English and 76 in Spanish).

- encourage students to use partner activities without game mats (**Word Swap, Spelling Tic-Tac-Toe, Circle Dot**) and activities with game mats (**Meteor Attack, Rockets, Spelling Checkers, Spelling Soccer**). Directions for game-mat activities appear on each game mat. Directions for all other activities are found in the **Spelling Process Handbook** (pages 7–21).

NOTE: These activities and games can be used to practice any spelling list.

A Practice Option

SPELLING STUDY STRATEGY

Generations of spelling scholars have researched the most productive way to study spelling words. The most consistently reliable method is the easy but effective **Spelling Study Strategy**. Once students master the basic steps of this look-say-cover-see-write-check-rewrite strategy, they can practice any spelling words independently, anywhere. (Directions appear in the **Spelling Process Handbook,** student pages 7–21. This activity is appropriate for practicing any spelling list.)

· · · · · · · MASTERING WORDS · · · · · · ·

STEP 6 Practice Your Spelling List Independently
Choose at least three activities to practice your spelling list.

Need Help?
Read the **Spelling Process Handbook** (pages 7–21).

Game Mats	With a Partner	On Your Own	At Home
 ○ Rockets ○ Spelling Soccer	 ○ Spelling Tic-Tac-Toe ○ Word Swap	 ○ Flip Folder ○ Spelling Study Strategy	 ○ Take Your List Home

Practice the Spelling Strategy

In each sentence, find the clue word or words that are spelled like a **Strategy Word**. Then write the **Strategy Word** that fits the sentence.

Strategy Words

fifth
tomorrow
instead
clothing
carpet
wouldn't
suit
threw
student
raise

1. Kareem wants to borrow my bike __. **tomorrow**
2. My dog tried to chew the ball I __. **threw**
3. In a car, a pet might scratch the __. **carpet**
4. Buy bread __ of rolls. **instead**
5. Don't spill the fruit on your best __! **suit**
6. The sign printed on the __ bin read, "Clothes only." **clothing**
7. Has the __ studied for the test? **student**
8. If you knew you shouldn't, then you __! **wouldn't**
9. To __ a good puppy, praise it often. **raise**
10. Is that gift the __ one Ruth has opened? **fifth**

STEP 7 Focus on Writing

A. Proofread the Writing of Others

This activity provides proofreading practice in a variety of formats, including popular standardized test formats.

B. Proofread Your Own Writing

Students return to their own writing, armed with strategies to identify and collect words they need to know how to spell, and make an authentic link between spelling and writing.

C. A Writing Idea: An Ad

This suggestion for a more extended writing activity provides opportunities for students to write in different genres for a variety of purposes and modes.

STEP 8 Check Your Weekly Progress

▶ Take the Test

Remind students that they can take a practice test before the final test on their spelling lists. To find the testing procedure that is right for you, refer to page Z12.

▶ Check Your Goal

Have students compare their tests to their spelling lists. Did they spell all the **Strategy Words** on their spelling lists correctly?

▶ Graph Your Progress

Ask students to graph the number correct (student page 175 for softbound users; **Teacher Resource Book** page 123 for hardbound users).

▶ Save Missed Words

Tell students to write misspelled words on their lists of **Words I Need to Know How to Spell**. Remind students to verify spellings and to recycle these words on future weekly spelling lists.

· · · · · · DEVELOPING GOOD SPELLING HABITS · · · · · ·

STEP 7 Focus on Writing

A. Proofread the Writing of Others

Proofread the sales ad below. Decide which type of mistake, if any, appears in each underlined section.

> Come to our giant sale tomorrow! All clotheing will
> _____①_____ _____②_____
> be reduced by half! Get a new soot for just $50! Hurry
> _____③_____
> in early! you wouldn't want to miss this fantastic event!
> _____④_____

≡ Make a capital.
/ Make a small letter.
∧ Add something.
⌔ Take out something.
⊙ Add a period.
¶ New paragraph
(SP) Spelling error

1. A Spelling
   B Capitalization
   C Punctuation
   Ⓓ No mistake

2. Ⓐ Spelling
   B Capitalization
   C Punctuation
   D No mistake

3. Ⓐ Spelling
   B Capitalization
   C Punctuation
   D No mistake

4. A Spelling
   Ⓑ Capitalization
   C Punctuation
   D No mistake

B. Proofread Your Own Writing

Proofread something you have written. If you are not sure a word is spelled correctly, try one of these strategies:
1. Think of a word you know how to spell that rhymes.
2. Think of a word with a similar meaning.
3. Think of a word that has the same spelling pattern.

Write the correct spelling of any misspelled words. Add these words to **Words I Need to Know How to Spell**.

C. A Writing Idea: An Ad

Dream up a product of the future. What will it be like? Write an ad for the product that might appear in a newspaper or magazine. Be persuasive! Proofread your ad for errors in spelling, capitalization, and punctuation.

STEP 8 Check Your Weekly Progress

▶ **Take the Test**
Ready? Practice test first.

▶ **Check Your Goal**
Check to see if you met your learning goal.

▶ **Graph Your Progress**
Graph your score for this week's test.

▶ **Save Missed Words**
Write the words you missed in your list of **Words I Need to Know How to Spell.**

Hunt Words

Remind students to continuously hunt words that they wish to learn how to spell and to write these words in **Words I Need to Know How to Spell**.

qu, squ

ENGAGING IN THE PROCESS

MATERIALS

Student Edition: Pages 68–71   **Teacher Edition:** Pages T68A–T71

Materials to help students practice their spelling lists:
- **Flip Folders**
- Copies of **Flip Folder Practice Sheet** (**Teacher Resource Book,** page 51)
- **Take Your List Home** (in *Spell It–Write!*)

Home News, **Teacher Resource Book,** pages 77 in English and 78 in Spanish)
- Game Mats Featured in This Unit: **Spelling Checkers, Spelling Soccer**

ENGAGING IN THE PROCESS

GOALS

SPELLING GOALS

Students will

- identify and spell words with the spelling patterns **qu** and **squ**.

- sort words according to the spelling patterns **qu** and **squ**.

- develop an understanding of how the spellings of words can change over time.

- use the spelling process of finding words, inspecting words, and mastering words as they develop good spelling habits to become better writers.

WRITING GOALS

Students will

- proofread a writing sample.

- proofread a piece of their own writing for misspelled words with the patterns **qu** and **squ**.

- write an expressive paragraph.

ENGAGING IN THE PROCESS

MANAGEMENT

Pacing	Notes	Quick Pick Management Option
Period 1 Finding Words (Steps 1–3)	If you wish to add **Teacher Words,** write them on the chalkboard. Sources for more words include: **More Words for Hungry Word Hunters** (page T68), content and theme-related words, or words of your choice.	Assign the list of **Pattern Words** to the whole class. Add the Blue List (**More Words for Hungry Word Hunters,** student page 164) for a more challenging list.
Period 2 Inspecting Words (Steps 4 and 5)	Students write the **Pattern Words** to complete **Explore the Spelling Pattern.**	Assign **Explore the Spelling Pattern** and **Focus on Word Study.**
Period 3 Mastering Words (Step 6) **Period 4** Developing Good Spelling Habits (Step 7)	These two periods can be allocated between selected **Mastering Words** activities and proofreading and writing activities in **Focus on Writing.**	Assign two or three activities to the whole class. Familiarize students with choosing their own activities at their own pace.
Period 5 Assessment (Step 8)	Gradually try different peer-testing options to find the style that best fits your class.	Test the class on the same, whole-class list.

Understanding Language Differences

Spanish Speakers

English words spelled with **qu** often correspond in meaning to Spanish words spelled with **cua**. For example, **quarter** is equivalent to **cuarto; square** is equivalent to **cuadrado.**

In other English words, **qu** may correspond with Spanish **g**. For example, **equal** is the counterpart of **igual.** In still other examples, **qu** is present in corresponding words in both languages: **liquid** and **liquido** (pronounced **\lee-KEE-doh**). Native Spanish speakers may confuse the Spanish and English spellings for some of these words.

Native Spanish speakers may have trouble pronouncing words with the initial **squ** blend. This letter combination does not occur at the beginning of words in Spanish. Care should be taken to model the pronunciation of this combination for students from Spanish-speaking backgrounds.

Some English sounds simply do not occur in Spanish; therefore, the bilingual learner will have difficulty hearing and producing the sounds. You might consult the school speech therapist to get suggestions for exercises to develop unfamiliar sounds in students' speech.

Helping Students Acquiring English

Write the word **quarter** on the chalkboard, using a different color of chalk for the letters **qu.** Display a quarter as you read the word aloud to students, pointing to each letter in turn. Explain that the letters **qu** stand for the beginning sounds in **quarter.** Follow a similar procedure for **square,** drawing a square on the chalkboard and labeling it, using a different color of chalk for the letters **squ.** Present the remaining words, grouping **qu** words with **quarter** and **squ** words with **square.**

Meeting Diverse Needs

Less Able Spellers

Students who have difficulty learning to spell may benefit from peer assistance in correcting spelling miscues in their writing. Before writing a final copy, a student can share his or her paper with a peer editor who locates and circles suspected misspellings. The paper is returned to the author, who uses the feedback to verify spellings and make the necessary corrections on the final copy.

More Able Spellers

Ask students who are strong spellers to select one of their spelling words. Then challenge them to develop as many new words as they can by adding prefixes and suffixes to the spelling word. Ask them to explain how the meaning (and spelling) of the original word changed with each addition.

Ask students to copy their lists in the **Take Your List Home** section of the *Spell It–Write!* Home News page for this lesson. Not only does this page provide a convenient way for families to share a student's spelling list, but it also provides a number of opportunities for families to be involved in students' spelling growth. It has a statement of the week's spelling pattern or strategy, a valuable spelling study strategy, and a suggested home spelling practice activity.

Teacher Resource Book, page 77

Teacher Resource Book, page 78

FINDING WORDS

STEP 1 Build Your Spelling List

Students will build their spelling lists with **Pattern Words, Teacher Words,** and **Your Words.** Students should study a minimum of twelve new words each week.

Find Your Pattern Words

- Pretest the students on these words.
- Tell students to write each misspelled pretest word on their spelling lists.

Add Teacher Words

- Select words for students to add to their spelling lists. Choose words from **More Words for Hungry Word Hunters** (on this page and on student page 164), words related to a theme or content area, or words students often misspell.

Add Your Words

- Ask students to pick words from their lists of **Words I Need to Know How to Spell** and their writing.
- Tell students to write these words on their spelling lists.

STEP 2 Write Your Spelling List

Remind students to verify all spellings. (Ask students to see **Strategies for Checking Your Spelling** in the back of the student edition.)

STEP 3 Set Your Learning Goal

Tell students to count the words on their spelling lists. This total is their learning goal. It may vary depending on ability, individual goals, and the difficulty of spelling words.

MORE WORDS FOR HUNGRY WORD HUNTERS

BLUE LIST

Pattern Words Above Level

equally
liquid
quarrel
quart
question
quiz
quote
squash
squeeze
squirt

Other Pattern Words

quaint
quake
quartz
quill
quilt
quiver
squad
squawk
squid
squint

Math Pattern Word

quotient

Science Pattern Word

earthquake

Social Studies Pattern Words

aqueduct
equator

These lists also appear on page 164 in the student edition and page 18 in the **Teacher Resource Book.**

SPELLING PATTERN

12

qu, squ

Your Spelling List

_____
_____
_____
_____
_____
_____
_____
_____
_____
_____
_____
_____
_____
_____
_____
_____
_____
_____
_____
_____

FINDING WORDS

STEP 1 Build Your Spelling List

Find Your Pattern Words

Take the pretest.
Write misspelled words on your spelling list.

Add Teacher Words

Teachers may add:
- More **Pattern Words** • Content Words • Theme Words

Add Your Words

Pick words from:
- **Words I Need to Know How to Spell** • Writing • Reading

Pattern Words

1. **quite**	Mr. Jackson is **quite** tall, even taller than Dad.
2. **square**	Can you draw a **square** without a ruler?
3. **queen**	The **queen** bee does not make honey.
4. **quarter**	Do you have a **quarter** and a penny in your pocket?
5. **squeak**	My shoes **squeak** loudly when I walk.
6. **quick**	If you are **quick**, you can catch that bug.
7. **quiet**	Please be **quiet** while the baby is sleeping.
8. **squeal**	Did you hear that pig **squeal**?
9. **quit**	Why did you **quit** the soccer team?
10. **equal**	Do ten dimes **equal** one dollar?

STEP 2 Write Your Spelling List

STEP 3 Set Your Learning Goal

My spelling list has _____ words for me to learn.

There are some words I always misspell when I write. I'll add them to my spelling list until I get them right!

Hmmm. That makes sense. Knowing those words will help you write better, too.

PATTERN MINI-LESSON

NOTE: The **Explore the Spelling Pattern** activity on page 69 is a self-directed mini-lesson. If you wish to supplement that activity with direct instruction, use the following mini-lesson.

* **Write** the **Pattern Words** from page 68 on the chalkboard. Say each word aloud and ask the class to repeat it.

* **Ask** students whether they can find the same two letters together in every word. (Possible response: *All the words contain the letters qu.*) You may wish to tell students that in English words, **q** is always followed by **u**. You may also wish to point out that some of the words on this week's list begin with **squ**. (The letter **s** is the only letter that combines with **qu** to form a blend.)

* **Read** the Spelling Pattern on page 69 with the class.

* **Write** the headings **qu** and **squ** on the chalkboard. Encourage students to provide other words that contain **qu** and **squ**. List these suggestions on the chalkboard under the appropriate heading. You may wish to include examples from **More Words for Hungry Word Hunters** (on student page 164 and page T68). Remind students that they may add any of these words to **Words I Need to Know How to Spell**.

 Explore the Spelling Pattern
Sorting Words

A. Making a word sort can help you inspect words. Sort the **Pattern Words** into two groups. Use the words below to guide your sort. Make sure you write each **Pattern Word** once.

Try sorting the **Pattern Words** in other ways. How many words are nouns?

1. quite	2. square
quite	square
queen	squeak
quarter	squeal
quick	
quiet	
quit	
equal	

B. Do a word hunt to find other words that have the spelling pattern **qu** or **squ**. Look in your reading, in your writing, and in **Words I Need to Know How to Spell**. Add the words you find to your word sort.

 Focus on Word Study
Changes in Spelling

Spelling changes over time. After the Norman king, William the Conqueror, conquered England in 1066, Norman scribes made many changes in Old English spellings. One change substituted **qu** for the Old English **cw**. If William had lost the Battle of Hastings, we might still spell **queen** as **cwene**!

Write the **Pattern Words** that came from these old words.

1. cwic   quick
2. aequalis   equal
3. skvala   squeal

▼▼▼▼▼▼▼▼▼▼▼▼
Spelling Pattern
• Listen to **quite**. The beginning sounds are spelled **qu**.

• Listen to **square**. The beginning sounds are spelled **squ**.
· · · · · · · · · · · · · · ·

 Explore the Spelling Pattern

Sorting Words

This activity is a self-directed mini-lesson on this week's **Spelling Pattern**.

Focus on Word Study

Changes in Spelling

This activity is intended to stimulate students' interest in words and to help them become more enthusiastic word hunters.

Spelling Process Handbook

Students who need to review any part of the spelling process, including practice options, should refer to the **Spelling Process Handbook** (pages 7–21).

MASTERING WORDS

STEP 6 Practice Your Spelling List Independently

Ask the students to choose activities to practice their spelling words and to master this week's **Spelling Pattern**. Students should complete at least three activities each week. You may wish to:

- assign **Practice the Spelling Pattern** to all students to reinforce this week's **Spelling Pattern**.

- involve students' families by assigning **Take Your List Home** for this lesson (**Teacher Resource Book,** pages 77 in English and 78 in Spanish).

- encourage students to use partner activities without game mats (**Word Swap, Spelling Tic-Tac-Toe, Circle Dot**) and activities with game mats (**Meteor Attack, Rockets, Spelling Checkers, Spelling Soccer**). Directions for game-mat activities appear on each game mat. Directions for all other activities are found in the **Spelling Process Handbook** (pages 7–21).

NOTE: These activities and games can be used to practice any spelling list.

SPELLING CHECKERS

Students will "jump" at the chance to play **Spelling Checkers**, a game mat that combines spelling practice with the popular board game. And because students write on the board with dry-erase markers to record their progress, game pieces are not needed. This game is especially appropriate spelling practice for auditory and visual learners. (Directions appear on the **Spelling Checkers** game mat. This activity is appropriate for practicing any spelling list.)

MASTERING WORDS

STEP 6 Practice Your Spelling List Independently
Choose at least three activities to practice your spelling list.

You can practice any spelling list with these activities.

Game Mats		With a Partner		On Your Own		At Home
○ Spelling Soccer	○ Spelling Checkers	○ Circle Dot	○ Word Swap	○ Flip Folder	○ Spelling Study Strategy	○ Take Your List Home

Practice the Spelling Pattern

Write the **Pattern Word** that fits the clue. Don't forget to write the **u** after the **q**. Then circle **qu** or **squ** in each word you wrote.

Pattern Words

quite
square
queen
quarter
squeak
quick
quiet
squeal
quit
equal

1. still; silent — ⓠuiet
2. 6 + 4 and 7 + 3 — eⓠual
3. something mice do — ⓢqueak
4. female head of a country — ⓠueen
5. twenty-five cents — ⓠuarter
6. stop doing something — ⓠuit
7. fast — ⓠuick
8. figure with four equal sides — ⓢquare
9. something pigs do — ⓢqueal
10. very — ⓠuite

DEVELOPING GOOD SPELLING HABITS

7 Focus on Writing

A. Proofread the Writing of Others

This activity provides proofreading practice in a variety of formats, including popular standardized test formats.

B. Proofread Your Own Writing

Students return to their own writing, armed with strategies to identify and collect words they need to know how to spell, and make an authentic link between spelling and writing.

C. A Writing Idea: A Description

This suggestion for a more extended writing activity provides opportunities for students to write in different genres for a variety of purposes and modes.

8 Check Your Weekly Progress

▶ Take the Test

Remind students that they can take a practice test before the final test on their spelling lists. To find the testing procedure that is right for you, refer to page Z12.

▶ Check Your Goal

Have students compare their tests to their spelling lists. Did they spell all the **Pattern Words** on their spelling lists correctly?

▶ Graph Your Progress

Ask students to graph the number correct (student page 175 for softbound users; **Teacher Resource Book** page 123 for hardbound users).

▶ Save Missed Words

Tell students to write misspelled words on their lists of **Words I Need to Know How to Spell**. Remind students to verify spellings and to recycle these words on future weekly spelling lists.

DEVELOPING GOOD SPELLING HABITS

7 Focus on Writing

A. Proofread the Writing of Others

Proofread the paragraph Ella wrote about a trip to the zoo. The underlined words are not spelled right. Look at the list of spellings and decide which spelling is correct. Write the correct spelling of the word.

A zoo is not a quite¹ place! In a kwarter² of an hour there, you can hear a lot of different noises. Some animals, like the pigs and monkeys, skweal³! The busy seals splash and play in a big sqaure⁴ pool.

≡ Make a capital.
/ Make a small letter.
∧ Add something.
ℓ Take out something.
⊙ Add a period.
¶ New paragraph
SP Spelling error

1. kwite
   kwiet
   quiet
   ___quiet___

3. squeel
   squeal
   skweel
   ___squeal___

2. quarter
   qaurter
   kwater
   ___quarter___

4. skware
   sqware
   square
   ___square___

B. Proofread Your Own Writing

In English words, **q** is always followed by **u**. Some words begin with **squ**. Go to your most recent writing. Look for any misspelled words that have the pattern **qu** or **squ**. Write them correctly in **Words I Need to Know How to Spell**.

C. A Writing Idea: A Description

On a quiet night you can hear many different sounds. Write a paragraph describing the sounds you hear on a quiet night. When you are finished writing, check to see if you've spelled all the words correctly.

8 Check Your Weekly Progress

▶ **Take the Test**
Ready? Practice test first.

▶ **Check Your Goal**
Check to see if you met your learning goal.

▶ **Graph Your Progress**
Graph your score for this week's test.

▶ **Save Missed Words**
Write the words you missed in your list of **Words I Need to Know How to Spell**.

Hunt Words

Remind students to continuously hunt words that they wish to learn how to spell and to write these words in **Words I Need to Know How to Spell**.

SPELLING PATTERN 13
Silent Consonants

ENGAGING IN THE PROCESS — MATERIALS

Student Edition: Pages 72–75   **Teacher Edition:** Pages T72A–T75

Materials to help students practice their spelling lists:

- **Flip Folders**
- Copies of **Flip Folder Practice Sheet** (**Teacher Resource Book,** page 51)
- **Take Your List Home** (in *Spell It–Write!*)

Home News, **Teacher Resource Book,** pages 79 in English and 80 in Spanish)
- Game Mats Featured in This Unit: **Meteor Attack, Spelling Checkers**

ENGAGING IN THE PROCESS — GOALS

SPELLING GOALS

Students will

- understand that some words are spelled with silent consonants.
- sort words according to their silent consonants.
- develop an understanding of how the pronunciations of words can change over time.
- use the spelling process of finding words, inspecting words, and mastering words as they develop good spelling habits to become better writers.

WRITING GOALS

Students will

- hunt for words with silent consonants in a piece of their own writing.
- write an informative how-to paragraph.

ENGAGING IN THE PROCESS — MANAGEMENT

Pacing	Notes	Quick Pick Management Option
Period 1 Finding Words (Steps 1–3)	If you wish to add **Teacher Words,** write them on the chalkboard. Sources for more words include: **More Words for Hungry Word Hunters** (page T72), content and theme-related words, or words of your choice.	Assign the list of **Pattern Words** to the whole class. Add the Red List (**More Words for Hungry Word Hunters,** student page 165) for a longer list. Add the Blue List (**More Words for Hungry Word Hunters**) for a more challenging list.
Period 2 Inspecting Words (Steps 4 and 5)	Students write the **Pattern Words** to complete **Explore the Spelling Pattern**.	Assign **Explore the Spelling Pattern** and **Focus on Word Study**.
Period 3 Mastering Words (Step 6) **Period 4** Developing Good Spelling Habits (Step 7)	These two periods can be allocated between selected **Mastering Words** activities and proofreading and writing activities in **Focus on Writing**.	Assign two or three activities to the whole class. Familiarize students with choosing their own activities at their own pace.
Period 5 Assessment (Step 8)	Gradually try different peer-testing options to find the style that best fits your class.	Test the class on the same, whole-class list.

Understanding Language Differences

Spanish Speakers

Spanish does not really have "silent" letters. However, some letters may not be pronounced in casual speech, especially at the end of a word. For example, **Madrid** may become \mah-dree\.

In most words, silent letters are there because of archaic pronunciations. Silent letters cause special problems for students who are learning English as a second language. These students often have no way of knowing how these words are actually pronounced by English speakers. In addition, depending on the writing system of their first language, students may not be familiar with the concept of silent letters. This makes modeling the pronunciations even more important.

You may wish to present pairs of words having a common meaning base and a common letter that is silent in one member of the pair but pronounced in the other. For example, the **g** is silent in **sign** but is pronounced in **signal**. Similar pairs are **crumb** and **crumble**, **limb** and **limber**, and **design** and **designate**.

Helping Students Acquiring English

Tape a picture of a knife to the chalkboard, and write the word **knife** under the picture, using a different color of chalk for the letter **k**. Read the word aloud, and discuss its spelling. Guide students to understand that the letter **k** does not stand for a sound in **knife;** it is silent. Follow a similar procedure for the remaining **Pattern Words**.

Meeting Diverse Needs

Less Able Spellers

How many new spelling words should teachers expect students with special needs to learn each week? This is a difficult question to answer because the number varies from student to student. The *Spell It–Write!* authors recommend that students with special needs learn at least six to twelve new spelling words each week.

More Able Spellers

Challenge students who are strong spellers to locate five to ten words whose spelling and/or meaning they do not know and to add these words to **Words I Need to Know How to Spell**. Students should also be asked to find the meanings they do not know and to use each word in an appropriate way orally.

ENGAGING
IN THE
PROCESS

INVOLVING
FAMILIES

Ask students to copy their lists in the **Take Your List Home** section of the *Spell It–Write!* Home News page for this lesson. Not only does this page provide a convenient way for families to share a student's spelling list, but it also provides a number of opportunities for families to be involved in students' spelling growth. It has a statement of the week's spelling pattern or strategy, a valuable spelling study strategy, and a suggested home spelling practice activity.

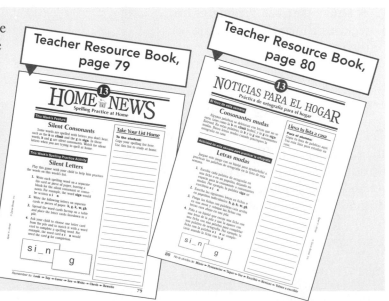

FINDING WORDS

STEP 1 Build Your Spelling List

Students will build their spelling lists with **Pattern Words, Teacher Words,** and **Your Words**. Students should study a minimum of twelve new words each week.

Find Your Pattern Words
- Pretest the students on these words.
- Tell students to write each misspelled pretest word on their spelling lists.

Add Teacher Words
- Select words for students to add to their spelling lists. Choose words from **More Words for Hungry Word Hunters** (on this page and on student page 165), words related to a theme or content area, or words students often misspell.

Add Your Words
- Ask students to pick words from their lists of **Words I Need to Know How to Spell** and their writing.
- Tell students to write these words on their spelling lists.

STEP 2 Write Your Spelling List

Remind students to verify all spellings. (Ask students to see **Strategies for Checking Your Spelling** in the back of the student edition.)

STEP 3 Set Your Learning Goal

Tell students to count the words on their spelling lists. This total is their learning goal. It may vary depending on ability, individual goals, and the difficulty of spelling words.

T72 UNIT 13

MORE WORDS FOR HUNGRY WORD HUNTERS

─RED LIST─ Pattern Words Below Level	─BLUE LIST─ Pattern Words Above Level	Other Pattern Words	Science Pattern Word
bought	although	bomb	height
fight	crumb	gnat	
high	design	knack	**Social Studies Pattern Word**
knot	gnaw	kneel	freight
know	knight	knob	
lamb	knock	knuckle	
might	limb	numb	
thumb	through	plumber	
wrap	wring	tomb	
	wrist	wreck	

These lists also appear on page 165 in the student edition and page 19 in the **Teacher Resource Book**.

FINDING WORDS

SPELLING PATTERN

13

Silent Consonants

Your Spelling List

_____
_____
_____
_____
_____
_____
_____
_____
_____
_____
_____
_____
_____
_____
_____
_____
_____
_____
_____

STEP 1 Build Your Spelling List

Find Your Pattern Words
Take the pretest.
Write misspelled words on your spelling list.

Add Teacher Words
Teachers may add:
• More **Pattern Words** • Content Words • Theme Words

Add Your Words
Pick words from:
• **Words I Need to Know How to Spell** • Writing • Reading

Pattern Words

1. **climb**	Jane can **climb** to the top of the tree.
2. **sign**	The **sign** on the fence read "Keep Out!"
3. **knife**	A sharp **knife** is not a toy.
4. **wrote**	Deb **wrote** a poem for her grandfather.
5. **flight**	The first airplane **flight** lasted only twelve seconds!
6. **wrong**	Was your answer right or **wrong**?
7. **knee**	Jake scraped his **knee** when he fell.
8. **comb**	You should not share your **comb**.
9. **written**	The speech was **written** long ago.
10. **sight**	Bats do not have poor **sight**.

STEP 2 Write Your Spelling List

STEP 3 Set Your Learning Goal

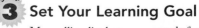

My spelling list has _____ words for me to learn.

> You know, hunting words is getting to be something I do all the time.

> Me, too! I went to the movies yesterday, and when I got home, I added three new words to my **Words I Need to Know How to Spell**.

INSPECTING WORDS

PATTERN MINI-LESSON

NOTE: The **Explore the Spelling Pattern** activity on page 73 is a self-directed mini-lesson. If you wish to supplement that activity with direct instruction, use the following mini-lesson.

* **Write** the **Pattern Words** from page 72 on the chalkboard.

* **Tell** students that these words are alike in that they all have one or more silent consonants.

* **Ask** why silent letters might cause spelling problems. (Possible response: *Letters that aren't pronounced might be left out when the words are spelled.*)

* **Call** on volunteers to identify the silent consonants in each word. As students name the silent letters, underline them in the words on the chalkboard.

* **Explain** that in all the words except **climb, comb, sight,** and **flight,** the silent consonant is part of a two-letter combination in which the first consonant is silent. Then ask how the silent letters in **climb** and **comb** are different. (Response: *In these words, the second consonant in the pair is silent.*) Ask how **sight** and **flight** are different. (Response: *Two consonants, g and h, are silent.*)

* **Read** the **Spelling Pattern** on page 73 with the class.

* **Encourage** students to give examples of other words they know that have silent consonants. You may also wish to write on the chalkboard examples from **More Words for Hungry Word Hunters** (on student page 165 and page T72). Remind students that they may add any of these words to **Words I Need to Know How to Spell**.

INSPECTING WORDS

 Explore the Spelling Pattern
Sorting Words

A. Making a word sort can help you inspect words. Look for the silent consonant in each **Pattern Word**. Then sort the **Pattern Words**. Use the words below to guide your sort. Make sure you write each **Pattern Word** once.

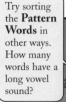 Try sorting the **Pattern Words** in other ways. How many words have a long vowel sound?

1. knife
knife
knee

2. climb
climb
comb

3. wrote
wrote
wrong
written

4. flight
flight
sight

5. sign
sign

B. With a partner, do a word hunt to find other words that have silent consonants. Think them up, or look in your writing or **Words I Need to Know How to Spell**. Sort the words according to their silent consonants.

 Focus on Word Study
Changes in Pronunciation

Hundreds of years ago English speakers pronounced the **k** in **knife**, the **b** in **comb**, and the **g** and **h** in **flight**. Now when we pronounce these words, some of the letters are silent.

Write the silent consonants in each word.

1. lamb __b__
2. knot __k__
3. wrap __w__
4. bright __gh__
5. height __gh__
6. light __gh__
7. autumn __n__
8. might __gh__

▼▼▼▼▼▼▼▼▼▼▼▼
Spelling Pattern
Some words are spelled with letters you don't hear, such as the **b** in **climb** and the **g** in **sign**. In these words, **b** and **g** are silent consonants.

 Explore the Spelling Pattern

Sorting Words

This activity is a self-directed mini-lesson on this week's **Spelling Pattern**.

 Focus on Word Study

Changes in Pronunciation

This activity is intended to stimulate students' interest in words and to help them become more enthusiastic word hunters.

Spelling Process Handbook

Students who need to review any part of the spelling process, including practice options, should refer to the **Spelling Process Handbook** (pages 7–21).

MASTERING WORDS

STEP 6 Practice Your Spelling List Independently

Ask the students to choose activities to practice their spelling words and to master this week's **Spelling Pattern**. Students should complete at least three activities each week. You may wish to:

- assign **Practice the Spelling Pattern** to all students to reinforce this week's **Spelling Pattern**.

- involve students' families by assigning **Take Your List Home** for this lesson (**Teacher Resource Book,** pages 79 in English and 80 in Spanish).

- encourage students to use partner activities without game mats (**Word Swap, Spelling Tic-Tac-Toe, Circle Dot**) and activities with game mats (**Meteor Attack, Rockets, Spelling Checkers, Spelling Soccer**). Directions for game-mat activities appear on each game mat. Directions for all other activities are found in the **Spelling Process Handbook** (pages 7–21).

NOTE: These activities and games can be used to practice any spelling list.

A Practice Option

CIRCLE DOT

Circles and dots become powerful learning tools in this simple, effective activity. Each student works with a partner to attempt —and then correct—the spelling of each word on his or her list. As the student corrects, he or she marks a dot for each correct letter and a circle for each error. Because **Circle Dot** makes discrete errors visible, students can practice their spelling words strategically by focusing on the part(s) of the spelling that most challenges them. (Directions appear in the **Spelling Process Handbook**, student pages 7–21. This activity is appropriate for practicing any spelling list.)

MASTERING WORDS

STEP 6 Practice Your Spelling List Independently

Choose at least three activities to practice your spelling list.

Copy your words carefully when you take your list home.

Game Mats	With a Partner	On Your Own	At Home
○ Spelling Checkers ○ Meteor Attack	○ Circle Dot ○ Spelling Tic-Tac-Toe	○ Flip Folder ○ Spelling Study Strategy	○ Take Your List Home

Practice the Spelling Pattern

Decide which letter or letter pair from the box completes each **Pattern Word**. Write the word. Then circle the silent consonants in the words you wrote.

Pattern Words

climb
sign
knife
wrote
flight
wrong
knee
comb
written
sight

b	g	gh	k	w

1. Ana __rote that note on the chalkboard.   ⓦrote
2. Don't let the puppy out of your si__t.   siⓖⓗt
3. It's hard to admit you're __rong.   ⓦrong
4. I forgot to com__ my hair this morning.   comⓑ
5. The si__n in the window read "Closed."   siⓖn
6. You will never see a penguin in fli__t.   fliⓖⓗt
7. I fell and scraped my __nee.   ⓚnee
8. We plan to clim__ that mountain!   climⓑ
9. The note was __ritten in green ink.   ⓦritten
10. Always handle a __nife carefully.   ⓚnife

STEP 7 Focus on Writing

A. Hunt Spelling Words in Your Writing

This activity equips students with a specific strategy for increasing students' consciousness of targeted spelling patterns and strategies in their own writing. It also enables them to collect words for spelling study.

B. A Writing Idea: A How-to

This suggestion for a more extended writing activity provides opportunities for students to write in different genres for a variety of purposes and modes.

STEP 8 Check Your Weekly Progress

▶ Take the Test

Remind students that they can take a practice test before the final test on their spelling lists. To find the testing procedure that is right for you, refer to page Z12.

▶ Check Your Goal

Have students compare their tests to their spelling lists. Did they spell all the **Pattern Words** on their spelling lists correctly?

▶ Graph Your Progress

Ask students to graph the number correct (student page 175 for softbound users; **Teacher Resource Book** page 123 for hardbound users).

▶ Save Missed Words

Tell students to write misspelled words on their lists of **Words I Need to Know How to Spell**. Remind students to verify spellings and to recycle these words on future weekly spelling lists.

· · · · · · · · DEVELOPING GOOD SPELLING HABITS · · · · · · · ·

STEP 7 Focus on Writing

A. Hunt Spelling Words in Your Writing

Choose some of your most recent writing. Work with a spelling partner to look for words with silent consonants. Use two columns like these to record what you found in your writing.

Column 1	Column 2
I spelled these **silent consonants** words correctly.	I misspelled these **silent consonants** words.
Answers will vary.	Answers will vary.

≡ Make a capital.
／ Make a small letter.
∧ Add something.
℮ Take out something.
⊙ Add a period.
¶ New paragraph
(SP) Spelling error

Add the words you wrote in Column 2 to **Words I Need to Know How to Spell**.

B. A Writing Idea: A How-to

Choose a useful object (such as a knife or a comb) and write directions for how to use it—but don't tell what it is! Explain the right way and the wrong way to use the object. Use lots of details. Read your directions to a partner. Can your partner guess what the object is?

STEP 8 Check Your Weekly Progress

▶ Take the Test
Ready? Practice test first.

▶ Check Your Goal
Check to see if you met your learning goal.

▶ Graph Your Progress
Graph your score for this week's test.

▶ Save Missed Words
Write the words you missed in your list of **Words I Need to Know How to Spell**.

Hunt Words

Remind students to continuously hunt words that they wish to learn how to spell and to write these words in **Words I Need to Know How to Spell**.

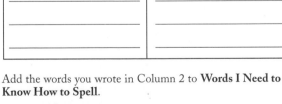

ENGAGING IN THE PROCESS

MATERIALS

Student Edition: Pages 76–79   **Teacher Edition:** Pages T76A–T79

Materials to help students practice their spelling lists:

- **Flip Folders**
- Copies of **Flip Folder Practice Sheet** (**Teacher Resource Book,** page 51)
- **Take Your List Home** (in *Spell It–Write!* Home News, **Teacher Resource Book,** pages 81 in English and 82 in Spanish)

- Game Mats Featured in This Unit: **Meteor Attack, Rockets**
- Unit 14 **Hands-on Word Sort Cards** (Grade 4 **Hands-on Word Sort Card Book**) and Unit 14 **Hands-on Word Sort Sheet** (**Teacher Resource Book,** page 42)

ENGAGING IN THE PROCESS

GOALS

SPELLING GOALS

Students will

- recognize and spell words with **ge** and **dge**.
- sort words according to the spelling patterns **ge** and **dge**.
- develop an understanding of how the meanings of words can change over time.
- use the spelling process of finding words, inspecting words, and mastering words as they develop good spelling habits to become better writers.

WRITING GOALS

Students will

- proofread a writing sample.
- proofread a piece of their own writing for misspelled words with **ge** and **dge**.
- write an expressive paragraph.

ENGAGING IN THE PROCESS

MANAGEMENT

Pacing	Notes	Quick Pick Management Option
Period 1 Finding Words (Steps 1–3)	If you wish to add **Teacher Words,** write them on the chalkboard. Sources for more words include: **More Words for Hungry Word Hunters** (page T76), content and theme-related words, or words of your choice.	Assign the list of **Pattern Words** to the whole class. Add the Blue List (**More Words for Hungry Word Hunters,** student page 165) for a more challenging list.
Period 2 Inspecting Words (Steps 4 and 5)	Students write the **Pattern Words** to complete **Explore the Spelling Pattern.**	Assign **Explore the Spelling Pattern** and **Focus on Word Study.**
Period 3 Mastering Words (Step 6) **Period 4** Developing Good Spelling Habits (Step 7)	These two periods can be allocated between selected **Mastering Words** activities and proofreading and writing activities in **Focus on Writing.**	Assign two or three activities to the whole class. Familiarize students with choosing their own activities at their own pace.
Period 5 Assessment (Step 8)	Gradually try different peer-testing options to find the style that best fits your class.	Test the class on the same, whole-class list.

Understanding Language Differences

English spells \j\ in a variety of ways—**j, g, dge**—as the mini-lesson explains. Linguists call this kind of sound an **affricate**. Affricates are complicated sounds because they combine two different kinds of consonant sounds to form one sound. The **ch**\ affricate is a combination of **t**\ and **sh**\. The **j**\ affricate is a combination of **d**\ and **zh**\.

Not all languages have affricate consonants. Spanish has the **ch**\ affricate, but **j**\ occurs only in some dialects. The word **yo** (**I**) is pronounced **joh**\ by some South Americans.

If students who are learning English as a second language have difficulty with these sounds, ask them to practice combining the two parts of the affricate sound to form one sound: **d**\ + **zh**\ = **j**\.

Helping Students Acquiring English

Create "cheerleading" teams. Invite each team to make up a cheer for one or more of the **Pattern Words** on page 76. Tell them to spell out the word twice and repeat the word at least four times during the cheer. Each team leader will write the team's **Pattern Word** on the chalkboard and then the team will lead the whole class in repeating the cheer. For instance, "E-D-G-E-edge, edge-E-D-G-E-edge, edge!" Continue until all the words have been presented.

Meeting Diverse Needs

Less Able Spellers

Some students who have difficulty learning to spell also struggle with handwriting. As a result, they often do not want to write words as they are learning to spell them. They prefer instead to say the letters out loud as part of the study process.

Emphasize to these students that writing will help them remember how to spell the word because they can "feel" how the word is made as they write it. Unless a student has motor difficulties, encourage him or her to use writing, instead of oral spelling, to practice new spelling words. Periodically check to see if these children use writing as part of the study process. Acknowledge and reinforce their use of writing as an element in the study process.

More Able Spellers

Ask stronger spellers to select one word from their weekly spelling lists and locate as many synonyms and antonyms for that word as they can. Ask them to examine the word pairs for similarities in spelling. If students have used prefixes to generate their synonyms and antonyms, encourage them to discuss the meaning of each prefix and use the prefixes to generate other words.

Ask students to copy their lists in the **Take Your List Home** section of the *Spell It–Write!* Home News page for this lesson. Not only does this page provide a convenient way for families to share a student's spelling list, but it also provides a number of opportunities for families to be involved in students' spelling growth. It has a statement of the week's spelling pattern or strategy, a valuable spelling study strategy, and a suggested home spelling practice activity.

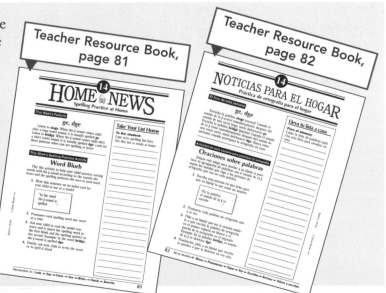

FINDING WORDS

STEP 1 Build Your Spelling List

Students will build their spelling lists with **Pattern Words, Teacher Words,** and **Your Words.** Students should study a minimum of twelve new words each week.

Find Your Pattern Words

- Pretest the students on these words.
- Tell students to write each misspelled pretest word on their spelling lists.

Add Teacher Words

- Select words for students to add to their spelling lists. Choose words from **More Words for Hungry Word Hunters** (on this page and on student page 165), words related to a theme or content area, or words students often misspell.

Add Your Words

- Ask students to pick words from their lists of **Words I Need to Know How to Spell** and their writing.
- Tell students to write these words on their spelling lists.

STEP 2 Write Your Spelling List

Remind students to verify all spellings. (Ask students to see **Strategies for Checking Your Spelling** in the back of the student edition.)

STEP 3 Set Your Learning Goal

Tell students to count the words on their spelling lists. This total is their learning goal. It may vary depending on ability, individual goals, and the difficulty of spelling words.

MORE WORDS FOR HUNGRY WORD HUNTERS

┌─BLUE LIST─┐

Pattern Words Above Level	Other Pattern Words
average	arrange
barge	college
dodge	damage
fudge	fidget
gadget	grudge
message	hedge
oblige	knowledge
pledge	ledger
range	lodge
ridge	wedge
stranger	
wage	

Science Pattern Word

plumage

Social Studies Pattern Word

heritage

These lists also appear on page 165 in the student edition and page 20 in the **Teacher Resource Book.**

· · · · · · · · · · FINDING WORDS · · · · · · · · · ·

SPELLING PATTERN

14

ge, dge

Your Spelling List

_____
_____
_____
_____
_____
_____
_____
_____
_____
_____
_____
_____
_____
_____
_____
_____
_____
_____
_____
_____
_____

STEP 1 Build Your Spelling List

Find Your Pattern Words

Take the pretest.
Write misspelled words on your spelling list.

Add Teacher Words

Teachers may add:
- More **Pattern Words** • Content Words • Theme Words

Add Your Words

Pick words from:
- **Words I Need to Know How to Spell** • Writing • Reading

Pattern Words

1. bridge	The **bridge** fell into the river.
2. stage	Who built the **stage** for the show?
3. village	The houses in the **village** are small.
4. rage	The bull was in a wild **rage**!
5. strange	The football player did a **strange** dance.
6. badge	She is wearing a police officer's **badge**.
7. package	That **package** came in the mail.
8. engage	James won't **engage** in dangerous games.
9. judge	Mrs. Smith will **judge** pies at the fair.
10. charge	Who is in **charge** here?
11. edge	Don't go near the **edge** of the cliff.
12. danger	The hunted spy's life was in **danger**.

STEP 2 Write Your Spelling List

STEP 3 Set Your Learning Goal

My spelling list has _____ words for me to learn.

> I like doing different things. Once we know all the activities, we'll be able to choose the ones we want to do.

> The teacher assigns a different practice activity to the class every week.

PATTERN MINI-LESSON

NOTE: The **Explore the Spelling Pattern** activity on page 77 is a self-directed mini-lesson. If you wish to supplement that activity with direct instruction, use the following mini-lesson.

* **Read** the **Spelling Pattern** on page 77. Explain that it will guide the **Hands-on Word Sort**.

* **Display** the **?** card and the **Hands-on Word Sort Cards** for Unit 14. Keep blank cards and a marker handy to make new cards.

* **Say** each guide word, pointing to the underlined letters. (Guide words are labeled "Master Word" on the **Word Sort Card**.) Help students to see that when \j\ is preceded by a short vowel sound, it is usually spelled **dge;** when it is preceded by a long vowel sound, it is spelled **ge**.

* **Sort** the words based on their spelling patterns. Model your decision making: "In **badge,** a short vowel sound comes before the \j\ sound, and the \j\ sound is spelled **dge,** so I'll put **badge** under **bridge**." Challenge students to explain why **village, strange, package, charge,** and **danger** do not fit either pattern. (Possible response: *The vowel sound before \j\ in* **village** *and* **package** *is neither* **long** *nor* **short** *a. In* **strange, danger,** *and* **charge,** *the \j\ is preceded by another consonant.*) For the completed word sort, see the **Answer Card** for this unit in the **Hands-on Word Sort Card Book.**

* **Duplicate** the **Hands-on Word Sort Sheet** for Unit 14 (**Teacher Resource Book,** page 42). Ask students to cut the words on the sheet apart and practice sorting the words with a partner or independently.

· · · · · · · · · · · INSPECTING WORDS · · · · · · · · · · · ·

STEP 4 Explore the Spelling Pattern
Sorting Words

A. Find a partner. Take turns reading the **Pattern Words** out loud. Sort the **Pattern Words** into three groups. Write each **Pattern Word** with the guide word that has the same sound and spelling pattern. If a word doesn't fit with a guide word, put it with the question mark. Make sure you write each **Pattern Word** once.

You may wish to use **Hands-on Word Sort Cards** and the **Hands-on Word Sort Sheet** for this unit.

1. bridge (short vowel + dge)	2. stage (long vowel + ge)	3. ? (other vowels + ge)
bridge	stage	village
badge	rage	strange
judge	engage	package
edge		charge
		danger

B. Do a word hunt with a partner to find other words that have the **j** sound spelled **dge** or **ge**. Look in **Words I Need to Know How to Spell** and in your writing. Sort the words you find by sound and spelling pattern.

STEP 5 Focus on Word Study
Word History

The word **danger** comes from an ancient Latin word that meant "master" or "lord." In Medieval French, the word meant "a lord's power."

Match the words **village, package,** and **strange** with the meanings they had long ago.

1. of, relating to, or characteristic of another country _____ strange

2. a farm _____ village

3. a burden _____ package

▼▼▼▼▼▼▼▼▼▼▼▼▼▼
Spelling Pattern

• Listen to **bridge**. When the **j** sound comes right after a short vowel sound, it is usually spelled **dge**.

• Listen to **stage**. When the **j** sound comes right after a long vowel sound, it is usually spelled **ge**.

· · · · · · · · · · · · · · · ·

STEP 4 Explore the Spelling Pattern
Sorting Words

This activity is a self-directed mini-lesson on this week's **Spelling Pattern**.

STEP 5 Focus on Word Study
Word History

This activity is intended to stimulate students' interest in words and to help them become more enthusiastic word hunters.

Spelling Process Handbook

Students who need to review any part of the spelling process, including practice options, should refer to the **Spelling Process Handbook** (pages 7–21).

MASTERING WORDS

Practice Your Spelling List Independently
STEP 6

Ask the students to choose activities to practice their spelling words and to master this week's **Spelling Pattern**. Students should complete at least three activities each week. You may wish to:

- assign **Practice the Spelling Pattern** to all students to reinforce this week's **Spelling Pattern**.

- involve students' families by assigning **Take Your List Home** for this lesson (**Teacher Resource Book**, pages 81 in English and 82 in Spanish).

- encourage students to use partner activities without game mats (**Word Swap, Spelling Tic-Tac-Toe, Circle Dot**) and activities with game mats (**Meteor Attack, Rockets, Spelling Checkers, Spelling Soccer**). Directions for game-mat activities appear on each game mat. Directions for all other activities are found in the **Spelling Process Handbook** (pages 7–21).

NOTE: These activities and games can be used to practice any spelling list.

METEOR ATTACK

Students will attack spelling words with enthusiasm as they pair up to play **Meteor Attack**. Partners take turns spelling and writing their spelling words as they "destroy" meteors and collect points. The more words they spell correctly, the more points they collect. It's great fun, and great spelling practice, especially for auditory and visual learners. (Directions appear on the **Meteor Attack** game mat. This activity is appropriate for practicing any spelling list.)

· · · · · · · · · MASTERING WORDS · · · · · · · · ·

Practice Your Spelling List Independently
STEP 6
Choose at least three activities to practice your spelling list.

It's fun to try different practice activities.

Game Mats	With a Partner	On Your Own	At Home
Meteor Attack ○ Rockets	Word Swap ○ Spelling Tic-Tac-Toe	Flip Folder ○ Spelling Study Strategy	Take Your List Home

Practice the Spelling Pattern

One word in each sentence is missing the letters that spell the **j** sound. Decide what letters are missing, then write the whole word. Use the **Pattern Words** to check your spelling.

Pattern Words

bridge
stage
village
rage
strange
badge
package
engage
judge
charge
edge
danger

1. The ju___ wore a long black robe.   **judge**
2. A villa___ is a very small town.   **village**
3. The leader wore a gold ba___.   **badge**
4. Try to stay out of dan___r.   **danger**
5. The river needs a new bri___.   **bridge**
6. What is that stran___ looking bug?   **strange**
7. Lani danced on the sta___.   **stage**
8. The char___ for the pizza was $5.00.   **charge**
9. Guess what is in this packa___!   **package**
10. Listen to the storm ra___ outside!   **rage**
11. The knife had a very sharp e___.   **edge**
12. Will the birds enga___ the cat's attention?   **engage**

DEVELOPING GOOD SPELLING HABITS

STEP 7 Focus on Writing

A. Proofread the Writing of Others

This activity provides proofreading practice in a variety of formats, including popular standardized test formats.

B. Proofread Your Own Writing

Students return to their own writing, armed with strategies to identify and collect words they need to know how to spell, and make an authentic link between spelling and writing.

C. A Writing Idea: A Description

This suggestion for a more extended writing activity provides opportunities for students to write in different genres for a variety of purposes and modes.

STEP 8 Check Your Weekly Progress

▶ Take the Test

Remind students that they can take a practice test before the final test on their spelling lists. To find the testing procedure that is right for you, refer to page Z12.

▶ Check Your Goal

Have students compare their tests to their spelling lists. Did they spell all the **Pattern Words** on their spelling lists correctly?

▶ Graph Your Progress

Ask students to graph the number correct (student page 175 for softbound users; **Teacher Resource Book** page 123 for hardbound users).

▶ Save Missed Words

Tell students to write misspelled words on their lists of **Words I Need to Know How to Spell**. Remind students to verify spellings and to recycle these words on future weekly spelling lists.

· · · · · · · · · · · DEVELOPING GOOD SPELLING HABITS · · · · · · · · · ·

STEP 7 Focus on Writing

A. Proofread the Writing of Others

Proofread the report that Kevin wrote. Find the eight misspelled words. Write each word correctly.

How to Build a Bridg

First, someone has to be in chardge of the work to make sure it is done right. Then that person can engaje other workers. The person who is boss has to check every staje of the work.

You have to be careful when you build a bridg. You don't want to put people in danjer. You can't just judge the distance across a river. You have to measure it from one edje to the other.

≡ Make a capital.
/ Make a small letter.
∧ Add something.
⌒ Take out something.
⊙ Add a period.
¶ New paragraph
(SP) Spelling error

1. ___Bridge___   5. ___bridge___
2. ___charge___   6. ___danger___
3. ___engage___   7. ___judge___
4. ___stage___   8. ___edge___

B. Proofread Your Own Writing

The **j** sound may be spelled **dge** as in **bridge** or **ge** as in **stage**. Go to your most recent writing. Look for words with these patterns that you may have misspelled. Add these words to **Words I Need to Know How to Spell**.

C. A Writing Idea: A Description

Imagine you have wrapped a surprise package for a friend. Write a paragraph describing the surprise, but don't tell what it is. Ask a partner to read what you have written and guess what your package contains.

STEP 8 Check Your Weekly Progress

▶ Take the Test
Ready? Practice test first.

▶ Check Your Goal
Check to see if you met your learning goal.

▶ Graph Your Progress
Graph your score for this week's test.

▶ Save Missed Words
Write the words you missed in your list of **Words I Need to Know How to Spell**.

Hunt Words

Remind students to continuously hunt words that they wish to learn how to spell and to write these words in **Words I Need to Know How to Spell**.

Use Spelling Clues

ENGAGING IN THE PROCESS — MATERIALS

Student Edition: Pages 80–83   **Teacher Edition:** Pages T80A–T83

Materials to help students practice their spelling lists:
- **Flip Folders**
- Copies of **Flip Folder Practice Sheet** (**Teacher Resource Book,** page 51)
- **Take Your List Home** (in *Spell It–Write!*

Home News, **Teacher Resource Book,** pages 83 in English and 84 in Spanish)
- Games Mats Featured in This Unit: **Rockets, Spelling Soccer**

ENGAGING IN THE PROCESS — GOALS

SPELLING GOALS

Students will

- understand that a saying can help them remember the spellings of words they find difficult.

- develop sayings to help them remember how to spell difficult words.

- develop an understanding of how the meanings of words can change as words move from one language to another over time.

- use the spelling process to become better writers.

WRITING GOALS

Students will

- proofread a writing sample.

- proofread a piece of their own writing for misspelled words and develop spelling clues for the words.

- write a persuasive paragraph.

ENGAGING IN THE PROCESS — MANAGEMENT

Pacing	Notes	Quick Pick Management Option
Period 1 Finding Words (Steps 1–3)	If you wish to add **Teacher Words,** write them on the chalkboard. Sources for more words include: **More Words for Hungry Word Hunters** (page T80), content and theme-related words, or words of your choice.	Assign the list of **Strategy Words** to the whole class. Add the Red List (**More Words for Hungry Word Hunters,** student page 166) for a longer list. Add the Blue List (**More Words for Hungry Word Hunters**) for a more challenging list.
Period 2 Inspecting Words (Steps 4 and 5)	Students write the **Strategy Words** to complete **Explore the Spelling Strategy**.	Assign **Explore the Spelling Strategy** and **Focus on Word Study**.
Period 3 Mastering Words (Step 6) **Period 4** Developing Good Spelling Habits (Step 7)	These two periods can be allocated between selected **Mastering Words** activities and proofreading and writing activities in **Focus on Writing**.	Assign two or three activities to the whole class. Familiarize students with choosing their own activities at their own pace.
Period 5 Assessment (Step 8)	Gradually try different peer-testing options to find the style that best fits your class.	Test the class on the same, whole-class list.

Understanding Language Differences

Eighth and **eight** are examples of just how complicated English spelling can be. There are several reasons for such unusual spellings. The first is that spelling is conservative. We are likely to continue to spell words as we have in the past, even though the pronunciation may have changed over the course of time. The **gh** in **eight** is there for a reason: Old English had a sound that modern English no longer has. It is the sound represented by **ch** in the German word **lch** (**I**) or the Scottish word **loch** (**lake**). In Old English this sound was usually spelled **gh,** as in **light** and **laugh,** but today these letters are either silent or pronounced as **\f\.**

Another reason for unexpected spellings is that before spelling became standardized, people from different regions spelled words as they pronounced them.

Helping Students Acquiring English

Encourage native English-speaking peers to work in pairs or groups with students acquiring English to make up mnemonics (memory aids) for spelling the words on this week's list that they can both act out and recite. For example, to remember the spelling of the word **whole,** they might act out filling a hole with sand at the beach, while saying, "I filled in the <u>wh</u>ole hole <u>w</u>ith sand."

Meeting Diverse Needs

For Less Able Spellers

Mnemonics are a great tool for helping students—especially students who struggle with spelling—remember the spelling of words. (A mnemonic is a saying to help students remember the spelling of a particular word. For example, "**Eight** is the **eighth** number" can help students remember how to spell **eighth.**) However, it is important to emphasize that a person can remember only a relatively small number of mnemonics, so mnemonics are not the entire answer to becoming a successful speller. Encourage students to use mnemonics only for words that are especially difficult for them.

For More Able Spellers

Challenge students to find as many words within another word as they can by rearranging letters. For example, **captain** contains **cap, cat, can, pat, pan, tap, tan, apt, act, pact,** and **pain**. As students become more adept with this activity, challenge them to manipulate the letters of target words mentally and respond without first writing the words on paper.

Ask students to copy their lists in the **Take Your List Home** section of the *Spell It–Write!* Home News page for this lesson. Not only does this page provide a convenient way for families to share a student's spelling list, but it also provides a number of opportunities for families to be involved in students' spelling growth. It has a statement of the week's spelling pattern or strategy, a valuable spelling study strategy, and a suggested home spelling practice activity.

Teacher Resource Book, page 83

Teacher Resource Book, page 84

MORE WORDS FOR HUNGRY WORD HUNTERS

RED LIST Strategy Words Below Level	BLUE LIST Strategy Words Above Level
another	business
every	capital
everywhere	diamond
forgot	exercise
once	handsome
paid	piece
party	principal
right	receive
safety	soldier
summer	theater

Math Strategy Words

duet	sphere	trio
fiftieth	subtraction	

Science Strategy Words

density	pulse	spinach
height	smog	stomach
lizard	solar	strength

Social Studies Strategy Words

colony	inlet	prairie
depot	island	scene
diagram	kayak	tornado
freight	lava	
fuel	oboe	

These lists also appear on page 166 in the student edition and page 21 in the **Teacher Resource Book.**

STEP 1 Build Your Spelling List

Students will build their spelling lists with **Strategy Words, Teacher Words,** and **Your Words.** Students should study a minimum of twelve new words each week.

Find Your Strategy Words
• Pretest the students on these words.

• Tell students to write each mis-spelled pretest word on their spelling lists.

Add Teacher Words
• Select words for students to add to their spelling lists. Choose words from **More Words for Hungry Word Hunters** (on this page and on student page 166), words related to a theme or content area, or words students often misspell.

Add Your Words
• Ask students to pick words from their lists of **Words I Need to Know How to Spell** and their writing.

• Tell students to write these words on their spelling lists.

STEP 2 Write Your Spelling List

Remind students to verify all spellings. (Ask students to see **Strategies for Checking Your Spelling** in the back of the student edition.)

STEP 3 Set Your Learning Goal

Tell students to count the words on their spelling lists. This total is their learning goal. It may vary depending on ability, individual goals, and the difficulty of spelling words.

SPELLING STRATEGY

15

Use Spelling Clues

Your Spelling List

_____
_____
_____
_____
_____
_____
_____
_____
_____
_____
_____
_____
_____
_____
_____
_____
_____
_____
_____
_____
_____

STEP 1 Build Your Spelling List

Find Your Strategy Words

Take the pretest.
Write misspelled words on your spelling list.

Add Teacher Words

Teachers may add:
• More **Strategy Words** • Content Words • Theme Words

Add Your Words

Pick words from:
• **Words I Need to Know How to Spell** • Writing • Reading

Strategy Words

1. field	The plow was stuck in the corn **field**.
2. caught	Rosa **caught** the biggest fish in the pond.
3. tried	Wayne **tried** to take a picture of the fish.
4. whole	The **whole** class went to the farm.
5. eighth	My sister is in the **eighth** grade.
6. doctor	You should see a **doctor** if you are sick.
7. young	A **young** cat is called a kitten.
8. clothes	Please put your clean **clothes** in the closet.
9. though	**Though** April is small, she is quite strong.
10. captain	The **captain** gave orders to the crew.

STEP 2 Write Your Spelling List

STEP 3 Set Your Learning Goal

My spelling list has _____ words for me to learn.

You know, if you want to be a better word hunter, you should reread your **Spelling Process Handbook.**

I already did. It's got some great tips that are really helpful.

STRATEGY MINI-LESSON

NOTE: ▶ The **Explore the Spelling Strategy** activity on page 81 is a self-directed mini-lesson. If you wish to supplement that activity with direct instruction, use the following mini-lesson.

* **Tell** students you are going to show them another way to remember how to spell a word.

* **Ask** a student to read aloud the **Spelling Strategy** on page 81. Explain how to use the strategy: "First, choose a word that is especially difficult for you to spell. Decide which part of the word is giving you trouble. Then make up a saying that will help you remember the hard part. Repeat the saying several times so that you will remember it. Write the saying on a piece of paper and put it in your pocket. Take it out and read it several times a day until you are sure you will not forget it."

* **Model** how to use the strategy with the word **fourth**. Write **forth** and **fourth** on the chalkboard. Say, "I can never remember which one of these words means 'the one after the third.'" Ask students if they have any ideas to help you. If no one responds, write "**Four** is the **four**th number."

* **Tell** students to choose a word from their list that is hard for them to spell. Ask each student to compose a memory aid for this word.

* **Encourage** students to share any memory aids they use that consist of sayings. You may wish to write on the chalkboard examples from **More Words for Hungry Word Hunters** (on student page 166 and page T80) and work with the class to devise memory aids for some of them. Remind students that they may add any of these words to **Words I Need to Know How to Spell**.

········ INSPECTING WORDS ········

STEP 4 Explore the Spelling Strategy
Use a Spelling Clue

A. Write the **Strategy Word** that fits each sentence. Use the underlined letters as clues to the spellings. Then circle the letters in the **Strategy Word** that match the underlined letters.

1. I __ the ball after you <u>taught</u> me how.

2. The __ stood in the <u>rain</u> on the ship.

3. <u>Who</u> ate the __ pie?

4. <u>Tie</u> the horse in the __.

5. <u>I</u>, <u>Ed</u>, __ to sleep in the bed.

6. <u>You</u> are __.

7. W<u>eigh</u> the __ sleigh.

8. The __ opened the <u>do</u>or in the clinic.

9. I <u>thought</u> you were gone, __ I knew you were here.

10. __ are made from <u>cloth</u>.

c(augh)t
capt(ai)n
(wh)ole
f(ie)ld
tr(ie)d
(you)ng
(eigh)th
doct(or)
(though)
(Cloth)es

B. Look in **Words I Need to Know How to Spell** to find other words that have hard parts. Write a clue sentence for each word to help you remember its spelling.

STEP 5 Focus on Word Study
Word History

The word **captain** comes from the Latin word **capitaneus,** meaning "chief." And **chief** comes from **caput,** meaning "head." But before these words became part of English, they traveled to France to become **capitain,** meaning "captain." The captain or chief is the head of a group of people.

Write the **Strategy Word** that came from these earlier words.

1. **doctour,** meaning "teacher, learned man" ___ doctor

2. **feld,** meaning "flat and broad" ___ field

3. **hal,** meaning "entire, healthy" ___ whole

▼▼▼▼▼▼▼▼▼▼▼▼▼▼▼
Spelling Strategy
You can make up a sentence with a clue to help you remember a word that's hard for you to spell.
▪▪▪▪▪▪▪▪▪▪▪▪▪▪▪

STEP 4 Explore the Spelling Strategy

Use a Spelling Clue
This activity is a self-directed mini-lesson on this week's **Spelling Strategy**.

STEP 5 Focus on Word Study

Word History
This activity is intended to stimulate students' interest in words and to help them become more enthusiastic word hunters.

Spelling Process Handbook

Students who need to review any part of the spelling process, including practice options, should refer to the **Spelling Process Handbook** (pages 7–21).

STEP 6 Practice Your Spelling List Independently

Ask the students to choose activities to practice their spelling words and to master this week's **Spelling Strategy**. Students should complete at least three activities each week. You may wish to:

• assign **Practice the Spelling Strategy** to all students to reinforce this week's **Spelling Strategy**.

• involve students' families by assigning **Take Your List Home** for this lesson (**Teacher Resource Book**, pages 83 in English and 84 in Spanish).

• encourage students to use partner activities without game mats (**Word Swap, Spelling Tic-Tac-Toe, Circle Dot**) and activities with game mats (**Meteor Attack, Rockets, Spelling Checkers, Spelling Soccer**). Directions for game-mat activities appear on each game mat. Directions for all other activities are found in the **Spelling Process Handbook** (pages 7–21).

> NOTE: ▶ These activities and games can be used to practice any spelling list.

A Practice Option

SPELLING SOCCER

Partners or teams can practice their spelling words as they compete in **Spelling Soccer**. Modeled after the game that is gaining popularity in the United States for both boys and girls, **Spelling Soccer** takes spelling practice to the soccer field. It'll be "hands off" poor spelling scores after students, especially auditory and visual learners, discover **Spelling Soccer**. (Directions appear on the **Spelling Soccer** game mat. This activity is appropriate for practicing any spelling list.)

STEP 6 Practice Your Spelling List Independently

Choose at least three activities to practice your spelling list.

> Hunt words in your writing and reading! Add words you want to learn to **Words I Need to Know How to Spell**.

Game Mats	With a Partner	On Your Own	At Home
○ Rockets ○ Spelling Soccer	○ Circle Dot ○ Word Swap	○ Flip Folder ○ Spelling Study Strategy	○ Take Your List Home

✏️ Practice the Spelling Strategy

Write a **Strategy Word** that fits each clue. The clue can be a rhyming word, a word with a similar spelling pattern, or a word connected to the **Strategy Word** by meaning.

Strategy Words

field
caught
tried
whole
eighth
doctor
young
clothes
though
captain

Rhyming Word

1. dough   **though**
2. cried   **tried**
3. stole   **whole**
4. shield   **field**

Similar Spelling Pattern

5. bargain **captain**
6. freight **eighth**
7. daughter **caught**
8. actor   **doctor**

Meaning

9. youth   **young**
10. clothing **clothes**

DEVELOPING GOOD SPELLING HABITS

STEP 7 Focus on Writing

A. Proofread the Writing of Others
This activity provides proofreading practice in a variety of formats, including popular standardized test formats.

B. Proofread Your Own Writing
Students return to their own writing, armed with strategies to identify and collect words they need to know how to spell, and make an authentic link between spelling and writing.

C. A Writing Idea: A Review
This suggestion for a more extended writing activity provides opportunities for students to write in different genres for a variety of purposes and modes.

STEP 8 Check Your Weekly Progress

▶ Take the Test
Remind students that they can take a practice test before the final test on their spelling lists. To find the testing procedure that is right for you, refer to page Z12.

▶ Check Your Goal
Have students compare their tests to their spelling lists. Did they spell all the **Strategy Words** on their spelling lists correctly?

▶ Graph Your Progress
Ask students to graph the number correct (student page 175 for softbound users; **Teacher Resource Book** page 123 for hardbound users).

▶ Save Missed Words
Tell students to write misspelled words on their lists of **Words I Need to Know How to Spell**. Remind students to verify spellings and to recycle these words on future weekly spelling lists.

DEVELOPING GOOD SPELLING HABITS

STEP 7 Focus on Writing

A. Proofread the Writing of Others
Proofread the paragraph below. Decide what type of mistake, if any, appears in each underlined section.

it was the eighth inning of the baseball game. Luisa
①
was on first base. Mary hit a fly ball to left feild. Luisa
②
started to run. A player on the other team caught the

ball and threw it to second base. The umpire yelled,

"Safe!" Then Pam, the capten of our team, hit a home
③
run. The hole team cheered wildly.
④

≡ Make a capital.
/ Make a small letter.
∧ Add something.
℮ Take out something.
⊙ Add a period.
¶ New paragraph
(SP) Spelling error

1. A Spelling
   (B) Capitalization
   C Punctuation
   D No mistake

2. (A) Spelling
   B Capitalization
   C Punctuation
   D No mistake

3. (A) Spelling
   B Capitalization
   C Punctuation
   D No mistake

4. (A) Spelling
   B Capitalization
   C Punctuation
   D No mistake

B. Proofread Your Own Writing
Spelling clues can help you remember words that are hard to spell. Find a word that you misspelled in your recent writing. Make up a spelling clue to remember the spelling. Write the word correctly in **Words I Need to Know How to Spell**.

C. A Writing Idea: A Review
Write a short paragraph about a book or a movie you like. Tell what happens and why you liked it. Try to get your readers to like it, too! Tell them why they should see the movie or read the book.

STEP 8 Check Your Weekly Progress

▶ Take the Test
Ready? Practice test first.

▶ Check Your Goal
Check to see if you met your learning goal.

▶ Graph Your Progress
Graph your score for this week's test.

▶ Save Missed Words
Write the words you missed in your list of **Words I Need to Know How to Spell**.

Hunt Words
Remind students to continuously hunt words that they wish to learn how to spell and to write these words in **Words I Need to Know How to Spell**.

Possessives

ENGAGING IN THE PROCESS — MATERIALS

Student Edition: Pages 84–87   **Teacher Edition:** Pages T84A–T87

Materials to help students practice their spelling lists:

- **Flip Folders**
- Copies of **Flip Folder Practice Sheet** (**Teacher Resource Book,** page 51)
- **Take Your List Home** (in *Spell It–Write!*

Home News, **Teacher Resource Book,** pages 85 in English and 86 in Spanish)

- Game Mats Featured in This Unit: **Spelling Checkers, Spelling Soccer**

ENGAGING IN THE PROCESS — GOALS

SPELLING GOALS

Students will

- transfer knowledge that possession can be designated by adding ' or 's to words to spell possessive forms of words.
- complete a chart of singular and plural possessive words.
- develop an understanding of how the spellings of words can change over time.
- use the spelling process of finding words, inspecting words, and mastering words as they develop good spelling habits to become better writers.

WRITING GOALS

Students will

- proofread a writing sample.
- proofread a piece of their own writing for misspelled possessives.
- write an expressive short story.

ENGAGING IN THE PROCESS — MANAGEMENT

Pacing	Notes	Quick Pick Management Option
Period 1 Finding Words (Steps 1–3)	If you wish to add **Teacher Words,** write them on the chalkboard. Sources for more words include: **More Words for Hungry Word Hunters** (page T84), content and theme-related words, or words of your choice.	Assign the list of **Pattern Words** to the whole class. Add the Red List (**More Words for Hungry Word Hunters,** student page 166) for a longer list. Add the Blue List (**More Words for Hungry Word Hunters**) for a more challenging list.
Period 2 Inspecting Words (Steps 4 and 5)	Students write the **Pattern Words** to complete **Explore the Spelling Pattern.**	Assign **Explore the Spelling Pattern** and **Focus on Word Study.**
Period 3 Mastering Words (Step 6) **Period 4** Developing Good Spelling Habits (Step 7)	These two periods can be allocated between selected **Mastering Words** activities and proofreading and writing activities in **Focus on Writing.**	Assign two or three activities to the whole class. Familiarize students with choosing their own activities at their own pace.
Period 5 Assessment (Step 8)	Gradually try different peer-testing options to find the style that best fits your class.	Test the class on the same, whole-class list.

Understanding Language Differences

Spanish Speakers

Spanish does not use the possessive inflection **'s**. Instead, it uses the preposition **of**, as in "el amigo de Juan," literally "the friend of Juan," when English speakers would use "Juan's friend."

English has two devices to show possession. One is the focus of this unit, the possessive inflection **'s**, as in "the child's toy." The other device uses the preposition **of**: "the toy of the child." How do we decide which device to use? Most American English speakers instinctively use the inflected form with human nouns. For example, we say "my father's foot," but we do not say "the bed's foot." Instead, we say "the foot of the bed."

Helping Students Acquiring English

Introduce the meanings of the base words of the **Pattern Words** using photographs and magazine illustrations. To help students grasp the possessive inflection, ask them to draw a picture of a person and an item or items belonging to the person. Then help them label the pictures. For example, a picture of a girl and a picture of shoes might be labeled "the girl's shoes." Have students read the labels aloud, pointing to the apostrophe as they say each possessive word.

Meeting Diverse Needs

Less Able Spellers

Peer tutoring and cooperative learning activities are effective in improving the spelling achievement of students with spelling difficulties, including children with special needs. However, the effectiveness of these procedures can be undermined if students are unclear about their individual roles and responsibilities.

Be sure to establish ground rules about how children are to talk and interact with each other during peer tutoring and cooperative learning activities. Examples of appropriate rules include:

- Partners don't use unkind language.
- Say spelling words clearly for partners during spelling practice.

Always model the steps children will use to complete the cooperative activity. Provide necessary assistance as children carry out the activity.

More Able Spellers

Challenge students to brainstorm lists of nouns and exchange them with a partner. Students are to add **'** or **'s** to each noun to make it a possessive noun and then add a word naming something that might be possessed by that noun, for example, "elephant's trunk."

Ask students to copy their lists in the **Take Your List Home** section of the *Spell It–Write!* Home News page for this lesson. Not only does this page provide a convenient way for families to share a student's spelling list, but it also provides a number of opportunities for families to be involved in students' spelling growth. It has a statement of the week's spelling pattern or strategy, a valuable spelling study strategy, and a suggested home spelling practice activity.

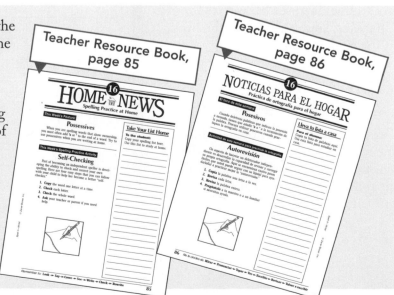

FINDING WORDS

MORE WORDS FOR HUNGRY WORD HUNTERS

RED LIST — Pattern Words Below Level	BLUE LIST — Pattern Words Above Level	Other Pattern Words
baby's	author's	couples'
boy's	dentist's	daughter's
boys'	farmer's	fathers'
dog's	judges'	fish's
girl's	mayor's	friend's
girls'	runners'	nephew's
horses'	scientists'	parents'
kittens'	teacher's	poets'
man's	teachers'	sons'
men's	travelers'	umpires'

These lists also appear on page 166 in the student edition and page 22 in the **Teacher Resource Book**.

STEP 1 Build Your Spelling List

Students will build their spelling lists with **Pattern Words, Teacher Words,** and **Your Words**. Students should study a minimum of twelve new words each week.

Find Your Pattern Words

- Pretest the students on these words.
- Tell students to write each misspelled pretest word on their spelling lists.

Add Teacher Words

- Select words for students to add to their spelling lists. Choose words from **More Words for Hungry Word Hunters** (on this page and on student page 166), words related to a theme or content area, or words students often misspell.

Add Your Words

- Ask students to pick words from their lists of **Words I Need to Know How to Spell** and their writing.
- Tell students to write these words on their spelling lists.

STEP 2 Write Your Spelling List

Remind students to verify all spellings. (Ask students to see **Strategies for Checking Your Spelling** in the back of the student edition.)

STEP 3 Set Your Learning Goal

Tell students to count the words on their spelling lists. This total is their learning goal. It may vary depending on ability, individual goals, and the difficulty of spelling words.

SPELLING PATTERN

16

Possessives

Your Spelling List

STEP 1 Build Your Spelling List

Find Your Pattern Words
Take the pretest.
Write misspelled words on your spelling list.

Add Teacher Words
Teachers may add:
- More **Pattern Words** • Content Words • Theme Words

Add Your Words
Pick words from:
- **Words I Need to Know How to Spell** • Writing • Reading

Pattern Words

1.	**brother's**	My little **brother's** wagon is red.
2.	**brothers'**	My two **brothers'** friends stayed late.
3.	**mother's**	Today is my **mother's** birthday.
4.	**father's**	Have you read my **father's** book?
5.	**sisters'**	My two older **sisters'** husbands play basketball with me.
6.	**doctor's**	The **doctor's** coat hung on a hook.
7.	**nurses'**	**Nurses'** uniforms come in all sizes.
8.	**animals'**	We are studying **animals'** homes.
9.	**child's**	The **child's** room was full of toys.
10.	**children's**	Look at the **children's** pictures.

STEP 2 Write Your Spelling List

STEP 3 Set Your Learning Goal

My spelling list has _____ words for me to learn.

I always take a practice test before the final test. I want to be sure I'm really ready.

This week I'm practicing with a friend. And I'll be ready!

PATTERN MINI-LESSON

NOTE: The **Explore the Spelling Pattern** activity on page 85 is a self-directed mini-lesson. If you wish to supplement that activity with direct instruction, use the following mini-lesson.

* **Write** the **Pattern Words** from page 84 on the chalkboard. Say each word aloud, and ask students to repeat it.

* **Explain** that an apostrophe or **'s** is added at the end of a word to show that something belongs to someone.

NOTE: If students mention contractions, explain that **'s** is often used in contractions to take the place of **is** or **has**.

* **Ask** students to tell you which words on the chalkboard are singular and which words are plural. Point to each word and ask students to call out "singular" or "plural." (Responses: *Plural words are* **brothers', sisters', nurses', animals', children's;** *singular words are* **brother's, mother's, father's, doctor's, child's.**)

* **Invite** students to make a generalization about the formation of words that show ownership. (Possible response: *If a word is singular, add* **'s**. *If a word is plural and does not end in* **s**, *add* **'s**. *If a word is plural and ends in* **s**, *add just an apostrophe after the* **s**.)

* **Read** the **Spelling Pattern** on page 85 with the class.

* **Encourage** students to hunt for other possessive words. Write students' examples on the chalkboard, listing singular possessives in one column and plural possessives in another. You may wish to include examples from **More Words for Hungry Word Hunters** (on student page 166 and page T84). Remind students that they may add any of these words to **Words I Need to Know How to Spell**.

· · · · · · · · · · · · · · INSPECTING WORDS · · · · · · · · · · · · · ·

 STEP 4

Explore the Spelling Pattern
Completing a Chart

A. Use **Pattern Words** to complete a chart of singular and plural words that show ownership.

Base Word	Belonging to One (Singular Possessive)		Belonging to More Than One (Plural Possessive)	
doctor	1.	doctor's		doctors'
nurse		nurse's	2.	nurses'
animal		animal's	3.	animals'
mother	4.	mother's		mothers'
father	5.	father's		fathers'
sister		sister's	6.	sisters'
brother	7.	brother's	8.	brothers'
child	9.	child's	10.	children's

B. Do a word hunt to find other words that show ownership. Sort the words you find the way the chart does.

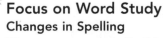 **STEP 5**

Focus on Word Study
Changes in Spelling

We use an apostrophe in English to show that a letter has been left out of a word. Long ago, many English words were spelled with **-es** at the end to show ownership. Now we write **brother's** instead of **brotheres**.

Match **fox's, man's,** and **ship's** with the old spelling of the possessive form.

1. mannes   man's
2. foxes   fox's
3. scipes   ship's

▼▼▼▼▼▼▼▼▼▼▼▼▼▼▼

Spelling Pattern
When you are spelling words that show ownership, you must often add **'s** or **'** to the end of a word.
· · · · · · · · · · · · · ·

 STEP 4

Explore the Spelling Pattern

Completing a Chart

This activity is a self-directed mini-lesson on this week's **Spelling Pattern**.

 STEP 5

Focus on Word Study

Changes in Spelling

This activity is intended to stimulate students' interest in words and to help them become more enthusiastic word hunters.

> ### Spelling Process Handbook
> Students who need to review any part of the spelling process, including practice options, should refer to the **Spelling Process Handbook** (pages 7–21).

MASTERING WORDS

STEP 6 Practice Your Spelling List Independently

Ask the students to choose activities to practice their spelling words and to master this week's **Spelling Pattern**. Students should complete at least three activities each week. You may wish to:

- assign **Practice the Spelling Pattern** to all students to reinforce this week's **Spelling Pattern**.

- involve students' families by assigning **Take Your List Home** for this lesson (**Teacher Resource Book,** pages 85 in English and 86 in Spanish).

- encourage students to use partner activities without game mats (**Word Swap, Spelling Tic-Tac-Toe, Circle Dot**) and activities with game mats (**Meteor Attack, Rockets, Spelling Checkers, Spelling Soccer**). Directions for game-mat activities appear on each game mat. Directions for all other activities are found in the **Spelling Process Handbook** (pages 7–21).

NOTE: These activities and games can be used to practice any spelling list.

A Practice Option

SPELLING TIC-TAC-TOE

Just about anyone knows how to play tic-tac-toe. And now this strategic game of **X**'s and **O**'s teams up with spelling words to make spelling practice fun! Partners can practice spelling words with **Spelling Tic-Tac-Toe** on any scrap of paper. And because partners spell words aloud and visually check errors against correct spellings, **Spelling Tic-Tac-Toe** appeals to both visual and auditory learners. (Directions appear in the **Spelling Process Handbook,** student pages 7–21. This activity is appropriate for practicing any spelling list.)

・・・・・・・ MASTERING WORDS ・・・・・・・

STEP 6 Practice Your Spelling List Independently

Choose at least three activities to practice your spelling list.

Need Help? Read the **Spelling Process Handbook** (pages 7–21).

Game Mats		With a Partner		On Your Own		At Home
○ Spelling Checkers	○ Spelling Soccer	○ Circle Dot	○ Spelling Tic-Tac-Toe	○ Flip Folder	○ Spelling Study Strategy	○ Take Your List Home

Practice the Spelling Pattern

Read each phrase and write the correct **Pattern Word**.

Pattern Words

brother's
brothers'
mother's
father's
sisters'
doctor's
nurses'
animals'
child's
children's

1. shoes that belong to my brother	**brother's**	shoes
2. bikes that belong to my brothers	**brothers'**	bikes
3. cages that belong to animals	**animals'**	cages
4. car that belongs to my mother	**mother's**	car
5. toy that belongs to the child	**child's**	toy
6. caps that belong to the nurses	**nurses'**	caps
7. tools that belong to my father	**father's**	tools
8. swings that belong to the children	**children's**	swings
9. rings that belong to my sisters	**sisters'**	rings
10. coat that belongs to the doctor	**doctor's**	coat

DEVELOPING GOOD SPELLING HABITS

STEP 7 Focus on Writing

A. Proofread the Writing of Others

This activity provides proofreading practice in a variety of formats, including popular standardized test formats.

B. Proofread Your Own Writing

Students return to their own writing, armed with strategies to identify and collect words they need to know how to spell, and make an authentic link between spelling and writing.

C. A Writing Idea: A Story

This suggestion for a more extended writing activity provides opportunities for students to write in different genres for a variety of purposes and modes.

STEP 8 Check Your Weekly Progress

▶ Take the Test

Remind students that they can take a practice test before the final test on their spelling lists. To find the testing procedure that is right for you, refer to page Z12.

▶ Check Your Goal

Have students compare their tests to their spelling lists. Did they spell all the **Pattern Words** on their spelling lists correctly?

▶ Graph Your Progress

Ask students to graph the number correct (student page 175 for softbound users; **Teacher Resource Book** page 123 for hardbound users).

▶ Save Missed Words

Tell students to write misspelled words on their lists of **Words I Need to Know How to Spell**. Remind students to verify spellings and to recycle these words on future weekly spelling lists.

· · · · · · · DEVELOPING GOOD SPELLING HABITS · · · · · · ·

STEP 7 Focus on Writing

A. Proofread the Writing of Others

Proofread Ramon's letter. Decide which underlined words are spelled correctly and which are misspelled. Write **c** for "correct" or **m** for "misspelled." Beside each **m**, write the correct spelling.

Dear Benji,

My brother Tomas made a volcano for a childrens'[1]

science fair. Tomas and the volcano went to the fair in

my father's[2] truck. My two sisters and I rode in my

mothers'[3] car. I liked the farm animals best. The

animals'[4] owners told us about caring for the animals.

My two sister's[5] favorite things were a weather station

and a model rocket. Guess what! My brothers'[6] volcano

won a prize.

Your friend,
Ramon

1. _m_ children's   4. _c_
2. _c_   5. _m_ sisters'
3. _m_ mother's   6. _m_ brother's

Make a capital.
Make a small letter.
Add something.
Take out something.
Add a period.
New paragraph
SP Spelling error

B. Proofread Your Own Writing

Words that show ownership are often spelled with **'s** or **'** at the end. Check your most recent writing for words that show ownership. Correct any misspelled words you find.

C. A Writing Idea: A Story

Some animals have escaped from the zoo! Write a short story about the animals' adventure. Proofread your story to see if you've spelled all the words correctly.

STEP 8 Check Your Weekly Progress

▶ Take the Test
Ready? Practice test first.

▶ Check Your Goal
Check to see if you met your learning goal.

▶ Graph Your Progress
Graph your score for this week's test.

▶ Save Missed Words
Write the words you missed in your list of **Words I Need to Know How to Spell**.

Hunt Words

Remind students to continuously hunt words that they wish to learn how to spell and to write these words in **Words I Need to Know How to Spell**.

NOTE: **Check Your Progress** is not a spelling unit, but some teachers prefer to spend a week on these activities.

Day One: Administer **Review Test**.

Day Two: Check **Review Test**. Use **Spelling Pattern Mastery Chart** to find each student's mastery level.

Day Three: Reteach as needed.

Day Four: Complete **Check Your Writing**.

Day Five: Complete **Check Your Strategies**.

Check Your Spelling

1. Administer the **Review Test** to all students. Dictation sentences appear on page T89. (The words in italics are also from the previous eight units.) Administer the words **in the order** in which they are presented here.

2. Ask students to check their tests as you spell each word and/or write the correct spelling on the board.

3. Ask students to circle the number of each correctly spelled word.

4. Review the categories on the **Spelling Pattern Mastery Chart** (page 88). As you review each pattern, ask students to find the corresponding items on their tests. Based on the number of words correct for each pattern, ask the students to determine their level of mastery for that pattern.

Reteaching Strategies

• Reteach the **Pattern Mini-Lesson** on the patterns students have not mastered.

• Ask students to record the words they missed in **Words I Need to Know How to Spell** for recycling into future spelling lists.

• Record the patterns students have not mastered. Include words with these patterns on future spelling lists.

Check Your Writing

1. Consider teaching the **Proofreading Strategy Mini-Lesson** (page T89).

2. Ask students to choose several pieces of their writing.

3. Ask students to work with a partner to proofread their writing and hunt words with each spelling pattern. They should record misspelled words in **Words I Need to Know How to Spell**.

Check Your Strategies

1. Read each question aloud. Remind the students that they should think about their use of each strategy in the past eight weeks and answer "Yes," "No," or "Sometimes."

2. Use these questions as the focus of a student-teacher conference. You may also wish to use **Strategy Assessment** (pages 120 and 121 in the **Teacher Resource Book**).

Check Your

✓ Check Your Spelling

Here is a fun way to review your progress on spelling patterns. First, take the review test your teacher will give you. Then, check your test.

Review Test

1	quarter
2	royal
3	engage
4	children's
5	noise
6	clue
7	choose
8	sign
9	knee
10	judge
11	equal
12	around
13	brother's
14	written
15	square
16	crowd
17	huge
18	package
19	brothers'
20	news

Spelling Pattern Mastery Chart

Which words did you spell correctly? Use this chart to find your mastery level for each spelling pattern.

Pattern	All Correct	Most Correct	None Correct
ou, ow, oi, oy 2 5 12 16			
Long u: u-C-e, ue, oo, ew 6 7 17 20			
qu, squ 1 11 15			
Silent Consonants 8 9 14			
ge, dge 3 10 18			
Possessives 4 13 19			

All Correct: Pattern Mastered
Most Correct: Pattern Partly Mastered
None Correct: Keep Working on the Pattern

PROOFREADING STRATEGY MINI-LESSON

* **Write** the title **Read It Backwards** on the chalkboard.

* **Explain** to students that they can use a strategy called **Read It Backwards** to proofread very short pieces of their writing, such as signs or lists that others will read. They will work with a partner to look at the last word of the text, check the spelling, and then move to the next-to-last word.

* **Tell** students that proofreading in this way helps them "tune out" the meaning of the words and concentrate on spelling accuracy.

* **Demonstrate** the strategy by asking a volunteer to work with you at the chalkboard. Point to the word "Backwards," and slide your finger along as your partner reads each word softly aloud.

* **Tell** students that they should circle any word if they are unsure of its spelling. After they verify the spelling, they should write the correct spelling above the misspelled word.

* **Remind** students that they may refer to **Strategies for Checking Your Spelling** in the back of the student edition.

Progress

Choose three recent samples of your writing. Use a grid that looks like this. Work with a partner to check your writing for words that match each pattern.

✓ Check Your Writing

Spelling Pattern Writing Chart	Column 1 I spelled these Pattern Words correctly.	Column 2 I misspelled these Pattern Words.
ou, ow, oi, oy		
Long u: u-C-e, ue, oo, ew		
qu, squ		
Silent Consonants		
ge, dge		
Possessives		

Write the words in Column 2 in your **Words I Need to Know How to Spell**.

✓ Check Your Strategies

Self-regulation

Ask yourself each of these questions. Do you answer "Yes," "No," or "Sometimes" to each question?

- Do I add words from **Words I Need to Know How to Spell** to my spelling list each week?
- Is the number of words I add right for me?
- When I practice my words, do I choose activities that help me learn my words?
- Do I take self-tests and practice tests to see if I know my words?

Dictation Sentences

1. **quarter** – The *whole* class *tried* to attend but only a **quarter** were allowed to go.
2. **royal** – *Due* to the weather only a *thousand* people saw the *queen* and the **royal** family.
3. **engage** – Please don't **engage** in games at the *wrong* time.
4. **children's** – *Tomorrow* the *group* will see the **children's** concert.
5. **noise** – The **noise** from the many *animals'* barn was *quite* loud.
6. **clue** – Sam *wrote* a **clue** on the *edge* of the *bridge*.
7. **choose** – He decided to **choose** a *suit instead* of a *balloon*.
8. **sign** – She *drew* a **sign** on the *stage* door.
9. **knee** – The *student* hurt her **knee** jumping into the *pool*.
10. **judge** – The *fifth* thief was *caught* and sent to the **judge**.
11. **equal** – The *young* man didn't see the *danger* as **equal** to the reward.
12. **around** – In summer we walk **around** in *clothing* that is *cool*.
13. **brother's** – The *captain* of my **brother's** team sent him onto the *field*.
14. **written** – *Though* she was sure she had **written** each *vowel* correctly, she checked again.
15. **square** – The people worked hard not to *spoil* the *village* **square**.
16. **crowd** – The **crowd** *wouldn't* be *quiet* and listen.
17. **huge** – We *threw* a **huge** party for my *mother's* birthday.
18. **package** – The **package** contained a *comb*, a *knife*, and face *powder*.
19. **brothers'** – My two **brothers'** friends sat on the *carpet* and saw a *strange sight*.
20. **news** – The *eighth* winning *tune* made the **news** in my *father's* paper.

Unusual Plurals

ENGAGING IN THE PROCESS MATERIALS

Student Edition: Pages 90–93   **Teacher Edition:** Pages T90A–T93

Materials to help students practice their spelling lists:

- **Flip Folders**
- Copies of **Flip Folder Practice Sheet** (**Teacher Resource Book,** page 51)
- **Take Your List Home** (in *Spell It–Write!*

Home News, **Teacher Resource Book,** pages 87 in English and 88 in Spanish)
- Game Mats Featured in This Unit: **Meteor Attack, Spelling Checkers**

ENGAGING IN THE PROCESS GOALS

SPELLING GOALS

Students will

- transfer knowledge that some plural words are formed in unusual ways to spell irregular plurals.

- develop an understanding of how the spellings of words can change as words pass from one language into another.

- use the spelling process of finding words, inspecting words, and mastering words as they develop good spelling habits to become better writers.

WRITING GOALS

Students will

- proofread a writing sample.

- proofread a piece of their own writing for misspelled irregular plural words.

- write tongue twisters.

ENGAGING IN THE PROCESS MANAGEMENT

Pacing	Notes	Quick Pick Management Option
Period 1 Finding Words (Steps 1–3)	If you wish to add **Teacher Words,** write them on the chalkboard. Sources for more words include: **More Words for Hungry Word Hunters** (page T90), content and theme-related words, or words of your choice.	Assign the list of **Pattern Words** to the whole class. Add the Red List (**More Words for Hungry Word Hunters,** student page 167) for a longer list. Add the Blue List (**More Words for Hungry Word Hunters**) for a more challenging list.
Period 2 Inspecting Words (Steps 4 and 5)	Students write the **Pattern Words** to complete **Explore the Spelling Pattern.**	Assign **Explore the Spelling Pattern** and **Focus on Word Study.**
Period 3 Mastering Words (Step 6) **Period 4** Developing Good Spelling Habits (Step 7)	These two periods can be allocated between selected **Mastering Words** activities and proofreading and writing activities in **Focus on Writing.**	Assign two or three activities to the whole class. Familiarize students with choosing their own activities at their own pace.
Period 5 Assessment (Step 8)	Gradually try different peer-testing options to find the style that best fits your class.	Test the class on the same, whole-class list.

ENGAGING
IN THE
PROCESS
INDIVIDUAL
NEEDS

Understanding Language Differences

As children, native English speakers go through a stage of language development during which they regularize irregular plurals. During this stage, they will say **mouses** instead of **mice** and **foots** or **feets** for **feet**. Students who are learning English as a second language do this as well. In helping these students grasp the concept of irregular plurals, it will be helpful to tell them that these words do not use the usual **s** to form the plural.

Helping Students Acquiring English

Place a picture of a goose on the chalk rail and label it **goose**. Read the word aloud and have students repeat it and then spell the word as you point to each letter. Provide a picture of several geese, or ask student volunteers to draw a simple picture, labeling the picture **geese**. Draw attention to the fact that the word for more than one **goose** is not formed by adding **s** to **goose**. Repeat this procedure for the remaining **Pattern Words**, using photographs, magazine or chalkboard illustrations, and realia (potatoes, tomatoes).

Meeting Diverse Needs

Less Able Spellers

Students with severe spelling difficulties may benefit from finger spelling. Here's how this strategy works.

As students say each letter when they practice a new spelling word, they make the associated sign for that letter from American English Sign Language (i.e., the manual alphabet used by people with hearing impairments). Similar to tracing and writing the letters in a word during spelling practice, finger spelling involves the motor modality in the process of learning new spellings.

Of course, before they can use finger spelling to help learn new words, students must first learn the manual alphabet. Fortunately, this task is enjoyed by most children, and they often master the alphabet readily.

More Able Spellers

Challenge students to develop a collection of words with unusual plural forms. Students' collections might include:

- words from Latin roots: **antenna, antennae; alumnus, alumni; datum, data;**
- words from Greek roots: **analysis, analyses; bacterium, bacteria;**
- words with changed spellings: **mouse, mice; child, children; die, dice; tooth, teeth;**
- words with the same singular and plural forms: **moose, sheep, deer.**

ENGAGING
IN THE
PROCESS
INVOLVING
FAMILIES

Ask students to copy their lists in the **Take Your List Home** section of the *Spell It–Write!* Home News page for this lesson. Not only does this page provide a convenient way for families to share a student's spelling list, but it also provides a number of opportunities for families to be involved in students' spelling growth. It has a statement of the week's spelling pattern or strategy, a valuable spelling study strategy, and a suggested home spelling practice activity.

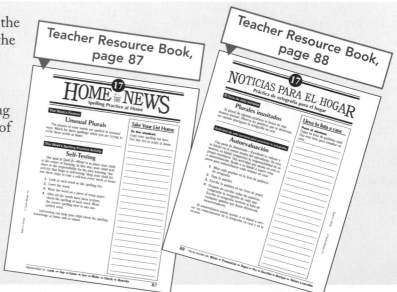

Teacher Resource Book, page 87

Teacher Resource Book, page 88

FINDING WORDS

STEP 1 Build Your Spelling List

Students will build their spelling lists with **Pattern Words, Teacher Words,** and **Your Words.** Students should study a minimum of twelve new words each week.

Find Your Pattern Words

- Pretest the students on these words.

- Tell students to write each misspelled pretest word on their spelling lists.

Add Teacher Words

- Select words for students to add to their spelling lists. Choose words from **More Words for Hungry Word Hunters** (on this page and on student page 167), words related to a theme or content area, or words students often misspell.

Add Your Words

- Ask students to pick words from their lists of **Words I Need to Know How to Spell** and their writing.

- Tell students to write these words on their spelling lists.

STEP 2 Write Your Spelling List

Remind students to verify all spellings. (Ask students to see **Strategies for Checking Your Spelling** in the back of the student edition.)

STEP 3 Set Your Learning Goal

Tell students to count the words on their spelling lists. This total is their learning goal. It may vary depending on ability, individual goals, and the difficulty of spelling words.

MORE WORDS FOR HUNGRY WORD HUNTERS

RED LIST	BLUE LIST	Other Pattern	Science Pattern Words
Pattern Words Below Level	Pattern Words Above Level	Words	antenna
child	echoes	gentlemen	antennae
children	heroes	oboes	cactus
deer	mosquitoes	radios	cacti
feet	scissors		stimulus
foot	series		stimuli
man	sisters-in-law		
men	species		**Social Studies Pattern Words**
mice	spoonfuls		oasis
mouse	studios		oases
sheep	volcanoes		

These lists also appear on page 167 in the student edition and page 23 in the **Teacher Resource Book.**

SPELLING PATTERN

17

Unusual Plurals

Your Spelling List

_____
_____
_____
_____
_____
_____
_____
_____
_____
_____
_____
_____
_____
_____
_____
_____
_____
_____

STEP 1 Build Your Spelling List

Find Your Pattern Words
Take the pretest.
Write misspelled words on your spelling list.

Add Teacher Words
Teachers may add:
- More **Pattern Words** • Content Words • Theme Words

Add Your Words
Pick words from:
- **Words I Need to Know How to Spell** • Writing • Reading

Pattern Words

1.	**goose**	That **goose** will bite!
2.	**woman**	That blonde **woman** is my aunt.
3.	**oxen**	Two **oxen** were pulling the plow.
4.	**pianos**	There are two grand **pianos** on the stage.
5.	**potatoes**	How many **potatoes** should we cook?
6.	**geese**	**Geese** fly south in the fall.
7.	**ox**	Paul Bunyan had an **ox** named Babe.
8.	**rodeos**	Bronco riding is popular at **rodeos**.
9.	**women**	The two **women** started a business.
10.	**tomatoes**	The **tomatoes** grew ripe on the vine.

STEP 2 Write Your Spelling List

STEP 3 Set Your Learning Goal

My spelling list has _____ words for me to learn.

When I build my spelling list, I'm more aware of the words and patterns I'm learning.

And I think I'm more aware of using my spelling words when I write in other classes. Spelling and writing go together!

PATTERN MINI-LESSON

NOTE: The **Explore the Spelling Pattern** activity on page 91 is a self-directed mini-lesson. If you wish to supplement that activity with direct instruction, use the following mini-lesson.

* **Write** on the chalkboard this sentence: "The mother goose chased the three baby goose around the yard." Invite a volunteer to read the sentence aloud. Ask the class to find the error. (Response: *There is more than one baby goose, but the singular form is used.*)

* **Ask** students how they should change the second word **goose** to make it mean "more than one." (Response: *Change oo to ee.*)

* **Write** the **Pattern Words** from page 90 on the chalkboard. Read each word aloud, and ask students to repeat it.

* **Ask** students to tell whether each word on the chalkboard is singular or plural.

* **Ask** students which words on the list form the plural by adding only **-s**. (Response: *pianos, rodeos*) Ask which words form the plural by adding **-es**. (Response: *potatoes, tomatoes*)

* **Invite** volunteers to explain how the other plurals are formed. (Possible responses: *For **woman**, the a changes to e. For **goose**, the letters oo change to ee. For **ox**, the letters en are added to the end of the word.*)

* **Ask** students to read the **Spelling Pattern** on page 91 with you.

* **Write** "One" and "More Than One" on the chalkboard. Ask students to provide other examples of unusual plurals. List students' suggestions under the appropriate heading.

········ INSPECTING WORDS ········

Explore the Spelling Pattern
Adding or Changing Letters

A. Use the clues to write the singular and plural **Pattern Words**.

	One	More Than One
1. musical instrument	piano	pianos
2. Western show	rodeo	rodeos
3. fruit	tomato	tomatoes
4. vegetable	potato	potatoes
5–6. female person	woman	women
7–8. bird	goose	geese
9–10. animal	ox	oxen

B. Which plural **Pattern Words** do not add **-s** or **-es** to the base word? Write these words.

11. ___oxen___   12. ___geese___   13. ___women___

Focus on Word Study
Words From Other Languages

In the New World, Christopher Columbus met the Taino people. They ate a kind of potato they called **batata**. Later, Columbus returned to Spain, where the word for **potato** was spelled **papa**. Over many years, **batatas** and **papas** combined to make the English word **potatoes**.

Here are some **Pattern Words** in different languages. Write their English spellings.

1. ganso (Spanish)   ___goose___
2. os (Dutch), Ochse (German)   ___ox___
3. tomatl (Aztec)   ___tomatoes___
4. rodeos (Spanish)   ___rodeos___

▼▼▼▼▼▼▼▼▼▼▼▼▼▼
Spelling Pattern
The plurals of some words are spelled in unusual ways.
■ ■ ■ ■ ■ ■ ■ ■ ■ ■ ■ ■

Explore the Spelling Pattern

Adding or Changing Letters
This activity is a self-directed mini-lesson on this week's **Spelling Pattern**.

Focus on Word Study

Words From Other Languages
This activity is intended to stimulate students' interest in words and to help them become more enthusiastic word hunters.

Spelling Process Handbook

Students who need to review any part of the spelling process, including practice options, should refer to the **Spelling Process Handbook** (pages 7–21).

MASTERING WORDS

ewary

ewary

Practice Your Spelling List Independently

STEP 6

Ask the students to choose activities to practice their spelling words and to master this week's **Spelling Pattern**. Students should complete at least three activities each week. You may wish to:

- assign **Practice the Spelling Pattern** to all students to reinforce this week's **Spelling Pattern**.

- involve students' families by assigning **Take Your List Home** for this lesson (**Teacher Resource Book,** pages 87 in English and 88 in Spanish).

- encourage students to use partner activities without game mats (**Word Swap, Spelling Tic-Tac-Toe, Circle Dot**) and activities with game mats (**Meteor Attack, Rockets, Spelling Checkers, Spelling Soccer**). Directions for game-mat activities appear on each game mat. Directions for all other activities are found in the **Spelling Process Handbook** (pages 7–21).

NOTE: These activities and games can be used to practice any spelling list.

A Practice Option

WORD SWAP

Word Swap is an extremely simple but effective partner spelling study strategy. Students simply swap spelling lists and quiz each other. (This activity is also an effective way to introduce students to key aspects of peer testing.) And as in all partnered practice activities, students reap the benefits of exposure to two spelling lists—their own and their partner's. It's a painless spelling bonus! (Directions appear in the **Spelling Process Handbook,** student pages 7–21. This activity is appropriate for practicing any spelling list.)

MASTERING WORDS

STEP 6 Practice Your Spelling List Independently
Choose at least three activities to practice your spelling list.

You can practice any spelling list with these activities.

Game Mats	With a Partner	On Your Own	At Home
Spelling Checkers · Meteor Attack	Spelling Tic-Tac-Toe · Word Swap	Flip Folder · Spelling Study Strategy	Take Your List Home

✏ Practice the Spelling Pattern

Read the riddles. Write the **Pattern Word** that fits each riddle.

Pattern Words

goose
woman
oxen
pianos
potatoes
geese
ox
rodeos
women
tomatoes

1. We have eyes but cannot see. ___potatoes___
2. We have keys but cannot unlock things. ___pianos___
3. I am not a car horn, but I honk. ___goose___
4. I am a cow's cousin. ___ox___
5. We grow on a vine. ___tomatoes___
6. We show roping and riding events. ___rodeos___
7. Sometimes we fly in a V-shape. ___geese___
8. We are more than one of riddle 4. ___oxen___
9. I am a grown-up girl. ___woman___
10. We are more than one of riddle 9. ___women___

STEP 7 Focus on Writing

A. Proofread the Writing of Others

This activity provides proofreading practice in a variety of formats, including popular standardized test formats.

B. Proofread Your Own Writing

Students return to their own writing, armed with strategies to identify and collect words they need to know how to spell, and make an authentic link between spelling and writing.

C. A Writing Idea: Tongue Twisters

This suggestion for a more extended writing activity provides opportunities for students to write in different genres for a variety of purposes and modes.

STEP 8 Check Your Weekly Progress

▶ Take the Test

Remind students that they can take a practice test before the final test on their spelling lists. To find the testing procedure that is right for you, refer to page Z12.

▶ Check Your Goal

Have students compare their tests to their spelling lists. Did they spell all the **Pattern Words** on their spelling lists correctly?

▶ Graph Your Progress

Ask students to graph the number correct (student page 176 for softbound users; **Teacher Resource Book** page 123 for hardbound users).

▶ Save Missed Words

Tell students to write misspelled words on their lists of **Words I Need to Know How to Spell**. Remind students to verify spellings and to recycle these words on future weekly spelling lists.

· · · · · · · · DEVELOPING GOOD SPELLING HABITS · · · · · · · ·

STEP 7 Focus on Writing

A. Proofread the Writing of Others

Proofread these six silly tongue twisters. Each underlined word is a misspelled plural. Write the correct spelling of each one.

1. Tony put ten <u>tomatos</u> on toast.

   tomatoes

2. Many mashed <u>potatose</u> make a mountain.

   potatoes

3. Foxes and <u>oxes</u> danced on the boxes.

   oxen

4. Six pink pigs played six pink <u>pianoes</u>.

   pianos

5. It's rough riding and roping at <u>rodeoes</u>.

   rodeos

6. Twelve <u>gooses</u> twirled twelve twigs.

   geese

B. Proofread Your Own Writing

The plurals of some words are spelled in unusual ways. Proofread a piece of writing you have completed recently. Look for plurals with unusual spellings that you might have misspelled. Add these words to your **Words I Need to Know How to Spell**.

C. A Writing Idea: Tongue Twisters

Write your own silly tongue twisters! Check your writing to see if you've spelled unusual plurals correctly. Share your tongue twisters with a partner.

≡ Make a capital.
／ Make a small letter.
∧ Add something.
✗ Take out something.
⊙ Add a period.
¶ New paragraph
(SP) Spelling error

STEP 8 Check Your Weekly Progress

▶ **Take the Test**
Ready? Practice test first.

▶ **Check Your Goal**
Check to see if you met your learning goal.

▶ **Graph Your Progress**
Graph your score for this week's test.

▶ **Save Missed Words**
Write the words you missed in your list of **Words I Need to Know How to Spell**.

Hunt Words

Remind students to continuously hunt words that they wish to learn how to spell and to write these words in **Words I Need to Know How to Spell**.

EXPRESSIVE

ENGAGING *IN THE* **PROCESS** **MATERIALS**

Student Edition: Pages 94–97   **Teacher Edition:** Pages T94A–T97

Materials to help students practice their spelling lists:

- **Flip Folders**
- Copies of **Flip Folder Practice Sheet** (**Teacher Resource Book,** page 51)
- **Take Your List Home** (in *Spell It–Write!* Home News, **Teacher Resource Book,** pages 89 in English and 90 in Spanish)

- Game Mats Featured in This Unit: **Meteor Attack, Rockets**
- Unit 18 **Hands-on Word Sort Cards** (**Grade 4 Hands-on Word Sort Card Book**) and Unit 18 **Hands-on Word Sort Sheet** (**Teacher Resource Book,** page 43)

ENGAGING *IN THE* **PROCESS** **GOALS**

SPELLING GOALS

Students will

- understand that meaning relationships can influence spelling, and use that understanding to spell words with certain patterns.
- sort words according to spelling patterns.
- recognize that some English words have evolved from Latin words.
- use the spelling process to become better writers.

WRITING GOALS

Students will

- proofread a writing sample.
- proofread a piece of their own writing for misspelled words with the short **e** sound spelled **ea** and **e**.
- write an expressive postcard.

ENGAGING *IN THE* **PROCESS** **MANAGEMENT**

Pacing	Notes	Quick Pick Management Option
Period 1 Finding Words (Steps 1–3)	If you wish to add **Teacher Words,** write them on the chalkboard. Sources for more words include: **More Words for Hungry Word Hunters** (page T94), content and theme-related words, or words of your choice.	Assign the list of **Pattern Words** to the whole class. Add the Red List (**More Words for Hungry Word Hunters,** student page 167) for a longer list.
Period 2 Inspecting Words (Steps 4 and 5)	Students write the **Pattern Words** to complete **Explore the Spelling Pattern.**	Assign **Explore the Spelling Pattern** and **Focus on Word Study.**
Period 3 Mastering Words (Step 6) **Period 4** Developing Good Spelling Habits (Step 7)	These two periods can be allocated between selected **Mastering Words** activities and proofreading and writing activities in **Focus on Writing.**	Assign two or three activities to the whole class. Familiarize students with choosing their own activities at their own pace.
Period 5 Assessment (Step 8)	Gradually try different peer-testing options to find the style that best fits your class.	Test the class on the same, whole-class list.

Understanding Language Differences

Students who are learning English as a second language are likely to be challenged by the words on this week's lists because they may be unsure about how the derived words (**health** from **heal,** for example) are pronounced.

These students are often as unsure of the spoken language as they are of the written language. They may rely on the spellings of words to give them clues about the spoken language. They may assume, for example, that because **heal** is pronounced with a **long e,** **health** must also be pronounced with a **long e.**

Pronounce and write these unexpected forms for your students.

Helping Students Acquiring English

Write the word **heal** on the chalkboard, using colored chalk for the letters **ea,** and pronounce the word. Add the letters **th** to **heal** to make **health,** and pronounce the word. Have students repeat the word after you. Then, point back and forth quickly between the two words, having students chant the words aloud as you point. Continue this procedure until all the words (**sweep, swept; peel, peeled; deal, dealt; sleep, slept; deep, depth; clean, cleanse; weep, wept; kneel, knelt; leap, leapt; creep, crept; mean, meant**) have been pronounced.

Meeting Diverse Needs

Less Able Spellers

Students with special needs, especially those with learning disabilities, often describe good writing as "spelling words correctly on the first draft." For this reason, an important instructional goal for these students is to help them develop a more balanced view of the role of spelling in writing.

Emphasize the importance of content and meaning when writing a first draft. Provide external assistance, such as electronic spell checkers and peer-spelling editors, to help students complete their final drafts successfully.

More Able Spellers

Challenge students to use their spelling list to build a compact crossword puzzle. A compact crossword puzzle takes as few spaces horizontally and vertically as possible. Invite students to include words that are not on their spelling lists in order to make more efficient use of the space. (**Teacher Resource Book** page 54 provides a crossword puzzle grid.)

Ask students to copy their lists in the **Take Your List Home** section of the *Spell It–Write!* Home News page for this lesson. Not only does this page provide a convenient way for families to share a student's spelling list, but it also provides a number of opportunities for families to be involved in students' spelling growth. It has a statement of the week's spelling pattern or strategy, a valuable spelling study strategy, and a suggested home spelling practice activity.

Teacher Resource Book, page 89

Teacher Resource Book, page 90

FINDING WORDS

Step 1 Build Your Spelling List

Students will build their spelling lists with **Pattern Words, Teacher Words,** and **Your Words.** Students should study a minimum of twelve new words each week.

Find Your Pattern Words

• Pretest the students on these words.

• Tell students to write each misspelled pretest word on their spelling lists.

Add Teacher Words

• Select words for students to add to their spelling lists. Choose words from **More Words for Hungry Word Hunters** (on this page and on student page 167), words related to a theme or content area, or words students often misspell.

Add Your Words

• Ask students to pick words from their lists of **Words I Need to Know How to Spell** and their writing.

• Tell students to write these words on their spelling lists.

Step 2 Write Your Spelling List

Remind students to verify all spellings. (Ask students to see **Strategies for Checking Your Spelling** in the back of the student edition.)

Step 3 Set Your Learning Goal

Tell students to count the words on their spelling lists. This total is their learning goal. It may vary depending on ability, individual goals, and the difficulty of spelling words.

MORE WORDS FOR HUNGRY WORD HUNTERS

RED LIST
Pattern Words Below Level

breath
fed
felt
kept
led
left
met

These lists also appear on page 167 in the student edition and page 24 in the **Teacher Resource Book.**

SPELLING PATTERN

18

Patterns That Show Meaning

Your Spelling List

_____
_____
_____
_____
_____
_____
_____
_____
_____
_____
_____
_____
_____
_____
_____
_____
_____
_____
_____

FINDING WORDS

Step 1 Build Your Spelling List

Find Your Pattern Words
Take the pretest.
Write misspelled words on your spelling list.

Add Teacher Words
Teachers may add:
• More **Pattern Words** • Content Words • Theme Words

Add Your Words
Pick words from:
• **Words I Need to Know How to Spell** • Writing • Reading

Pattern Words

1.	health	Taking care of your **health** is important.
2.	swept	We **swept** the leaves out of the garage.
3.	peeled	Maria **peeled** ten pounds of potatoes.
4.	dealt	Who **dealt** the cards last?
5.	slept	The cat **slept** under the porch.
6.	depth	The **depth** of this pool is six feet.
7.	cleanse	**Cleanse** the cut carefully.
8.	wept	The winners **wept** for joy.
9.	knelt	The nurse **knelt** down to help the child.
10.	leapt	The lizard **leapt** onto the turtle's back.
11.	crept	The worm **crept** across the road.
12.	meant	Isabel **meant** to call her grandmother.

Step 2 Write Your Spelling List

Step 3 Set Your Learning Goal

My spelling list has _____ words for me to learn.

> Yeah, and if I understand that pattern, I can spell other words with the same spelling pattern.

> The **Pattern Words** list helps me see the same spelling pattern in a whole group of words.

PATTERN MINI-LESSON

NOTE: The **Explore the Spelling Pattern** activity on page 95 is a self-directed mini-lesson. If you wish to supplement that activity with direct instruction, use the following mini-lesson.

* **Read** the **Spelling Pattern** on page 95 with students. Explain that it will guide the **Hands-on Word Sort**.

* **Display** the **?** card and the **Hands-on Word Sort Cards** for Unit 18. Keep blank cards and a marker handy to make new cards.

* **Say** each guide word, pointing to the underlined letters. (Guide words are labeled "Master Word" on the **Word Sort Card**.) Explain that if a **long e** sound is spelled **ea**, as in **mean**, the **short e** sound in a related word, such as **meant**, will usually be spelled **ea**. If a **long e** sound is spelled **ee**, as in **sweep**, the **short e** sound in a related word, such as **swept**, will be spelled **e**.

* **Sort** the words based on their spelling patterns. Model your decision making: "The word **meant** is formed from **mean**, just as **health** is formed from **heal**, so I'll write **meant** under **health**."

* **Tell** students to place words that do not fit the patterns under the question mark. Challenge students to explain why **peeled** does not fit. (Response: *According to the pattern, the past tense of peel should be pelt.*) For the completed word sort, see the **Answer Card** for this unit in the **Hands-on Word Sort Card Book**.

* **Duplicate** the **Hands-on Word Sort Sheet** for Unit 18 (**Teacher Resource Book,** page 43). Ask students to cut the words on the sheet apart and practice sorting the words with a partner or independently.

· · · · · · · · · INSPECTING WORDS · · · · · · · · ·

Explore the Spelling Pattern
Sorting Words

A. Find a partner. Take turns reading the **Pattern Words** out loud. Match each **Pattern Word** with the word below that has the same spelling pattern. If a word doesn't fit, put it with the question mark. Make sure you write each **Pattern Word** once.

> You may wish to use **Hands-on Word Sort Cards** and the **Hands-on Word Sort Sheet** for this unit.

1. health	2. swept	3. ?
health	swept	peeled
dealt	slept	
cleanse	depth	
leapt	wept	
meant	knelt	
	crept	

B. Think of other words to add to each list. Look at your writing and in **Words I Need to Know How to Spell.**

Focus on Word Study
Words From Latin

The English word **peeled** has a base word **(peel)** that comes from the Latin word **pilare**. The meaning of **pilare** is "to make bald." You make a potato "bald" when you peel it.

Match the words **enormous, large,** and **giant** with the Latin words they come from.

1. largus   large
2. gigas   giant
3. enormis   enormous

▼ ▼ ▼ ▼ ▼ ▼ ▼ ▼ ▼ ▼ ▼ ▼

Spelling Pattern

* Listen to **mean** and **meant**. If the **long e** sound in a base word is spelled **ea** (**mean**), then the **short e** sound in related words is spelled **ea** (**meant**).

* Listen to **sweep** and **swept**. If the **long e** sound is spelled **ee** (**sweep**), the **short e** sound in related words is spelled **e** (**swept**).

· · · · · · · · · · · · · · ·

Explore the Spelling Pattern
Sorting Words

This activity is a self-directed mini-lesson on this week's **Spelling Pattern**.

Focus on Word Study
Words From Latin

This activity is intended to stimulate students' interest in words and to help them become more enthusiastic word hunters.

Spelling Process Handbook

Students who need to review any part of the spelling process, including practice options, should refer to the **Spelling Process Handbook** (pages 7–21).

Practice Your Spelling List Independently

Ask the students to choose activities to practice their spelling words and to master this week's **Spelling Pattern**. Students should complete at least three activities each week. You may wish to:

- assign **Practice the Spelling Pattern** to all students to reinforce this week's **Spelling Pattern**.

- involve students' families by assigning **Take Your List Home** for this lesson (**Teacher Resource Book**, pages 89 in English and 90 in Spanish).

- encourage students to use partner activities without game mats (**Word Swap, Spelling Tic-Tac-Toe, Circle Dot**) and activities with game mats (**Meteor Attack, Rockets, Spelling Checkers, Spelling Soccer**). Directions for game-mat activities appear on each game mat. Directions for all other activities are found in the **Spelling Process Handbook** (pages 7–21).

NOTE: These activities and games can be used to practice any spelling list.

ROCKETS

Can you figure out the spelling word before your partner "blasts off"? That's the challenge for students as they play **Rockets**. Students will develop their knowledge of common spelling patterns as they make strategic guesses to visualize spellings and complete words. It's a countdown to spelling success with **Rockets**. (Directions appear on the **Rockets** game mat. This activity is appropriate for practicing any spelling list.)

Practice Your Spelling List Independently

Choose at least three activities to practice your spelling list.

> Copy your words carefully when you take your list home.

Game Mats	With a Partner	On Your Own	At Home
○ Meteor Attack ○ Rockets	○ Circle Dot ○ Word Swap	○ Flip Folder ○ Spelling Study Strategy	○ Take Your List Home

Practice the Spelling Pattern

For each base word below, write the related **Pattern Word**.

Pattern Words

health
swept
peeled
dealt
slept
depth
cleanse
wept
knelt
leapt
crept
meant

1. **Base Word:** creep _____ crept
2. **Base Word:** knee _____ knelt
3. **Base Word:** deal _____ dealt
4. **Base Word:** deep _____ depth
5. **Base Word:** clean _____ cleanse
6. **Base Word:** weep _____ wept
7. **Base Word:** heal _____ health
8. **Base Word:** peel _____ peeled
9. **Base Word:** sweep _____ swept
10. **Base Word:** leap _____ leapt
11. **Base Word:** mean _____ meant
12. **Base Word:** sleep _____ slept

DEVELOPING GOOD SPELLING HABITS

STEP 7 Focus on Writing

A. Proofread the Writing of Others

This activity provides proofreading practice in a variety of formats, including popular standardized test formats.

B. Proofread Your Own Writing

Students return to their own writing, armed with strategies to identify and collect words they need to know how to spell, and make an authentic link between spelling and writing.

C. A Writing Idea: A Postcard

This suggestion for a more extended writing activity provides opportunities for students to write in different genres for a variety of purposes and modes.

STEP 8 Check Your Weekly Progress

▶ Take the Test

Remind students that they can take a practice test before the final test on their spelling lists. To find the testing procedure that is right for you, refer to page Z12.

▶ Check Your Goal

Have students compare their tests to their spelling lists. Did they spell all the **Pattern Words** on their spelling lists correctly?

▶ Graph Your Progress

Ask students to graph the number correct (student page 176 for softbound users; **Teacher Resource Book** page 123 for hardbound users).

▶ Save Missed Words

Tell students to write misspelled words on their lists of **Words I Need to Know How to Spell**. Remind students to verify spellings and to recycle these words on future weekly spelling lists.

· · · · · DEVELOPING GOOD SPELLING HABITS · · · · ·

STEP 7 Focus on Writing

A. Proofread the Writing of Others

Proofread the following paragraph. Decide which type of mistake, if any, appears in each underlined part.

Sue sent a postcard from camp. She said that she had <u>ment to write</u> sooner. Sue slept in a cabin with six
①
campers. Each day a camper <u>sweept the floor</u> of the cabin.
②
When it was Sue's turn, a caterpillar <u>crept up the broom</u>
③
and onto her <u>hand. sue said</u>, "It tickled!"
④

≡ Make a capital.
╱ Make a small letter.
∧ Add something.
ℓ Take out something.
⊙ Add a period.
¶ New paragraph
(SP) Spelling error

1. Ⓐ Spelling
   B Capitalization
   C Punctuation
   D No mistake

2. Ⓐ Spelling
   B Capitalization
   C Punctuation
   D No mistake

3. A Spelling
   B Capitalization
   C Punctuation
   Ⓓ No mistake

4. A Spelling
   Ⓑ Capitalization
   C Punctuation
   D No mistake

B. Proofread Your Own Writing

When a base word has a **long e** sound spelled **ea (mean)**, the **short e** in related words is also spelled **ea (meant)**. Look for words with the **short e** sound in your most recent writing. Add misspelled words to **Words I Need to Know How to Spell**.

C. A Writing Idea: A Postcard

Think about a place you have visited. Write a postcard to a relative telling what you did. Draw a picture on the front of the card. Before you send it, check your spelling.

STEP 8 Check Your Weekly Progress

▶ **Take the Test**
Ready? Practice test first.

▶ **Check Your Goal**
Check to see if you met your learning goal.

▶ **Graph Your Progress**
Graph your score for this week's test.

▶ **Save Missed Words**
Write the words you missed in your list of **Words I Need to Know How to Spell**.

Hunt Words

Remind students to continuously hunt words that they wish to learn how to spell and to write these words in **Words I Need to Know How to Spell**.

ENGAGING IN THE PROCESS — MATERIALS

Student Edition: Pages 98–101   **Teacher Edition:** Pages T98A–T101

Materials to help students practice their spelling lists:

- **Flip Folders**
- Copies of **Flip Folder Practice Sheet** (**Teacher Resource Book,** page 51)
- **Take Your List Home** (in *Spell It–Write!*

Home News, **Teacher Resource Book,** pages 91 in English and 92 in Spanish)
- Game Mats Featured in This Unit: **Rockets, Spelling Soccer**

ENGAGING IN THE PROCESS — GOALS

SPELLING GOALS

Students will

- transfer knowledge that the suffixes **-ful, -less, -ly, -ment,** and **-ness** can be added to words to form new words.
- sort words according to their suffixes.
- develop an understanding of how the meanings of words can change over time.
- use the spelling process of finding words, inspecting words, and mastering words as they develop good spelling habits to become better writers.

WRITING GOALS

Students will

- hunt for words made by adding the suffixes **-ful, -ly, -ness, -ment,** or **-less** to a base word in a piece of their own writing.
- write an expressive paragraph.

ENGAGING IN THE PROCESS — MANAGEMENT

Pacing	Notes	Quick Pick Management Option
Period 1 Finding Words (Steps 1–3)	If you wish to add **Teacher Words,** write them on the chalkboard. Sources for more words include: **More Words for Hungry Word Hunters** (page T98), content and theme-related words, or words of your choice.	Assign the list of **Pattern Words** to the whole class. Add the Red List (**More Words for Hungry Word Hunters,** student page 168) for a longer list. Add the Blue List (**More Words for Hungry Word Hunters**) for a more challenging list.
Period 2 Inspecting Words (Steps 4 and 5)	Students write the **Pattern Words** to complete **Explore the Spelling Pattern.**	Assign **Explore the Spelling Pattern** and **Focus on Word Study.**
Period 3 Mastering Words (Step 6) **Period 4** Developing Good Spelling Habits (Step 7)	These two periods can be allocated between selected **Mastering Words** activities and proofreading and writing activities in **Focus on Writing.**	Assign two or three activities to the whole class. Familiarize students with choosing their own activities at their own pace.
Period 5 Assessment (Step 8)	Gradually try different peer-testing options to find the style that best fits your class.	Test the class on the same, whole-class list.

Understanding Language Differences

In casual speech, American English speakers often use the same form for both adjectives and adverbs. For example, instead of using the adverbs **really** and **slowly** to say, "I always drive really slowly at night," some speakers would say, "I always drive real slow at night." In written language, it is still considered important to use the **-ly** form for these adverbs.

Some students who are learning English as a second language may have trouble with the more complicated spellings in this unit, including **really, illness, brightly, friendly,** and **greatly**. Silent letters (**brightly**), vowel digraphs (**friendly, greatly**), and double consonants (**really, illness**) are concepts that will require frequent oral and written practice.

Helping Students Acquiring English

Explain that word parts can be added to words to make new words. Then write the word **pain** on the chalkboard, pronounce it, and discuss its meaning. Using a different color of chalk, add the suffix **-ful** to **pain,** explaining what you are doing. Pronounce the word **painful,** have students repeat the word, and discuss its meaning. Follow a similar procedure to introduce **painless,** emphasizing the way the new suffix changes the meaning, and then go on to introduce the remaining **Pattern Words**.

Meeting Diverse Needs

Less Able Spellers

Students with attention deficit and hyperactivity disorders may enjoy improved performance when color is used to highlight an important feature of a task. In spelling, color can be used to highlight the part of the word the child is having difficulty remembering. (The child should practice the word initially to determine which part presents the greatest challenge.) The addition of color to this "hard part" may make the word easier for the child to remember.

Avoid presenting the entire word in color or practicing writing the word with colored pens. Too much color may prove distracting for some children with attention deficit disorder.

More Able Spellers

Ask students who are strong spellers to select one of their spelling words. Then challenge them to develop as many new words as they can by adding prefixes and suffixes to the base word. Ask them to explain how the meaning (and spelling) of the original word changed with the addition of each prefix and suffix.

Ask students to copy their lists in the **Take Your List Home** section of the *Spell It–Write!* Home News page for this lesson. Not only does this page provide a convenient way for families to share a student's spelling list, but it also provides a number of opportunities for families to be involved in students' spelling growth. It has a statement of the week's spelling pattern or strategy, a valuable spelling study strategy, and a suggested home spelling practice activity.

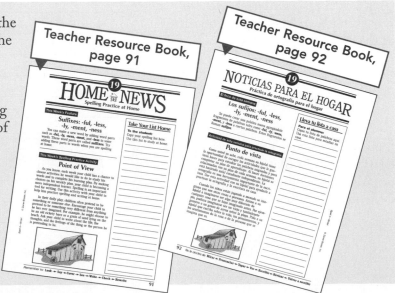

FINDING WORDS

STEP 1 Build Your Spelling List

Students will build their spelling lists with **Pattern Words, Teacher Words,** and **Your Words**. Students should study a minimum of twelve new words each week.

Find Your Pattern Words

• Pretest the students on these words.

• Tell students to write each misspelled pretest word on their spelling lists.

Add Teacher Words

• Select words for students to add to their spelling lists. Choose words from **More Words for Hungry Word Hunters** (on this page and on student page 168), words related to a theme or content area, or words students often misspell.

Add Your Words

• Ask students to pick words from their lists of **Words I Need to Know How to Spell** and their writing.

• Tell students to write these words on their spelling lists.

STEP 2 Write Your Spelling List

Remind students to verify all spellings. (Ask students to see **Strategies for Checking Your Spelling** in the back of the student edition.)

STEP 3 Set Your Learning Goal

Tell students to count the words on their spelling lists. This total is their learning goal. It may vary depending on ability, individual goals, and the difficulty of spelling words.

T98 UNIT 19

MORE WORDS FOR HUNGRY WORD HUNTERS

RED LIST — Pattern Words Below Level	BLUE LIST — Pattern Words Above Level	Other Pattern Words	Math Pattern Words
badly	agreement	directly	equally
brightly	blindness	endless	measurement
friendly	cloudless	especially	
greatly	cordless	fitness	**Science Pattern Word**
kindly	government	powerful	hardness
loudly	harmful	skillful	
mainly	proudly	thankless	**Social Studies Pattern Word**
mostly	sickness	thickness	amendment
partly	suddenly	treatment	
softly	thoughtful	wonderment	

These lists also appear on page 168 in the student edition and page 25 in the **Teacher Resource Book**.

············ FINDING WORDS ············

SPELLING PATTERN

19

**Suffixes:
-ful, -less, -ly,
-ment, -ness**

Your Spelling List

STEP 1 Build Your Spelling List

Find Your Pattern Words
Take the pretest.
Write misspelled words on your spelling list.

Add Teacher Words
Teachers may add:
• More **Pattern Words** • Content Words • Theme Words

Add Your Words
Pick words from:
• **Words I Need to Know How to Spell** • Writing • Reading

Pattern Words

1. **really**   I **really** enjoyed reading *Charlotte's Web*.
2. **cheerful**   Yellow is a **cheerful** color.
3. **painless**   Getting a haircut is **painless**.
4. **shipment**   Send this **shipment** of clothes today.
5. **illness**   Chicken pox is a common **illness**.
6. **enjoyment** Eric builds kites for **enjoyment**.
7. **slowly**   The snake **slowly** slid down the tree.
8. **helpless**   The **helpless** bird was in danger.
9. **painful**   The cut on my finger was **painful**.
10. **darkness** The **darkness** of the night surrounded us.

STEP 2 Write Your Spelling List

STEP 3 Set Your Learning Goal

My spelling list has _____ words for me to learn.

Sometimes our teacher adds the Red List or the Blue List from **More Words for Hungry Word Hunters** to our spelling lists.

Uh-huh. And sometimes our teacher adds the social studies words we'll write during the week.

98 UNIT 19

PATTERN MINI-LESSON

NOTE: The **Explore the Spelling Pattern** activity on page 99 is a self-directed mini-lesson. If you wish to supplement that activity with direct instruction, use the following mini-lesson.

* **Write** the words **real** and **really** on the chalkboard. Ask how **real** was changed to make **really**. (Possible responses: *The suffix -ly was added; the part of speech changed from adjective to adverb; the meaning changed.*)

* **Write** the **Pattern Words** from page 98 on the chalkboard. Pronounce each word and ask students to repeat it.

* **Ask** students what these words have in common. (Response: *Each word has a suffix.*)

* **Model** separating the suffix from the base word by drawing a vertical line between the **l**'s in **really**. Circle the suffix.

* **Ask** volunteers to do the same for the remaining words.

* **Assign** each word on the chalkboard to a pair of students. Tell partners to write two sentences for the word—one sentence using the base word and one sentence using the word with the suffix.

NOTE: You may wish to point out the meaning of each suffix: **-ful** means "full of," **-ly** means "in a (certain) way" or "like," **-less** means "without," **-ment** means "the act of (do)ing," **-ness** means "state of being."

* **Read** the **Spelling Pattern** on page 99 with students.

* **Write** these headings on the chalkboard: **-ful, -less, -ly, -ment, -ness**. Encourage students to give examples of other words with these suffixes. Write students' words under the appropriate headings.

········· INSPECTING WORDS ·········

 Explore the Spelling Pattern
Sorting Words

A. Making a word sort can help you inspect words. Sort the **Pattern Words** according to the ending in the word. Use the words below to guide your sort. Make sure you write each **Pattern Word** once.

Try sorting the **Pattern Words** in other ways. Which words have double letters?

1. **cheerful**	3. **really**	5. **illness**
cheerful	really	illness
painful	slowly	darkness

2. **painless**	4. **shipment**	
painless	shipment	
helpless	enjoyment	

B. What other words can you find that end with the suffixes **-ful, -ly, -ness, -ment,** or **-less**? Look in your writing and in **Words I Need to Know How to Spell**. Trade words with a partner and make your own word sort.

 Focus on Word Study
Changes in Meaning

The first meaning of the English word **cheer** was "face." At that time, **face** meant "be cheerful" or "put on a happy face." Later, the meaning of **cheer** changed to "gladness" or "happiness."

Each of these old words is related to a **Pattern Word**. Read the meaning for each old word and write the related **Pattern Word**.

1. enjoyne (rejoice, be glad) ___enjoyment___
2. peine (punishment, penalty) ___painful___
3. slowe (sluggish, not quick) ___slowly___

Spelling Pattern

You can make a new word by adding word parts, such as **-ful, -ly, -ness, -ment,** and **-less,** to some words. These word parts are called **suffixes**.

 Explore the Spelling Pattern

Sorting Words

This activity is a self-directed mini-lesson on this week's **Spelling Pattern**.

Focus on Word Study

Changes in Meaning

This activity is intended to stimulate students' interest in words and to help them become more enthusiastic word hunters.

Spelling Process Handbook

Students who need to review any part of the spelling process, including practice options, should refer to the **Spelling Process Handbook** (pages 7–21).

MASTERING WORDS

STEP 6 Practice Your Spelling List Independently

Ask the students to choose activities to practice their spelling words and to master this week's **Spelling Pattern**. Students should complete at least three activities each week. You may wish to:

- assign **Practice the Spelling Pattern** to all students to reinforce this week's **Spelling Pattern**.

- involve students' families by assigning **Take Your List Home** for this lesson (**Teacher Resource Book**, pages 91 in English and 92 in Spanish).

- encourage students to use partner activities without game mats (**Word Swap, Spelling Tic-Tac-Toe, Circle Dot**) and activities with game mats (**Meteor Attack, Rockets, Spelling Checkers, Spelling Soccer**). Directions for game-mat activities appear on each game mat. Directions for all other activities are found in the **Spelling Process Handbook** (pages 7–21).

NOTE: These activities and games can be used to practice any spelling list.

A Practice Option

FLIP FOLDER

The **Flip Folder** is a fun practice activity that is especially effective for kinesthetic learners. While **Flip Folder** is similar to the Have-a-Go strategy, the techniques differ in that the first step in **Flip Folder** is to look at the correct spelling. Students then cover that spelling, visualize it, and attempt at recreate it. When they lift the flap and compare their attempt to the correct spelling, they receive immediate feedback—vital for correcting mistakes and retaining correct spellings. (Directions appear in the **Spelling Process Handbook,** student pages 7–21, and on the **Flip Folder** itself. This activity is appropriate for practicing any spelling list.)

MASTERING WORDS

STEP 6 Practice Your Spelling List Independently
Choose at least three activities to practice your spelling list.

It's fun to try different practice activities.

Game Mats		With a Partner		On Your Own		At Home
○ Rockets	○ Spelling Soccer	○ Circle Dot	○ Spelling Tic-Tac-Toe	○ Flip Folder	○ Spelling Study Strategy	○ Take Your List Home

✏️ Practice the Spelling Pattern

Write the **Pattern Word** that is defined by each phrase.

Pattern Words

really
cheerful
painless
shipment
illness
enjoyment
slowly
helpless
painful
darkness

1. act of enjoying — **enjoyment**
2. state of being ill — **illness**
3. full of cheer — **cheerful**
4. without pain — **painless**
5. in a real way — **really**
6. without help — **helpless**
7. when it is dark; state of being dark — **darkness**
8. full of pain — **painful**
9. in a slow way — **slowly**
10. act of shipping; something that is shipped — **shipment**

DEVELOPING GOOD SPELLING HABITS

STEP 7 Focus on Writing

A. Hunt Spelling Words in Your Writing

This activity equips students with a specific strategy for increasing students' consciousness of targeted spelling patterns and strategies in their own writing. It also enables them to collect words for spelling study.

B. A Writing Idea: A Paragraph

This suggestion for a more extended writing activity provides opportunities for students to write in different genres for a variety of purposes and modes.

STEP 8 Check Your Weekly Progress

▶ **Take the Test**

Remind students that they can take a practice test before the final test on their spelling lists. To find the testing procedure that is right for you, refer to page Z12.

▶ **Check Your Goal**

Have students compare their tests to their spelling lists. Did they spell all the **Pattern Words** on their spelling lists correctly?

▶ **Graph Your Progress**

Ask students to graph the number correct (student page 176 for softbound users; **Teacher Resource Book** page 123 for hardbound users).

▶ **Save Missed Words**

Tell students to write misspelled words on their lists of **Words I Need to Know How to Spell**. Remind students to verify spellings and to recycle these words on future weekly spelling lists.

· · · · · · · · · DEVELOPING GOOD SPELLING HABITS · · · · · · · · ·

STEP 7 Focus on Writing

A. Hunt Spelling Words in Your Writing

Work with a spelling partner to hunt through your writing for words that were made by adding a suffix to a base word. Look especially for words with these suffixes: **-ful, -ly, -ness, -ment, -less**. Write the words you find in two columns like these.

Column 1	Column 2
I spelled these **base word + suffix** words correctly.	I misspelled these **base word + suffix** words.
Answers will vary.	Answers will vary.

If you can't find any words that were made by adding a suffix to a base word, choose a different piece of writing.

Add the words you wrote in Column 2 to **Words I Need to Know How to Spell**.

B. A Writing Idea: A Paragraph

Have you ever felt cheerful or helpless? Choose any **Pattern Word** that is about a feeling. Write a paragraph to explain when you've experienced this feeling. Check your writing to see if you've spelled all the words correctly.

≡ Make a capital.
/ Make a small letter.
∧ Add something.
℮ Take out something.
⊙ Add a period.
¶ New paragraph
(SP) Spelling error

STEP 8 Check Your Weekly Progress

▶ **Take the Test**
Ready? Practice test first.

▶ **Check Your Goal**
Check to see if you met your learning goal.

▶ **Graph Your Progress**
Graph your score for this week's test.

▶ **Save Missed Words**
Write the words you missed in your list of **Words I Need to Know How to Spell**.

Hunt Words

Remind students to continuously hunt words that they wish to learn how to spell and to write these words in **Words I Need to Know How to Spell**.

ENGAGING IN THE PROCESS

MATERIALS

Student Edition: Pages 102–105 **Teacher Edition:** Pages T102A–T105

Materials to help students practice their spelling lists:
- **Flip Folders**
- Copies of **Flip Folder Practice Sheet** (**Teacher Resource Book,** page 51)
- Take Your List Home (in *Spell It–Write!*

Home News, **Teacher Resource Book,** pages 93 in English and 94 in Spanish)
- Games Mats Featured in This Unit: **Spelling Checkers, Spelling Soccer**

ENGAGING IN THE PROCESS

GOALS

SPELLING GOALS

Students will

- understand that a dictionary is a valuable spelling tool.
- use a dictionary to find other forms of base words.
- explore similar spellings and meanings of words in English and other languages.
- use the spelling process of finding words, inspecting words, and mastering words as they develop good spelling habits to become better writers.

WRITING GOALS

Students will

- proofread a writing sample.
- proofread a piece of their own writing for misspelled words that are different forms of other words.
- write expressive dialogue for a cartoon.

ENGAGING IN THE PROCESS

MANAGEMENT

Pacing	Notes	Quick Pick Management Option
Period 1 Finding Words (Steps 1–3)	If you wish to add **Teacher Words,** write them on the chalkboard. Sources for more words include: **More Words for Hungry Word Hunters** (page T102), content and theme-related words, or words of your choice.	Assign the list of **Strategy Words** to the whole class. Add the Red List (**More Words for Hungry Word Hunters,** student page 168) for a longer list. Add the Blue List (**More Words for Hungry Word Hunters**) for a more challenging list.
Period 2 Inspecting Words (Steps 4 and 5)	Students write the **Strategy Words** to complete **Explore the Spelling Strategy.**	Assign **Explore the Spelling Strategy** and **Focus on Word Study.**
Period 3 Mastering Words (Step 6) **Period 4** Developing Good Spelling Habits (Step 7)	These two periods can be allocated between selected **Mastering Words** activities and proofreading and writing activities in **Focus on Writing.**	Assign two or three activities to the whole class. Familiarize students with choosing their own activities at their own pace.
Period 5 Assessment (Step 8)	Gradually try different peer-testing options to find the style that best fits your class.	Test the class on the same, whole-class list.

ENGAGING
IN THE
PROCESS
INDIVIDUAL
NEEDS

Understanding Language Differences

Spanish Speakers

Students from Spanish-speaking backgrounds who are familiar with Spanish dictionaries may encounter some initial confusion when they pick up an English dictionary. Although Spanish and English dictionaries are basically similar, there are some differences. Most Spanish dictionaries treat **ch** as a separate letter—the fourth letter of the alphabet (between **c** and **d**). Similarly, the combination **ll** is treated as a separate letter falling between **l** and **m**. This means that **champú** (**shampoo**) comes after **curso** (**course**) and that **llama** follows **luz** (**light**). If your students are already literate in Spanish, ask them to look up in an English dictionary words beginning with **ch** (**chair, child,** and so on) to be sure they understand how an English dictionary is organized.

Helping Students Acquiring English

Display a dictionary, and discuss its organization and features with students. Pair less fluent speakers with more fluent partners. Give each pair a dictionary, and ask them to look up each **Strategy Word** and discuss its meaning. Refer students to **Strategies for Checking Your Spelling** in the back of the student edition for a sample dictionary entry.

Meeting Diverse Needs

Less Able Spellers

An effective technique in teaching students with special needs is called "reinforcement, contingent upon performance." For example, providing incentives, such as stickers, may result in improvement on weekly spelling tests. Similarly, awarding points for using cooperative learning activities as intended may also lead to better scores on weekly spelling quizzes.

Children can also be encouraged to develop their own system of self-reinforcement and determine for themselves how they will reward themselves for meeting their weekly spelling goal.

More Able Spellers

Challenge students to use the **Strategy Words** to build a crossword puzzle. Encourage students to include other forms of the words they find in the dictionary. For clues, students should use the dictionary definitions of the words they include. (**Teacher Resource Book** page 54 provides a crossword puzzle grid.)

ENGAGING
IN THE
PROCESS
INVOLVING
FAMILIES

Ask students to copy their lists in the **Take Your List Home** section of the *Spell It–Write!* Home News page for this lesson. Not only does this page provide a convenient way for families to share a student's spelling list, but it also provides a number of opportunities for families to be involved in students' spelling growth. It has a statement of the week's spelling pattern or strategy, a valuable spelling study strategy, and a suggested home spelling practice activity.

FINDING WORDS

. . . . FINDING WORDS . . . .

STEP 1 Build Your Spelling List

Students will build their spelling lists with **Strategy Words, Teacher Words,** and **Your Words.** Students should study a minimum of twelve new words each week.

Find Your Strategy Words

• Pretest the students on these words.

• Tell students to write each misspelled pretest word on their spelling lists.

Add Teacher Words

• Select words for students to add to their spelling lists. Choose words from **More Words for Hungry Word Hunters** (on this page and on student page 168), words related to a theme or content area, or words students often misspell.

Add Your Words

• Ask students to pick words from their lists of **Words I Need to Know How to Spell** and their writing.

• Tell students to write these words on their spelling lists.

STEP 2 Write Your Spelling List

Remind students to verify all spellings. (Ask students to see **Strategies for Checking Your Spelling** in the back of the student edition.)

STEP 3 Set Your Learning Goal

Tell students to count the words on their spelling lists. This total is their learning goal. It may vary depending on ability, individual goals, and the difficulty of spelling words.

MORE WORDS FOR HUNGRY WORD HUNTERS

RED LIST
Strategy Words Below Level

begin
brave
busy
carry
lady
lie
pretty
think
tooth
write

BLUE LIST
Strategy Words Above Level

argue
buffalo
describe
foggy
freeze
industry
marry
panel
plod
straight

Science Strategy Words

behavior
digestion
hardness
prospector

Social Studies Strategy Words

boundary
crafts
tourist

These lists also appear on page 168 in the student edition and page 26 in the **Teacher Resource Book.**

SPELLING STRATEGY

20

Using a Dictionary

Your Spelling List

_____
_____
_____
_____
_____
_____
_____
_____
_____
_____
_____
_____
_____
_____
_____
_____
_____
_____
_____
_____
_____

. . . . **FINDING WORDS** . . . .

STEP 1 Build Your Spelling List

Find Your Strategy Words

Take the pretest.
Write misspelled words on your spelling list.

Add Teacher Words

Teachers may add:
• More **Strategy Words** • Content Words • Theme Words

Add Your Words

Pick words from:
• **Words I Need to Know How to Spell** • Writing • Reading

Strategy Words

1. **country** — My cousin lives out in the **country,** far away from any city.
2. **zero** — One minus one equals **zero.**
3. **scare** — Loud thunder will **scare** our dog.
4. **speak** — Did you **speak** to the new girl today?
5. **rough** — Sara hurt her knee on the **rough** rocks.
6. **picnic** — Who invited ants to our **picnic**?
7. **company** — My bird keeps me **company** at home.
8. **scar** — Shawn has a **scar** on his chin.
9. **gentle** — Please be **gentle** with the baby.
10. **reply** — Send a **reply** to the invitation soon.

STEP 2 Write Your Spelling List

STEP 3 Set Your Learning Goal

My spelling list has _____ words for me to learn.

 I always go through stuff I've written, especially in language arts and science, for words I need to know how to spell.

 What's a good way to find words for your spelling list?

STRATEGY MINI-LESSON

NOTE: The **Explore the Spelling Strategy** activity on page 103 is a self-directed mini-lesson. If you wish to supplement that activity with direct instruction, use the following mini-lesson. Dictionaries, as available, should be distributed for use with the mini-lesson.

* **Help** students brainstorm what uses a dictionary may have. (Possible responses: *to find the meaning of a word; to check spelling*)

* **Tell** students they can also use a dictionary to spell other forms of words. Explain that another form of **country** is **countries**. Provide dictionaries and ask students to look up **countries**. Ask several volunteers to explain how and where they found the word **countries**. (Possible response: *The word countries can be found by looking up country; countries is found within the entry for country.*) If no one can find **countries,** model the procedure to follow.

* **Divide** the class into groups. Assign each group one of the remaining **Strategy Words** on page 102. Challenge students to see how many other forms they can find in the dictionary for the assigned word. Make a list on the chalkboard of the words they find. Emphasize that to find these words in a dictionary, they must look up the simplest form of the word.

* **Use** students' responses to discuss the types of words that might be found under a given entry word. These might include some kinds of plurals, some words with **-ed** and **-ing** endings, and other parts of speech.

* **Ask** students to read the **Spelling Strategy** on page 103 with you. Call on volunteers to summarize the **Spelling Strategy** in their own words.

· · · · · · · · · · INSPECTING WORDS · · · · · · · · · ·

 STEP 4 **Explore the Spelling Strategy**
Looking Up Words

A. A dictionary lists entry words alphabetically. Looking up a word in the dictionary can help you spell other forms of the word. The words in each item below are other forms of a **Strategy Word**. Write the **Strategy Word** you would look up in the dictionary to find these other forms.

1. roughly, roughness   **rough**
2. picnicking, picnicker   **picnic**
3. replies, replying   **reply**
4. scarred, scarring   **scar**
5. gentler, gentlest   **gentle**
6. zeros or zeroes   **zero**
7. companies   **company**
8. scared, scares   **scare**
9. countries, countryish   **country**
10. speaking, spoke   **speak**

B. Use a dictionary to find other words that have different forms. Write each word you find and its different forms.

STEP 5 **Focus on Word Study**
Words From Other Languages

If you can spell **zero,** you are writing in three languages! In English, French, and Italian, **zero** has the same spelling and the same meaning.

Compare the spellings of these number words. Which letters are the same in all three languages?

English	French	Spanish	
1. one	un	uno	n
2. three	trois	tres	t and r
3. six	six	seis	s and i

▼ ▼ ▼ ▼ ▼ ▼ ▼ ▼ ▼ ▼ ▼ ▼
Spelling Strategy
You can use the dictionary to find the spelling of another form of a word. You can find the spelling of **countries** by looking up **country**.
· · · · · · · · · · · · · ·

 STEP 4 **Explore the Spelling Strategy**
Looking Up Words

This activity is a self-directed mini-lesson on this week's **Spelling Strategy.**

 STEP 5 **Focus on Word Study**
Words From Other Languages

This activity is intended to stimulate students' interest in words and to help them become more enthusiastic word hunters.

Spelling Process Handbook
Students who need to review any part of the spelling process, including practice options, should refer to the **Spelling Process Handbook** (pages 7–21).

MASTERING WORDS

A Practice Option

STEP 6 — Practice Your Spelling List Independently

Ask the students to choose activities to practice their spelling words and to master this week's **Spelling Strategy**. Students should complete at least three activities each week. You may wish to:

• assign **Practice the Spelling Strategy** to all students to reinforce this week's **Spelling Strategy**.

• involve students' families by assigning **Take Your List Home** for this lesson (**Teacher Resource Book**, pages 93 in English and 94 in Spanish).

• encourage students to use partner activities without game mats (**Word Swap, Spelling Tic-Tac-Toe, Circle Dot**) and activities with game mats (**Meteor Attack, Rockets, Spelling Checkers, Spelling Soccer**). Directions for game-mat activities appear on each game mat. Directions for all other activities are found in the **Spelling Process Handbook** (pages 7–21).

NOTE: These activities and games can be used to practice any spelling list.

SPELLING CHECKERS

Students will "jump" at the chance to play **Spelling Checkers,** a game mat that combines spelling practice with the popular board game. And because students write on the board with dry-erase markers to record their progress, game pieces are not needed. This game is especially appropriate spelling practice for auditory and visual learners. (Directions appear on the **Spelling Checkers** game mat. This activity is appropriate for practicing any spelling list.)

· · · · · · · · · · · · · · · · **MASTERING WORDS** · · · · · · · · · · · · · · · ·

STEP 6 — Practice Your Spelling List Independently
Choose at least three activities to practice your spelling list.

*Hunt words in your writing and reading! Add words you want to learn to **Words I Need to Know How to Spell**.*

Game Mats	With a Partner	On Your Own	At Home
○ Spelling Soccer ○ Spelling Checkers	○ Spelling Tic-Tac-Toe ○ Word Swap	○ Flip Folder ○ Spelling Study Strategy	○ Take Your List Home

Practice the Spelling Strategy

In the sentences below, each underlined word is another form of a **Strategy Word**. Write the related **Strategy Word** that fits each sentence.

Strategy Words

country
zero
scare
speak
rough
picnic
company
scar
gentle
reply

1. Our cat likes a __ touch, so please pat it <u>gently</u>. — **gentle**

2. Did Maryann __ before everyone else <u>replied</u>? — **reply**

3. At our class __ we <u>picnicked</u> on the grass. — **picnic**

4. This __ makes more toys than those two <u>companies</u>. — **company**

5. I'll __ after he has <u>spoken</u>. — **speak**

6. These stones are __, but those stones are even <u>rougher</u>. — **rough**

7. Is this __ bigger than some other <u>countries</u>? — **country**

8. My dog has one __ on his nose and two <u>scars</u> on his left ear. — **scar**

9. What does one __ plus two <u>zeroes</u> equal? — **zero**

10. You will __ everyone with that <u>scary</u> mask! — **scare**

DEVELOPING GOOD SPELLING HABITS

STEP 7 Focus on Writing

A. Proofread the Writing of Others

This activity provides proofreading practice in a variety of formats, including popular standardized test formats.

B. Proofread Your Own Writing

Students return to their own writing, armed with strategies to identify and collect words they need to know how to spell, and make an authentic link between spelling and writing.

C. A Writing Idea: A Cartoon

This suggestion for a more extended writing activity provides opportunities for students to write in different genres for a variety of purposes and modes.

STEP 8 Check Your Weekly Progress

▶ Take the Test

Remind students that they can take a practice test before the final test on their spelling lists. To find the testing procedure that is right for you, refer to page Z12.

▶ Check Your Goal

Have students compare their tests to their spelling lists. Did they spell all the **Strategy Words** on their spelling lists correctly?

▶ Graph Your Progress

Ask students to graph the number correct (student page 176 for softbound users; **Teacher Resource Book** page 123 for hardbound users).

▶ Save Missed Words

Tell students to write misspelled words on their lists of **Words I Need to Know How to Spell**. Remind students to verify spellings and to recycle these words on future weekly spelling lists.

· · · · DEVELOPING GOOD SPELLING HABITS · · · ·

STEP 7 Focus on Writing

A. Proofread the Writing of Others

Proofread the invitation. Choose the correct spelling for each underlined word. Write the correct spelling.

You are invited to a picnik¹. It will be this Saturday at

Brookside Park in the kountry². Come at 2:00.

We will play games, paddle a canoe, and eat. I promise

zerro³ ants! Please replie⁴ by Tuesday.

≡ Make a capital.
/ Make a small letter.
⌃ Add something.
⌇ Take out something.
⊙ Add a period.
¶ New paragraph
(sp) Spelling error

1. picknic   picnick   picnic
   picnic
   _____

2. countrey   contry   country
   country
   _____

3. zero   zeroe   zerow
   zero
   _____

4. rieply   reply   repply
   reply
   _____

B. Proofread Your Own Writing

Proofread your last piece of writing. Did you misspell any words that are different forms of other words? Use a dictionary to check related spellings.

C. A Writing Idea: A Cartoon

Draw a cartoon of two people at a picnic. Write the words they say to each other in speech balloons. When you are finished, role-play your cartoon with a spelling partner. Take turns reading each character's dialogue.

STEP 8 Check Your Weekly Progress

▶ **Take the Test**
Ready? Practice test first.

▶ **Check Your Goal**
Check to see if you met your learning goal.

▶ **Graph Your Progress**
Graph your score for this week's test.

▶ **Save Missed Words**
Write the words you missed in your list of **Words I Need to Know How to Spell**.

Hunt Words

Remind students to continuously hunt words that they wish to learn how to spell and to write these words in **Words I Need to Know How to Spell**.

Homographs

Student Edition: Pages 106–109   **Teacher Edition:** Pages T106A–T109

Materials to help students practice their spelling lists:
- **Flip Folders**
- Copies of **Flip Folder Practice Sheet** (**Teacher Resource Book**, pages 51)
- **Take Your List Home** (in *Spell It–Write!*

Home News, **Teacher Resource Book,** pages 95 in English and 96 in Spanish)
- Game Mats Featured in This Unit: **Meteor Attack, Spelling Checkers**

SPELLING GOALS

Students will

- understand the concept of stress, or accent, in pronunciation.
- transfer knowledge that homographs are spelled the same but have different pronunciations and meanings.
- explore the concept that language users invent new words as the need to convey new meanings arises.
- use the spelling process to become better writers.

WRITING GOALS

Students will

- proofread a writing sample.
- proofread a piece of their own writing for misspelled words that are homographs.
- write a persuasive paragraph.

Pacing	Notes	Quick Pick Management Option
Period 1 Finding Words (Steps 1–3)	If you wish to add **Teacher Words,** write them on the chalkboard. Sources for more words include: **More Words for Hungry Word Hunters** (page T106), content and theme-related words, or words of your choice.	Assign the list of **Pattern Words** to the whole class. Add the Red List (**More Words for Hungry Word Hunters,** student page 169) for a longer list. Add the Blue List (**More Words for Hungry Word Hunters**) for a more challenging list.
Period 2 Inspecting Words (Steps 4 and 5)	Students write the **Pattern Words** to complete **Explore the Spelling Pattern.**	Assign **Explore the Spelling Pattern** and **Focus on Word Study.**
Period 3 Mastering Words (Step 6) **Period 4** Developing Good Spelling Habits (Step 7)	These two periods can be allocated between selected **Mastering Words** activities and proofreading and writing activities in **Focus on Writing.**	Assign two or three activities to the whole class. Familiarize students with choosing their own activities at their own pace.
Period 5 Assessment (Step 8)	Gradually try different peer-testing options to find the style that best fits your class.	Test the class on the same, whole-class list.

Understanding Language Differences

Spanish Speakers

Spanish speakers may be challenged by English homographs ending in **se** (**use, close, refuse, excuse**) because the final sound may be pronounced \z\ or \s\, depending on the desired meaning. It will be helpful if students from Spanish-speaking backgrounds practice pronouncing these words and practice using each pronunciation in sentences. This can be done in peer groups or with a tape recorder.

Any students from non-English-speaking backgrounds will need special help learning the meanings and pronunciations for the homographs on this week's lists. It will be helpful to model the pronunciations and to use the words in sentences: "The **desert** is hot and dry." "You shouldn't **desert** a friend."

Helping Students Acquiring English

Model a simple homograph from the Red List, such as **bow** (bowing to students and then pantomiming the use of a bow and arrow) to be sure the concept is clear. Then create sentence strips that use each homograph in context. Use illustrations wherever possible. Have pairs of students work together to practice saying each sentence aloud with the correct pronunciation of the homograph.

Meeting Diverse Needs

Less Able Spellers

Students who have difficulty with spelling may benefit from activities that connect new knowledge with knowledge they already possess. For example, a word that the child already knows how to spell, such as **head,** can be used to introduce other, more difficult words, such as **thread, spread,** and **bread**.

Similarly, a familiar word, such as the child's name, can be used to introduce a tricky spelling pattern. For example, **<u>Kate</u>** will more readily remember how to spell a homograph such as **sep<u>arate</u>** when the relationship with her name is pointed out.

More Able Spellers

Encourage students to maintain a chart or an alphabetized card file of homographs, beginning with the **Pattern Words** from this unit and adding other words they come across in their reading. Entries should include both words in the homograph pair with, for each, a pronunciation example using capital letters to show stress (e.g., **DESert, deSERT**), the definition, and an example sentence. Students may also include illustrations when appropriate.

Ask students to copy their lists in the **Take Your List Home** section of the *Spell It–Write!* Home News page for this lesson. Not only does this page provide a convenient way for families to share a student's spelling list, but it also provides a number of opportunities for families to be involved in students' spelling growth. It has a statement of the week's spelling pattern or strategy, a valuable spelling study strategy, and a suggested home spelling practice activity.

Teacher Resource Book, page 95

Teacher Resource Book, page 96

MORE WORDS FOR HUNGRY WORD HUNTERS

RED LIST — Pattern Words Below Level	BLUE LIST — Pattern Words Above Level	Other Pattern Words	Science Pattern Word
bow	address	buffet	bass
close	associate	compact	
does	contest	conduct	
dove	entrance	console	
lead	estimate	contract	
live	primer	convert	
sow	progress	convict	
tear	project	extract	
use	rebel	invalid	
wind	subject	wound	

These lists also appear on page 169 in the student edition and page 27 in the **Teacher Resource Book.**

STEP 1 Build Your Spelling List

Students will build their spelling lists with **Pattern Words, Teacher Words,** and **Your Words.** Students should study a minimum of twelve new words each week.

Find Your Pattern Words

• Pretest the students on these words.

• Tell students to write each misspelled pretest word on their spelling lists.

Add Teacher Words

• Select words for students to add to their spelling lists. Choose words from **More Words for Hungry Word Hunters** (on this page and on student page 169), words related to a theme or content area, or words students often misspell.

Add Your Words

• Ask students to pick words from their lists of **Words I Need to Know How to Spell** and their writing.

• Tell students to write these words on their spelling lists.

STEP 2 Write Your Spelling List

Remind students to verify all spellings. (Ask students to see **Strategies for Checking Your Spelling** in the back of the student edition.)

STEP 3 Set Your Learning Goal

Tell students to count the words on their spelling lists. This total is their learning goal. It may vary depending on ability, individual goals, and the difficulty of spelling words.

SPELLING PATTERN

21

Homographs

Your Spelling List

STEP 1 Build Your Spelling List

Find Your Pattern Words
Take the pretest.
Write misspelled words on your spelling list.

Add Teacher Words
Teachers may add:
• More **Pattern Words** • Content Words • Theme Words

Add Your Words
Pick words from:
• **Words I Need to Know How to Spell** • Writing • Reading

Pattern Words

1. **desert** — It's hot in the **desert** during the day, but it can get cold at night.
2. **record** — Do you have a **record** of what you saw?
3. **present** — My puppy was a birthday **present**.
4. **produce** — I can **produce** proof that she is wrong.
5. **refuse** — I **refuse** to play down by the river.
6. **object** — Do not throw that **object** away.
7. **content** — The cat seems **content** in your lap.
8. **minute** — I will be there in one **minute**.
9. **excuse** — Please **excuse** me for being rude.
10. **separate** — **Separate** the cans from the bottles.

STEP 2 Write Your Spelling List

STEP 3 Set Your Learning Goal

My spelling list has _____ words for me to learn.

> I use a blank bookmark and write down words I want to spell as I read. Later, I put them in my **Words I Need to Know How to Spell**.

> It's easy to be a word hunter when you're writing, but how about when you're reading?

PATTERN MINI-LESSON

NOTE: The **Explore the Spelling Pattern** activity on page 107 is a self-directed mini-lesson. If you wish to supplement that activity with direct instruction, use the following mini-lesson.

* **Write** these two sentences on the chalkboard: "The desert is hot and dry." "Amanda will never desert her friends." Ask students to explain the two meanings of **desert**. Ask how the word is pronounced in each sentence. Explain that the stress—or accent—shifts (**DESert, deSERT**) and that the accented syllable is the one we say more strongly.

* **Ask** students to open their books to page 106. Divide the class in half. Ask one half to say the second word in the list of **Pattern Words** with the accent on the first syllable: **REcord**. Then ask the other half to pronounce the same word, accenting the second syllable: **reCORD**. Follow this procedure for each word except **excuse** and **separate**.

* **Ask** students to explain how the two pronunciations for **excuse** and **separate** differ. (Response: *In **excuse**, the s is pronounced either \s\ or \z\. In **separate**, the last **a** has a long vowel sound or a schwa sound.*) Remind students that the change in pronunciation signals a change in meaning.

* **Tell** students that words that are spelled the same but have different meanings and different pronunciations are called **homographs**.

* **Have** students read the **Spelling Pattern** on page 107 with you.

* **Encourage** students to hunt other homographs. Write these words on the chalkboard. Remind students that they may add any of these words to **Words I Need to Know How to Spell**.

· · · · · INSPECTING WORDS · · · · ·

 4 Explore the Spelling Pattern
Thinking About Sound and Meaning

A. Read the meanings below. Write the **Pattern Word** that has both meanings.

Column A	Column B	
1. to leave	very dry place	desert
2. to put on tape	information on a subject	record
3. to give	gift	present
4. to make	fruits and vegetables	produce
5. to say no	trash	refuse
6. to be against	goal	object
7. satisfied	thing or meaning inside something	content
8. sixty seconds	tiny	minute
9. to remove blame from	reason for failing to do something	excuse
10. to put in different places	apart	separate

B. Pronounce each **Pattern Word** in two different ways. Which meaning above does each pronunciation go with?

 5 Focus on Word Study
Invented Words

Word meanings can change as people need to talk about new things. A **record** originally meant something on paper. After the phonograph was invented, people used the word **record** in a different way. Today we listen to compact discs instead of records.

Sometimes people make up new words to talk about new inventions. Write an invented word to complete each sentence.

1. The ___zipper___ on my jacket is stuck.

2. Make the popcorn in the ___microwave___.

3. What's your favorite ___television___ show?

▼▼▼▼▼▼▼▼▼▼▼
Spelling Pattern
Words that are spelled the same but have different pronunciations and meanings are called **homographs**.
▪▪▪▪▪▪▪▪▪▪▪

---

 4 Explore the Spelling Pattern

Thinking About Sound and Meaning
This activity is a self-directed mini-lesson on this week's **Spelling Pattern**.

 5 Focus on Word Study

Invented Words
This activity is intended to stimulate students' interest in words and to help them become more enthusiastic word hunters.

Spelling Process Handbook
Students who need to review any part of the spelling process, including practice options, should refer to the **Spelling Process Handbook** (pages 7–21).

A Practice Option

Step 6 Practice Your Spelling List Independently

Ask the students to choose activities to practice their spelling words and to master this week's **Spelling Pattern**. Students should complete at least three activities each week. You may wish to:

- assign **Practice the Spelling Pattern** to all students to reinforce this week's **Spelling Pattern**.

- involve students' families by assigning **Take Your List Home** for this lesson (**Teacher Resource Book**, pages 95 in English and 96 in Spanish).

- encourage students to use partner activities without game mats (**Word Swap, Spelling Tic-Tac-Toe, Circle Dot**) and activities with game mats (**Meteor Attack, Rockets, Spelling Checkers, Spelling Soccer**). Directions for game-mat activities appear on each game mat. Directions for all other activities are found in the **Spelling Process Handbook** (pages 7–21).

NOTE: These activities and games can be used to practice any spelling list.

Generations of spelling scholars have researched the most productive way to study spelling words. The most consistently reliable method is the easy but effective **Spelling Study Strategy**. Once students master the basic steps of this look-say-cover-see-write-check-rewrite strategy, they can practice any spelling words independently, anywhere. (Directions appear in the **Spelling Process Handbook,** student pages 7–21. This activity is appropriate for practicing any spelling list.)

· · · · · · · · · · · · MASTERING WORDS · · · · · · · · · · · ·

Step 6 Practice Your Spelling List Independently

Choose at least three activities to practice your spelling list.

Need Help? Read the Spelling Process Handbook (pages 7–21).

Game Mats

 ○ Spelling Checkers
 ○ Meteor Attack

With a Partner

 ○ Circle Dot
 ○ Word Swap

On Your Own

 ○ Flip Folder
 ○ Spelling Study Strategy

At Home

 ○ Take Your List Home

Practice the Spelling Pattern

The same spelling can have two meanings. To complete each sentence, write the **Pattern Word** that fits in both places in the sentence. The first one is done as an example.

Pattern Words

desert
record
present
produce
refuse
object
content
minute
excuse
separate

1. I __ to live near a __ dump. — **refuse**
2. Gilda was __ with the story's __. — **content**
3. It'll take a __ to make the __ correction. — **minute**
4. I will __ the birthday __. — **present**
5. Mom will __ you if you give her an __. — **excuse**
6. I __ to this __ on my desk. — **object**
7. __ the paper from the plastic and put them into __ bins. — **Separate**
8. I helped __ a song for the __. — **record**
9. Did you __ your group in the __? — **desert**
10. The farmers __ delicious __. — **produce**

Now read each sentence to yourself. Listen to how you pronounced the **Pattern Word** two different ways in each sentence.

STEP 7 Focus on Writing

A. Proofread the Writing of Others

This activity provides proofreading practice in a variety of formats, including popular standardized test formats.

B. Proofread Your Own Writing

Students return to their own writing, armed with strategies to identify and collect words they need to know how to spell, and make an authentic link between spelling and writing.

C. A Writing Idea: A Paragraph

This suggestion for a more extended writing activity provides opportunities for students to write in different genres for a variety of purposes and modes.

STEP 8 Check Your Weekly Progress

▶ Take the Test

Remind students that they can take a practice test before the final test on their spelling lists. To find the testing procedure that is right for you, refer to page Z12.

▶ Check Your Goal

Have students compare their tests to their spelling lists. Did they spell all the **Pattern Words** on their spelling lists correctly?

▶ Graph Your Progress

Ask students to graph the number correct (student page 176 for softbound users; **Teacher Resource Book** page 123 for hardbound users).

▶ Save Missed Words

Tell students to write misspelled words on their lists of **Words I Need to Know How to Spell**. Remind students to verify spellings and to recycle these words on future weekly spelling lists.

DEVELOPING GOOD SPELLING HABITS

STEP 7 Focus on Writing

A. Proofread the Writing of Others

Proofread the paragraph about Dan's story. Decide whether each underlined word is misspelled or spelled correctly. If it is correct, write **c**. If it is misspelled, write **m** and the correct spelling.

> Dan wrote a story about his dream. He remembered that he and his family were in the <u>desert</u>.[1] Then suddenly he was alone and in a <u>seperate</u>[2] place. But he felt safe and <u>cantent</u>,[3] not lost and lonely. Although he could not <u>produse</u>[4] all the events of the dream, he was able to <u>record</u>[5] part of what happened. He even remembered some fairly <u>minoot</u>[6] details.

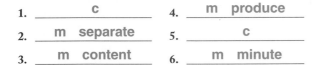

≡ Make a capital.
/ Make a small letter.
∧ Add something.
ℓ Take out something.
⊙ Add a period.
¶ New paragraph
(SP) Spelling error

1. ____c____
2. __m separate__
3. __m content__
4. __m produce__
5. ____c____
6. __m minute__

B. Proofread Your Own Writing

Words that are homographs don't sound alike, so it's easy to forget that they are spelled alike! Go to your most recent writing. Look for words that are homograph pairs. Check to see whether you used the same spelling for the different pronunciations and meanings.

C. A Writing Idea: A Paragraph

Is there ever an excuse for not recycling? Write a paragraph that tells why people should separate their refuse at all times. Or tell about times when people might be excused from recycling, and present your reasons.

PERSUASIVE

STEP 8 Check Your Weekly Progress

▶ **Take the Test**
Ready? Practice test first.

▶ **Check Your Goal**
Check to see if you met your learning goal.

▶ **Graph Your Progress**
Graph your score for this week's test.

▶ **Save Missed Words**
Write the words you missed in your list of **Words I Need to Know How to Spell**.

Hunt Words

Remind students to continuously hunt words that they wish to learn how to spell and to write these words in **Words I Need to Know How to Spell**.

SPELLING PATTERN 22

en, in, on, an Words

ENGAGING  **MATERIALS**

Student Edition: Pages 110–113   **Teacher Edition:** Pages T110A–T113

Materials to help students practice their spelling lists:

- **Flip Folders**
- Copies of **Flip Folder Practice Sheet** (**Teacher Resource Book,** page 51)
- **Take Your List Home** (in *Spell It–Write!* Home News, **Teacher Resource Book,** pages 97 in English and 98 in Spanish)

- **Game Mats Featured in This Unit: Meteor Attack, Rockets**
- Unit 22 **Hands-on Word Sort Cards** (Grade 4 **Hands-on Word Sort Card Book**) and Unit 22 **Hands-on Word Sort Sheet** (**Teacher Resource Book,** page 44)

ENGAGING **GOALS**

SPELLING GOALS

Students will

- transfer knowledge of unaccented **en, in, on,** and **an** to spell words that end with these syllables.

- sort words according to the spelling pattern of their last syllable.

- explore the concept that special sayings called "idioms" don't always mean exactly what the words say.

- use the spelling process to become better writers.

WRITING GOALS

Students will

- proofread a writing sample.

- proofread a piece of their own writing for misspelled words ending with **en, in, on,** and **an.**

- write an expressive story.

ENGAGING  **MANAGEMENT**

Pacing	Notes	Quick Pick Management Option
Period 1 Finding Words (Steps 1–3)	If you wish to add **Teacher Words,** write them on the chalkboard. Sources for more words include: **More Words for Hungry Word Hunters** (page T110), content and theme-related words, or words of your choice.	Assign the list of **Pattern Words** to the whole class. Add the Red List (**More Words for Hungry Word Hunters,** student page 169) for a longer list. Add the Blue List (**More Words for Hungry Word Hunters**) for a more challenging list.
Period 2 Inspecting Words (Steps 4 and 5)	Students write the **Pattern Words** to complete **Explore the Spelling Pattern.**	Assign **Explore the Spelling Pattern** and **Focus on Word Study.**
Period 3 Mastering Words (Step 6) **Period 4** Developing Good Spelling Habits (Step 7)	These two periods can be allocated between selected **Mastering Words** activities and proofreading and writing activities in **Focus on Writing.**	Assign two or three activities to the whole class. Familiarize students with choosing their own activities at their own pace.
Period 5 Assessment (Step 8)	Gradually try different peer-testing options to find the style that best fits your class.	Test the class on the same, whole-class list.

Understanding Language Differences

Spanish Speakers

Native Spanish speakers in your class may be able to take advantage of related Spanish words to spell a few words on this week's lists. In a few cases, the word that is difficult to spell in English is pronounced distinctly in Spanish, and the spelling is easy to figure out. Examples from the **Pattern Words** include **dozen** (Spanish form **docena**) and **organ** (Spanish form **órgano**). Examples from the Red List include **dragon** (Spanish form **dragón**) and **person** (Spanish form **persona**). Your awareness of these cognates, or similar forms, could help ease the spelling task for Spanish-speaking students.

Although the **t** in **often** (Red List) is usually silent in American English speech, some speakers choose to pronounce the **t** because it is present in the spelling. Although this is not the most common pronunciation, it may help spellers to include the \t\ sound as they say the word to themselves.

The combination of consonants in the middle of **pumpkin** (**mpk**) can be difficult for some speakers to pronounce. As a result, some American English speakers simplify the word to \pun-kin\. This simplification can cause spelling confusion. Model precise pronunciation and ask students to repeat it.

Helping Students Acquiring English

You may wish to use the **Hands-on Word Sort Cards** to present the **Pattern Words**. Alternatively, you may wish to write the words on the chalkboard and underline **en, in, on,** or **an** with colored chalk as you pronounce each word distinctly. Have students repeat the words after you. If you are using the **Hands-on Word Sort Cards,** place them along the chalk rail. Then name a word and call on a volunteer to choose the correct card, hold it up, and say the word.

Meeting Diverse Needs

Less Able Spellers

Students who have difficulty with spelling, including students with special needs, may not fully learn or retain all the spelling skills they are taught. It is a good idea to maintain a learning record for each child, noting whether particular spelling strategies, skills, or patterns are applied consistently, usually, or are developing. (**Strategy Assessment,** pages 120-121 in the *Spell It–Write!* **Teacher Resource Book,** may also be helpful.)

More Able Spellers

Encourage students who are strong spellers to locate words that have the final schwa-**n** sound but do not end in **en, in, on,** or **an,** such as **ocean.**

Ask students to copy their lists in the **Take Your List Home** section of the *Spell It–Write!* Home News page for this lesson. Not only does this page provide a convenient way for families to share a student's spelling list, but it also provides a number of opportunities for families to be involved in students' spelling growth. It has a statement of the week's spelling pattern or strategy, a valuable spelling study strategy, and a suggested home spelling practice activity.

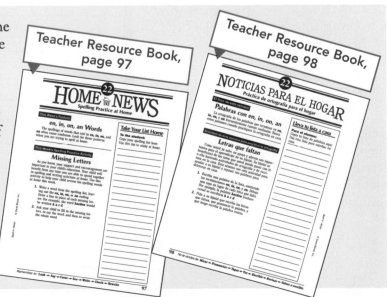

FINDING WORDS

STEP 1 Build Your Spelling List

Students will build their spelling lists with **Pattern Words, Teacher Words,** and **Your Words**. Students should study a minimum of twelve new words each week.

Find Your Pattern Words

• Pretest the students on these words.

• Tell students to write each misspelled pretest word on their spelling lists.

Add Teacher Words

• Select words for students to add to their spelling lists. Choose words from **More Words for Hungry Word Hunters** (on this page and on student page 169), words related to a theme or content area, or words students often misspell.

Add Your Words

• Ask students to pick words from their lists of **Words I Need to Know How to Spell** and their writing.

• Tell students to write these words on their spelling lists.

STEP 2 Write Your Spelling List

Remind students to verify all spellings. (Ask students to see **Strategies for Checking Your Spelling** in the back of the student edition.)

STEP 3 Set Your Learning Goal

Tell students to count the words on their spelling lists. This total is their learning goal. It may vary depending on ability, individual goals, and the difficulty of spelling words.

T110 UNIT 22

MORE WORDS FOR HUNGRY WORD HUNTERS

RED LIST Pattern Words Below Level	BLUE LIST Pattern Words Above Level	Other Pattern Words	Social Studies Pattern Word
cabin	citizen	American	swollen
dragon	common	cinnamon	
even	frozen	fasten	
given	gelatin	Indian	
kitten	linen	Mexican	
often	margin	onion	
person	oven	origin	
raisin	oxygen	prison	
robin	poison	satin	
seven	pollen	specimen	
taken	slogan		
wagon	violin		

These lists also appear on page 169 in the student edition and page 28 in the **Teacher Resource Book**.

FINDING WORDS

SPELLING PATTERN
22
en, in, on, an Words

Your Spelling List

STEP 1 Build Your Spelling List

Find Your Pattern Words
Take the pretest.
Write misspelled words on your spelling list.

Add Teacher Words
Teachers may add:
• More **Pattern Words** • Content Words • Theme Words

Add Your Words
Pick words from:
• **Words I Need to Know How to Spell** • Writing • Reading

Pattern Words

1. **chicken**	We will have **chicken** and rice tonight.
2. **pumpkin**	We picked the biggest **pumpkin**!
3. **cotton**	This shirt is made of **cotton**.
4. **organ**	My sister is learning to play the **organ**.
5. **harden**	We are waiting for the clay to **harden**.
6. **cousin**	I went to the fair with my **cousin**.
7. **sudden**	The car came to a **sudden** stop.
8. **wooden**	Use a **wooden** spoon to stir the soup.
9. **dozen**	Joy bought a **dozen** eggs at the market.
10. **basin**	Fill the **basin** with water.
11. **kitchen**	Good smells came from the **kitchen**.
12. **broken**	Luisa swept up the **broken** glass.

STEP 2 Write Your Spelling List

STEP 3 Set Your Learning Goal

My spelling list has _____ words for me to learn.

Which game mat is your favorite?

I was stuck on **Meteor Attack** for a while. But then I discovered **Rockets**.

110 UNIT 22

PATTERN MINI-LESSON

NOTE: The **Explore the Spelling Pattern** activity on page 111 is a self-directed mini-lesson. If you wish to supplement that activity with direct instruction, use the following mini-lesson.

* **Read** the **Spelling Pattern** on page 111. Explain that it will guide the **Hands-on Word Sort**.

* **Display** the **Hands-on Word Sort Cards** for Unit 22. Keep blank cards and a marker ready to make new cards.

* **Say** each guide word, pointing to the underlined letters. (Guide words are labeled "Master Word" on the **Word Sort Card**.)

* **Sort** the words according to the spelling of the schwa-n sound. Model your decision making: "The word **harden** ends with **e-n**, so I'll put **harden** under **chicken**." For the completed word sort, see the **Answer Card** for this unit in the **Hands-on Word Sort Card Book**.

* **Ask** for other examples for each category. Invite volunteers to print words on cards and add them to the **Hands-on Word Sort**. Underline the spelling pattern in the final syllable. You may wish to include examples from **More Words for Hungry Word Hunters** (on student page 169 and page T110).

* **Ask** how the finished **Hands-on Word Sort** relates to the **Spelling Pattern**. Leave the **Hands-on Word Sort** in place until the end of the period. Remind students that they may add any of these words to **Words I Need to Know How to Spell**.

* **Duplicate** the **Hands-on Word Sort Sheet** for Unit 22 (**Teacher Resource Book,** page 44). Ask students to cut the words on the sheet apart and practice sorting the words with a partner or independently.

· · · · INSPECTING WORDS · · · ·

Step 4 Explore the Spelling Pattern
Sorting Words

A. Find a spelling partner. Take turns reading the **Pattern Words** out loud. Sort the **Pattern Words** into four groups. Use the words below to guide your sort. Make sure you write each **Pattern Word** once.

You may wish to use **Hands-on Word Sort Cards** and the **Hands-on Word Sort Sheet** for this unit.

1. chicken	2. pumpkin	3. cotton
chicken	pumpkin	cotton
harden	cousin	
sudden	basin	
wooden		**4. organ**
dozen		organ
kitchen		
broken		

B. Ask a family member to join you in a word hunt at home. Find telephone messages or shopping lists. Are the words that end in **an, en, in,** and **on** spelled correctly? If you find a word with a spelling error, spell it correctly or find out how to spell it. Sort the words you find.

▼▼▼▼▼▼▼▼▼▼▼▼

Spelling Pattern
The spelling of words that end in **en, in, on,** and **an** is often confused.
· · · · · · · · · · · ·

Step 5 Focus on Word Study
Idioms

Like other languages, English has expressions called idioms. Idioms are special sayings that don't mean what the actual words say. For example, people who say, "You're chicken!" aren't calling you a barnyard bird. They're saying you're afraid to do something.

Choose a word to complete each idiom.

1. If you can't take the heat, get out of the (kitchen, pumpkin). ___ kitchen
2. Don't take any (sudden, wooden) nickels. ___ wooden
3. My cooking can't hold a (candle, metal) to Tom's. ___ candle

---

Step 4 Explore the Spelling Pattern
Sorting Words

This activity is a self-directed mini-lesson on this week's **Spelling Pattern**.

Step 5 Focus on Word Study
Idioms

This activity is intended to stimulate students' interest in words and to help them become more enthusiastic word hunters.

> **Spelling Process Handbook**
>
> Students who need to review any part of the spelling process, including practice options, should refer to the **Spelling Process Handbook** (pages 7–21).

MASTERING WORDS

Practice Your Spelling List Independently

STEP 6

Ask the students to choose activities to practice their spelling words and to master this week's **Spelling Pattern**. Students should complete at least three activities each week. You may wish to:

- assign **Practice the Spelling Pattern** to all students to reinforce this week's **Spelling Pattern**.

- involve students' families by assigning **Take Your List Home** for this lesson (**Teacher Resource Book,** pages 97 in English and 98 in Spanish).

- encourage students to use partner activities without game mats (**Word Swap, Spelling Tic-Tac-Toe, Circle Dot**) and activities with game mats (**Meteor Attack, Rockets, Spelling Checkers, Spelling Soccer**). Directions for game-mat activities appear on each game mat. Directions for all other activities are found in the **Spelling Process Handbook** (pages 7–21).

NOTE: These activities and games can be used to practice any spelling list.

CIRCLE DOT

Circles and dots become powerful learning tools in this simple, effective activity. Each student works with a partner to attempt —and then correct—the spelling of each word on his or her list. As the student corrects, he or she marks a dot for each correct letter and a circle for each error. Because **Circle Dot** makes discrete errors visible, students can practice their spelling words strategically by focusing on the part(s) of the spelling that most challenges them. (Directions appear in the **Spelling Process Handbook,** student pages 7–21. This activity is appropriate for practicing any spelling list.)

MASTERING WORDS

STEP 6 Practice Your Spelling List Independently

Choose at least three activities to practice your spelling list.

You can practice any spelling list with these activities.

Game Mats	With a Partner	On Your Own	At Home

- ○ Meteor Attack
- ○ Rockets
- ○ Circle Dot
- ○ Spelling Tic-Tac-Toe
- ○ Flip Folder
- ○ Spelling Study Strategy
- ○ Take Your List Home

✏️ Practice the Spelling Pattern

Write the **Pattern Word** that fits each clue. Then circle **en, in, on,** or **an** in each word you wrote.

Pattern Words

chicken
pumpkin
cotton
organ
harden
cousin
sudden
wooden
dozen
basin
kitchen
broken

1. **Clue:** place to prepare food
   kitch**en**

2. **Clue:** a family member
   cous**in**

3. **Clue:** barnyard animal
   chick**en**

4. **Clue:** musical instrument
   org**an**

5. **Clue:** container for liquid
   bas**in**

6. **Clue:** in need of repair
   brok**en**

7. **Clue:** to become hard
   hard**en**

8. **Clue:** quick and unexpected
   sudd**en**

9. **Clue:** twelve of anything
   doz**en**

10. **Clue:** made of wood
    wood**en**

11. **Clue:** a kind of cloth
    cott**on**

12. **Clue:** large, round, orange fruit
    pump**kin**

7 Focus on Writing

A. Proofread the Writing of Others
This activity provides proofreading practice in a variety of formats, including popular standardized test formats.

B. Proofread Your Own Writing
Students return to their own writing, armed with strategies to identify and collect words they need to know how to spell, and make an authentic link between spelling and writing.

C. A Writing Idea: A Story
This suggestion for a more extended writing activity provides opportunities for students to write in different genres for a variety of purposes and modes.

8 Check Your Weekly Progress

▶ Take the Test
Remind students that they can take a practice test before the final test on their spelling lists. To find the testing procedure that is right for you, refer to page Z12.

▶ Check Your Goal
Have students compare their tests to their spelling lists. Did they spell all the **Pattern Words** on their spelling lists correctly?

▶ Graph Your Progress
Ask students to graph the number correct (student page 176 for softbound users; **Teacher Resource Book** page 123 for hardbound users).

▶ Save Missed Words
Tell students to write misspelled words on their lists of **Words I Need to Know How to Spell**. Remind students to verify spellings and to recycle these words on future weekly spelling lists.

· · · · · · · DEVELOPING GOOD SPELLING HABITS · · · · · · ·

7 Focus on Writing

A. Proofread the Writing of Others
Proofread the paragraph. Decide which type of mistake, if any, appears in each underlined part.

> As a hobby, my cousin Jessica carves wood. Her
>
> wooden pumpken is great! Last year Jessica sold a dozen
>   ①   ②
>
> of these carvings at Thanksgiving time. People also like
>
> the chickon she carves. We put some of her wood
>   ③
>
> carvings on our kitchin walls.
>   ④

Proofreading marks:
- ≡ Make a capital.
- / Make a small letter.
- ∧ Add something.
- ⊙ Take out something.
- ⊙ Add a period.
- ¶ New paragraph
- (SP) Spelling error

1. Ⓐ Spelling
   B Capitalization
   C Punctuation
   D No mistake

2. A Spelling
   B Capitalization
   C Punctuation
   Ⓓ No mistake

3. Ⓐ Spelling
   B Capitalization
   C Punctuation
   D No mistake

4. Ⓐ Spelling
   B Capitalization
   C Punctuation
   D No mistake

B. Proofread Your Own Writing
Look at your latest writing. Did you spell **an, en, in,** and **on** words correctly? If you find misspelled words, add them to **Words I Need to Know How to Spell**.

C. A Writing Idea: A Story
Develop a story map or plan for a tale. Come up with an idea or brainstorm ideas based on these titles: "Stolen Pumpkin," "The Broken Basin," or "A Dozen Cousins." Use your map to write the story.

8 Check Your Weekly Progress

▶ Take the Test
Ready? Practice test first.

▶ Check Your Goal
Check to see if you met your learning goal.

▶ Graph Your Progress
Graph your score for this week's test.

▶ Save Missed Words
Write the words you missed in your list of **Words I Need to Know How to Spell.**

Hunt Words
Remind students to continuously hunt words that they wish to learn how to spell and to write these words in **Words I Need to Know How to Spell.**

ENGAGING IN THE PROCESS

MATERIALS

Student Edition: Pages 114–117   **Teacher Edition:** Pages T114A–T117

Materials to help students practice their spelling lists:
- **Flip Folders**
- Copies of **Flip Folder Practice Sheet** (**Teacher Resource Book,** page 51)
- **Take Your List Home** (in *Spell It–Write!*

Home News, **Teacher Resource Book,** pages 99 in English and 100 in Spanish)
- Game Mats Featured in This Unit: **Rockets, Spelling Soccer**

ENGAGING IN THE PROCESS

GOALS

SPELLING GOALS

Students will

- recognize that words ending in the suffixes -**er** and -**or** often mean "one who (does something)."

- sort words according to the suffixes -**er** and -**or**.

- explore the concept that words can have multiple meanings.

- use the spelling process of finding words, inspecting words, and mastering words as they develop good spelling habits to become better writers.

WRITING GOALS

Students will

- hunt for words with the suffixes -**er** and -**or** in pieces of their own writing.

- write an informative paragraph.

ENGAGING IN THE PROCESS

MANAGEMENT

Pacing	Notes	Quick Pick Management Option
Period 1 Finding Words (Steps 1–3)	If you wish to add **Teacher Words,** write them on the chalkboard. Sources for more words include: **More Words for Hungry Word Hunters** (page T114), content and theme-related words, or words of your choice.	Assign the list of **Pattern Words** to the whole class. Add the Red List (**More Words for Hungry Word Hunters,** student page 170) for a longer list. Add the Blue List (**More Words for Hungry Word Hunters**) for a more challenging list.
Period 2 Inspecting Words (Steps 4 and 5)	Students write the **Pattern Words** to complete **Explore the Spelling Pattern.**	Assign **Explore the Spelling Pattern** and **Focus on Word Study.**
Period 3 Mastering Words (Step 6) **Period 4** Developing Good Spelling Habits (Step 7)	These two periods can be allocated between selected **Mastering Words** activities and proofreading and writing activities in **Focus on Writing.**	Assign two or three activities to the whole class. Familiarize students with choosing their own activities at their own pace.
Period 5 Assessment (Step 8)	Gradually try different peer-testing options to find the style that best fits your class.	Test the class on the same, whole-class list.

Understanding Language Differences

Spanish Speakers

The Spanish equivalent for the **-er** suffix is **-or**. Because English has both **-er** and **-or** forms, native Spanish speakers could guess wrong about English spellings, especially for words in which the **-er** suffix is used. English and Spanish equivalents for some of the words on this week's lists are **worker** (**trabajador**), **player** (**jugador**), **reader** (**lector**), and **driver** (**conductor**) from the Red List, as well as the word **writer** (**escritor**). Your sensitivity to this particular need of Spanish-speaking students will help as they learn the intricacies of English spelling.

Helping Students Acquiring English

Write the **Pattern Word** base words horizontally across the chalkboard. Beneath each base word, draw a stick figure and label it with the appropriate **Pattern Word,** writing the **-er** or **-or** suffix in colored chalk. Lead students to chorally repeat, for example, "Speak. This is a speaker," as you point to the words and the figures. Then have students work in pairs to make up sentences using the base word and the **-er** or **-or** form of the **Pattern Word** (e.g., "I write. I am a writer.").

Meeting Diverse Needs

Less Able Spellers

Sometimes students with spelling difficulties are asked to write correctly five (or even ten) times the words they misspelled in their writing. We would encourage you not to initiate such a practice with your students. Children often see this as a punishment and, as a result, may develop negative attitudes about spelling and their spelling capabilities. They may also avoid using words in their writing that they are not certain how to spell, thus reducing the richness of vocabulary in their writing.

More Able Spellers

Ask students who are strong spellers to select one of their spelling words. Then challenge them to develop as many new words as they can by adding prefixes and suffixes to the spelling word. Ask them to explain how the meaning (and spelling) of the original word changed with the addition of each prefix and suffix.

Ask students to copy their lists in the **Take Your List Home** section of the *Spell It–Write!* Home News page for this lesson. Not only does this page provide a convenient way for families to share a student's spelling list, but it also provides a number of opportunities for families to be involved in students' spelling growth. It has a statement of the week's spelling pattern or strategy, a valuable spelling study strategy, and a suggested home spelling practice activity.

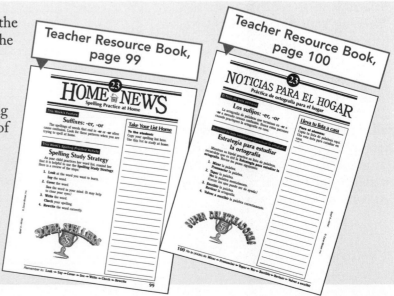

Teacher Resource Book, page 99

Teacher Resource Book, page 100

FINDING WORDS

STEP 1 Build Your Spelling List

Students will build their spelling lists with **Pattern Words, Teacher Words,** and **Your Words.** Students should study a minimum of twelve new words each week.

Find Your Pattern Words

• Pretest the students on these words.

• Tell students to write each misspelled pretest word on their spelling lists.

Add Teacher Words

• Select words for students to add to their spelling lists. Choose words from **More Words for Hungry Word Hunters** (on this page and on student page 170), words related to a theme or content area, or words students often misspell.

Add Your Words

• Ask students to pick words from their lists of **Words I Need to Know How to Spell** and their writing.

• Tell students to write these words on their spelling lists.

STEP 2 Write Your Spelling List

Remind students to verify all spellings. (Ask students to see **Strategies for Checking Your Spelling** in the back of the student edition.)

STEP 3 Set Your Learning Goal

Tell students to count the words on their spelling lists. This total is their learning goal. It may vary depending on ability, individual goals, and the difficulty of spelling words.

MORE WORDS FOR HUNGRY WORD HUNTERS

RED LIST — Pattern Words Below Level	BLUE LIST — Pattern Words Above Level	Other Pattern Words	Social Studies Pattern Words
actor	director	creditor	explorer
driver	drummer	dancer	prospector
farmer	gardener	dreamer	reaper
leader	governor	hiker	trawler
player	juggler	instructor	
reader	pitcher	jeweler	
rider	professor	jogger	
sailor	settler	operator	
teacher	traveler	senator	
worker	treasurer	skater	

These lists also appear on page 170 in the student edition and page 29 in the **Teacher Resource Book.**

························ FINDING WORDS ························

SPELLING PATTERN

23

**Suffixes:
-er, -or**

Your Spelling List

_____
_____
_____
_____
_____
_____
_____
_____
_____
_____
_____
_____
_____
_____
_____
_____
_____
_____
_____
_____

STEP 1 Build Your Spelling List

Find Your Pattern Words
Take the pretest.
Write misspelled words on your spelling list.

Add Teacher Words
Teachers may add:
• More **Pattern Words** • Content Words • Theme Words

Add Your Words
Pick words from:
• **Words I Need to Know How to Spell** • Writing • Reading

Pattern Words

1. **speaker** — Dr. Barr will be the **speaker** tonight.
2. **visitor** — We had a **visitor** in our school today.
3. **listener** — It's important to be a good **listener**.
4. **owner** — My uncle is the **owner** of that car.
5. **writer** — I want to be a **writer** when I grow up.
6. **editor** — The **editor** changed the news story.
7. **stranger** — Never get into a car with a **stranger**.
8. **inventor** — Benjamin Franklin was an **inventor**.
9. **officer** — A police **officer** spoke to our class.
10. **ruler** — Who is the **ruler** of that country?

STEP 2 Write Your Spelling List

STEP 3 Set Your Learning Goal

My spelling list has _____ words for me to learn.

It's easy for me to practice test with a friend.

The **Spelling Process Handbook** has good directions on practice testing.

INSPECTING WORDS

PATTERN MINI-LESSON

NOTE: The **Explore the Spelling Pattern** activity on page 115 is a self-directed mini-lesson. If you wish to supplement that activity with direct instruction, use the following mini-lesson.

* **Write** the **Pattern Words** from page 114 on the chalkboard. Say each word aloud and ask students to repeat it.

* **Ask** students to study the words on the chalkboard and offer observations about the endings of these words. (Response: *All the words end with* -er *or* -or.)

* **Ask** students to identify the base word in each word on the chalkboard. Circle the base words as students identify them. Tell the students that the suffix changes the meaning of each base word. The word changes to mean "one who." For example, a speaker is one who speaks.

* **Call on** volunteers to define each word by completing the phrase "one who . . . ."

* **Ask** students what is similar about these base words: **write, strange, office, rule**. (Response: *Each word ends in* **silent e**.) Explain that when these words are changed to mean "one who . . . " they always end in **-er**, never **-or**. Ask what happens when **-er** is added to these words. (Response: *The final* **e** *is dropped before the suffix is added*.)

* **Read** the **Spelling Pattern** on page 115 with students.

* **Write** the headings **-er** and **-or** on the chalkboard. Encourage students to provide other words that mean "one who . . . ," and list their suggestions under the appropriate heading. Remind students that they may add any of these words to **Words I Need to Know How to Spell**.

Explore the Spelling Pattern
Sorting Words

A. Word sorts help you to inspect words. Sort the **Pattern Words** into two groups. Use each word's ending and the words below to guide your sort. Make sure to write each **Pattern Word** once.

1. speaker	2. visitor
speaker	visitor
listener	editor
owner	inventor
writer	
stranger	
officer	
ruler	

B. Work with a partner to find other words that end in **-er** or **-or**. Think them up and look in your writing and in **Words I Need to Know How to Spell**. Sort the words you find.

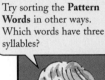

Try sorting the **Pattern Words** in other ways. Which words have three syllables?

▼ ▼ ▼ ▼ ▼ ▼ ▼ ▼ ▼ ▼ ▼ ▼ ▼ ▼
Spelling Pattern
The spelling of words that end in **-er** or **-or** is often confused.
▪ ▪ ▪ ▪ ▪ ▪ ▪ ▪ ▪ ▪ ▪ ▪ ▪ ▪

Focus on Word Study
Multiple Meanings

Some words have many different meanings, depending on how they are used. A **ruler** can be either the leader of a country or a stick that measures 12 inches.

Write **change, tie,** or **check** to complete each pair of sentences.

1. The race ended in a __.
   We bought Dad a new __.   tie

2. Do you have __ for a dollar?
   I'll __ my clothes now.   change

3. Our __ totaled $12.79.
   Did you __ for misspelled words? check

Explore the Spelling Pattern

Sorting Words

This activity is a self-directed mini-lesson on this week's **Spelling Pattern**.

Focus on Word Study

Multiple Meanings

This activity is intended to stimulate students' interest in words and to help them become more enthusiastic word hunters.

Spelling Process Handbook

Students who need to review any part of the spelling process, including practice options, should refer to the **Spelling Process Handbook** (pages 7–21).

MASTERING WORDS

Practice Your Spelling List Independently
STEP 6

Ask the students to choose activities to practice their spelling words and to master this week's **Spelling Pattern**. Students should complete at least three activities each week. You may wish to:

- assign **Practice the Spelling Pattern** to all students to reinforce this week's **Spelling Pattern**.

- involve students' families by assigning **Take Your List Home** for this lesson (**Teacher Resource Book, pages 99 in English and 100 in Spanish**).

- encourage students to use partner activities without game mats (**Word Swap, Spelling Tic-Tac-Toe, Circle Dot**) and activities with game mats (**Meteor Attack, Rockets, Spelling Checkers, Spelling Soccer**). Directions for game-mat activities appear on each game mat. Directions for all other activities are found in the **Spelling Process Handbook** (pages 7–21).

NOTE: These activities and games can be used to practice any spelling list.

SPELLING SOCCER

Partners or teams can practice their spelling words as they compete in **Spelling Soccer**. Modeled after the game that is gaining popularity in the United States for both boys and girls, **Spelling Soccer** takes spelling practice to the soccer field. It'll be "hands off" poor spelling scores after students, especially auditory and visual learners, discover **Spelling Soccer**. (Directions appear on the **Spelling Soccer** game mat. This activity is appropriate for practicing any spelling list.)

MASTERING WORDS

Practice Your Spelling List Independently
STEP 6

Choose at least three activities to practice your spelling list.

Copy your words carefully when you take your list home.

Game Mats		With a Partner		On Your Own		At Home
Rockets	Spelling Soccer	Spelling Tic-Tac-Toe	Word Swap	Flip Folder	Spelling Study Strategy	Take Your List Home

Practice the Spelling Pattern

Decide whether to add **-er** or **-or** to each word below to make a word that names a person. Then write the new word and circle the **-er** or **-or** ending. Use the **Pattern Words** to check your spelling.

Pattern Words

speaker
visitor
listener
owner
writer
editor
stranger
inventor
officer
ruler

1. speak + __ = __   speak**er**
2. strange + __ = __   strang**er**
3. visit + __ = __   visit**or**
4. listen + __ = __   listen**er**
5. rule + __ = __   rul**er**
6. edit + __ = __   edit**or**
7. write + __ = __   writ**er**
8. own + __ = __   own**er**
9. office + __ = __   offic**er**
10. invent + __ = __   invent**or**

DEVELOPING GOOD SPELLING HABITS

 **Focus on** Writing

A. Hunt Spelling Words in Your Writing

This activity equips students with a specific strategy for increasing students' consciousness of targeted spelling patterns and strategies in their own writing. It also enables them to collect words for spelling study.

B. A Writing Idea: A Comparison

This suggestion for a more extended writing activity provides opportunities for students to write in different genres for a variety of purposes and modes.

STEP 8 Check Your Weekly Progress

▶ **Take the Test**

Remind students that they can take a practice test before the final test on their spelling lists. To find the testing procedure that is right for you, refer to page Z12.

▶ **Check Your Goal**

Have students compare their tests to their spelling lists. Did they spell all the **Pattern Words** on their spelling lists correctly?

▶ **Graph Your Progress**

Ask students to graph the number correct (student page 176 for softbound users; **Teacher Resource Book** page 123 for hardbound users).

▶ **Save Missed Words**

Tell students to write misspelled words on their lists of **Words I Need to Know How to Spell**. Remind students to verify spellings and to recycle these words on future weekly spelling lists.

· · · · · · DEVELOPING GOOD SPELLING HABITS · · · · · ·

STEP 7 Focus on Writing

A. Hunt Spelling Words in Your Writing

With a spelling partner, look back at pieces of your latest writing. Hunt for all the words that end in **-er** or **-or**. Use two columns like these to write the words you find.

Column 1	Column 2
I spelled these -er and -or words correctly.	I misspelled these -er and -or words.
Answers will vary.	**Answers will vary.**

If you didn't find any **-er** or **-or** words, check another piece of writing.

Add the words you wrote in Column 2 to your **Words I Need to Know How to Spell**.

B. A Writing Idea: A Comparison

Write a paragraph comparing and contrasting two careers or jobs. For example, you might compare the working hours and tasks of an author with those of a baker. As you proofread your paragraph, check to be sure you spelled all the words correctly.

≡ Make a capital.
／ Make a small letter.
∧ Add something.
ℓ Take out something.
⊙ Add a period.
¶ New paragraph
(SP) Spelling error

STEP 8 Check Your Weekly Progress

▶ **Take the Test**
Ready? Practice test first.

▶ **Check Your Goal**
Check to see if you met your learning goal.

▶ **Graph Your Progress**
Graph your score for this week's test.

▶ **Save Missed Words**
Write the words you missed in your list of **Words I Need to Know How to Spell**.

Hunt Words

Remind students to continuously hunt words that they wish to learn how to spell and to write these words in **Words I Need to Know How to Spell**.

Student Edition: Pages 118–121   **Teacher Edition:** Pages T118A–T121

Materials to help students practice their spelling lists:

- **Flip Folders**
- Copies of **Flip Folder Practice Sheet** (**Teacher Resource Book,** page 51)
- **Take Your List Home** (in *Spell It–Write!*

Home News, **Teacher Resource Book,** pages 101 in English and 102 in Spanish)
- Game Mats Featured in This Unit: **Spelling Checkers, Spelling Soccer**

SPELLING GOALS

Students will

- transfer knowledge that the schwa-**r** sound may be spelled **er, ir,** and **ur** to spell words with **r**-controlled **e, i,** and **u.**

- sort words according to the spelling of the schwa-**r** sound.

- develop an understanding of how a common root word can evolve over time into an entire word family of related words.

- use the spelling process to become better writers.

WRITING GOALS

Students will

- proofread a writing sample.

- proofread a piece of their own writing for misspelled words with **r**-controlled vowels **e, i,** and **u.**

- write an informative list.

Pacing	Notes	Quick Pick Management Option
Period 1 Finding Words (Steps 1–3)	If you wish to add **Teacher Words,** write them on the chalkboard. Sources for more words include: **More Words for Hungry Word Hunters** (page T118), content and theme-related words, or words of your choice.	Assign the list of **Pattern Words** to the whole class. Add the Red List (**More Words for Hungry Word Hunters,** student page 170) for a longer list. Add the Blue List (**More Words for Hungry Word Hunters**) for a more challenging list.
Period 2 Inspecting Words (Steps 4 and 5)	Students write the **Pattern Words** to complete **Explore the Spelling Pattern.**	Assign **Explore the Spelling Pattern** and **Focus on Word Study.**
Period 3 Mastering Words (Step 6) **Period 4** Developing Good Spelling Habits (Step 7)	These two periods can be allocated between selected **Mastering Words** activities and proofreading and writing activities in **Focus on Writing.**	Assign two or three activities to the whole class. Familiarize students with choosing their own activities at their own pace.
Period 5 Assessment (Step 8)	Gradually try different peer-testing options to find the style that best fits your class.	Test the class on the same, whole-class list.

Understanding Language Differences

Some speakers of American English along the southern and eastern coasts of the United States leave out \r\ after a vowel in spoken language. For example, **herd** is pronounced \hud\, **germs** is pronounced \jumz\, and so on. For some speakers, **burn** and **bun** sound the same or similar, as do **turn** and **ton**. It is important for students who omit \r\ in these words to be aware of its inclusion in the written forms.

Helping Students Acquiring English

Write the words **clerk, shirt,** and **turtle** on the chalkboard, using a different color of chalk for the spellings **er, ir,** and **ur**. Introduce the meanings of the **Pattern Words** in appropriate ways, using pictures and gestures. Then invite volunteers to come up and add one **Pattern Word** at a time (using colored chalk for **er, ir,** and **ur**) to the correct column until all the words are on the chalkboard.

Meeting Diverse Needs

Less Able Spellers

Students who have difficulty learning to spell, including students with special needs, may benefit from techniques that make the association between a sound and its corresponding letter pattern more memorable. For example, tell students that the "r-r-r" sound a growling dog makes is often spelled **er** as in **cl<u>er</u>k, ir** as in **sh<u>ir</u>t,** or **ur** as in **t<u>ur</u>tle**.

More Able Spellers

Ask stronger spellers to select one word from their weekly spelling list and locate as many synonyms and antonyms for that word as they can. Ask them to examine the word pairs for similarities in spelling. If students have used prefixes or suffixes to generate their synonyms and antonyms, encourage them to discuss the meaning of each prefix and use the prefixes to generate other words.

Ask students to copy their lists in the **Take Your List Home** section of the *Spell It–Write!* Home News page for this lesson. Not only does this page provide a convenient way for families to share a student's spelling list, but it also provides a number of opportunities for families to be involved in students' spelling growth. It has a statement of the week's spelling pattern or strategy, a valuable spelling study strategy, and a suggested home spelling practice activity.

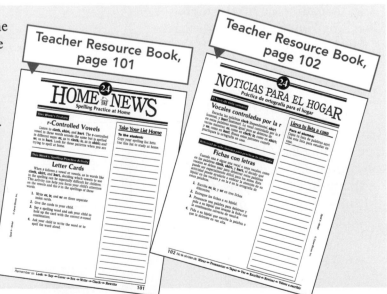

Teacher Resource Book, page 101

Teacher Resource Book, page 102

FINDING WORDS

STEP 1 Build Your Spelling List

Students will build their spelling lists with **Pattern Words, Teacher Words,** and **Your Words.** Students should study a minimum of twelve new words each week.

Find Your Pattern Words

- Pretest the students on these words.
- Tell students to write each misspelled pretest word on their spelling lists.

Add Teacher Words

- Select words for students to add to their spelling lists. Choose words from **More Words for Hungry Word Hunters** (on this page and on student page 170), words related to a theme or content area, or words students often misspell.

Add Your Words

- Ask students to pick words from their lists of **Words I Need to Know How to Spell** and their writing.
- Tell students to write these words on their spelling lists.

STEP 2 Write Your Spelling List

Remind students to verify all spellings. (Ask students to see **Strategies for Checking Your Spelling** in the back of the student edition.)

STEP 3 Set Your Learning Goal

Tell students to count the words on their spelling lists. This total is their learning goal. It may vary depending on ability, individual goals, and the difficulty of spelling words.

MORE WORDS FOR HUNGRY WORD HUNTERS

RED LIST Pattern Words Below Level	BLUE LIST Pattern Words Above Level	Other Pattern Words	Science Pattern Words
bird	burglar	alert	circuit
birthday	current	burnt	exert
burn	curve	disturb	
dirt	dirty	external	**Social Studies Pattern Words**
fur	further	fern	cursive
germs	service	internal	govern
herd	stern	murmur	jury
perch	terms	squirm	permafrost
third	thirst	squirrel	
turn	twirl	turkey	

These lists also appear on page 170 in the student edition and page 30 in the **Teacher Resource Book.**

· · · · · FINDING WORDS · · · · · · ·

SPELLING PATTERN

24

r-Controlled Vowels

Your Spelling List

_____
_____
_____
_____
_____
_____
_____
_____
_____
_____
_____
_____
_____
_____
_____
_____
_____
_____

STEP 1 Build Your Spelling List

Find Your Pattern Words

Take the pretest.
Write misspelled words on your spelling list.

Add Teacher Words

Teachers may add:
- More **Pattern Words** • Content Words • Theme Words

Add Your Words

Pick words from:
- **Words I Need to Know How to Spell** • Writing • Reading

Pattern Words

1. **clerk**	I gave five dollars to the **clerk**.
2. **shirt**	My new cotton **shirt** has blue stripes.
3. **hurt**	Did the cat **hurt** the mouse?
4. **serve**	I will **serve** the apple pie later.
5. **turtle**	I found a green **turtle** down by the river.
6. **circus**	The **circus** is coming to town.
7. **term**	The president serves a four-year **term**.
8. **firm**	This tomato is too **firm**.
9. **return**	I must **return** this book to Anna.
10. **burst**	The bubble **burst** on the grass.

STEP 2 Write Your Spelling List

STEP 3 Set Your Learning Goal

My spelling list has _____ words for me to learn.

I really think I'm improving as a speller this year.

I *know* I'm getting better because I graph my progress every week.

INSPECTING WORDS

PATTERN MINI-LESSON

NOTE: ▶ The **Explore the Spelling Pattern** activity on page 119 is a self-directed mini-lesson. If you wish to supplement that activity with direct instruction, use the following mini-lesson.

* Write the **Pattern Words** from page 118 on the chalkboard. Invite volunteers to read the words aloud.

* Ask students what sound they hear in every word. (Response: \er\) Ask students to identify the letters that spell those sounds. (Response: *er, ir, ur*) Underline the appropriate letters in each word on the chalkboard. You may wish to compare the spellings for \er\ in this unit with the spellings for \er\ in Unit 23.

* Explain that **er, ir,** and **ur** are three possible spellings of \er\.

* Ask a volunteer to read aloud the **Spelling Pattern** on page 119.

* Write er, ir, and **ur** as headings on the chalkboard. Encourage students to suggest other words that contain \er\, and write their suggestions under the appropriate heading. If students suggest words in which \er\ is spelled in other ways, write these words in a separate column as exceptions. Such spellings might include **or** (word, work), **ear** (learn, early), and **ar** (sugar, dollar).

* Point out that the **ar** spelling occurs only in unaccented syllables. You may wish to include examples from **More Words for Hungry Word Hunters** (on student page 170 and page T118). Remind students that they may add any of these words to **Words I Need to Know How to Spell.**

· · · · · · · · · INSPECTING WORDS · · · · · · · · ·

STEP 4 Explore the Spelling Pattern
Sorting Words

A. One way to inspect words is by sorting them. Sort the **Pattern Words** into three groups. Use the underlined spelling patterns in the words below to guide your sort. Make sure you write each **Pattern Word** once.

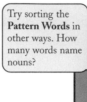

Try sorting the **Pattern Words** *in other ways. How many words name nouns?*

1. clerk	2. shirt	3. hurt
clerk	shirt	hurt
serve	circus	turtle
term	firm	return
		burst

B. Look in your reading, in your writing, and in **Words I Need to Know How to Spell** to find other words with **er, ir,** or **ur.** Sort the words you find by spelling pattern.

STEP 5 Focus on Word Study
Word History

The word **circus** has been spelled the same way since ancient times. Long ago it meant "circle" or "ring." In fact, the ancient city of Rome had a huge ring called the Circus Maximus. It was the site of exciting horse races.

Write the word in each pair that probably shares some of its meaning and spelling history with **circus.**

1. circle, cook   circle
2. circular, cream   circular
3. crane, circumference   circumference

▼▼▼▼▼▼▼▼▼▼▼▼
Spelling Pattern
Listen to **clerk, shirt,** and **hurt.** The **r**-controlled vowel in these words sounds the same but is spelled in different ways: **er,** as in **clerk; ir,** as in **shirt;** and **ur,** as in **hurt.**
· · · · · · · · · · · ·

STEP 4 Explore the Spelling Pattern
Sorting Words

This activity is a self-directed mini-lesson on this week's **Spelling Pattern.**

STEP 5 Focus on Word Study
Word History

This activity is intended to stimulate students' interest in words and to help them become more enthusiastic word hunters.

Spelling Process Handbook

Students who need to review any part of the spelling process, including practice options, should refer to the **Spelling Process Handbook** (pages 7–21).

MASTERING WORDS

A Practice Option

Practice Your Spelling List Independently
STEP 6

Ask the students to choose activities to practice their spelling words and to master this week's **Spelling Pattern**. Students should complete at least three activities each week. You may wish to:

- assign **Practice the Spelling Pattern** to all students to reinforce this week's **Spelling Pattern**.

- involve students' families by assigning **Take Your List Home** for this lesson (**Teacher Resource Book,** pages 101 in English and 102 in Spanish).

- encourage students to use partner activities without game mats (**Word Swap, Spelling Tic-Tac-Toe, Circle Dot**) and activities with game mats (**Meteor Attack, Rockets, Spelling Checkers, Spelling Soccer**). Directions for game-mat activities appear on each game mat. Directions for all other activities are found in the **Spelling Process Handbook** (pages 7–21).

NOTE: These activities and games can be used to practice any spelling list.

WORD SWAP

Word Swap is an extremely simple but effective partner spelling study strategy. Students simply swap spelling lists and quiz each other. (This activity is also an effective way to introduce students to key aspects of peer testing.) And as in all partnered practice activities, students reap the benefits of exposure to two spelling lists—their own and their partner's. It's a painless spelling bonus! (Directions appear in the **Spelling Process Handbook,** student pages 7–21. This activity is appropriate for practicing any spelling list.)

· · · · · · · · · · · MASTERING WORDS · · · · · · · · · · ·

STEP 6 Practice Your Spelling List Independently
Choose at least three activities to practice your spelling list.

It's fun to try different practice activities.

Game Mats		With a Partner		On Your Own		At Home
○ Spelling Soccer	○ Spelling Checkers	○ Circle Dot	○ Word Swap	○ Flip Folder	○ Spelling Study Strategy	○ Take Your List Home

Practice the Spelling Pattern

In each set of words below, decide which words are misspelled and which word is spelled correctly. Write the correctly spelled word. Use the **Pattern Words** to check your spelling.

Pattern Words

clerk
shirt
hurt
serve
turtle
circus
term
firm
return
burst

1. ferm	firm	furm		firm
2. serve	sirve	surve		serve
3. berst	birst	burst		burst
4. clerk	clirk	clurk		clerk
5. cercus	circus	curcus		circus
6. hert	hirt	hurt		hurt
7. tertle	tirtle	turtle		turtle
8. term	tirm	turm		term
9. shert	shirt	shurt		shirt
10. retern	retirn	return		return

DEVELOPING GOOD SPELLING HABITS

STEP 7 Focus on Writing

A. Proofread the Writing of Others

This activity provides proofreading practice in a variety of formats, including popular standardized test formats.

B. Proofread Your Own Writing

Students return to their own writing, armed with strategies to identify and collect words they need to know how to spell, and make an authentic link between spelling and writing.

C. A Writing Idea: A List

This suggestion for a more extended writing activity provides opportunities for students to write in different genres for a variety of purposes and modes.

STEP 8 Check Your Weekly Progress

▶ Take the Test

Remind students that they can take a practice test before the final test on their spelling lists. To find the testing procedure that is right for you, refer to page Z12.

▶ Check Your Goal

Have students compare their tests to their spelling lists. Did they spell all the **Pattern Words** on their spelling lists correctly?

▶ Graph Your Progress

Ask students to graph the number correct (student page 176 for softbound users; **Teacher Resource Book** page 123 for hardbound users).

▶ Save Missed Words

Tell students to write misspelled words on their lists of **Words I Need to Know How to Spell**. Remind students to verify spellings and to recycle these words on future weekly spelling lists.

DEVELOPING GOOD SPELLING HABITS

STEP 7 Focus on Writing

A. Proofread the Writing of Others

Read the want ads below. Find the six misspelled words. Write the correct spelling of each one.

Wanted: Clirk to work 8–5 in shert stockroom.

Wanted: Cercus seeks animal trainer for performing tertle and seal.

Wanted: Small law furm looking for short-tirm help.

≡ Make a capital.
/ Make a small letter.
∧ Add something.
_ Take out something.
⊙ Add a period.
¶ New paragraph
(SP) Spelling error

1. _____Clerk_____
2. _____shirt_____
3. _____Circus_____
4. _____turtle_____
5. _____firm_____
6. _____term_____

B. Proofread Your Own Writing

Look for some of the words from this lesson in your own writing. Also look for other words with the **r**-controlled spelling pattern, as in **shirt, hurt,** and **term.** Did you spell the words correctly? Did you find words to add to **Words I Need to Know How to Spell**?

C. A Writing Idea: A List

Suppose you were at home with someone who got hurt or became sick, and no one else was there to help. What would you do? Write a list of three or more steps you could take on your own. Include at least one emergency phone number you would call. Combine your list with your classmates' lists to create a bulletin board titled ER (Emergency Rules).

STEP 8 Check Your Weekly Progress

▶ Take the Test
Ready? Practice test first.

▶ Check Your Goal
Check to see if you met your learning goal.

▶ Graph Your Progress
Graph your score for this week's test.

▶ Save Missed Words
Write the words you missed in your list of **Words I Need to Know How to Spell.**

Hunt Words

Remind students to continuously hunt words that they wish to learn how to spell and to write these words in **Words I Need to Know How to Spell**.

> **NOTE:** **Check Your Progress** is not a spelling unit, but some teachers prefer to spend a week on these activities.
>
> **Day One:** Administer **Review Test**.
>
> **Day Two:** Check **Review Test**. Use **Spelling Pattern Mastery Chart** to find each student's mastery level.
>
> **Day Three:** Reteach as needed.
>
> **Day Four:** Complete **Check Your Writing**.
>
> **Day Five:** Complete **Check Your Strategies**.

Check Your Spelling

1. Administer the **Review Test** to all students. Dictation sentences appear on page T123. (The words in italics are also from the previous eight units.) Administer the words **in the order** in which they are presented here.

2. Ask students to check their tests as you spell each word and/or write the correct spelling on the board.

3. Ask students to circle the number of each correctly spelled word.

4. Review the categories on the **Spelling Pattern Mastery Chart** (page 122). As you review each pattern, ask students to find the corresponding items on their tests. Based on the number of words correct for each pattern, ask the students to determine their level of mastery for that pattern.

Reteaching Strategies

• Reteach the **Pattern Mini-Lesson** on the patterns students have not mastered.

• Ask students to record the words they missed in **Words I Need to Know How to Spell** for recycling into future spelling lists.

• Record the patterns students have not mastered. Include words with these patterns on future spelling lists.

T122 Check Your Progress

Check Your Writing

1. Consider teaching the **Proofreading Strategy Mini-Lesson** (page T123).

2. Ask students to choose several pieces of their writing.

3. Ask students to work with a partner to proofread their writing and hunt words with each spelling pattern. They should record misspelled words in **Words I Need to Know How to Spell**.

Check Your Strategies

1. Read each question aloud. Remind the students that they should think about their use of each strategy in the past eight weeks and answer "Yes," "No," or "Sometimes."

2. Use these questions as the focus of a student-teacher conference. You may also wish to use **Strategy Assessment** (pages 120 and 121 in the **Teacher Resource Book**).

Check Your

✓ Check Your Spelling

Here is a fun way to review your progress on spelling patterns. First, take the review test your teacher will give you. Then, check your test.

Review Test

1. pianos
2. turtle
3. inventor
4. separate
5. potatoes
6. listener
7. return
8. painless
9. minute
10. women
11. circus
12. dozen
13. health
14. officer
15. kitchen
16. really
17. cousin
18. depth
19. cleanse
20. desert

Spelling Pattern Mastery Chart

Which words did you spell correctly? Use this chart to find your mastery level for each spelling pattern.

Pattern	All Correct	Most Correct	None Correct
Unusual Plurals 1 5 10			
Patterns That Show Meaning 13 18 19			
-ful, -less, -ly, -ment, -ness 8 16			
Homographs 4 9 20			
en, in, on, an Words 12 15 17			
Suffixes: -er, -or 3 6 14			
r-Controlled Vowels 2 7 11			

All Correct: Pattern Mastered
Most Correct: Pattern Partly Mastered
None Correct: Keep Working on the Pattern

PROOFREADING STRATEGY MINI-LESSON

* **Write** the title **Box It In** on the chalkboard.

* **Explain** that students can use a strategy called **Box It In** to proofread their writing. They will work with a partner to surround each word with fingers or pieces of paper, check the spelling, and then move on to the next word.

* **Tell** students that proofreading in this way will help them concentrate on the spelling accuracy of each word.

* **Demonstrate** the strategy by asking a volunteer to work with you at the chalkboard. Place your hands or pieces of paper around the word "Box," and then do the same for each word as your partner reads, "Box-It-In."

* **Tell** students that they should circle any word if they are unsure of its spelling. After they verify the spelling, they should write the correct spelling above the misspelled word.

* **Remind** students that they may refer to **Strategies for Checking Your Spelling** in the back of the student edition.

Progress

Choose three recent samples of your writing. Use a grid that looks like this. Work with a partner to check your writing for words that match each pattern.

✓ Check Your Writing

Spelling Pattern Writing Chart	Column 1 I spelled these Pattern Words correctly.	Column 2 I misspelled these Pattern Words.
Unusual Plurals		
Patterns That Show Meaning		
-ful, -less, -ly, -ment, -ness		
Homographs		
en, in, on, an Words		
Suffixes: -er, -or		
r-Controlled Vowels		

Write the words in Column 2 in your **Words I Need to Know How to Spell**.

✓ Check Your Strategies

Self-regulation

Ask yourself each of these questions. Do you answer "Yes," "No," or "Sometimes" to each question?

• Do I add words from **Words I Need to Know How to Spell** to my spelling list each week?

• Is the number of words I add right for me?

• When I practice my words, do I choose activities that help me learn my words?

• Do I take self-tests and practice tests to see if I know my words?

Dictation Sentences

1. **pianos** – The *company* accepted the *shipment* of two **pianos**.
2. **turtle** – The **turtle** *crept slowly* across the *rough* ground.
3. **inventor** – The **inventor** made a machine that would *produce cotton* material.
4. **separate** – The *owner* will **separate** the *chicken* from the *geese*.
5. **potatoes** – Mama will *serve peeled* **potatoes** and *tomatoes*.
6. **listener** – The **listener** *wept* with *enjoyment* of the story.
7. **return** – **Return** the *oxen* when you have *dealt* with the field.
8. **painless** – During her *illness*, the *woman* looked for **painless** treatment.
9. **minute** – The ants found the **minute** scraps left from our *picnic* in the *country*.
10. **women** – The **women** are making a *cheerful* quilt and a new *shirt* to *present* to the *visitor*.
11. **circus** – The *stranger leapt* at the chance to join the **circus**.
12. **dozen** – We have *swept* a **dozen** *wooden* floors.
13. **health** – It would not *hurt* your **health** to wash your hands in this *basin*.
14. **officer** – The **officer** did not *excuse* the *clerk* for breaking the law.
15. **kitchen** – We *meant* to clean the *pumpkin* in the **kitchen**.
16. **really** – Do you **really** think the *ox* has *broken* the door?
17. **cousin** – My **cousin** played the *organ* last *term* in school.
18. **depth** – The light couldn't cut the **depth** of the *sudden darkness*.
19. **cleanse** – Don't *refuse* to **cleanse** the *painful* cut or it will leave a *scar*.
20. **desert** – The *writer* told of **desert** flowers that *burst* into bloom after storms.

SPELLING PATTERN 25

Words Ending With al, il, le

ENGAGING IN THE PROCESS — MATERIALS

Student Edition: Pages 124–127 **Teacher Edition:** Pages T124A–T127

Materials to help students practice their spelling lists:

- **Flip Folders**
- Copies of **Flip Folder Practice Sheet** (**Teacher Resource Book,** page 51)
- **Take Your List Home** (in *Spell It–Write!*

Home News, **Teacher Resource Book,** pages 103 in English and 104 in Spanish)
- Game Mats Featured in This Unit: **Meteor Attack, Spelling Checkers**

ENGAGING IN THE PROCESS — GOALS

SPELLING GOALS

Students will

- transfer knowledge of the spelling patterns **-al, -il,** and **-le** to spell words with these patterns.

- sort words according to the spelling patterns **-al, -il,** and **-le**.

- explore the concept that "word cousins" are words that share a common root, yet have developed different meanings and spellings over time.

- use the spelling process to become better writers.

WRITING GOALS

Students will

- hunt for words ending with **-al, -il,** and **-le** in a piece of their own writing.

- write an informative letter.

ENGAGING IN THE PROCESS — MANAGEMENT

Pacing	Notes	Quick Pick Management Option
Period 1 Finding Words (Steps 1–3)	If you wish to add **Teacher Words,** write them on the chalkboard. Sources for more words include: **More Words for Hungry Word Hunters** (page T124), content and theme-related words, or words of your choice.	Assign the list of **Pattern Words** to the whole class. Add the Red List (**More Words for Hungry Word Hunters,** student page 171) for a longer list. Add the Blue List (**More Words for Hungry Word Hunters**) for a more challenging list.
Period 2 Inspecting Words (Steps 4 and 5)	Students write the **Pattern Words** to complete **Explore the Spelling Pattern.**	Assign **Explore the Spelling Pattern** and **Focus on Word Study.**
Period 3 Mastering Words (Step 6) **Period 4** Developing Good Spelling Habits (Step 7)	These two periods can be allocated between selected **Mastering Words** activities and proofreading and writing activities in **Focus on Writing.**	Assign two or three activities to the whole class. Familiarize students with choosing their own activities at their own pace.
Period 5 Assessment (Step 8)	Gradually try different peer-testing options to find the style that best fits your class.	Test the class on the same, whole-class list.

Understanding Language Differences

Spanish Speakers

The words **animal** (Red List), **metal, simple,** and **hospital** are spelled the same in Spanish as in English. Spanish speakers will also find Spanish words similar to English as they spell **candle** (**candela**) and **April** (**abril**).

Many students who are learning English as a second language may be able to make use of their first language to spell certain words on this week's lists. For example, French speakers will recognize similarities between these English words and their French equivalents: **uncle** (**oncle**), **circle** (**cercle**), **metal** (**métal**), **hospital** (**hôpital**), **April** (**avril**), **example** (**exemple**). Some words, including **animal, total,** and **simple,** are spelled the same in English and French.

Helping Students Acquiring English

Write each **Pattern Word** on a separate card, using a different color for the **-al, -il,** and **-le** spellings. Display one card at a time. Pronounce the word and use appropriate means to convey the word's meaning. Read the word again, and ask students to repeat it after you. Have students spell the word with you. Provide students with letter tiles, and let them construct and break apart each **Pattern Word** several times.

Meeting Diverse Needs

Less Able Spellers

Students who have difficulty learning to spell, including students with special needs, may benefit from correction activities that provide immediate feedback and focus attention on the part of the word that was misspelled.

First ask the child to check the spelling of the misspelled word and circle the misspelled part in red. Encourage the child to study the difference between the misspelled word and the correct spelling. Ask the child to practice spelling the word correctly and to circle the part of the word that was misspelled originally.

The practice activity **Circle Dot** is another concrete way to draw students' attention to the parts of words they have misspelled. **Circle Dot** is described in the **Spelling Process Handbook** (pages 7–21).

More Able Spellers

Encourage students who are strong spellers to locate words that rhyme with words ending in **al, il,** or **le** but in which the final sound is not spelled in one of these ways, e.g., **beautiful**. Students may wish to find out about the history of these "spelling violators" as a way to explain the variation in spelling.

Ask students to copy their lists in the **Take Your List Home** section of the *Spell It–Write!* Home News page for this lesson. Not only does this page provide a convenient way for families to share a student's spelling list, but it also provides a number of opportunities for families to be involved in students' spelling growth. It has a statement of the week's spelling pattern or strategy, a valuable spelling study strategy, and a suggested home spelling practice activity.

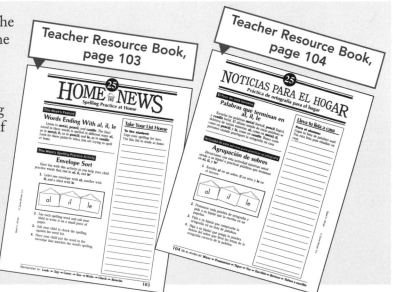

FINDING WORDS

STEP 1 Build Your Spelling List

Students will build their spelling lists with **Pattern Words, Teacher Words,** and **Your Words**. Students should study a minimum of twelve new words each week.

Find Your Pattern Words
• Pretest the students on these words.

• Tell students to write each misspelled pretest word on their spelling lists.

Add Teacher Words
• Select words for students to add to their spelling lists. Choose words from **More Words for Hungry Word Hunters** (on this page and on student page 171), words related to a theme or content area, or words students often misspell.

Add Your Words
• Ask students to pick words from their lists of **Words I Need to Know How to Spell** and their writing.

• Tell students to write these words on their spelling lists.

STEP 2 Write Your Spelling List

Remind students to verify all spellings. (Ask students to see **Strategies for Checking Your Spelling** in the back of the student edition.)

STEP 3 Set Your Learning Goal

Tell students to count the words on their spelling lists. This total is their learning goal. It may vary depending on ability, individual goals, and the difficulty of spelling words.

T124 UNIT 25

MORE WORDS FOR HUNGRY WORD HUNTERS

RED LIST
Pattern Words Below Level

animal
castle
circle
uncle

BLUE LIST
Pattern Words Above Level

ample
council
final
freckle
general
marble
possible
pupil
scramble
several

Other Pattern Words

ankle
evil
festival
loyal
normal
peril
rural
sparkle
stencil
wrinkle

Math Pattern Words

equal   ordinal
numeral

Science Pattern Words

fossil   pistil
petal   wobble

Social Studies Pattern Words

chuckle   local
civil   natural
coastal

These lists also appear on page 171 in the student edition and page 31 in the **Teacher Resource Book**.

SPELLING PATTERN

25 UNIT

Words Ending With al, il, le

Your Spelling List

_____
_____
_____
_____
_____
_____
_____
_____
_____
_____
_____
_____
_____
_____
_____
_____
_____
_____
_____
_____

· · · · · · · · FINDING WORDS · · · · · · · ·

STEP 1 Build Your Spelling List

Find Your Pattern Words
Take the pretest.
Write misspelled words on your spelling list.

Add Teacher Words
Teachers may add:
• More **Pattern Words** • Content Words • Theme Words

Add Your Words
Pick words from:
• **Words I Need to Know How to Spell** • Writing • Reading

Pattern Words

1.	metal	**Metal** can melt if it gets hot enough.
2.	pencil	I can't find my **pencil** anywhere.
3.	candle	The light of a **candle** is not bright.
4.	total	What was the **total** of the bill?
5.	simple	The math problem was **simple**.
6.	example	You can be a good **example** for others.
7.	hospital	I visited my friend in the **hospital**.
8.	single	There isn't a **single** apple left.
9.	April	My dog Duke was born in **April**.
10.	handle	Turn the **handle** to open the door.

STEP 2 Write Your Spelling List

STEP 3 Set Your Learning Goal

My spelling list has _____ words for me to learn.

> I'm really aware of the words I need for writing, so I always have *more* than three words to add every week.

> Our teacher asks us to add at least three words from our own writing to our spelling lists each week.

PATTERN MINI-LESSON

NOTE: The **Explore the Spelling Pattern** activity on page 125 is a self-directed mini-lesson. If you wish to supplement that activity with direct instruction, use the following mini-lesson.

* **Write** the **Pattern Words** from page 124 on the chalkboard. Call on volunteers to pronounce each word. Ask students to identify the three pairs of letters that end these words.

* **Write** these headings on the chalkboard: **-al, -il, -le**. Ask students to identify the words in the list that should be placed under each heading.

* **Lead** a discussion on ways students can remember which spelling—**al, il,** or **le**—should be used in each word. (Possible responses: *Look the word up in a dictionary; try to picture the word; practice spelling the word often; memorize the correct spelling.*)

* **Ask** students to read the **Spelling Pattern** on page 125 with you.

* **Encourage** students to provide other examples of words that end with the schwa-l sound. (Possible responses: **dental, sandal, signal, spiral, gerbil, stencil, utensil, ankle, dimple, jingle, pickle, turtle, whistle**) List these words on the chalkboard under the appropriate heading. You may wish to include examples from **More Words for Hungry Word Hunters** (on student page 171 and page T124). Remind students that they may add any of these words to **Words I Need to Know How to Spell**.

······· INSPECTING WORDS ·······

 Explore the Spelling Pattern
Sorting Words

A. Sort the **Pattern Words** into three groups. Use the words below to guide your sort. Make sure you write each **Pattern Word** once.

Try sorting the **Pattern Words** in other ways. How many words begin with a vowel?

1. met<u>al</u>	2. penc<u>il</u>	3. cand<u>le</u>
metal	pencil	candle
total	April	simple
hospital		example
		single
		handle

B. You can sort the **Pattern Words** by the number of syllables in each word. Write the **Pattern Words** that have three syllables.

example	hospital

C. Look in your writing and in **Words I Need to Know How to Spell** to find other words that end with **al, il,** or **le**. Add the words you find to the word sort.

5 Focus on Word Study
Word Cousins

What do **hospital** and **hotel** have in common? They're "word cousins" that come from the same "parent word." Word cousins share the same root but have developed different meanings and spellings over time.

Write the word cousins **clock–cloak, poodle–puddle,** or **salami–salad** to complete each sentence.

1. The black __ sat in the muddy __ .
2. Do you want a __ sandwich or a spinach __ ?
3. As the __ struck ten, he put on his silk __ .

poodle	puddle
salami	salad
clock	cloak

▼▼▼▼▼▼▼▼▼▼▼▼

Spelling Pattern

Listen to **metal, pencil,** and **candle**. The final sound in these words is spelled in different ways: **al,** as in **metal; il,** as in **pencil;** and **le,** as in **candle**.

■ ■ ■ ■ ■ ■ ■ ■ ■ ■ ■

 Explore the Spelling Pattern

Sorting Words

This activity is a self-directed mini-lesson on this week's **Spelling Pattern**.

 Focus on Word Study

Word Cousins

This activity is intended to stimulate students' interest in words and to help them become more enthusiastic word hunters.

Spelling Process Handbook

Students who need to review any part of the spelling process, including practice options, should refer to the **Spelling Process Handbook** (pages 7–21).

MASTERING WORDS

A Practice Option

Practice Your Spelling List Independently

STEP 6

Ask the students to choose activities to practice their spelling words and to master this week's **Spelling Pattern**. Students should complete at least three activities each week. You may wish to:

- assign **Practice the Spelling Pattern** to all students to reinforce this week's **Spelling Pattern**.

- involve students' families by assigning **Take Your List Home** for this lesson (**Teacher Resource Book**, pages 103 in English and 104 in Spanish).

- encourage students to use partner activities without game mats (**Word Swap, Spelling Tic-Tac-Toe, Circle Dot**) and activities with game mats (**Meteor Attack, Rockets, Spelling Checkers, Spelling Soccer**). Directions for game-mat activities appear on each game mat. Directions for all other activities are found in the **Spelling Process Handbook** (pages 7–21).

NOTE: These activities and games can be used to practice any spelling list.

SPELLING TIC-TAC-TOE

Just about anyone knows how to play tic-tac-toe. And now this strategic game of **X**'s and **O**'s teams up with spelling words to make spelling practice fun! Partners can practice spelling words with **Spelling Tic-Tac-Toe** on any scrap of paper. And because partners spell words aloud and visually check errors against correct spellings, **Spelling Tic-Tac-Toe** appeals to both visual and auditory learners. (Directions appear in the **Spelling Process Handbook**, student pages 7–21. This activity is appropriate for practicing any spelling list.)

· · · · · · · MASTERING WORDS · · · · · · ·

STEP 6 Practice Your Spelling List Independently
Choose at least three activities to practice your spelling list.

*Hunt words in your writing and reading! Add words you want to learn to **Words I Need to Know How to Spell**.*

Game Mats

○ Spelling Checkers   ○ Meteor Attack

With a Partner

○ Circle Dot   ○ Spelling Tic-Tac-Toe

On Your Own

○ Flip Folder   ○ Spelling Study Strategy

At Home

○ Take Your List Home

 Practice the Spelling Pattern

The words below have lost their ending letters. Rewrite the whole word. Circle the letters that were missing. Use the **Pattern Words** to check your spelling.

Pattern Words

metal
pencil
candle
total
simple
example
hospital
single
April
handle

1. simp __   simp(le)
2. Apr __   Apr(il)
3. tot __   tot(al)
4. examp __   examp(le)
5. sing __   sing(le)
6. met __   met(al)
7. penc __   penc(il)
8. hand __   hand(le)
9. hospit __   hospit(al)
10. cand __   cand(le)

DEVELOPING GOOD SPELLING HABITS

STEP 7 — Focus on Writing

A. Hunt Spelling Words in Your Writing

This activity equips students with a specific strategy for increasing students' consciousness of targeted spelling patterns and strategies in their own writing. It also enables them to collect words for spelling study.

B. A Writing Idea: A Friendly Letter

This suggestion for a more extended writing activity provides opportunities for students to write in different genres for a variety of purposes and modes.

STEP 8 — Check Your Weekly Progress

▶ Take the Test

Remind students that they can take a practice test before the final test on their spelling lists. To find the testing procedure that is right for you, refer to page Z12.

▶ Check Your Goal

Have students compare their tests to their spelling lists. Did they spell all the **Pattern Words** on their spelling lists correctly?

▶ Graph Your Progress

Ask students to graph the number correct (student page 176 for softbound users; **Teacher Resource Book** page 123 for hardbound users).

▶ Save Missed Words

Tell students to write misspelled words on their lists of **Words I Need to Know How to Spell**. Remind students to verify spellings and to recycle these words on future weekly spelling lists.

• • • • • DEVELOPING GOOD SPELLING HABITS • • • • •

STEP 7 — Focus on Writing

A. Hunt Spelling Words in Your Writing

Choose some of your most recent writing. Work with a spelling partner to look for words that end with **al, il,** or **le**. Use two columns like these to record the words you find.

Column 1	Column 2
I spelled these **al, il,** and **le** words correctly.	I misspelled these **al, il,** and **le** words.
Answers will vary.	Answers will vary.
_____	_____
_____	_____
_____	_____
_____	_____
_____	_____
_____	_____

If you can't find any **al, il,** or **le** words, choose a different piece of writing.

Add the words you wrote in Column 2 to **Words I Need to Know How to Spell**.

B. A Writing Idea: A Friendly Letter

Write a letter to a friend. Invite your friend to join you on a camping trip next April. Remind your friend to pack lightweight, simple, and useful items, and give a few examples of what your friend should bring along. Proofread your letter to be sure you've spelled all the words correctly.

≡ Make a capital.
／ Make a small letter.
∧ Add something.
℆ Take out something.
⊙ Add a period.
¶ New paragraph
(SP) Spelling error

STEP 8 — Check Your Weekly Progress

▶ Take the Test
Ready? Practice test first.

▶ Check Your Goal
Check to see if you met your learning goal.

▶ Graph Your Progress
Graph your score for this week's test.

▶ Save Missed Words
Write the words you missed in your list of **Words I Need to Know How to Spell**.

Hunt Words

Remind students to continuously hunt words that they wish to learn how to spell and to write these words in **Words I Need to Know How to Spell**.

More Words Ending With le

ENGAGING *IN THE* **PROCESS**

MATERIALS

Student Edition: Pages 128–131   **Teacher Edition:** Pages T128A–T131

Materials to help students practice their spelling lists:

- **Flip Folders**
- Copies of **Flip Folder Practice Sheet** (**Teacher Resource Book,** page 51)
- **Take Your List Home** (in *Spell It–Write!* Home News, **Teacher Resource Book,** pages 105 in English and 106 in Spanish)

- Game Mats Featured in This Unit: **Meteor Attack, Rockets**
- Unit 26 **Hands-on Word Sort Cards** (Grade 4 **Hands-on Word Sort Card Book**) and Unit 26 **Hands-on Word Sort Sheet** (**Teacher Resource Book,** page 45)

ENGAGING *IN THE* **PROCESS**

GOALS

SPELLING GOALS

Students will

- transfer knowledge of the short vowel-consonant-consonant-**le** and long vowel-consonant-**le** spelling patterns to spell words with these patterns.
- sort words according to their spelling patterns.
- understand that some words have similar, yet not identical, meanings.
- use the spelling process to become better writers.

WRITING GOALS

Students will

- proofread a writing sample.
- proofread a piece of their own writing for misspelled words ending with **le**.
- write an expressive poem.

ENGAGING *IN THE* **PROCESS**

MANAGEMENT

Pacing	Notes	Quick Pick Management Option
Period 1 Finding Words (Steps 1–3)	If you wish to add **Teacher Words,** write them on the chalkboard. Sources for more words include: **More Words for Hungry Word Hunters** (page T128), content and theme-related words, or words of your choice.	Assign the list of **Pattern Words** to the whole class. Add the Red List (**More Words for Hungry Word Hunters,** student page 171) for a longer list. Add the Blue List (**More Words for Hungry Word Hunters**) for a more challenging list.
Period 2 Inspecting Words (Steps 4 and 5)	Students write the **Pattern Words** to complete **Explore the Spelling Pattern.**	Assign **Explore the Spelling Pattern** and **Focus on Word Study.**
Period 3 Mastering Words (Step 6) **Period 4** Developing Good Spelling Habits (Step 7)	These two periods can be allocated between selected **Mastering Words** activities and proofreading and writing activities in **Focus on Writing.**	Assign two or three activities to the whole class. Familiarize students with choosing their own activities at their own pace.
Period 5 Assessment (Step 8)	Gradually try different peer-testing options to find the style that best fits your class.	Test the class on the same, whole-class list.

Understanding Language Differences

Spanish Speakers

Native Spanish speakers may be misled by the **e** in the **-le** ending and may attempt to pronounce this syllable so that it sounds like **lay**. For example, **saddle, bubble,** and **battle** might be pronounced **sad-lay**\, **bub-lay**\, and **bat-lay**\. The reason is that in Spanish, the letter **e** stands for the English **long a,** as in **play**. Make sure your students are pronouncing these words correctly.

Helping Students Acquiring English

Write the **Pattern Words** on the chalkboard. To help students recall the spelling patterns in this unit, teach them little chants. For example:

Short vowel, double "tt"
bat/tle-ket/tle
Long vowel, single "t"
ti/tle-bee/tle

Replace the **t**'s with other appropriate letters and create new chants for words like **saddle, bubble,** and **middle.** Then have pairs of students use the **Hands-on Word Sort Cards** as flash cards to reinforce the **Pattern Words**.

Meeting Diverse Needs

Less Able Spellers

Students with special needs are more likely than their peers to attribute their classroom successes and failures to luck or innate ability rather than effort or hard work.

When students do well on an end-of-the-week spelling test, ask them to identify the study procedures they used to get ready for this test. Emphasize how these techniques and their hard work helped them do well on the test.

You may also wish to ask students to keep a process log in which they maintain a record of the study techniques they implement each week. Periodically ask them to share with their peers the study technique that was most useful for them.

More Able Spellers

Challenge students who are strong spellers to locate five to ten words that they do not know the spelling and/or meaning of and to add these words to their weekly spelling lists. Students should also be asked to find the meanings they do not know and to use each word in an appropriate way orally.

Ask students to copy their lists in the **Take Your List Home** section of the *Spell It–Write!* Home News page for this lesson. Not only does this page provide a convenient way for families to share a student's spelling list, but it also provides a number of opportunities for families to be involved in students' spelling growth. It has a statement of the week's spelling pattern or strategy, a valuable spelling study strategy, and a suggested home spelling practice activity.

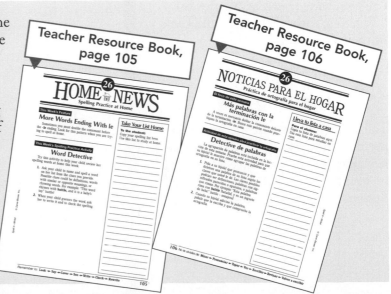

FINDING WORDS

STEP 1 Build Your Spelling List

Students will build their spelling lists with **Pattern Words, Teacher Words,** and **Your Words**. Students should study a minimum of twelve new words each week.

Find Your Pattern Words
- Pretest the students on these words.
- Tell students to write each misspelled pretest word on their spelling lists.

Add Teacher Words
- Select words for students to add to their spelling lists. Choose words from **More Words for Hungry Word Hunters** (on this page and on student page 171), words related to a theme or content area, or words students often misspell.

Add Your Words
- Ask students to pick words from their lists of **Words I Need to Know How to Spell** and their writing.
- Tell students to write these words on their spelling lists.

STEP 2 Write Your Spelling List

Remind students to verify all spellings. (Ask students to see **Strategies for Checking Your Spelling** in the back of the student edition.)

STEP 3 Set Your Learning Goal

Tell students to count the words on their spelling lists. This total is their learning goal. It may vary depending on ability, individual goals, and the difficulty of spelling words.

T128 UNIT 26

MORE WORDS FOR HUNGRY WORD HUNTERS

RED LIST Pattern Words Below Level	BLUE LIST Pattern Words Above Level	Other Pattern Words	Social Studies Pattern Word
able	bridle	brittle	recycle
apple	bugle	idle	
bottle	doodle	meddle	
couple	double	snuggle	
little	giggle	wriggle	
maple	juggle		
people	multiple		
puddle	needle		
scribble	paddle		
table	pebble		
	settle		
	waffle		

These lists also appear on page 171 in the student edition and page 32 in the **Teacher Resource Book.**

SPELLING PATTERN

26

More Words Ending With le

Your Spelling List

_____
_____
_____
_____
_____
_____
_____
_____
_____
_____
_____
_____
_____
_____
_____
_____

128 UNIT 26

FINDING WORDS

STEP 1 Build Your Spelling List

Find Your Pattern Words
Take the pretest.
Write misspelled words on your spelling list.

Add Teacher Words
Teachers may add:
- More **Pattern Words** • Content Words • Theme Words

Add Your Words
Pick words from:
- **Words I Need to Know How to Spell** • Writing • Reading

Pattern Words

1.	saddle	Amy sat high in the **saddle** on the horse.
2.	title	What is the **title** of that book?
3.	triple	Hank wants to do a **triple** flip someday.
4.	bubble	The **bubble** floated down to the grass.
5.	beetle	A **beetle** was crawling on the rose.
6.	trouble	Carla had **trouble** tying her shoe.
7.	battle	Which team will win the spelling **battle**?
8.	cycle	Most butterflies have a short life **cycle**.
9.	middle	My **middle** name is Anne.
10.	kettle	We boiled the water in a **kettle**.
11.	eagle	The **eagle** swooped down on the mouse.
12.	rattle	The baby's **rattle** fell under the crib.

STEP 2 Write Your Spelling List

STEP 3 Set Your Learning Goal

My spelling list has _____ words for me to learn.

I always add the whole **Pattern Words** list to my spelling list just to be sure I understand the pattern.

Really? I *still* add only the words I don't get right on the pretest.

PATTERN MINI-LESSON

NOTE: The **Explore the Spelling Pattern** activity on page 129 is a self-directed mini-lesson. If you wish to supplement that activity with direct instruction, use the following mini-lesson.

* **Read** the **Spelling Pattern** on page 129 together with the class. Explain that it will guide the **Hands-on Word Sort**.

* **Display** the **?** card and the **Hands-on Word Sort Cards** for Unit 26. Keep blank cards and a marker handy to make new cards.

* **Pronounce** each guide word. (Guide words are labeled "Master Word" on the **Word Sort Card**.) Ask students to listen for the first vowel sound and to note whether it is short or long. Point to the underlined letters. Ask students how the spelling patterns vary. (Response: *Saddle has a short vowel sound followed by a double consonant and le. Title has a* long vowel sound followed by a single consonant and *le*.)

* **Sort** the words according to their spelling pattern. Model your decision making: "The word **bubble** has a short vowel sound followed by a double consonant, so I'll put **bubble** under **saddle**."

* **Tell** students to place words that do not fit the patterns under the question mark. Challenge them to explain why **triple** and **trouble** do not fit. (Response: *The first syllable has a short vowel sound but is not followed by a double consonant*.) For the completed word sort, see the **Answer Card** for this unit in the **Hands-on Word Sort Card Book**.

* **Duplicate** the **Hands-on Word Sort Sheet** for Unit 26 (**Teacher Resource Book,** page 45). Ask students to cut the words on the sheet apart and practice sorting the words with a partner or independently.

· · · · · INSPECTING WORDS · · · · ·

Explore the Spelling Pattern
Sorting Words

A. Find a spelling partner. Take turns reading the **Pattern Words** out loud. Sort the **Pattern Words** into three groups. Use the words below to guide your sort. If a word doesn't fit with a guide word, put it with the question mark. Make sure you write each **Pattern Word** once.

> You may wish to use **Hands-on Word Sort Cards** and the **Hands-on Word Sort Sheet** for this unit.

1. saddle (short vowel–double consonant + le)	2. title (long vowel–single consonant + le)	3. ?
saddle	title	triple
bubble	beetle	trouble
battle	cycle	
middle	eagle	
kettle		
rattle		

B. Ask a family member to do a word hunt with you at home. Find notes or messages. Are the words that end in **le** spelled correctly? If you find a word with a spelling error, spell it correctly or find out how to spell it. Sort the words you find by sound and spelling pattern.

▼ ▼ ▼ ▼ ▼ ▼ ▼ ▼ ▼ ▼ ▼ ▼
Spelling Pattern
Sometimes you must double the consonant before the **-le** ending.
■ ■ ■ ■ ■ ■ ■ ■ ■ ■ ■

Focus on Word Study
Near Synonyms

Battle and **fight** have similar meanings, but there is a bit of difference between them. Two armies of ants take part in a battle, but it takes only two ants to have a fight.

Write these word pairs to complete each sentence: **name–title** or **saddle–seat**.

1. She put the __ on the horse so she could have a safe __.
saddle   seat

2. His __ was Joe but his __ was Dr. Smith.
name   title

Explore the Spelling Pattern
Sorting Words

This activity is a self-directed mini-lesson on this week's **Spelling Pattern**.

Focus on Word Study

Near Synonyms

This activity is intended to stimulate students' interest in words and to help them become more enthusiastic word hunters.

Spelling Process Handbook

Students who need to review any part of the spelling process, including practice options, should refer to the **Spelling Process Handbook** (pages 7–21).

A Practice Option

STEP 6 Practice Your Spelling List Independently

Ask the students to choose activities to practice their spelling words and to master this week's **Spelling Pattern**. Students should complete at least three activities each week. You may wish to:

• assign **Practice the Spelling Pattern** to all students to reinforce this week's **Spelling Pattern**.

• involve students' families by assigning **Take Your List Home** for this lesson (**Teacher Resource Book, pages 105 in English and 106 in Spanish**).

• encourage students to use partner activities without game mats (**Word Swap, Spelling Tic-Tac-Toe, Circle Dot**) and activities with game mats (**Meteor Attack, Rockets, Spelling Checkers, Spelling Soccer**). Directions for game-mat activities appear on each game mat. Directions for all other activities are found in the **Spelling Process Handbook** (pages 7–21).

NOTE: These activities and games can be used to practice any spelling list.

FLIP FOLDER

The **Flip Folder** is a fun practice activity that is especially effective for kinesthetic learners. While **Flip Folder** is similar to the Have-a-Go strategy, the techniques differ in that the first step in **Flip Folder** is to look at the correct spelling. Students then cover that spelling, visualize it, and attempt to recreate it. When they lift the flap and compare their attempt to the correct spelling, they receive immediate feedback—vital for correcting mistakes and retaining correct spellings. (Directions appear in the **Spelling Process Handbook**, student pages 7–21, and on the **Flip Folder** itself. This activity is appropriate for practicing any spelling list.)

MASTERING WORDS

STEP 6 Practice Your Spelling List Independently
Choose at least three activities to practice your spelling list.

Need Help? Read the Spelling Process Handbook (pages 7–21).

Game Mats		With a Partner		On Your Own		At Home
○ Meteor Attack	○ Rockets	○ Spelling Tic-Tac-Toe	○ Word Swap	○ Flip Folder	○ Spelling Study Strategy	○ Take Your List Home

Practice the Spelling Pattern

Use the clues to unscramble each **Pattern Word**. Write each word. Circle the doubled consonant in six of the words.

Pattern Words
saddle
title
triple
bubble
beetle
trouble
battle
cycle
middle
kettle
eagle
rattle

1. **Clue:** kind of cooking pot
l e t t k e
ke**tt**le

2. **Clue:** name
e t i l t
title

3. **Clue:** kind of bird
g a e e l
eagle

4. **Clue:** baby's toy
l t a r t e
ra**tt**le

5. **Clue:** beginning, ___, end
d i l m e d
mi**dd**le

6. **Clue:** kind of insect
e l t e e b
beetle

7. **Clue:** seat on a horse
d s a e l d
sa**dd**le

8. **Clue:** three times
p r i t e l
triple

9. **Clue:** contest or fight
e t t b a l
ba**tt**le

10. **Clue:** a series that is repeated
l c c e y
cycle

11. **Clue:** bother or difficulty
u e t l o r b
trouble

12. **Clue:** pocket of air
b e b l u b
bu**bb**le

DEVELOPING GOOD SPELLING HABITS

STEP 7 Focus on Writing

A. Proofread the Writing of Others

This activity provides proofreading practice in a variety of formats, including popular standardized test formats.

B. Proofread Your Own Writing

Students return to their own writing, armed with strategies to identify and collect words they need to know how to spell, and make an authentic link between spelling and writing.

C. A Writing Idea: A Poem

This suggestion for a more extended writing activity provides opportunities for students to write in different genres for a variety of purposes and modes.

STEP 8 Check Your Weekly Progress

▶ Take the Test

Remind students that they can take a practice test before the final test on their spelling lists. To find the testing procedure that is right for you, refer to page Z12.

▶ Check Your Goal

Have students compare their tests to their spelling lists. Did they spell all the **Pattern Words** on their spelling lists correctly?

▶ Graph Your Progress

Ask students to graph the number correct (student page 176 for softbound users; **Teacher Resource Book** page 123 for hardbound users).

▶ Save Missed Words

Tell students to write misspelled words on their lists of **Words I Need to Know How to Spell**. Remind students to verify spellings and to recycle these words on future weekly spelling lists.

· · · · DEVELOPING GOOD SPELLING HABITS · · · ·

STEP 7 Focus on Writing

A. Proofread the Writing of Others

Help a group of students proofread the invitation they wrote. Find the six misspelled words. Write them correctly.

You're Invited!

Come and meet Ms. Bowman, author of *Saving the Eaggle* and *The Life Cycl of the Beetel*. She will be in the Middle School library on May 2. She will read from her latest book, *Tripple Troubble*. Hope you can be there!

1. _____ Eagle
2. _____ Cycle
3. _____ Beetle
4. _____ Middle
5. _____ Triple
6. _____ Trouble

≡ Make a capital.
／ Make a small letter.
∧ Add something.
ℓ Take out something.
⊙ Add a period.
¶ New paragraph
SP Spelling error

B. Proofread Your Own Writing

Many words end with **le,** but not all of them have double consonants before the **le** ending. Go to your most recent writing. Look for words with this pattern that you may have misspelled. Add these words to **Words I Need to Know How to Spell**.

C. A Writing Idea: A Poem

Write a poem about a beetle, an eagle, a rattlesnake—or any other kind of creature. Give your poem an interesting title. Combine your poem with your classmates' poems in a class book titled *Poems Featuring Creatures*.

EXPRESSIVE

STEP 8 Check Your Weekly Progress

▶ Take the Test
Ready? Practice test first.

▶ Check Your Goal
Check to see if you met your learning goal.

▶ Graph Your Progress
Graph your score for this week's test.

▶ Save Missed Words
Write the words you missed in your list of **Words I Need to Know How to Spell**.

Hunt Words

Remind students to continuously hunt words that they wish to learn how to spell and to write these words in **Words I Need to Know How to Spell**.

Look for the Vowels

ENGAGING IN THE PROCESS — MATERIALS

Student Edition: Pages 132–135   **Teacher Edition:** Pages T132A–T135

Materials to help students practice their spelling lists:
- **Flip Folders**
- Copies of **Flip Folder Practice Sheet** (**Teacher Resource Book,** page 51)
- **Take Your List Home** (in *Spell It–Write!*

Home News, **Teacher Resource Book,** pages 107 in English and 108 in Spanish)
- Game Mats Featured in This Unit: **Rockets, Spelling Soccer**

ENGAGING IN THE PROCESS — GOALS

SPELLING GOALS

Students will

- develop a spelling strategy to help them spell new words.

- understand that a syllable must have at least one vowel.

- develop an understanding that many English words come from Latin words and evolve over time.

- use the spelling process to become better writers.

WRITING GOALS

Students will

- proofread a writing sample.

- proofread a piece of their own writing for misspelled words containing syllables with missing vowel letters.

- write an expressive letter.

ENGAGING IN THE PROCESS — MANAGEMENT

Pacing	Notes	Quick Pick Management Option
Period 1 Finding Words (Steps 1–3)	If you wish to add **Teacher Words,** write them on the chalkboard. Sources for more words include: **More Words for Hungry Word Hunters** (page T132), content and theme-related words, or words of your choice.	Assign the list of **Strategy Words** to the whole class. Add the Red List (**More Words for Hungry Word Hunters,** student page 172) for a longer list. Add the Blue List (**More Words for Hungry Word Hunters**) for a more challenging list.
Period 2 Inspecting Words (Steps 4 and 5)	Students write the **Strategy Words** to complete **Explore the Spelling Strategy**.	Assign **Explore the Spelling Strategy** and **Focus on Word Study**.
Period 3 Mastering Words (Step 6) **Period 4** Developing Good Spelling Habits (Step 7)	These two periods can be allocated between selected **Mastering Words** activities and proofreading and writing activities in **Focus on Writing**.	Assign two or three activities to the whole class. Familiarize students with choosing their own activities at their own pace.
Period 5 Assessment (Step 8)	Gradually try different peer-testing options to find the style that best fits your class.	Test the class on the same, whole-class list.

Understanding Language Differences

Counting syllables is a useful strategy in many cases. In some cases, however, it may be misleading. For example, a word like **interesting** has four syllables for some speakers but only three for others: **in-trust-ing**\. Other examples include such words as **temperature** (**tem-pruh-cher**\) and **laboratory** (**lab-ruh-tor-ee**\). You will want to encourage your students to check doubtful spellings in a dictionary.

Helping Students Acquiring English

Present the word **together,** either by writing it on the chalkboard or on a 3" x 5" card, and discuss its meaning. Pronounce the word, and ask students to repeat it. Next, ask them to clap for every vowel sound they hear as you say the word again. Ask how many vowel sounds are in **together**. (Response: *three*) Draw lines between the syllables, and explain that the number of vowel sounds is the same as the number of syllables, or word parts. Continue this procedure until all the **Strategy Words** have been introduced. Discuss the **Spelling Strategy** on page 133, guiding students to understand how this strategy can help them spell words with more than one syllable.

Meeting Diverse Needs

Less Able Spellers

Students with special needs do not always spontaneously use the spelling strategies they are taught in school. However, they are more likely to use these strategies if they see their teachers using them.

When doing directed writing lessons in class, be sure to note when you are using a particular strategy and model its use as you think out loud. For example, if you wish to remind students that they can often spell a word by relating it to a rhyming word, model that technique out loud: "I'm not sure how to spell **stable,** but the first sounds are the same as in **star,** so **stable** must begin with **s-t** like **star.** And **stable** rhymes with **able,** so I'll try that spelling: **a-b-l-e**. I can check my spelling later."

Look for opportunities to encourage students to use the spelling strategies you have taught. Encourage students to keep a record or a log, noting when strategies were used.

More Able Spellers

Challenge students to find as many words within another word as they can by rearranging letters. For example, **discover** contains **is, cove(s), cover(s), over, side, score, red, rice,** and many other words. As students become more adept with this activity, challenge them to respond without first writing the words on paper.

Ask students to copy their lists in the **Take Your List Home** section of the *Spell It–Write!* Home News page for this lesson. Not only does this page provide a convenient way for families to share a student's spelling list, but it also provides a number of opportunities for families to be involved in students' spelling growth. It has a statement of the week's spelling pattern or strategy, a valuable spelling study strategy, and a suggested home spelling practice activity.

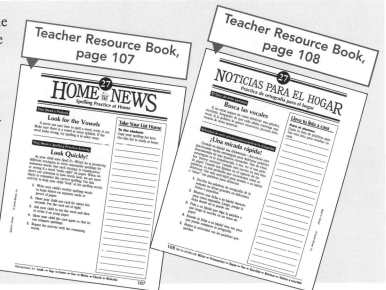

FINDING WORDS

STEP 1 Build Your Spelling List

Students will build their spelling lists with **Strategy Words, Teacher Words,** and **Your Words**. Students should study a minimum of twelve new words each week.

Find Your Strategy Words

- Pretest the students on these words.
- Tell students to write each misspelled pretest word on their spelling lists.

Add Teacher Words

- Select words for students to add to their spelling lists. Choose words from **More Words for Hungry Word Hunters** (on this page and on student page 172), words related to a theme or content area, or words students often misspell.

Add Your Words

- Ask students to pick words from their lists of **Words I Need to Know How to Spell** and their writing.
- Tell students to write these words on their spelling lists.

STEP 2 Write Your Spelling List

Remind students to verify all spellings. (Ask students to see **Strategies for Checking Your Spelling** in the back of the student edition.)

STEP 3 Set Your Learning Goal

Tell students to count the words on their spelling lists. This total is their learning goal. It may vary depending on ability, individual goals, and the difficulty of spelling words.

MORE WORDS FOR HUNGRY WORD HUNTERS

┌RED LIST┐ Strategy Words Below Level	┌BLUE LIST┐ Strategy Words Above Level	Other Strategy Words
almost	alligator	apology
along	area	credit
basket	deposit	dinosaur
behind	important	discuss
hundred	material	enormous
morning	president	mention
number	problem	passenger
penny	skiing	reward
sister	umbrella	silent
yesterday	western	supply

Math Strategy Words

arithmetic	product
century	zero

Science Strategy Words

acid	formula
atom	hospital
battery	level
chemical	planet
clinic	solid

Social Studies Strategy Words

altitude	laughter
cargo	monument
hogan	pilgrim

These lists also appear on page 172 in the student edition and page 33 in the **Teacher Resource Book**.

FINDING WORDS

SPELLING STRATEGY

27

Look for the Vowels

Your Spelling List

_____
_____
_____
_____
_____
_____
_____
_____
_____
_____
_____
_____
_____
_____
_____
_____
_____
_____

STEP 1 Build Your Spelling List

Find Your Strategy Words

Take the pretest.
Write misspelled words on your spelling list.

Add Teacher Words

Teachers may add:
- More **Strategy Words** • Content Words • Theme Words

Add Your Words

Pick words from:
- **Words I Need to Know How to Spell** • Writing • Reading

Strategy Words

1. **together** — Let's go to the store **together**.
2. **parent** — Which **parent** did you ask—Mom or Dad?
3. **remember** — It's hard to **remember** phone numbers.
4. **during** — You must be quiet **during** a test.
5. **discover** — When did you **discover** the mistake?
6. **bottom** — Kenny swam to the **bottom** of the pool.
7. **until** — Wait **until** the light turns green.
8. **radio** — **Radio** programs were popular in the 1920s.
9. **idea** — Whose **idea** was this?
10. **apartment** — We are moving to a new **apartment**.

STEP 2 Write Your Spelling List

STEP 3 Set Your Learning Goal

My spelling list has _____ words for me to learn.

When we come to class on Monday, the words our teacher wants to add to our spelling lists are written on the chalkboard.

I like that! Then that part of my list is already done.

STRATEGY MINI-LESSON

NOTE: ► The **Explore the Spelling Strategy** activity on page 133 is a self-directed mini-lesson. If you wish to supplement that activity with direct instruction, use the following mini-lesson.

* **Review** these spelling strategies: write a word to see if it looks right; use rhyming words or word parts; find small words in larger words; make up phrases to use as memory aids.

* **Tell** students that there is another way to use the strategy of writing out a word to see if it looks right.

* **Write** the words **together** and **parent** on the chalkboard. Ask students how many vowel sounds they hear in each word. (Response: *three in **together**, two in **parent***) Remind students that the number of vowel sounds is the same as the number of syllables. Ask students to notice that there is at least one vowel letter in each syllable.

* **Say** the word **remember**. Ask students how many syllables they hear. (Response: *three*) Then ask a volunteer to attempt to spell the word. Write that student's spelling on the chalkboard. Ask the class if this spelling has at least one vowel in each syllable. Make any corrections. Follow the same procedure with the remaining words.

* **Read** aloud with students the **Spelling Strategy** on page 133. Emphasize that one way to check the spelling of a word is to make sure there is a vowel in every syllable.

* **Include** examples from **More Words for Hungry Word Hunters** (on student page 172 and page T132), if desired. Remind students that they may add any of these words to **Words I Need to Know How to Spell**.

· · · INSPECTING WORDS · · ·

STEP 4 Explore the Spelling Strategy
Checking Vowels

A. Find a partner. Take turns reading each **Strategy Word** out loud slowly, by syllables. Listen for each vowel sound. How many syllables does each **Strategy Word** have? (Hint: To see how many syllables the **Strategy Word** has, count the vowel sounds.) Write the **Strategy Word** with the heading it matches.

Remember, count the vowel sounds to find the number of syllables.

Syllables

Two Syllables	Three Syllables
1. parent	2. together
parent	together
during	remember
bottom	discover
until	radio
	idea
	apartment

B. Look in **Words I Need to Know How to Spell** and your writing to find other words with more than one syllable.

STEP 5 Focus on Word Study
Words From Latin

Even ancient Latin was a changing language. A very early Latin word, **parere**, meant "to give birth." A later word, **parentes**, came to mean "mothers or fathers." So the word **parent** has two parents from ancient Latin!

Which **Strategy Words** come from these Latin words?

1. durare, meaning "to last" ___during___
2. rememorari, meaning "to mind" ___remember___
3. ad partem, meaning "to one side or part" ___apartment___

▼▼▼▼▼▼▼▼▼▼▼▼
Spelling Strategy
If you're not sure how to spell a word, write it out. Make sure there is a vowel in every syllable. If the word looks wrong, try spelling it in other ways.
· · · · · · · · · · · · · · ·

STEP 4 Explore the Spelling Strategy

Checking Vowels

This activity is a self-directed mini-lesson on this week's **Spelling Strategy**.

STEP 5 Focus on Word Study

Words From Latin

This activity is intended to stimulate students' interest in words and to help them become more enthusiastic word hunters.

Spelling Process Handbook

Students who need to review any part of the spelling process, including practice options, should refer to the **Spelling Process Handbook** (pages 7–21).

MASTERING WORDS

A Practice Option

Practice Your Spelling List Independently
STEP 6

Ask the students to choose activities to practice their spelling words and to master this week's **Spelling Strategy**. Students should complete at least three activities each week. You may wish to:

- assign **Practice the Spelling Strategy** to all students to reinforce this week's **Spelling Strategy**.

- involve students' families by assigning **Take Your List Home** for this lesson (**Teacher Resource Book, pages 107 in English and 108 in Spanish**).

- encourage students to use partner activities without game mats (**Word Swap, Spelling Tic-Tac-Toe, Circle Dot**) and activities with game mats (**Meteor Attack, Rockets, Spelling Checkers, Spelling Soccer**). Directions for game-mat activities appear on each game mat. Directions for all other activities are found in the **Spelling Process Handbook** (pages 7–21).

NOTE: These activities and games can be used to practice any spelling list.

TAKE YOUR LIST HOME

Maintaining the home-school connection is important to educational success. One way to involve families in students' spelling growth is to duplicate and send the *Spell It–Write!* Home News to families every week. First, each student copies his or her spelling list in the **Take Your List Home** section of the Home News page. Then students take the page home to share the list and to use the suggested home spelling practice activity. This page also includes a statement of the week's spelling strategy or pattern and a spelling study strategy. (A different Home News page—in both Spanish and English—is available for each *Spell It–Write!* unit in the **Teacher Resource Book**.)

· · · MASTERING WORDS · · ·

Practice Your Spelling List Independently
STEP 6

Choose at least three activities to practice your spelling list.

You can practice any spelling list with these activities.

Game Mats	With a Partner	On Your Own	At Home
Rockets / Spelling Soccer	Circle Dot / Word Swap	Flip Folder / Spelling Study Strategy	Take Your List Home

Practice the Spelling Strategy

In each set of words below, find the **Strategy Word** with the correct spelling. Write the **Strategy Word** correctly.

Strategy Words

together
parent
remember
during
discover
bottom
until
radio
idea
apartment

1.	raido	radio	radeo	**radio**
2.	idia	idee	idea	**idea**
3.	remember	rembr	remembr	**remember**
4.	bottum	bottm	bottom	**bottom**
5.	dering	during	durig	**during**
6.	apartmnt	aprtment	apartment	**apartment**
7.	discuvr	discouver	discover	**discover**
8.	until	untill	entil	**until**
9.	pairunt	parnt	parent	**parent**
10.	toogethr	together	togither	**together**

DEVELOPING GOOD SPELLING HABITS

STEP 7 Focus on Writing

A. Proofread the Writing of Others

This activity provides proofreading practice in a variety of formats, including popular standardized test formats.

B. Proofread Your Own Writing

Students return to their own writing, armed with strategies to identify and collect words they need to know how to spell, and make an authentic link between spelling and writing.

C. A Writing Idea: A Letter

This suggestion for a more extended writing activity provides opportunities for students to write in different genres for a variety of purposes and modes.

STEP 8 Check Your Weekly Progress

▶ Take the Test

Remind students that they can take a practice test before the final test on their spelling lists. To find the testing procedure that is right for you, refer to page Z12.

▶ Check Your Goal

Have students compare their tests to their spelling lists. Did they spell all the **Strategy Words** on their spelling lists correctly?

▶ Graph Your Progress

Ask students to graph the number correct (student page 176 for softbound users; **Teacher Resource Book** page 123 for hardbound users).

▶ Save Missed Words

Tell students to write misspelled words on their lists of **Words I Need to Know How to Spell**. Remind students to verify spellings and to recycle these words on future weekly spelling lists.

DEVELOPING GOOD SPELLING HABITS

STEP 7 Focus on Writing

A. Proofread the Writing of Others

Proofread the passage below. Decide which type of mistake, if any, appears in each underlined section.

We stood <u>togethar</u> on the hilltop, watching for
①
shooting stars. Nothing <u>happened until</u> we saw a bright
②
star streak through the sky. It went from the top of the

sky <u>to the bottm.</u> I'll always <u>remember that moment</u>
③ ④

≡ Make a capital.
／ Make a small letter.
‸ Add something.
⌒ Take out something.
⊙ Add a period.
¶ New paragraph
(sp) Spelling error

1. (A) Spelling
   B Capitalization
   C Punctuation
   D No mistake

2. A Spelling
   B Capitalization
   C Punctuation
   (D) No mistake

3. (A) Spelling
   B Capitalization
   C Punctuation
   D No mistake

4. A Spelling
   B Capitalization
   (C) Punctuation
   D No mistake

B. Proofread Your Own Writing

It can be easy to leave out vowel letters when you write words with more than one syllable. Read aloud a piece of your most recent writing. Make sure you wrote at least one vowel for each syllable in every word. If you are unsure of a spelling, try other ways to spell the word.

C. A Writing Idea: A Letter

Imagine that you are an alien visiting Earth. Write a letter home telling what you discover here. Try to use lots of words that have more than one syllable. Be sure to check your spelling. Then share your letter with another "alien"!

STEP 8 Check Your Weekly Progress

▶ **Take the Test**
Ready? Practice test first.

▶ **Check Your Goal**
Check to see if you met your learning goal.

▶ **Graph Your Progress**
Graph your score for this week's test.

▶ **Save Missed Words**
Write the words you missed in your list of **Words I Need to Know How to Spell**.

Hunt Words

Remind students to continuously hunt words that they wish to learn how to spell and to write these words in **Words I Need to Know How to Spell**.

SPELLING PATTERN 28

Compound Words

ENGAGING IN THE PROCESS — MATERIALS

Student Edition: Pages 136–139   **Teacher Edition:** Pages T136A–T139

Materials to help students practice their spelling lists:

- **Flip Folders**
- Copies of **Flip Folder Practice Sheet** (**Teacher Resource Book,** page 51)
- **Take Your List Home** (in *Spell It–Write!*

Home News, **Teacher Resource Book,** pages 109 in English and 110 in Spanish)
- Game Mats Featured in This Unit: **Spelling Checkers, Spelling Soccer**

ENGAGING IN THE PROCESS — GOALS

SPELLING GOALS

Students will

- transfer the knowledge that compound words are composed of two or more smaller words to spell compound words.
- learn about words that other languages have borrowed from English.
- use the spelling process of finding words, inspecting words, and mastering words as they develop good spelling habits to become better writers.

WRITING GOALS

Students will

- proofread a writing sample.
- proofread a piece of their own writing for misspelled compound words.
- write expressive slogans.

ENGAGING IN THE PROCESS — MANAGEMENT

Pacing	Notes	Quick Pick Management Option
Period 1 Finding Words (Steps 1–3)	If you wish to add **Teacher Words,** write them on the chalkboard. Sources for more words include: **More Words for Hungry Word Hunters** (page T136), content and theme-related words, or words of your choice.	Assign the list of **Pattern Words** to the whole class. Add the Red List (**More Words for Hungry Word Hunters,** student page 172) for a longer list. Add the Blue List (**More Words for Hungry Word Hunters**) for a more challenging list.
Period 2 Inspecting Words (Steps 4 and 5)	Students write the **Pattern Words** to complete **Explore the Spelling Pattern.**	Assign **Explore the Spelling Pattern** and **Focus on Word Study**.
Period 3 Mastering Words (Step 6) **Period 4** Developing Good Spelling Habits (Step 7)	These two periods can be allocated between selected **Mastering Words** activities and proofreading and writing activities in **Focus on Writing**.	Assign two or three activities to the whole class. Familiarize students with choosing their own activities at their own pace.
Period 5 Assessment (Step 8)	Gradually try different peer-testing options to find the style that best fits your class.	Test the class on the same, whole-class list.

Understanding Language Differences

Spanish Speakers

Spanish has some compound words. For example, the Spanish word **vaivén** (literally, "go come") means "seesaw." It is easy to create new words in English by combining words. But some languages, including Spanish, prefer to use affixes or phrases to form what in English would be a compound word. For example, **raincoat** in Spanish is **impermeable** ("not permeable"), and **sunbeam** is **rayo de sol** ("ray of sun").

An interesting linguistic note is that most two-syllable, noun + noun compounds are stressed on the first syllable. For example, the nouns **foot** and **ball** combine to make **FOOTball**.

Helping Students Acquiring English

For each **Pattern Word,** prepare two cards, one for each part of the compound word. Next, display a basketball, and name it for students. Place the cards for **basket** and **ball** close together on the chalk rail. Read the word **basketball,** and ask students to repeat it. Point out that the two words **basket** and **ball** have been joined together to make one word: **basketball.** On the chalkboard, write **basket + ball = basketball.** Follow a similar procedure to introduce the remaining **Pattern Words.**

Meeting Diverse Needs

Less Able Spellers

Students who have difficulty learning to spell may benefit from the use of a spell checker in a word processing computer program. While spell checkers can help children find many of their spelling miscues, they do not work well enough to rely on them completely. Some spelling miscues may not be identified because:

- they involve the correct spelling of other real words, such as homophones.
- the spell checker cannot recognize the word.
- the child fails to pick the correct spelling from the list of options.
- the word is not in the spell checker's "dictionary."

Discuss these limitations with children, and periodically check to see that the spell checker is used correctly.

More Able Spellers

Students might make up picture puzzles for compound words using plus and equal signs; for example: **drawing of star + drawing of fish =** (starfish). Students then exchange puzzles and solve the puzzles they receive.

Ask students to copy their lists in the **Take Your List Home** section of the *Spell It–Write!* Home News page for this lesson. Not only does this page provide a convenient way for families to share a student's spelling list, but it also provides a number of opportunities for families to be involved in students' spelling growth. It has a statement of the week's spelling pattern or strategy, a valuable spelling study strategy, and a suggested home spelling practice activity.

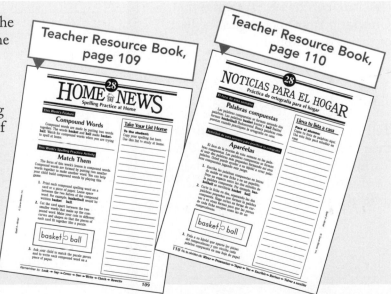

FINDING WORDS

STEP 1 Build Your Spelling List

Students will build their spelling lists with **Pattern Words, Teacher Words,** and **Your Words**. Students should study a minimum of twelve new words each week.

Find Your Pattern Words
• Pretest the students on these words.
• Tell students to write each misspelled pretest word on their spelling lists.

Add Teacher Words
• Select words for students to add to their spelling lists. Choose words from **More Words for Hungry Word Hunters** (on this page and on student page 172), words related to a theme or content area, or words students often misspell.

Add Your Words
• Ask students to pick words from their lists of **Words I Need to Know How to Spell** and their writing.
• Tell students to write these words on their spelling lists.

STEP 2 Write Your Spelling List

Remind students to verify all spellings. (Ask students to see **Strategies for Checking Your Spelling** in the back of the student edition.)

STEP 3 Set Your Learning Goal

Tell students to count the words on their spelling lists. This total is their learning goal. It may vary depending on ability, individual goals, and the difficulty of spelling words.

MORE WORDS FOR HUNGRY WORD HUNTERS

RED LIST
Pattern Words Below Level

afternoon
airplane
downtown
football
grandfather
grandmother
moonlight
something
sunshine
upstairs

BLUE LIST
Pattern Words Above Level

applesauce
cheerleader
headache
home run
homework
merry-go-round
peanut butter
post office
skyscraper
watermelon

Other Pattern Words

background
hindsight
outline
sister-in-law
throughout
typewriter
videotape
waterproof
wholesome
withdrawal

Science Pattern Words

cardboard   sunspot
earthquake   waterfall
grasshopper

Social Studies Pattern Words

aftershock   paperback
airport   railroad
freeway   sailboat
handmade   skyline
handwriting   sugarcane
highway   taxicab
landscape   timberline
outback   tugboat

These lists also appear on page 172 in the student edition and page 34 in the **Teacher Resource Book**.

SPELLING PATTERN

28

Compound Words

Your Spelling List

_____
_____
_____
_____
_____
_____
_____
_____
_____
_____
_____
_____
_____
_____
_____
_____
_____
_____
_____

STEP 1 Build Your Spelling List

Find Your Pattern Words
Take the pretest.
Write misspelled words on your spelling list.

Add Teacher Words
Teachers may add:
• More **Pattern Words** • Content Words • Theme Words

Add Your Words
Pick words from:
• **Words I Need to Know How to Spell** • Writing • Reading

Pattern Words

1.	**basketball**	Pass the **basketball** to me.
2.	**everybody**	**Everybody** moved into the hall.
3.	**breakfast**	You need to eat a good **breakfast**.
4.	**fireplace**	Put a fresh log in the **fireplace**.
5.	**good-bye**	I don't like to say **good-bye**.
6.	**flashlight**	Shine the **flashlight** over here.
7.	**peanut**	Can you eat just one **peanut**?
8.	**Thanksgiving**	**Thanksgiving** is always on a Thursday in November.
9.	**weekend**	I went camping last **weekend**.
10.	**T-shirt**	I painted a fish on my **T-shirt**.

STEP 2 Write Your Spelling List

STEP 3 Set Your Learning Goal

My spelling list has _____ words for me to learn.

> Sometimes I see some words that are really cool! I like to add them to my spelling list.

> Hey, I do that, too! And those are the very words that help make my writing more fun to read.

PATTERN MINI-LESSON

NOTE: The **Explore the Spelling Pattern** activity on page 137 is a self-directed mini-lesson. If you wish to supplement that activity with direct instruction, use the following mini-lesson.

* **Write** the **Pattern Words** from page 136 on the chalkboard. Invite volunteers to read the words aloud.

* **Point out** to students that each word is made up of two smaller words. Each **Pattern Word** is a compound word.

* **Ask** students how the two smaller words give a clue to the meaning of the compound word. (Possible response: *The meanings of the two smaller words are combined.*)

* **Discuss** with students how **good-bye** and **T-shirt** differ from the other words on the list. (Response: *Both **good-bye** and **T-shirt** are written with hyphens.*) You may wish to tell students that compounds written as one solid word, like **basketball,** are called "closed compounds," and those written with a hyphen, like **good-bye,** are called "hyphenated compounds." Compounds consisting of two separate words such as **home run, peanut butter,** and **post office** (on the Blue List in **More Words for Hungry Word Hunters**) are called "open compounds."

* **Read** the **Spelling Pattern** on page 137 aloud with students.

* **Encourage** students to hunt examples of other compound words. List these on the chalkboard. You may wish to include examples from **More Words for Hungry Word Hunters** (on student page 172 and page T136). Remind students that they may add any of these words to **Words I Need to Know How to Spell**.

 STEP 4 Explore the Spelling Pattern

Join Up!

A. Each **Pattern Word** is a compound word formed from two smaller words. Some are joined together, like **basketball**. Some have a hyphen between the parts, like **good-bye**. Decide which word from the box goes with each numbered word. Write the **Pattern Word**. Don't forget to write the hyphen when you need to!

body nut	giving place	end bye	ball shirt	fast light

1. week + __ = __weekend__
2. break + __ = __breakfast__
3. pea + __ = __peanut__
4. T- + __ = __T-shirt__
5. flash + __ = __flashlight__
6. every + __ = __everybody__
7. fire + __ = __fireplace__
8. good- + __ = __good-bye__
9. basket + __ = __basketball__
10. Thanks + __ = __Thanksgiving__

B. Do a word hunt in your writing and in **Words I Need to Know How to Spell** to find compound words that are joined together or have hyphens. See how many of each kind you can list.

STEP 5 Focus on Word Study

Borrowed English Words

Sometimes other languages borrow words from English. For example, the French had no word for the period from the end of school or work on Friday until Monday morning, so they borrowed the English word **weekend**. Sometimes the words borrowed by other languages are spelled differently. In Spanish, **beisbol** means "baseball."

Write the English word for the foreign spelling of each sport name.

1. futbol __football__
2. basquetbol __basketball__
3. tenis __tennis__

Spelling Pattern
Compound words are made by putting two words together. The words **basket** and **ball** make **basketball**.

 STEP 4 Explore the Spelling Pattern

Join Up!

This activity is a self-directed mini-lesson on this week's **Spelling Pattern**.

 STEP 5 Focus on Word Study

Borrowed English Words

This activity is intended to stimulate students' interest in words and to help them become more enthusiastic word hunters.

Spelling Process Handbook

Students who need to review any part of the spelling process, including practice options, should refer to the **Spelling Process Handbook** (pages 7–21).

MASTERING WORDS

STEP 6 Practice Your Spelling List Independently

Ask the students to choose activities to practice their spelling words and to master this week's **Spelling Pattern**. Students should complete at least three activities each week. You may wish to:

- assign **Practice the Spelling Pattern** to all students to reinforce this week's **Spelling Pattern**.

- involve students' families by assigning **Take Your List Home** for this lesson (**Teacher Resource Book**, pages 109 in English and 110 in Spanish).

- encourage students to use partner activities without game mats (**Word Swap, Spelling Tic-Tac-Toe, Circle Dot**) and activities with game mats (**Meteor Attack, Rockets, Spelling Checkers, Spelling Soccer**). Directions for game-mat activities appear on each game mat. Directions for all other activities are found in the **Spelling Process Handbook** (pages 7–21).

NOTE: These activities and games can be used to practice any spelling list.

A Practice Option

SPELLING TIC-TAC-TOE

Just about anyone knows how to play tic-tac-toe. And now this strategic game of **X**'s and **O**'s teams up with spelling words to make spelling practice fun! Partners can practice spelling words with **Spelling Tic-Tac-Toe** on any scrap of paper. And because partners spell words aloud and visually check errors against correct spellings, **Spelling Tic-Tac-Toe** appeals to both visual and auditory learners. (Directions appear in the **Spelling Process Handbook,** student pages 7–21. This activity is appropriate for practicing any spelling list.)

MASTERING WORDS

STEP 6 Practice Your Spelling List Independently

Copy your words carefully when you take your list home.

Choose at least three activities to practice your spelling list.

Game Mats	With a Partner	On Your Own	At Home
○ Spelling Soccer ○ Spelling Checkers	○ Circle Dot ○ Spelling Tic-Tac-Toe	○ Flip Folder ○ Spelling Study Strategy	○ Take Your List Home

Practice the Spelling Pattern

Write the **Pattern Word** that matches each clue.

Pattern Words

basketball
everybody
breakfast
fireplace
good-bye
flashlight
peanut
Thanksgiving
weekend
T-shirt

1. something to wear — **T-shirt**
2. shines in the dark — **flashlight**
3. place for burning logs — **fireplace**
4. Friday evening to Monday morning — **weekend**
5. dribble, pass, or shoot it — **basketball**
6. all the people — **everybody**
7. morning meal — **breakfast**
8. grows underground — **peanut**
9. holiday — **Thanksgiving**
10. farewell — **good-bye**

DEVELOPING GOOD SPELLING HABITS

STEP 7 Focus on Writing

A. Proofread the Writing of Others

This activity provides proofreading practice in a variety of formats, including popular standardized test formats.

B. Proofread Your Own Writing

Students return to their own writing, armed with strategies to identify and collect words they need to know how to spell, and make an authentic link between spelling and writing.

C. A Writing Idea: Slogans

This suggestion for a more extended writing activity provides opportunities for students to write in different genres for a variety of purposes and modes.

STEP 8 Check Your Weekly Progress

▶ Take the Test

Remind students that they can take a practice test before the final test on their spelling lists. To find the testing procedure that is right for you, refer to page Z12.

▶ Check Your Goal

Have students compare their tests to their spelling lists. Did they spell all the **Pattern Words** on their spelling lists correctly?

▶ Graph Your Progress

Ask students to graph the number correct (student page 176 for softbound users; **Teacher Resource Book** page 123 for hardbound users).

▶ Save Missed Words

Tell students to write misspelled words on their lists of **Words I Need to Know How to Spell**. Remind students to verify spellings and to recycle these words on future weekly spelling lists.

· · · · · · · · · · · DEVELOPING GOOD SPELLING HABITS · · · · · · · · · · ·

STEP 7 Focus on Writing

A. Proofread the Writing of Others

Proofread Lin's postcard from camp. Check the six underlined **Pattern Words**. If the compound word is spelled correctly, write **c**. If it is misspelled, write **m** and then write the word correctly. Remember, incorrectly joining the smaller words is as much a spelling error as using the wrong letters!

Dear Dana,

Today we cooked our breakfist¹ in the fire-place². I lost my flash light³ in the woods. I will be home this weekend⁴. But it will be hard to say good bye⁵ to everybody⁶ here.

Love,
Lin

≡ Make a capital.
/ Make a small letter.
∧ Add something.
ℯ Take out something.
⊙ Add a period.
¶ New paragraph
SP Spelling error

1. __m__ breakfast   4. _____ c
2. __m__ fireplace   5. __m__ good-bye
3. __m__ flashlight   6. _____ c

B. Proofread Your Own Writing

Compound words are formed by joining two words together, sometimes with a hyphen but usually without one. Look through a few pieces of your most recent writing to find compound words you may have misspelled. Correct any misspelled words and add them to **Words I Need to Know How to Spell**.

C. A Writing Idea: Slogans

Choose compound words and use them to write slogans for T-shirts. Use **Pattern Words** or other compound words you know. Use your imagination! Check your spelling when you're finished. Then, if you want to, copy your favorite slogan on a piece of paper and attach it to your favorite T-shirt.

STEP 8 Check Your Weekly Progress

▶ Take the Test
Ready? Practice test first.

▶ Check Your Goal
Check to see if you met your learning goal.

▶ Graph Your Progress
Graph your score for this week's test.

▶ Save Missed Words
Write the words you missed in your list of **Words I Need to Know How to Spell**.

Hunt Words

Remind students to continuously hunt words that they wish to learn how to spell and to write these words in **Words I Need to Know How to Spell**.

Suffixes: -ful, -less, -ly, -ment, -ness

ENGAGING IN THE PROCESS

MATERIALS

Student Edition: Pages 140–143   **Teacher Edition:** Pages T140A–T143

Materials to help students practice their spelling lists:
- **Flip Folders**
- Copies of **Flip Folder Practice Sheet** (**Teacher Resource Book,** page 51)
- **Take Your List Home** (in *Spell It–Write!*

Home News, **Teacher Resource Book,** pages 111 in English and 112 in Spanish)
- Game Mats Featured in This Unit: **Meteor Attack, Spelling Checkers**

ENGAGING IN THE PROCESS

GOALS

SPELLING GOALS

Students will

- demonstrate understanding of the idea that a final **silent e** is usually retained before a suffix beginning with a consonant.
- sort words according to the suffixes **-ful, -less, -ly, -ment,** and **-ness.**
- understand how suffixes have been used to change the meanings of words over time.
- use the spelling process to become better writers.

WRITING GOALS

Students will

- proofread a writing sample.
- proofread a piece of their own writing for misspelled words with the suffixes **-ful, -less, -ly, -ment,** and **-ness.**
- write an expressive description.

ENGAGING IN THE PROCESS

MANAGEMENT

Pacing	Notes	Quick Pick Management Option
Period 1 Finding Words (Steps 1–3)	If you wish to add **Teacher Words,** write them on the chalkboard. Sources for more words include: **More Words for Hungry Word Hunters** (page T140), content and theme-related words, or words of your choice.	Assign the list of **Pattern Words** to the whole class. Add the Blue List (**More Words for Hungry Word Hunters,** student page 173) for a more challenging list.
Period 2 Inspecting Words (Steps 4 and 5)	Students write the **Pattern Words** to complete **Explore the Spelling Pattern.**	Assign **Explore the Spelling Pattern** and **Focus on Word Study.**
Period 3 Mastering Words (Step 6) **Period 4** Developing Good Spelling Habits (Step 7)	These two periods can be allocated between selected **Mastering Words** activities and proofreading and writing activities in **Focus on Writing.**	Assign two or three activities to the whole class. Familiarize students with choosing their own activities at their own pace.
Period 5 Assessment (Step 8)	Gradually try different peer-testing options to find the style that best fits your class.	Test the class on the same, whole-class list.

Understanding Language Differences

Spanish Speakers

Spanish has equivalents for some of the suffixes in this unit. Spanish speakers may use these comparisons to learn the English forms.

English Suffix	Spanish Equivalent
-ly	-mente
-less	des-
-ment	-miento
-ness	-dad

English Example	Spanish Equivalent
lately	recientemente
careless	descuidado
movement	movimiento
gentleness	suavidad

Helping Students Acquiring English

Remind students that word parts can be added to words to make new words. Make a chart on the board of the suffixes **-ful, -less, -ly, -ment,** and **-ness** together with their meanings. Then write the word **late** on the chalkboard, pronounce it, and discuss its meaning. Using a different color of chalk, add the suffix **-ly** to **late,** explaining what you are doing. Pronounce the word **lately,** have students repeat the word, and discuss its meaning. Continue until all the **Pattern Words** have been introduced.

Meeting Diverse Needs

Less Able Spellers

Students who have difficulty learning to spell often have trouble locating misspellings in their written work. These children may benefit from learning to use one or more of the following strategies to help them locate spelling miscues.

- Start at the last word in a paper and read backward through the paper, one word at a time. Circle misspelled words.

- Place an index card over the first word in a paper, slide it forward one word at a time, and circle spelling miscues.

- Read the paper out loud, circling any words that are misspelled.

More Able Spellers

Ask students who are strong spellers to select one of their spelling words. Then challenge them to develop as many new words as they can by adding prefixes and suffixes to the base word. Ask them to explain how the meaning (and spelling) of the original word changed with the addition of each prefix and suffix.

Ask students to copy their lists in the **Take Your List Home** section of the *Spell It–Write!* Home News page for this lesson. Not only does this page provide a convenient way for families to share a student's spelling list, but it also provides a number of opportunities for families to be involved in students' spelling growth. It has a statement of the week's spelling pattern or strategy, a valuable spelling study strategy, and a suggested home spelling practice activity.

FINDING WORDS

 Build Your Spelling List

Students will build their spelling lists with **Pattern Words, Teacher Words,** and **Your Words**. Students should study a minimum of twelve new words each week.

Find Your Pattern Words

- Pretest the students on these words.
- Tell students to write each misspelled pretest word on their spelling lists.

Add Teacher Words

- Select words for students to add to their spelling lists. Choose words from **More Words for Hungry Word Hunters** (on this page and on student page 173), words related to a theme or content area, or words students often misspell.

Add Your Words

- Ask students to pick words from their lists of **Words I Need to Know How to Spell** and their writing.
- Tell students to write these words on their spelling lists.

2 **Write Your Spelling List**

Remind students to verify all spellings. (Ask students to see **Strategies for Checking Your Spelling** in the back of the student edition.)

3 **Set Your Learning Goal**

Tell students to count the words on their spelling lists. This total is their learning goal. It may vary depending on ability, individual goals, and the difficulty of spelling words.

MORE WORDS FOR HUNGRY WORD HUNTERS

BLUE LIST — Pattern Words Above Level	Other Pattern Words	Math Pattern Word
actively	advancement	measurement
amusement	barely	
arrangement	blameless	**Social Studies Pattern Word**
gentleness	completely	agreement
graceful	loosely	
hopeless	politely	
peaceful	priceless	
sincerely	puzzlement	
surely	scarcely	
wasteful	tireless	

These lists also appear on page 173 in the student edition and page 35 in the **Teacher Resource Book**.

SPELLING PATTERN

29

Suffixes: -ful, -less, -ly, -ment, -ness

Your Spelling List

_____
_____
_____
_____
_____
_____
_____
_____
_____
_____
_____
_____
_____
_____
_____

· · · · · · FINDING WORDS · · · · · · ·

1 **Build Your Spelling List**

Find Your Pattern Words
Take the pretest.
Write misspelled words on your spelling list.

Add Teacher Words
Teachers may add:
- More **Pattern Words** • Content Words • Theme Words

Add Your Words
Pick words from:
- **Words I Need to Know How to Spell** • Writing • Reading

Pattern Words

1. **lately**	Where have you been **lately**?
2. **careful**	Be **careful** as you cross the street.
3. **useless**	This broken pen is **useless**.
4. **movement**	I like the **movement** in this dance.
5. **strangeness**	The cat's **strangeness** bothers me.
6. **useful**	This book was **useful** for my project.
7. **careless**	Don't make **careless** mistakes.
8. **statement**	The mayor will make a **statement** to the reporters.
9. **hopeful**	She is **hopeful** she got an A.
10. **homeless**	He gave blankets to the **homeless**.

2 **Write Your Spelling List**

3 **Set Your Learning Goal**
My spelling list has _____ words for me to learn.

It's funny, but word hunting now seems to be a habit with me.

Me, too! Being a word hunter is something I can do all the time.

PATTERN MINI-LESSON

NOTE: The **Explore the Spelling Pattern** activity on page 141 is a self-directed mini-lesson. If you wish to supplement that activity with direct instruction, use the following mini-lesson.

* **Write** the **Pattern Words** from page 140 on the chalkboard. Pronounce each word and ask students to repeat it.

* **Ask** students what is similar about the words. (Possible response: *Each word has a suffix.*)

* **Invite** volunteers to identify each base word and to draw a line between the base word and the suffix. Ask students how each base word ends. (Possible response: *Each base word ends in e.*)

* **Point out** that each of these suffixes begins with a consonant. Explain that when a suffix beginning with a consonant is added to a base word ending in **e,** the spelling of the base word usually does not change.

* **Read** the **Spelling Pattern** on page 141 together with students.

NOTE: There are some classes of words in which final **e** is dropped before adding **-ly.** These include words ending in **ue** (**truly, duly**) and words ending in consonant-**le** (**simply, gently, cuddly,** and so on).

* **Write** these headings on the chalkboard: **-ful, -less, -ly, -ment, -ness.** Encourage students to offer other examples of words with these suffixes. Write the words under the appropriate headings. Circle the words in which the base word ends in **e.** You may wish to include examples from **More Words for Hungry Word Hunters** (on student page 173 and page T140). Remind students that they may add any of these words to **Words I Need to Know How to Spell**.

· · · · · INSPECTING WORDS · · · · ·

STEP 4 Explore the Spelling Pattern
Sorting Words

A. Sort the **Pattern Words** into five groups. Use the words below to guide your sort. Make sure you write each **Pattern Word** once. Then circle the suffix in each **Pattern Word**. Notice that each base word ends in **e.**

Try sorting the **Pattern Words** in other ways. How many words begin with a vowel?

1. careful
care(ful)
use(ful)
hope(ful)

2. useless
use(less)
care(less)
home(less)

3. movement
move(ment)
state(ment)

4. strangeness
strange(ness)

5. lately
late(ly)

B. Do a word hunt to find other words with the suffixes **-ful, -less, -ly, -ment,** and **-ness.** Add these words to your lists.

STEP 5 Focus on Word Study
Old English Suffixes

For at least a thousand years, suffixes have been added to English words to change their meaning. The Old English suffixes **-ness, -less,** and **-ful** are still useful today. Middle English borrowed many French suffixes, including **-ment.**

Add **-ful** and **-less** to each new word to make two new words.

1. taste	tasteful	tasteless
2. grace	graceful	graceless
3. shame	shameful	shameless
4. color	colorful	colorless

▼▼▼▼▼▼▼▼▼▼▼▼

Spelling Pattern
When you add a suffix beginning with a consonant, such as **-ful** or **-ness,** to a word that ends in **e,** you usually keep the **e.**

· · · · · · · · · · · · · · · · · · · ·

STEP 4 Explore the Spelling Pattern
Sorting Words

This activity is a self-directed mini-lesson on this week's **Spelling Pattern.**

STEP 5 Focus on Word Study
Old English Suffixes

This activity is intended to stimulate students' interest in words and to help them become more enthusiastic word hunters.

Spelling Process Handbook

Students who need to review any part of the spelling process, including practice options, should refer to the **Spelling Process Handbook** (pages 7–21).

MASTERING WORDS

 STEP 6 Practice Your Spelling List Independently

Ask the students to choose activities to practice their spelling words and to master this week's **Spelling Pattern**. Students should complete at least three activities each week. You may wish to:

- assign **Practice the Spelling Pattern** to all students to reinforce this week's **Spelling Pattern**.

- involve students' families by assigning **Take Your List Home** for this lesson (**Teacher Resource Book**, pages 111 in English and 112 in Spanish).

- encourage students to use partner activities without game mats (**Word Swap, Spelling Tic-Tac-Toe, Circle Dot**) and activities with game mats (**Meteor Attack, Rockets, Spelling Checkers, Spelling Soccer**). Directions for game-mat activities appear on each game mat. Directions for all other activities are found in the **Spelling Process Handbook** (pages 7–21).

> NOTE: These activities and games can be used to practice any spelling list.

SPELLING CHECKERS

Students will "jump" at the chance to play **Spelling Checkers**, a game mat that combines spelling practice with the popular board game. And because students write on the board with dry-erase markers to record their progress, game pieces are not needed. This game is especially appropriate spelling practice for auditory and visual learners. (Directions appear on the **Spelling Checkers** game mat. This activity is appropriate for practicing any spelling list.)

MASTERING WORDS

 STEP 6 Practice Your Spelling List Independently
Choose at least three activities to practice your spelling list.

It's fun to try different practice activities.

Game Mats	With a Partner	On Your Own	At Home
Spelling Checkers / Meteor Attack	Spelling Tic-Tac-Toe / Word Swap	Flip Folder / Spelling Study Strategy	Take Your List Home

 Practice the Spelling Pattern

Write the **Pattern Word** that fits each meaning. Use the underlined base word to help you.

Pattern Words

lately
careful
useless
movement
strangeness
useful
careless
statement
hopeful
homeless

Adjectives: Describing words that may end in **-ful** or **-less**

1. If you do a job with <u>care</u>, you are __.   careful

2. If you have <u>hope</u> about the future, you are __.   hopeful

3. If a dog has no <u>home</u>, it is __.   homeless

4. If a tool will be of <u>use</u>, it will be __.   useful

5. If you do not use enough <u>care</u>, you are __.   careless

6. If it's no <u>use</u> to complain, it is __.   useless

Nouns: Naming words that may end in **-ness** or **-ment**

7. If you <u>state</u> a fact, you make a __.   statement

8. If a story is <u>strange</u>, it has __.   strangeness

9. If you <u>move</u>, you make a __.   movement

Adverbs: Explaining words that may end in **-ly**

10. If you did it recently, or of <u>late</u>, you did it __.   lately

DEVELOPING GOOD SPELLING HABITS

STEP 7 Focus on Writing

A. Proofread the Writing of Others
This activity provides proofreading practice in a variety of formats, including popular standardized test formats.

B. Proofread Your Own Writing
Students return to their own writing, armed with strategies to identify and collect words they need to know how to spell, and make an authentic link between spelling and writing.

C. A Writing Idea: A Description
This suggestion for a more extended writing activity provides opportunities for students to write in different genres for a variety of purposes and modes.

STEP 8 Check Your Weekly Progress

▶ **Take the Test**
Remind students that they can take a practice test before the final test on their spelling lists. To find the testing procedure that is right for you, refer to page Z12.

▶ **Check Your Goal**
Have students compare their tests to their spelling lists. Did they spell all the **Pattern Words** on their spelling lists correctly?

▶ **Graph Your Progress**
Ask students to graph the number correct (student page 176 for softbound users; **Teacher Resource Book** page 123 for hardbound users).

▶ **Save Missed Words**
Tell students to write misspelled words on their lists of **Words I Need to Know How to Spell**. Remind students to verify spellings and to recycle these words on future weekly spelling lists.

· · · · · · · · · · · · · DEVELOPING GOOD SPELLING HABITS · · · · · · · · · · · · ·

STEP 7 Focus on Writing

A. Proofread the Writing of Others
Proofread the spelling tips. There's a word in each tip that is spelled wrong. Find the misspelled word and write the correct spelling.

1. When you add an ending to the word **care,** be carefull to keep the **e.**

2. Train your eye to notice the strangness of a word that is misspelled.

3. Don't be careliss when writing a word with a suffix. Spell the suffix correctly.

4. If you are not sure of a spelling, it's usefull to check the word in a dictionary.

1. _____careful_____
2. _____strangeness_____
3. _____careless_____
4. _____useful_____

≡ Make a capital.
/ Make a small letter.
∧ Add something.
℮ Take out something.
⊙ Add a period.
¶ New paragraph
SP Spelling error

B. Proofread Your Own Writing
Go to your most recent writing. Look for words that end in **-ful, -less, -ly, -ment,** and **-ness.** Make sure that you have spelled them correctly, especially if the base word ends in **e.** Did you keep the **e** wherever you should? Did you find words to add to **Words I Need to Know How to Spell**?

C. A Writing Idea: A Description
Words that end with **-ful** and **-less** are usually describing words, or adjectives. Think of a favorite character in a book you have read. Write a short paragraph describing that character. Try to use words ending in **-ful** and **-less** in your description. When you're finished, check your spelling.

STEP 8 Check Your Weekly Progress

▶ **Take the Test**
Ready? Practice test first.

▶ **Check Your Goal**
Check to see if you met your learning goal.

▶ **Graph Your Progress**
Graph your score for this week's test.

▶ **Save Missed Words**
Write the words you missed in your list of **Words I Need to Know How to Spell.**

Hunt Words
Remind students to continuously hunt words that they wish to learn how to spell and to write these words in **Words I Need to Know How to Spell.**

Changing y to i

Student Edition: Pages 144–147   **Teacher Edition:** Pages T144A–T147

Materials to help students practice their spelling lists:

- **Flip Folders**
- Copies of **Flip Folder Practice Sheet** (**Teacher Resource Book,** page 51)
- **Take Your List Home** (in *Spell It–Write!* Home News, **Teacher Resource Book,** pages 113 in English and 114 in Spanish)

- Game Mats Featured in This Unit: **Meteor Attack, Rockets**
- Unit 30 **Hands-on Word Sort Cards** (Grade 4 **Hands-on Word Sort Card Book**) and Unit 30 **Hands-on Word Sort Sheet** (**Teacher Resource Book,** page 46)

SPELLING GOALS

Students will

- transfer knowledge that when a suffix is added to a word ending in consonant-**y**, **y** is changed to **i**, but when a suffix is added to a word ending in vowel-**y**, **y** is not changed.

- sort words according to whether or not **y** is changed to **i** when a suffix is added.

- develop an understanding of the differences between British and American English.

- use the spelling process to become better writers.

WRITING GOALS

Students will

- hunt for **y** + suffix words in a piece of their own writing.

- write an informative comparison of two books.

Pacing	Notes	Quick Pick Management Option
Period 1 Finding Words (Steps 1–3)	If you wish to add **Teacher Words,** write them on the chalkboard. Sources for more words include: **More Words for Hungry Word Hunters** (page T144), content and theme-related words, or words of your choice.	Assign the list of **Pattern Words** to the whole class. Add the Red List (**More Words for Hungry Word Hunters,** student page 173) for a longer list. Add the Blue List (**More Words for Hungry Word Hunters**) for a more challenging list.
Period 2 Inspecting Words (Steps 4 and 5)	Students write the **Pattern Words** to complete **Explore the Spelling Pattern.**	Assign **Explore the Spelling Pattern** and **Focus on Word Study.**
Period 3 Mastering Words (Step 6) **Period 4** Developing Good Spelling Habits (Step 7)	These two periods can be allocated between selected **Mastering Words** activities and proofreading and writing activities in **Focus on Writing.**	Assign two or three activities to the whole class. Familiarize students with choosing their own activities at their own pace.
Period 5 Assessment (Step 8)	Gradually try different peer-testing options to find the style that best fits your class.	Test the class on the same, whole-class list.

Understanding Language Differences

Spanish Speakers

There are many kinds of \r\ sounds. Spanish has two. One is spelled with a single **r** and is called a "flapped **r,**" because the tongue flaps once in making it: **pero** (**but**). (Many British speakers pronounce the **r** in **very** and some other words with a flap. To American English speakers, it almost sounds as if they are saying "veddy.") The second Spanish **r** is called a "trilled **r,**" spelled with two **r**'s, in which the tongue flaps rapidly several times: **perro** (**dog**).

The \l\ and \r\ sounds are common in languages around the world. They are usually called "liquids" because they do not produce as much friction as most consonants do when we say them. However, there are many ways to produce these consonant sounds, and some are not really very "liquid."

Some languages, including French and German, use a gargling or uvular trill **r** sound, which is quite different from the American English **r** sound.

In English, \r\ and \l\ can occur in any position within a word, but in Japanese and Korean, for example, they cannot. This leads some Asian learners of English to pronounce \l\ in place of English \r\ when they encounter the letter **r** in unexpected positions.

Helping Students Acquiring English

Using magnetic letters or letter tiles, form the word **study**. Pronounce the word and discuss its meaning. Then ask students to watch what happens to **study** when you add **-es** to the word. Demonstrate changing the **y** to **i** before adding **-es**. Follow a similar procedure with the remaining **Pattern Words**.

Meeting Diverse Needs

Less Able Spellers

Students with special needs may benefit from learning to use self-instructions to help them manage their behavior during the spelling period or when studying words at home.

First, in concert with the student, identify any disruptive behavior. Then develop together a statement the child can use to help control the behavior, such as "Stop and think." Finally, model the use of the self-instruction, and ask the child to role play with you.

More Able Spellers

Encourage students to develop a chart or an alphabetized card file of words ending in **y** that provides examples of base words to which suffixes have been added. Students' entries should include words in these categories: consonant-**y** words in which **y** is changed to **i**; vowel-**y** words in which **y** is not changed to **i**; exceptions to these rules (e.g., **slyly**).

Ask students to copy their lists in the **Take Your List Home** section of the *Spell It–Write!* Home News page for this lesson. Not only does this page provide a convenient way for families to share a student's spelling list, but it also provides a number of opportunities for families to be involved in students' spelling growth. It has a statement of the week's spelling pattern or strategy, a valuable spelling study strategy, and a suggested home spelling practice activity.

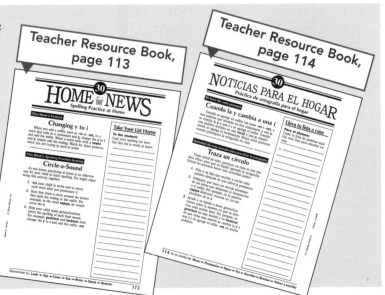

Teacher Resource Book, page 113

Teacher Resource Book, page 114

FINDING WORDS

STEP 1 Build Your Spelling List

Students will build their spelling lists with **Pattern Words, Teacher Words,** and **Your Words.** Students should study a minimum of twelve new words each week.

Find Your Pattern Words
- Pretest the students on these words.
- Tell students to write each misspelled pretest word on their spelling lists.

Add Teacher Words
- Select words for students to add to their spelling lists. Choose words from **More Words for Hungry Word Hunters** (on this page and on student page 173), words related to a theme or content area, or words students often misspell.

Add Your Words
- Ask students to pick words from their lists of **Words I Need to Know How to Spell** and their writing.
- Tell students to write these words on their spelling lists.

STEP 2 Write Your Spelling List

Remind students to verify all spellings. (Ask students to see **Strategies for Checking Your Spelling** in the back of the student edition.)

STEP 3 Set Your Learning Goal

Tell students to count the words on their spelling lists. This total is their learning goal. It may vary depending on ability, individual goals, and the difficulty of spelling words.

MORE WORDS FOR HUNGRY WORD HUNTERS

RED LIST Pattern Words Below Level	BLUE LIST Pattern Words Above Level	Other Pattern Words	Social Studies Pattern Words
angrily	denied	armies	hurried
busily	destroyed	driest	pities
buys	dirtiest	easiest	silliest
carries	laziness	factories	wittiest
cried	naughtier	funnier	
easier	obeyed	happier	
flies	rainiest	healthiest	
funniest	relies	heavier	
happiest	shyly	heaviest	
hurried	steadily	strawberries	
pays	sways		
stayed	tinier		

These lists also appear on page 173 in the student edition and page 36 in the **Teacher Resource Book.**

SPELLING PATTERN

30

Changing y to i

Your Spelling List

_____
_____
_____
_____
_____
_____
_____
_____
_____
_____
_____
_____
_____
_____
_____
_____
_____
_____
_____
_____

STEP 1 Build Your Spelling List

Find Your Pattern Words
Take the pretest.
Write misspelled words on your spelling list.

Add Teacher Words
Teachers may add:
- More **Pattern Words** • Content Words • Theme Words

Add Your Words
Pick words from:
- **Words I Need to Know How to Spell** • Writing • Reading

Pattern Words

1. **studies**	Joan **studies** every night.
2. **prettiest**	The **prettiest** flower is a rose.
3. **enjoys**	Tom **enjoys** listening to music.
4. **slyly**	The fox **slyly** tricked the hen.
5. **spied**	Linda **spied** the coin in the fountain.
6. **healthier**	What can you do to become **healthier**?
7. **fries**	Betty **fries** apples for dessert.
8. **luckiest**	Hank is the **luckiest** person I know.
9. **sprayed**	We **sprayed** air freshener in the car.
10. **worried**	Kenny is **worried** about his math test.
11. **happiness**	What does **happiness** mean to you?
12. **happily**	The police **happily** help people.

STEP 2 Write Your Spelling List

STEP 3 Set Your Learning Goal

My spelling list has _____ words for me to learn.

> Sorting words helps me look at how the spellings are the same in different words.

> I really like the word sorts that have **Hands-on Word Sort Cards.**

INSPECTING WORDS

PATTERN MINI-LESSON

> **NOTE:** The **Explore the Spelling Pattern** activity on page 145 is a self-directed mini-lesson. If you wish to supplement that activity with direct instruction, use the following mini-lesson.

* **Read** the **Spelling Pattern** on page 145 together with the class. Explain that it will guide the **Hands-on Word Sort**.

* **Display** the **?** card and the **Hands-on Word Sort Cards** for Unit 30. Keep blank cards and a marker handy to make new cards.

* **Pronounce** each guide word. (Guide words are labeled "Master Word" on the **Word Sort Card**.) Point to the under-lined letters, and then point to the base word. Ask students what difference they see between the two words. Establish that when a suffix is added to a word ending in a consonant and **y,** the **y** is changed to **i.**

> **NOTE:** Point out that this rule does not apply to the suffix **-ing.**

* **Sort** the words according to whether or not the **y** was changed to **i.** Model your decision making: "The base word of **prettiest** is **pretty.** When the suffix was added, the **y** was changed to **i.** So I'll put **prettiest** under **studies.**"

* **Tell** students to place words that do not fit the patterns under the question mark. Challenge students to explain why **slyly** does not fit. (Response: *The base word ends in a con-sonant and y, but the y is not changed to i.*) For the completed word sort, see the **Answer Card** for this unit in the **Hands-on Word Sort Card Book.**

* **Duplicate** the **Hands-on Word Sort Sheet** for Unit 30 (**Teacher Resource Book,** page 46). Ask students to cut the words on the sheet apart and practice sorting the words with a partner or independently.

· · · · · · · · · · INSPECTING WORDS · · · · · · · · · ·

STEP 4 Explore the Spelling Pattern
Sorting Words

A. Find a spelling partner. Take turns reading the **Pattern Words** out loud. Think about whether the spelling of each base word changes when an ending is added. Write each word with the guide word below that has the same spelling pattern. If a word doesn't fit, put it with the question mark. Be sure to write each **Pattern Word** once.

> You may wish to use **Hands-on Sort Cards Word** and the **Hands-on Sort Sheet** for this unit.

1. stud<u>ies</u> (study)

studies	healthier	worried
prettiest	fries	happiness
spied	luckiest	happily

2. enj<u>oys</u> (enjoy)

		3. ?
enjoys	sprayed	slyly

B. Work with a partner to do a word hunt. Look for words with a suffix added to a base word that ends in **y.** Which words, if any, were formed by changing the **y** to **i?** Which words kept the **y?** Add the words you find to your word sort.

STEP 5 Focus on Word Study
British and American English

The British people joke that "Americans haven't spoken English for years!" That's because there are differences between American English and British English. For example, an American eats "French fries," but a British person eats "chips."

Match the American word to the British word with the same meaning.

1. lift   <u>c</u>   **a.** potato chips

2. crisps   <u>a</u>   **b.** cookie

3. biscuit   <u>b</u>   **c.** elevator

▼▼▼▼▼▼▼▼▼▼▼▼▼
Spelling Pattern
* When you add a suffix, such as **-es** or **-est,** to a word that ends in a consonant and **y,** change the **y** to **i** and add the suffix.

* When a word ends with a vowel and **y,** simply add the ending.
· · · · · · · · · · · · · · · ·

STEP 4 Explore the Spelling Pattern
Sorting Words

This activity is a self-directed mini-lesson on this week's **Spelling Pattern.**

STEP 5 Focus on Word Study
British and American English

This activity is intended to stimulate students' interest in words and to help them become more enthusiastic word hunters.

Spelling Process Handbook

Students who need to review any part of the spelling process, including practice options, should refer to the **Spelling Process Handbook** (pages 7–21).

MASTERING WORDS

n

STEP 6 Practice Your Spelling List Independently

Ask the students to choose activities to practice their spelling words and to master this week's **Spelling Pattern**. Students should complete at least three activities each week. You may wish to:

- assign **Practice the Spelling Pattern** to all students to reinforce this week's **Spelling Pattern**.

- involve students' families by assigning **Take Your List Home** for this lesson (**Teacher Resource Book,** pages 113 in English and 114 in Spanish).

- encourage students to use partner activities without game mats (**Word Swap, Spelling Tic-Tac-Toe, Circle Dot**) and activities with game mats (**Meteor Attack, Rockets, Spelling Checkers, Spelling Soccer**). Directions for game-mat activities appear on each game mat. Directions for all other activities are found in the **Spelling Process Handbook** (pages 7–21).

> NOTE: These activities and games can be used to practice any spelling list.

age_ref id="12" />

A Practice Option

METEOR ATTACK

Students will attack spelling words with enthusiasm as they pair up to play **Meteor Attack**. Partners take turns spelling and writing their spelling words as they "destroy" meteors and collect points. The more words they spell correctly, the more points they collect. It's great fun, and great spelling practice, especially for auditory and visual learners. (Directions appear on the **Meteor Attack** game mat. This activity is appropriate for practicing any spelling list.)

· · · · · MASTERING WORDS · · · · ·

STEP 6 Practice Your Spelling List Independently

Choose at least three activities to practice your spelling list.

> Hunt words in your writing and reading! Add words you want to learn to **Words I Need to Know How to Spell**.

Game Mats	With a Partner	On Your Own	At Home
○ Meteor Attack ○ Rockets	○ Circle Dot ○ Word Swap	○ Flip Folder ○ Spelling Study Strategy	○ Take Your List Home

Practice the Spelling Pattern

In the math puzzles below, some of the letters you need to add or subtract are missing. To solve the puzzle, decide which letter or letters are missing. Write the **Pattern Word** and then circle the letter or letters that were missing.

Pattern Words

studies
prettiest
enjoys
slyly
spied
healthier
fries
luckiest
sprayed
worried
happiness
happily

1. enjoy + __ = __   enjoy(s)

2. spy − y + __ + ed = __   sp(i)ed

3. worry − y + __ + ed = __   worr(i)ed

4. happy − y + __ + ness = __   happ(i)ness

5. fry − y + i + __ __ = __   fri(es)

6. lucky − y + __ + est = __   luck(i)est

7. spray + __ __ = __   spray(ed)

8. healthy − y + __ + er = __   health(i)er

9. happy − y + i + __ __ = __   happi(ly)

10. sly + __ __ = __   sly(ly)

11. pretty − y + __ + est = __   prett(i)est

12. study − y + i + __ __ = __   studi(es)

T146 UNIT 30

146 UNIT 30

DEVELOPING GOOD SPELLING HABITS

STEP 7 Focus on Writing

A. Hunt Spelling Words in Your Writing

This activity equips students with a specific strategy for increasing students' consciousness of targeted spelling patterns and strategies in their own writing. It also enables them to collect words for spelling study.

B. A Writing Idea: A Comparison

This suggestion for a more extended writing activity provides opportunities for students to write in different genres for a variety of purposes and modes.

STEP 8 Check Your Weekly Progress

▶ Take the Test

Remind students that they can take a practice test before the final test on their spelling lists. To find the testing procedure that is right for you, refer to page Z12.

▶ Check Your Goal

Have students compare their tests to their spelling lists. Did they spell all the **Pattern Words** on their spelling lists correctly?

▶ Graph Your Progress

Ask students to graph the number correct (student page 176 for softbound users; **Teacher Resource Book** page 123 for hardbound users).

▶ Save Missed Words

Tell students to write misspelled words on their lists of **Words I Need to Know How to Spell**. Remind students to verify spellings and to recycle these words on future weekly spelling lists.

· · · · · · DEVELOPING GOOD SPELLING HABITS · · · · · ·

STEP 7 Focus on Writing

A. Hunt Spelling Words in Your Writing

Choose a few pieces of your latest writing. With a spelling partner, look for words with a suffix added to a base word that ends in **y**. Don't forget to check and see if **y** changed to **i**. Use two columns like these to record the words you find.

Column 1	Column 2
I spelled these **y + suffix** words correctly.	I misspelled these **y + suffix** words.
Answers will vary.	Answers will vary.

If you didn't find any **y + suffix** words, check another piece of writing.

Add the words you wrote in Column 2 to **Words I Need to Know How to Spell**.

B. A Writing Idea: A Comparison

Write a book review to compare and contrast two books you have read recently. Use words that show a comparison, such as **funnier** and **scariest**. When you are finished writing, check your spelling. Then post your review with your classmates' reviews on a bulletin board.

≡ Make a capital.
/ Make a small letter.
∧ Add something.
ℓ Take out something.
⊙ Add a period.
ዋ New paragraph
(SP) Spelling error

STEP 8 Check Your Weekly Progress

▶ Take the Test
Ready? Practice test first.

▶ Check Your Goal
Check to see if you met your learning goal.

▶ Graph Your Progress
Graph your score for this week's test.

▶ Save Missed Words
Write the words you missed in your list of **Words I Need to Know How to Spell**.

Hunt Words

Remind students to continuously hunt words that they wish to learn how to spell and to write these words in **Words I Need to Know How to Spell**.

Word Building

SPELLING PATTERN

ENGAGING
IN THE
PROCESS

MATERIALS

Student Edition: Pages 148–151   **Teacher Edition:** Pages T148A–T151

Materials to help students practice their spelling lists:

- **Flip Folders**
- Copies of **Flip Folder Practice Sheet** (**Teacher Resource Book,** page 51)
- **Take Your List Home** (in *Spell It–Write!*

Home News, **Teacher Resource Book,** pages 115 in English and 116 in Spanish)
- Game Mats Featured in This Unit: **Rockets, Spelling Soccer**

ENGAGING
IN THE
PROCESS

GOALS

SPELLING GOALS

Students will

- transfer knowledge that words can be built by adding prefixes and suffixes to base words.
- develop an understanding of how the meanings of words can change over time.
- use the spelling process of finding words, inspecting words, and mastering words as they develop good spelling habits to become better writers.

WRITING GOALS

Students will

- proofread a writing sample.
- proofread a piece of their own writing for misspelled words with prefixes and suffixes.
- write a persuasive ad.

ENGAGING
IN THE
PROCESS

MANAGEMENT

Pacing	Notes	Quick Pick Management Option
Period 1 Finding Words (Steps 1–3)	If you wish to add **Teacher Words,** write them on the chalkboard. Sources for more words include: **More Words for Hungry Word Hunters** (page T148), content and theme-related words, or words of your choice.	Assign the list of **Pattern Words** to the whole class. Add the Red List (**More Words for Hungry Word Hunters,** student page 174) for a longer list. Add the Blue List (**More Words for Hungry Word Hunters**) for a more challenging list.
Period 2 Inspecting Words (Steps 4 and 5)	Students write the **Pattern Words** to complete **Explore the Spelling Pattern.**	Assign **Explore the Spelling Pattern** and **Focus on Word Study.**
Period 3 Mastering Words (Step 6) **Period 4** Developing Good Spelling Habits (Step 7)	These two periods can be allocated between selected **Mastering Words** activities and proofreading and writing activities in **Focus on Writing.**	Assign two or three activities to the whole class. Familiarize students with choosing their own activities at their own pace.
Period 5 Assessment (Step 8)	Gradually try different peer-testing options to find the style that best fits your class.	Test the class on the same, whole-class list.

Understanding Language Differences

Prefixes are common to most Western European languages. Some prefixes and suffixes in the words on this week's lists correspond to affixes in Spanish, French, and German. For example, **pre-** and **re-** are used as prefixes in both Spanish and French. (In French, the spellings are **pré** and **ré**.) The prefix **un-** is found in German.

However, not all languages have prefixes. Chinese uses separate words instead. Students with this language background may require special attention to grasp the notion of adding affixes to a base word to express a change in meaning.

Helping Students Acquiring English

On the chalkboard or on chart paper, create a chart of the prefixes and suffixes used in this week's **Pattern Words,** together with their meanings. (See the **Pattern Mini-Lessons** on pages T99 and T149.) Next, write the word **test,** and discuss its meaning. Add the prefix **pre-** and the suffix **-ed** to **test,** using different colors of chalk. Pronounce the new word, **pretested.** Ask students to repeat the word, and discuss how the meaning of the word changed. Follow a similar procedure to introduce the remaining **Pattern Words.** Allow students to construct and take apart words using magnetic letters or letter tiles.

Meeting Diverse Needs

Less Able Spellers

Students with special needs, including children with attention deficit disorders, may have difficulty sustaining their attention during academic tasks such as spelling time. One way to help these students stay on-task is to ask them to self-assess their performance.

For example, when they study new spelling words, children can be asked to count and record the number of times they practice each word. Similarly, they can be asked to periodically record whether they are on- or off-task.

More Able Spellers

Challenge students to create antonyms for words by adding, subtracting, and switching prefixes or suffixes. To get students started, you might provide these examples of antonym pairs: **unfriendly-friendly, careless-careful.**

Ask students to copy their lists in the **Take Your List Home** section of the *Spell It–Write!* Home News page for this lesson. Not only does this page provide a convenient way for families to share a student's spelling list, but it also provides a number of opportunities for families to be involved in students' spelling growth. It has a statement of the week's spelling pattern or strategy, a valuable spelling study strategy, and a suggested home spelling practice activity.

Teacher Resource Book, page 115

Teacher Resource Book, page 116

FINDING WORDS

Build Your Spelling List

Students will build their spelling lists with **Pattern Words, Teacher Words,** and **Your Words**. Students should study a minimum of twelve new words each week.

Find Your Pattern Words
• Pretest the students on these words.
• Tell students to write each misspelled pretest word on their spelling lists.

Add Teacher Words
• Select words for students to add to their spelling lists. Choose words from **More Words for Hungry Word Hunters** (on this page and on student page 174), words related to a theme or content area, or words students often misspell.

Your Words
• Ask students to pick words from their lists of **Words I Need to Know How to Spell** and their writing.
• Tell students to write these words on their spelling lists.

Write Your Spelling List

Remind students to verify all spellings. (Ask students to see **Strategies for Checking Your Spelling** in the back of the student edition.)

Set Your Learning Goal

Tell students to count the words on their spelling lists. This total is their learning goal. It may vary depending on ability, individual goals, and the difficulty of spelling words.

MORE WORDS FOR HUNGRY WORD HUNTERS

RED LIST Pattern Words Below Level	BLUE LIST Pattern Words Above Level
bravely	breathlessly
colorful	prepayment
kindness	prerecorded
payment	previewing
prepay	replacement
preschool	sleeplessness
pretest	unemployment
reheat	unfitness
restless	unlikely
untied	usefulness

These lists also appear on page 174 in the student edition and page 37 in the **Teacher Resource Book.**

SPELLING PATTERN

31

Word Building

Your Spelling List

_____
_____
_____
_____
_____
_____
_____
_____
_____
_____
_____
_____
_____
_____
_____
_____

FINDING WORDS

Build Your Spelling List

Find Your Pattern Words
Take the pretest.
Write misspelled words on your spelling list.

Add Teacher Words
Teachers may add:
• More **Pattern Words** • Content Words • Theme Words

Add Your Words
Pick words from:
• **Words I Need to Know How to Spell** • Writing • Reading

Pattern Words

1. **pretested**	Toys are **pretested** for safety.
2. **cheerfully**	He **cheerfully** washed the dishes.
3. **unfriendly**	That growling bear is **unfriendly**.
4. **peacefulness**	I love the **peacefulness** of the quiet lake.
5. **restlessly**	Joan slept **restlessly** last night.
6. **preschooler**	My little brother is a **preschooler**.
7. **repayment**	This is the **repayment** of my loan.
8. **unkindness**	Your **unkindness** hurts others.
9. **forgetfulness**	Please forgive my **forgetfulness**.
10. **prepaying**	We saved money by **prepaying** the loan.

Write Your Spelling List

Set Your Learning Goal

My spelling list has _____ words for me to learn.

The really good thing about the practice activities is that I can use them to practice any words.

Yes, **Circle Dot** works every time with any spelling list.

INSPECTING WORDS

PATTERN MINI-LESSON

NOTE: The **Explore the Spelling Pattern** activity on page 149 is a self-directed mini-lesson. If you wish to supplement that activity with direct instruction, use the following mini-lesson.

* **Write** each of these word parts on separate cards: **pay, pre, ing, re, ment**. Challenge students to make as many words as possible from these word parts by using any two or three parts. (Possible responses: *prepay, repay, repaying, prepaying, payment, repayment, prepayment*) Write the words on the chalkboard.

* **Tell** students that the words on this week's list were made by building words with base words, prefixes, and suffixes.

* **Write** "Prefix," "Base Word," and "Suffix" as headings on the chalkboard. Remind students that a prefix comes before a base word and a suffix comes after a base word.

* **Ask** students to open their books to page 148. Invite volunteers to read the **Pattern Words** and divide them into prefixes, base words, and suffixes. Write each part under the correct heading.

* **Write** these words on the chalkboard: **prewash, precook, preheat, undo, unmake, untold, redo, remake, retold**. Establish that **pre-** means "before" or "ahead," **un-** means "do the opposite of" or "back," and **re-** means "again" or "back."

* **Review** the meanings of **-ful, -less, -ly, -ment,** and **-ness** on page T99.

* **Ask** students to read the **Spelling Pattern** on page 149.

* **Encourage** students to offer other examples of words with prefixes and suffixes. List these on the chalkboard.

· · · · · · INSPECTING WORDS · · · · · ·

STEP 4 Explore the Spelling Pattern
Thinking About Meaning

A. Write the **Pattern Word** that makes the best sense in each sentence. The base word in parentheses is a clue. Circle the prefix and box the suffix in each word you wrote. The first one is done for you.

1. The bank accepted my __. (pay) — (re)pay[ment]
2. Before a car is sold, it is __. (test) — (pre)test[ed]
3. The __ is almost ready for kindergarten. (school) — (pre)school[er]
4. Did his remark have an __ tone? (friend) — (un)friend[ly]
5. We __ did the unpacking. (cheer) — cheer[fully]
6. We are __ the bill before its due date. (pay) — (pre)pay[ing]
7. Their __ seemed very rude. (kind) — (un)kind[ness]
8. She is known for her calmness and __. (peace) — peace[fulness]
9. The baby tossed and turned __. (rest) — rest[lessly]
10. Did your __ make you late? (forget) — forget[fulness]

B. Have a contest with a partner to find more words with prefixes and suffixes. Look in your reading and in **Words I Need to Know How to Spell**. Set a time limit, and score one point for each prefix or suffix in words you list. Words with more parts are worth more points!

STEP 5 Focus on Word Study
Word History

Long ago, **teste** was a small container that was used in checking for gold and other precious metals. Over time, the word **test** came to mean any trial or examination.

Write the word **meat, disease,** or **governor** with its earlier meaning.

1. protector — governor
2. food — meat
3. discomfort — disease

STEP 4 Explore the Spelling Pattern
Thinking About Meaning
This activity is a self-directed mini-lesson on this week's **Spelling Pattern**.

STEP 5 Focus on Word Study
Word History
This activity is intended to stimulate students' interest in words and to help them become more enthusiastic word hunters.

▼▼▼▼▼▼▼▼▼▼▼
Spelling Pattern
Many words are formed by adding prefixes or suffixes to a base word.
· · · · · · · · · ·

Spelling Process Handbook
Students who need to review any part of the spelling process, including practice options, should refer to the **Spelling Process Handbook** (pages 7–21).

MASTERING WORDS

STEP 6 Practice Your Spelling List Independently

Ask the students to choose activities to practice their spelling words and to master this week's **Spelling Pattern**. Students should complete at least three activities each week. You may wish to:

- assign **Practice the Spelling Pattern** to all students to reinforce this week's **Spelling Pattern**.

- involve students' families by assigning **Take Your List Home** for this lesson (**Teacher Resource Book**, pages 115 in English and 116 in Spanish).

- encourage students to use partner activities without game mats (**Word Swap, Spelling Tic-Tac-Toe, Circle Dot**) and activities with game mats (**Meteor Attack, Rockets, Spelling Checkers, Spelling Soccer**). Directions for game-mat activities appear on each game mat. Directions for all other activities are found in the **Spelling Process Handbook** (pages 7–21).

NOTE: These activities and games can be used to practice any spelling list.

A Practice Option

ROCKETS

Can you figure out the spelling word before your partner "blasts off"? That's the challenge for students as they play **Rockets**. Students will develop their knowledge of common spelling patterns as they make strategic guesses to visualize spellings and complete words. It's a countdown to spelling success with **Rockets**. (Directions appear on the **Rockets** game mat. This activity is appropriate for practicing any spelling list.)

MASTERING WORDS

STEP 6 Practice Your Spelling List Independently

Choose at least three activities to practice your spelling list.

Need Help? Read the **Spelling Process Handbook** (pages 7–21).

Game Mats	With a Partner	On Your Own	At Home
○Rockets ○Spelling Soccer	○Circle Dot ○Spelling Tic-Tac-Toe	○Flip Folder ○Spelling Study Strategy	○Take Your List Home

Practice the Spelling Pattern

Look at each analogy and think about how the words relate to each other. Write the **Pattern Word** that goes with the other words to complete each analogy. The first one is done for you.

Pattern Words

pretested
cheerfully
unfriendly
peacefulness
restlessly
preschooler
repayment
unkindness
forgetfulness
prepaying

1. Prepay is to prepayment as repay is to __. **repayment**
2. Kindly is to unkindly as friendly is to __. **unfriendly**
3. Heated is to preheated as tested is to __. **pretested**
4. Helpful is to helpfulness as peaceful is to __. **peacefulness**
5. Careless is to carelessly as restless is to __. **restlessly**
6. Joyful is to joyfully as cheerful is to __. **cheerfully**
7. Preview is to previewing as prepay is to __. **prepaying**
8. Playful is to playfulness as forgetful is to __. **forgetfulness**
9. Fairness is to unfairness as kindness is to __. **unkindness**
10. Pretest is to pretester as preschool is to __. **preschooler**

DEVELOPING GOOD SPELLING HABITS

7 Focus on Writing

A. Proofread the Writing of Others

This activity provides proofreading practice in a variety of formats, including popular standardized test formats.

B. Proofread Your Own Writing

Students return to their own writing, armed with strategies to identify and collect words they need to know how to spell, and make an authentic link between spelling and writing.

C. A Writing Idea: An Ad

This suggestion for a more extended writing activity provides opportunities for students to write in different genres for a variety of purposes and modes.

8 Check Your Weekly Progress

▶ Take the Test

Remind students that they can take a practice test before the final test on their spelling lists. To find the testing procedure that is right for you, refer to page Z12.

▶ Check Your Goal

Have students compare their tests to their spelling lists. Did they spell all the **Pattern Words** on their spelling lists correctly?

▶ Graph Your Progress

Ask students to graph the number correct (student page 176 for softbound users; **Teacher Resource Book** page 123 for hardbound users).

▶ Save Missed Words

Tell students to write misspelled words on their lists of **Words I Need to Know How to Spell**. Remind students to verify spellings and to recycle these words on future weekly spelling lists.

· · · · · · · · · DEVELOPING GOOD SPELLING HABITS · · · · · · · · ·

7 Focus on Writing

A. Proofread the Writing of Others

Proofread these signs from a computer store. Decide which type of mistake, if any, appears in each underlined section.

If you are not happy, your money <u>will be cheerfully</u> refunded.
①

All our <u>computers are pretestid</u> before we sell them.
②

Our staff is not <u>unfriendly! we smile!</u>
③

Are you interested in <u>prepaying. See</u> the manager.
④

≡ Make a capital.
/ Make a small letter.
∧ Add something.
⌒ Take out something.
⊙ Add a period.
¶ New paragraph
(SP) Spelling error

1. A Spelling
   B Capitalization
   C Punctuation
   (D) No mistake

2. (A) Spelling
   B Capitalization
   C Punctuation
   D No mistake

3. A Spelling
   (B) Capitalization
   C Punctuation
   D No mistake

4. A Spelling
   B Capitalization
   (C) Punctuation
   D No mistake

B. Proofread Your Own Writing

Look through your recent writing for words with prefixes and suffixes. Use this strategy to check spelling: First make sure you have spelled each word part correctly. Then check the spelling of the whole word. Write misspelled words correctly in **Words I Need to Know How to Spell**.

C. A Writing Idea: An Ad

Write a radio ad for a computer store. Tell about a new kind of computer: What amazing things does it do? Who will want to buy it, and why? Swap ads with a classmate and read each other's ads aloud to the class.

8 Check Your Weekly Progress

▶ Take the Test
Ready? Practice test first.

▶ Check Your Goal
Check to see if you met your learning goal.

▶ Graph Your Progress
Graph your score for this week's test.

▶ Save Missed Words
Write the words you missed in your list of **Words I Need to Know How to Spell**.

Hunt Words

Remind students to continuously hunt words that they wish to learn how to spell and to write these words in **Words I Need to Know How to Spell**.

PERSUASIVE

SPELLING PATTERN 32   Word Building

ENGAGING IN THE PROCESS — MATERIALS

Student Edition: Pages 152–155   **Teacher Edition:** Pages T152A–T155

Materials to help students practice their spelling lists:
- **Flip Folders**
- Copies of **Flip Folder Practice Sheet** (**Teacher Resource Book,** page 51)
- **Take Your List Home** (in *Spell It–Write!*

Home News, **Teacher Resource Book,** pages 117 in English and 118 in Spanish)
- Game Mats Featured in This Unit: **Spelling Checkers, Spelling Soccer**

ENGAGING IN THE PROCESS — GOALS

SPELLING GOALS

Students will

- transfer knowledge that words can be built by adding prefixes and suffixes to base words.

- develop an understanding of how meanings and spellings of words can change over time.

- use the spelling process of finding words, inspecting words, and mastering words as they develop good spelling habits to become better writers.

WRITING GOALS

Students will

- proofread a writing sample.

- proofread a piece of their own writing for misspelled words with prefixes and suffixes.

- write a persuasive speech.

ENGAGING IN THE PROCESS — MANAGEMENT

Pacing	Notes	Quick Pick Management Option
Period 1 Finding Words (Steps 1–3)	If you wish to add **Teacher Words,** write them on the chalkboard. Sources for more words include: **More Words for Hungry Word Hunters** (page T152), content and theme-related words, or words of your choice.	Assign the list of **Pattern Words** to the whole class. Add the Red List (**More Words for Hungry Word Hunters,** student page 174) for a longer list. Add the Blue List (**More Words for Hungry Word Hunters**) for a more challenging list.
Period 2 Inspecting Words (Steps 4 and 5)	Students write the **Pattern Words** to complete **Explore the Spelling Pattern.**	Assign **Explore the Spelling Pattern** and **Focus on Word Study.**
Period 3 Mastering Words (Step 6) **Period 4** Developing Good Spelling Habits (Step 7)	These two periods can be allocated between selected **Mastering Words** activities and proofreading and writing activities in **Focus on Writing.**	Assign two or three activities to the whole class. Familiarize students with choosing their own activities at their own pace.
Period 5 Assessment (Step 8)	Gradually try different peer-testing options to find the style that best fits your class.	Test the class on the same, whole-class list.

Understanding Language Differences

Not all languages create words by adding affixes. However, most students from a Western European or Latin American language background will at least be familiar with the concept of adding prefixes to base words to express a change in meaning.

Helping Students Acquiring English

Review with students the meanings of the prefixes and suffixes presented in Units 19 and 31 and spelling changes that take place when suffixes are added to base words (drop final **silent e,** change **y** to **i**). Next, write all the **Pattern Words** on the chalkboard. Write the prefixes and suffixes for this unit (**re-, -ly, -un, -ness**) on separate cards, and place them in a box or a hat. Ask students to pick one card, take it up to the chalkboard and match the prefix or suffix to one of the matching **Pattern Words.** They should show the card to the class, and then read aloud the prefix or suffix and the matching **Pattern Word** they have chosen. The class should then respond chorally to repeat the same information. Continue until all the **Pattern Words** have been chosen at least once. (More than one **Pattern Word** may match each prefix or suffix.)

Meeting Diverse Needs

Less Able Spellers

During the summer break, students who have difficulty learning to spell, including students with special needs, often forget some of the spelling skills they have mastered during the school year. One way to minimize the effects of forgetting during summer break is to design a series of spelling activities and reviews that students can complete during summer break.

If your school offers summer programs, you may also want to give children an advanced start on next year's spelling program by providing instruction on upcoming spelling skills during the summer.

More Able Spellers

Encourage students to hunt unusual or intriguing words throughout the summer. Invite them to collect these words in a journal and organize them according to the different spelling patterns they include.

ENGAGING
IN THE
PROCESS
INVOLVING
FAMILIES

Ask students to copy their lists in the **Take Your List Home** section of the *Spell It–Write!* Home News page for this lesson. Not only does this page provide a convenient way for families to share a student's spelling list, but it also provides a number of opportunities for families to be involved in students' spelling growth. It has a statement of the week's spelling pattern or strategy, a valuable spelling study strategy, and a suggested home spelling practice activity.

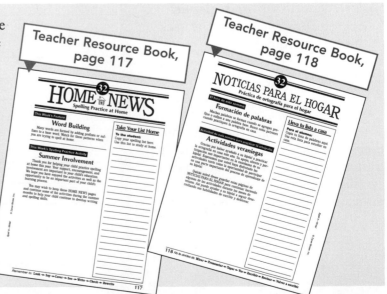

FINDING WORDS

STEP 1 Build Your Spelling List

Students will build their spelling lists with **Pattern Words, Teacher Words,** and **Your Words.** Students should study a minimum of twelve new words each week.

Find Your Pattern Words

• Pretest the students on these words.

• Tell students to write each misspelled pretest word on their spelling lists.

Add Teacher Words

• Select words for students to add to their spelling lists. Choose words from **More Words for Hungry Word Hunters** (on this page and on student page 174), words related to a theme or content area, or words students often misspell.

Add Your Words

• Ask students to pick words from their lists of **Words I Need to Know How to Spell** and their writing.

• Tell students to write these words on their spelling lists.

STEP 2 Write Your Spelling List

Remind students to verify all spellings. (Ask students to see **Strategies for Checking Your Spelling** in the back of the student edition.)

STEP 3 Set Your Learning Goal

Tell students to count the words on their spelling lists. This total is their learning goal. It may vary depending on ability, individual goals, and the difficulty of spelling words.

MORE WORDS FOR HUNGRY WORD HUNTERS

RED LIST — Pattern Words Below Level	BLUE LIST — Pattern Words Above Level
becoming	argument
changed	awfully
divided	loneliness
dried	probably
drying	rearrangement
easily	undying
lovelier	unfriendliness
loveliest	unhappiness
moving	unhurried
simply	unluckily

These lists also appear on page 174 in the student edition and page 38 in the **Teacher Resource Book.**

SPELLING PATTERN

32

Word Building

Your Spelling List

_____
_____
_____
_____
_____
_____
_____
_____
_____
_____
_____
_____
_____
_____
_____
_____
_____
_____
_____
_____

FINDING WORDS

STEP 1 Build Your Spelling List

Find Your Pattern Words
Take the pretest.
Write misspelled words on your spelling list.

Add Teacher Words
Teachers may add:
• More **Pattern Words** • Content Words • Theme Words

Add Your Words
Pick words from:
• **Words I Need to Know How to Spell** • Writing • Reading

Pattern Words

1. **rebuilding** — They are **rebuilding** the burned house.
2. **truly** — Tina is **truly** sorry she hurt you.
3. **beautiful** — This work of art is **beautiful**.
4. **unhappily** — We **unhappily** said good-bye to Joji.
5. **undivided** — We are one nation **undivided**.
6. **emptiness** — I felt an **emptiness** in my stomach before lunch.
7. **gently** — She **gently** lifted the hurt robin.
8. **rewriting** — We are **rewriting** the play.
9. **uneasily** — Fred sat **uneasily** in the chair.
10. **removing** — Mom is **removing** the old paint.

STEP 2 Write Your Spelling List

STEP 3 Set Your Learning Goal

My spelling list has _____ words for me to learn.

The spelling test lets me know how I'm doing every week.

I like **Check Your Progress** because it helps me check how well I remember important spelling patterns.

PATTERN MINI-LESSON

NOTE: The **Explore the Spelling Pattern** activity on page 153 is a self-directed mini-lesson. If you wish to supplement that activity with direct instruction, use the following mini-lesson.

* **Write** the following words on the chalkboard: **write, beauty, easy, empty, move, happy, build, divide, gentle, true**.

* **Ask** students to open their books to page 152. Call on volunteers to read the **Pattern Words** aloud. Ask students to find the base word on the chalkboard for each **Pattern Word**. As they identify each base word, write the corresponding **Pattern Word** beside it: **beauty-beautiful**.

* **Read** the **Spelling Pattern** on page 153 aloud with students.

* **Challenge** students to work in pairs to prepare formal rules for adding prefixes and suffixes to as many spelling words as they can. Ask each group to report its hypotheses to the class. Allow the class to confirm, reject, or revise the principles. Post the valid rules on a bulletin board with example words.

* **Ask** students to think of other words with prefixes and suffixes and to classify them according to the rules the class has established. You may wish to include examples from **More Words for Hungry Word Hunters** (on student page 174 and page T152). Remind students that they may add any of these words to **Words I Need to Know How to Spell**.

· · · · · · · · · INSPECTING WORDS · · · · · · · · ·

Explore the Spelling Pattern
Thinking About Meaning

A. Look at each sentence. Decide which **Pattern Word** fits the meaning of the sentence and is related to the underlined base word. Write the **Pattern Word**.

1. We stared into the ___ of the big <u>empty</u> cave.   emptiness

2. Yes, it's <u>true</u>, and I'm ___ sorry.   truly

3. The pizza came ___ , so let's <u>divide</u> it now.   undivided

4. Don't <u>move</u> the table without ___ the lamp.   removing

5. Those ___ roses add to the garden's <u>beauty</u>.   beautiful

6. Be <u>gentle</u> with the kitten and stroke its fur ___ .   gently

7. The stories I <u>write</u> are better after some ___ .   rewriting

8. Nobody ever sings "<u>Happy</u> Birthday" ___ !   unhappily

9. I waited ___ , knowing the test wouldn't be <u>easy</u>.   uneasily

10. ___ a sand castle is as much fun as <u>building</u> it!   Rebuilding

B. Look in **Words I Need to Know How to Spell** and in your writing to find other words formed by adding prefixes and suffixes to base words.

Focus on Word Study
Changes in Spelling and Meaning

The Old English word **emtig** meant "not busy." It also meant "not married"! Later, the word was spelled **empti**, and it meant "containing nothing." Now, we spell it **empty**.

Write the modern spelling of **drink, glove**, and **bed** with its Old English spelling.

1. bedd   bed

2. drincan   drink

3. glof   glove

▼ ▼ ▼ ▼ ▼ ▼ ▼ ▼ ▼ ▼ ▼ ▼ ▼

Spelling Pattern

Many words are formed by adding prefixes or suffixes to a base word.

· · · · · · · · · · · · · · · ·

Explore the Spelling Pattern
Thinking About Meaning

This activity is a self-directed mini-lesson on this week's **Spelling Pattern**.

Focus on Word Study

Changes in Spelling and Meaning

This activity is intended to stimulate students' interest in words and to help them become more enthusiastic word hunters.

Spelling Process Handbook

Students who need to review any part of the spelling process, including practice options, should refer to the **Spelling Process Handbook** (pages 7–21).

MASTERING WORDS

STEP 6 Practice Your Spelling List Independently

Ask the students to choose activities to practice their spelling words and to master this week's **Spelling Pattern**. Students should complete at least three activities each week. You may wish to:

- assign **Practice the Spelling Pattern** to all students to reinforce this week's **Spelling Pattern**.

- involve students' families by assigning **Take Your List Home** for this lesson (**Teacher Resource Book,** pages 117 in English and 118 in Spanish).

- encourage students to use partner activities without game mats (**Word Swap, Spelling Tic-Tac-Toe, Circle Dot**) and activities with game mats (**Meteor Attack, Rockets, Spelling Checkers, Spelling Soccer**). Directions for game-mat activities appear on each game mat. Directions for all other activities are found in the **Spelling Process Handbook** (pages 7–21).

NOTE: These activities and games can be used to practice any spelling list.

SPELLING SOCCER

Partners or teams can practice their spelling words as they compete in **Spelling Soccer.** Modeled after the game that is gaining popularity in the United States for both boys and girls, **Spelling Soccer** takes spelling practice to the soccer field. It'll be "hands off" poor spelling scores after students, especially auditory and visual learners, discover **Spelling Soccer.** (Directions appear on the **Spelling Soccer** game mat. This activity is appropriate for practicing any spelling list.)

· · · · · · · MASTERING WORDS · · · · · · ·

STEP 6 Practice Your Spelling List Independently

Choose at least three activities to practice your spelling list.

You can practice any spelling list with these activities.

Game Mats	With a Partner	On Your Own	At Home
○ Spelling Checkers ○ Spelling Soccer	○ Spelling Tic-Tac-Toe ○ Word Swap	○ Flip Folder ○ Spelling Study Strategy	○ Take Your List Home

Practice the Spelling Pattern

Solve the spelling problems below. Write the **Pattern Word** that completes each problem. Remember that the spelling of some base words will change when a suffix is added.

Pattern Words

rebuilding
truly
beautiful
unhappily
undivided
emptiness
gently
rewriting
uneasily
removing

1. re + build + ing = **rebuilding**
2. un + easy + ly = **uneasily**
3. re + write + ing = **rewriting**
4. beauty + ful = **beautiful**
5. un + divide + ed = **undivided**
6. true + ly = **truly**
7. gentle + ly = **gently**
8. re + move + ing = **removing**
9. empty + ness = **emptiness**
10. un + happy + ly = **unhappily**

STEP 7 Focus on **Writing**

A. Proofread the Writing of Others

This activity provides proofreading practice in a variety of formats, including popular standardized test formats.

B. Proofread Your Own Writing

Students return to their own writing, armed with strategies to identify and collect words they need to know how to spell, and make an authentic link between spelling and writing.

C. A Writing Idea: A Speech

This suggestion for a more extended writing activity provides opportunities for students to write in different genres for a variety of purposes and modes.

STEP 8 Check Your Weekly Progress

▶ Take the Test

Remind students that they can take a practice test before the final test on their spelling lists. To find the testing procedure that is right for you, refer to page Z12.

▶ Check Your Goal

Have students compare their tests to their spelling lists. Did they spell all the **Pattern Words** on their spelling lists correctly?

▶ Graph Your Progress

Ask students to graph the number correct (student page 176 for softbound users; **Teacher Resource Book** page 123 for hardbound users).

▶ Save Missed Words

Tell students to write misspelled words on their lists of **Words I Need to Know How to Spell**. Remind students to verify spellings and to recycle these words on future weekly spelling lists.

· · · · · · · DEVELOPING GOOD SPELLING HABITS · · · · · · · ·

STEP 7 Focus on **Writing**

A. Proofread the Writing of Others

When Ben wrote his speech, he misspelled some **Pattern Words**. Proofread Ben's speech and decide what he needs to do before adding the suffix in each underlined word. Then write the correct spelling.

> My name is Ben. May I please have your undivideed [1]
>
> attention? Unhappyly, [2] our park isn't a pleasant place to
>
> play. We can make it beautyful [3] again if we work
>
> together removeing [4] litter. I truely [5] hope you will help!

Make a capital.
Make a small letter.
Add something.
Take out something.
Add a period.
New paragraph
(SP) Spelling error

1. ☑ drop the **e** ☐ change **y** to **i** _____ undivided
2. ☐ drop the **e** ☑ change **y** to **i** _____ Unhappily
3. ☐ drop the **e** ☑ change **y** to **i** _____ beautiful
4. ☑ drop the **e** ☐ change **y** to **i** _____ removing
5. ☑ drop the **e** ☐ change **y** to **i** _____ truly

B. Proofread Your Own Writing

Proofread a piece of your most recent writing. When you find misspelled words with prefixes and suffixes, add them to **Words I Need to Know How to Spell**.

C. A Writing Idea: A Speech

Think of a problem you feel strongly about. It might be something about the environment or something in your school. Write a short speech that tells how you would fix the problem and why people should help you. Check your writing for spelling mistakes, and then share it.

PERSUASIVE

STEP 8 Check Your Weekly Progress

▶ **Take the Test**
Ready? Practice test first.

▶ **Check Your Goal**
Check to see if you met your learning goal.

▶ **Graph Your Progress**
Graph your score for this week's test.

▶ **Save Missed Words**
Write the words you missed in your list of **Words I Need to Know How to Spell**.

Hunt Words

Remind students to continuously hunt words that they wish to learn how to spell and to write these words in **Words I Need to Know How to Spell**.

CHECK YOUR PROGRESS

NOTE: **Check Your Progress** is not a spelling unit, but some teachers prefer to spend a week on these activities.

Day One: Administer **Review Test**.

Day Two: Check **Review Test**. Use **Spelling Pattern Mastery Chart** to find each student's mastery level.

Day Three: Reteach as needed.

Day Four: Complete **Check Your Writing**.

Day Five: Complete **Check Your Strategies**.

Check Your Spelling

1. Administer the **Review Test** to all students. Dictation sentences appear on page T157. (The words in italics are also from the previous eight units.) Administer the words **in the order** in which they are presented here.

2. Ask students to check their tests as you spell each word and/or write the correct spelling on the board.

3. Ask students to circle the number of each correctly spelled word.

4. Review the categories on the **Spelling Pattern Mastery Chart** (page 156). As you review each pattern, ask students to find the corresponding items on their tests. Based on the number of words correct for each pattern, ask the students to determine their level of mastery for that pattern.

Reteaching Strategies

• Reteach the **Pattern Mini-Lesson** on the patterns students have not mastered.

• Ask students to record the words they missed in **Words I Need to Know How to Spell** for recycling into future spelling lists.

• Record the patterns students have not mastered. Include words with these patterns on future spelling lists.

T156 Check Your Progress

Check Your Writing

1. Consider teaching the **Proofreading Strategy Mini-Lesson** (page T157).

2. Ask students to choose several pieces of their writing.

3. Ask students to work with a partner to proofread their writing and hunt words with each spelling pattern. They should record misspelled words in **Words I Need to Know How to Spell**.

Check Your Strategies

1. Read each question aloud. Remind the students that they should think about their use of each strategy in the past eight weeks and answer "Yes," "No," or "Sometimes."

2. Use these questions as the focus of a student-teacher conference. You may also wish to use **Strategy Assessment** (pages 120 and 121 in the **Teacher Resource Book**).

✓ **Check Your Spelling**

Check Your

Here is a fun way to review your progress on spelling patterns. First, take the review test your teacher will give you. Then, check your test.

Review Test

1	pretested
2	hospital
3	forgetfulness
4	candle
5	beautiful
6	good-bye
7	eagle
8	slyly
9	prettiest
10	battle
11	statement
12	trouble
13	unhappily
14	pencil
15	careful
16	emptiness
17	basketball
18	peacefulness
19	strangeness
20	healthier

Spelling Pattern Mastery Chart

Which words did you spell correctly? Use this chart to find your mastery level for each spelling pattern.

Pattern	All Correct	Most Correct	None Correct
Words Ending With al, il, le 2 4 14			
More Words Ending With le 7 10 12			
Compound Words 6 17			
-ful, -less, -ly, -ment, -ness 11 15 19			
Changing y to i 8 9 20			
Word Building 1 3 18			
Word Building 5 13 16			

All Correct: Pattern Mastered
Most Correct: Pattern Partly Mastered
None Correct: Keep Working on the Pattern

PROOFREADING STRATEGY MINI-LESSON

* **Write Partner Proofreading** on the chalkboard.

* **Explain** that students can use a strategy called **Partner Proofreading** to proofread their writing. One student will read aloud slowly and softly from a partner's paper, while the partner listens and looks carefully to check the spelling of each word.

* **Demonstrate** the strategy by asking a volunteer to work with you at the chalkboard. Point to the word "Partner," and slide your finger along

as your partner reads each word softly aloud, "Partner-Proofreading."

* **Tell** students that they should circle any word if they are unsure of its spelling. After they verify the spelling, they should write the correct spelling above the misspelled word.

* **Remind** students that they may refer to **Strategies for Checking Your Spelling** in the back of the student edition.

Progress

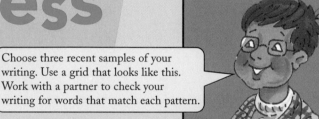

Choose three recent samples of your writing. Use a grid that looks like this. Work with a partner to check your writing for words that match each pattern.

✓ Check Your Writing

Spelling Pattern Writing Chart	Column 1 I spelled these Pattern Words correctly.	Column 2 I misspelled these Pattern Words.
Words Ending With al, il, le		
More Words Ending With le		
Compound Words		
-ful, -less, -ly, -ment, -ness		
Changing y to i		
Word Building		
Word Building		

Write the words in Column 2 in your **Words I Need to Know How to Spell**.

✓ Check Your Strategies

Self-regulation

Ask yourself each of these questions. Do you answer "Yes," "No," or "Sometimes" to each question?

- Do I add words from **Words I Need to Know How to Spell** to my spelling list each week?
- Is the number of words I add right for me?
- When I practice my words, do I choose activities that help me learn my words?
- Do I take self-tests and practice tests to see if I know my words?

Dictation Sentences

1. **pretested** – Sal **pretested** the *metal* to see if it really was *triple* strength.
2. **hospital** – *Everybody* knew that Joan was in the **hospital** over the *weekend*.
3. **forgetfulness** – His **forgetfulness** made it hard for him to *remember* where his *apartment* was.
4. **candle** – We burned a new **candle** *during Thanksgiving* dinner.
5. **beautiful** – We had the **beautiful** *idea* to plant flowers *together* in *April*.
6. **good-bye** – My *parents* said **good-bye** after *breakfast* and went to work.
7. **eagle** – The **eagle** saw a *beetle* in the *middle* of a leaf.
8. **slyly** – After *gently* opening the door, they **slyly** moved past the *bottom* step.
9. **prettiest** – She *cheerfully* wore her **prettiest** *T-shirt*.
10. **battle** – There was a **battle** over what to listen to *until* Mom shut the *radio* off.
11. **statement** – A *careless* **statement** isn't *simple* to *handle*.
12. **trouble** – We did *discover* the **trouble** with the *fireplace*.
13. **unhappily** – **Unhappily** the *movement* to help *homeless* people seems to be going slowly.
14. **pencil** – When *rewriting* his story, the *preschooler* used a **pencil**.
15. **careful** – **Careful** *studies* show some students prefer *fries* with lunch.
16. **emptiness** – Because of the can's **emptiness,** it is *useless* to try to make it *rattle*.
17. **basketball** – *Lately* he has *worried* that his *happiness* with **basketball** won't last.
18. **peacefulness** – He *truly enjoys* the feeling of *total* **peacefulness**.
19. **strangeness** – His new *title* made the **strangeness** of his new job worse.
20. **healthier** – Are apples that are *sprayed* **healthier** to eat?

SPELLING AND HANDWRITING

Explain to students that good handwriting will make their correct spelling easier to read. Remind them that even when all their words are spelled correctly, if the reader is not able to identify the letters they have written, the words may not be recognized as spelled correctly in their writing. Emphasize the importance of legible handwriting as part of their spelling efforts. A student's goal of mastering the spelling list must include the legible writing of that list.

To increase students' awareness of making their handwriting fully legible, point out these keys to legibility that will help them improve their written work.

• Size

Inconsistent size of letters in words can cause confusion to the reader. Students should try to make the size of their letters uniform. The lines and the space between the lines on their writing paper can help students learn to make the size of their letters consistent. Letters that are consistent in size are easier to read.

• Shape

Students should make their letters with consistent and proper shape. Being careful to form their letters well increases the readability of what they have written.

• Slant

Letters with a consistent, forward slant are easier to read than letters that slant randomly. Students should learn how to position their papers and hold their writing implements so that consistent, forward slant comes with ease.

• Spacing

Children can make their handwriting more legible by maintaining correct spacing between letters and between words. Crowded, uneven handwriting makes their papers difficult for others to read.

Spelling and Handwriting

Good handwriting makes it easier for others to understand your good ideas.

ERROR	INCORRECT		CORRECT	
1. a like u	a	soup	a	soap
2. e closed	e	receive	e	receive
3. d like cl	cl	clog	d	dog
4. o like a	a	sald	o	sold
5. a like ce	ce	stcmp	a	stamp
6. n like u	u	braud	n	brand

Cursive Alphabet

Aa Bb Cc Dd Ee Ff Gg
Hh Ii Jj Kk Ll Mm
Nn Oo Pp Qq Rr Ss Tt
Uu Vv Ww Xx Yy Zz

MORE WORDS FOR HUNGRY WORD HUNTERS

More Words for Hungry Word Hunters provides a resource for building spelling lists each week.

A group of lists is provided for each unit. The words on each group of lists all relate to the **Spelling Pattern** or **Spelling Strategy** that is the focus of that unit.

Words on the Red List are below grade level and words on the Blue List are above grade level. A context sentence is provided for each word on both Red Lists and Blue Lists. These sentences will help facilitate testing.

Occasionally a word will appear on both a Red List or a Blue List and a content words list. This repetition is to help students relate spelling words to other content areas.

More Words for Hungry Word Hunters also appears in the teacher edition and in the **Teacher Resource Book**.

UNIT 1 RED LIST

1. I like to read a book when I'm **alone**.
2. Aunt Kathy is going to eat **dinner** with us.
3. We will eat when the meat is **done**.
4. I am in the **fourth** grade.
5. Would you like **half** of my sandwich?
6. To whom did you write your **letter**?
7. This is a **real** plant, not a plastic one.
8. May we go to the beach **sometime** this summer?
9. Kevin likes to go sledding in the **winter**.
10. You can make the **world** a better place.

UNIT 1 BLUE LIST

1. We could see the camper's tent **among** the tall trees.
2. Butterflies **interest** me.
3. What **language** do you speak at home?
4. You can improve your grade with extra **practice**.
5. Sam must **prepare** a report for social studies class.
6. How many houses are on your paper **route**?
7. Your **sentence** is not complete without a predicate.
8. Every person is a **special** human being.
9. The bus **usually** comes at eight o'clock.
10. Karen went to the beach on **vacation**.

UNIT 2 RED LIST

1. I **can't** make this toy work right.
2. You **didn't** hear me, did you?
3. I **don't** think it's going to rain today.
4. **I'll** wait until you're ready to go.
5. **I'm** closer to the window than you are.
6. Jenny **isn't** in her seat.
7. Do you think **it's** going to rain today?
8. **I've** finished all my homework.
9. You **weren't** surprised at the news, were you?
10. Luis **won't** go to the park without me.

UNIT 2 BLUE LIST

1. Why **aren't** you coming with us?
2. Juan **hasn't** been here in two days.
3. Her parents **hadn't** given permission for her to go on the field trip.
4. **Here's** the glass of water you wanted.
5. **She's** going to feed the fish now.
6. **There's** no reason to get upset.
7. **We've** got enough beans to fill the jar.
8. **What's** that book about?
9. When did you say **you'd** be on vacation?
10. Tell me when **you've** finished writing your story.

MORE WORDS FOR

Hungry WORD Hunters

When you are building your spelling list each week, you might choose from these lists of additional words. These words match the pattern or strategy featured in each unit.

Unit 1	Other Strategy Words	Unit 2	Other Pattern Words
Spelling Is Important	annual	**Contractions**	he'd
	beauty		he'll
	biscuit		it'll
	exact		needn't
	honest		she'd
lone	million		she'll
dinner	neither		they'd
lone	scarce	can't	who'll
ourth	scary	didn't	
alf	touch	don't	
etter		I'll	
eal	**Math Strategy Words**	I'm	
ometime	array	isn't	
vinter	factor	it's	
vorld	problem	I've	
		weren't	
	Science Strategy Words	won't	
	fault		
mong	orbit		
nterest	polar	aren't	
anguage		hasn't	
ractice	**Social Studies Strategy Words**	hadn't	
repare	canal	here's	
oute	dune	she's	
entence	mesa	there's	
pecial	ocean	we've	
sually	swamp	what's	
acation		you'd	
		you've	

MORE WORDS FOR HUNGRY WORD HUNTERS *continued*

UNIT 3 RED LIST

1. Twins often look **alike**.
2. Is that mouse in the trap dead or **alive**?
3. Have you put **aside** some money for college?
4. I was **awake** during the thunderstorm.
5. Lin **became** ill after lunch.
6. Mrs. Wong asked the baker to **divide** the cake in half.
7. Who will **erase** the handwriting on the chalkboard?
8. Marching bands and floats will be in the **parade**.

UNIT 3 BLUE LIST

1. We will **arrive** in New York in one hour.
2. Did you **compose** that song?
3. Lu cannot **decide** which project to begin.
4. It is my greatest **desire** to fly a plane.
5. I can't believe you ate the **entire** pie!
6. Please don't **excite** the mother cat.
7. Please help me **locate** my lost math book.
8. The **oriole** flew to its nest in the oak tree.
9. You can **reduce** waste by recycling.
10. I **suppose** the train will be late again.

UNIT 4 RED LIST

1. Everyone feels **afraid** sometimes.
2. The kitten is **asleep** in the basket.
3. I saw a **beaver** swimming in the river.
4. There will be a **delay** in the game because of rain.
5. I am **feeling** happy today.
6. The **kangaroo** is an Australian animal.
7. A **raccoon** got into the trash can to look for food.
8. I will visit the dentist on **Tuesday**.

UNIT 4 BLUE LIST

1. The ball rolled **beneath** the couch.
2. **Coffee** beans grow in Brazil.
3. What does this box **contain**?
4. We will **continue** to save our empty cans.
5. The dentist told us how to prevent tooth **decay**.
6. Can you **explain** how to do this math problem?
7. His eyes are his best **feature**.
8. We celebrate our country's **freedom** on the Fourth of July.
9. I spilled the new **shampoo** in the sink.
10. Six birds were perched on the stone **statue**.

Unit 3 Long Vowels: V-C-e	Other Pattern Words	Unit 4 Long Vowels: Vowel Pairs	Other Pattern Words
alike alive aside awake became divide erase parade	celebrate cooperate fertilize generalize include operate polite populate recite require **Math Pattern Word** decade **Science Pattern Words** earthquake explode reptile **Social Studies Pattern Words** bauxite interstate landscape skyline sugarcane timberline vibrate	afraid asleep beaver delay feeling kangaroo raccoon Tuesday	charcoal decrease detain disagree eastern increase loosen obtain reclaim release **Math Pattern Wo[rd]** remainder **Science Pattern Words** beetle disease measles **Social Studies Pattern Words** freeway sailboat
arrive compose decide desire entire excite locate oriole reduce suppose		beneath coffee contain continue decay explain feature freedom shampoo statue	

1. John **closed** the door quietly.
2. The store is **closing** early because of the storm.
3. Julia is **flying** a kite in the park.
4. We were **getting** wet in the rain.
5. Are you **having** fun?
6. A raccoon is **living** in our doghouse.
7. My best friend **moved** to California.
8. We **rubbed** wax on our sled runners.
9. Kim is **sleeping** outdoors in a tent.
10. It **snowed** four inches last night.
11. The man **stopped** to tie his shoelace.
12. We'll be **stopping** at Marnie's house after the game.

1. Paul **admitted** he might have been mistaken.
2. The plane will be **arriving** soon.
3. At the **beginning** of the race, the runner fell.
4. Diane is **carrying** a basket of flowers.
5. Ken **decided** to go home early.
6. We are **deciding** what colors to use on our poster.
7. The children **enjoyed** the sunshine.
8. After we **finished** lunch, we played tag.
9. Our team **proved** we could win.
10. My sister is **quitting** her summer job.
11. Anita **wrapped** a towel around her wet hair.
12. We are **wrapping** Dad's birthday present.

1. I **also** have a new box of crayons.
2. I'm **always** ready to help a friend.
3. **Everyone** in my class is going to the zoo.
4. Did you bring **everything** we need for the picnic?
5. How many people are in your **family**?
6. Have you met the new **kids** next door?
7. I would **never** lie to you.
8. Do you know **where** Amanda lives?
9. **Would** you like to go with me to the library?
10. We will all be in the fifth grade next **year**.

1. Do you have a **complete** set of playing cards?
2. Most spiders are not **dangerous**.
3. Ms. Gomez has more **energy** than her students.
4. Have you ever met a **famous** movie star?
5. I've **forgotten** my notebook again!
6. Would a spider or a snake **frighten** you?
7. Our **neighbor** sometimes mows our lawn.
8. You shouldn't make a **promise** if you can't keep it.
9. Several children hurt **themselves** on the playground.
10. Do you know what your **weight** would be on the moon?

Unit 5

ngs: -ed, -ing

ed
ng
g
g
g
ed
ed
ing
ved
ped
ping

itted
ving
nning
ying
ded
ding
yed
shed
ved
ting
pped
pping

Other Pattern Words
continued
hiccupped
hiccupping
laughed
laughing
removed
trimmed
trimming

Math Pattern Words
divided
rating

Social Studies Pattern Words
climbing
farming
jogging
marched
sowing

Unit 6

Words Writers Use

also
always
everyone
everything
family
kids
never
where
would
year

complete
dangerous
energy
famous
forgotten
frighten
neighbor
promise
themselves
weight

Other Strategy Words
article
author
create
either
inform
listen
make-believe
movies
rather
serious

Science Strategy Word
stomach

Social Studies Strategy Words
blizzard
cactus
tropics

UNIT 7 RED LIST

1. I don't have one **cent** left in my pocket today.
2. I **knew** my dog would come when I called.
3. Nelda got a **new** pair of shoes yesterday.
4. That house looks very **plain** without flowers and bushes.
5. The **plane** had to make an emergency landing.
6. I **sent** a letter to my pen pal in France.
7. Please don't pull on the cat's **tail**.
8. The storyteller told a **tale** of long ago.
9. My strong brother was **weak** after the flu.
10. Sean saw that new movie last **week**.

UNIT 7 BLUE LIST

1. Maria is not **allowed** to have a dog.
2. The teacher asked us to read our poems **aloud**.
3. Throw **coarse** salt on the icy sidewalk.
4. I found several balls on the golf **course**.
5. Banks **loan** people money to buy houses.
6. Can you see that **lone** star in the northern sky?
7. I rode a gentle **mare** at the ranch.
8. My mom would like to be **mayor** of our city.
9. This belt is too big for my **waist**.
10. Try not to **waste** any of this paper.

UNIT 8 RED LIST

1. We'll leave when you are **all ready**.
2. Is it time for lunch **already**?
3. I watched a big black **ant** carrying a crumb.
4. My favorite **aunt** is taking me to lunch.
5. My tooth is **loose**.
6. How could you **lose** one shoe?
7. Tomás would rather swim **than** run.
8. My friends brought **their** sleeping bags to the slumber party.
9. Fido can lie down and **then** roll over.
10. Were you **there** when the plane landed?

UNIT 8 BLUE LIST

1. Felicia made an **angel** in the snow.
2. I had to draw a right **angle** on my test paper.
3. All this noise must **cease** now!
4. Do you eat **cereal** for breakfast?
5. My sister wore a **formal** gown to the party.
6. The **former** president made a speech.
7. When you buy something, you should get a **receipt**.
8. Chad followed his grandmother's **recipe** carefully.
9. If we **seize** the fort, our troops will win!
10. Read me the **serial** number on the box.

Unit 7 Homophones	Other Pattern Words	Unit 8 Using a Dictionary	Other Strategy Words
cent	guessed	all ready	borough
knew	guest	already	bridal
new	missed	ant	bridle
plain	mist	aunt	burrow
plane	passed	loose	colonel
sent	past	lose	country
tail	vain	than	county
tale	vane	their	kernel
weak	vein	then	naval
week		there	navel
	Math Pattern Word		
	sum (some)		**Math Strategy Words**
			liter
	Science Pattern Words		quartet
	bass (base)		sentence
	flu (flew)		
			Science Strategy Words
	Social Studies Pattern Words		blizzard
	ore (or)		digest
	seas (sees)		socket
	sowing (sewing)		
	steppe (step)		**Social Studies Strategy Word**
			station
allowed		angel	
aloud		angle	
coarse		cease	
course		cereal	
loan		formal	
lone		former	
mare		receipt	
mayor		recipe	
waist		seize	
waste		serial	

UNIT 9 RED LIST

1. Tell me **about** your best friend.
2. The **clown** had a big red nose.
3. I really **enjoy** going to the zoo.
4. I **found** a dollar on the way to school.
5. Do you **frown** when you are sad?
6. It is hard to dig into the frozen **ground**.
7. Seeing my grandma filled me with **joy**.
8. The **oil** in the river is killing the fish.
9. The **point** of this pencil is dull.
10. Where is the library in this **town**?

UNIT 9 BLUE LIST

1. Will you **allow** me to ride your bike?
2. Try to **avoid** stepping in the mud.
3. The cats like to sit next to Grandpa on the **couch**.
4. The **coward** was afraid of his own shadow.
5. Cold weather might **destroy** the orange crop.
6. There is a drinking **fountain** in the hall.
7. The baseball fans were very **noisy**.
8. A **noun** can be a person, a place, or a thing.
9. There is a large bell in the top of that tall **tower**.
10. The astronaut was eager to take her **voyage** to outer space.

UNIT 10 RED LIST

1. Yesterday Ellen wore **blue** shoes.
2. Our new kittens are tiny and **cute**.
3. There are only a **few** grapes left.
4. Feed the fish a little **food** while I'm gone.
5. Mark **grew** a watermelon in his garden.
6. Wearing a helmet while biking is an important safety **rule**.
7. There is no **school** on Saturday.
8. We had bean **soup** and corn bread for supper.
9. This large, padded chair is **too** soft.
10. The story I told you is **true**.
11. **You** are a very special person.
12. We saw some polar bears at the **zoo**.

UNIT 10 BLUE LIST

1. That joke did not **amuse** me.
2. Jamaal walked down the **avenue** to the pet store.
3. My dad wore a clown **costume** to the party.
4. There was **dew** on the grass this morning.
5. I play the **flute** in the marching band.
6. It is **foolish** to fish in a puddle.
7. Rachel is in a good **mood** today.
8. Firefighters learn to **rescue** people from burning buildings.
9. Carla had one **scoop** of strawberry ice cream.
10. This ring does not have any real **value**.
11. We have a **view** of the ocean from our window.
12. That club is for the town's **youth**.

Unit 9
..., ow, oi, oy

ut
vn
y
id
rn
und

at
n

w
d
ch
ard
roy
ntain
sy
n
er
age

Other Pattern Words
annoy
blouse
drown
however
loiter
oyster
poise
power
sour
trousers

Math Pattern Words
ounce
pound
thousand

Science Pattern Words
asteroid
compound
noise

Social Studies Pattern Words
boundary
flounder
mountain
mouth
oil
pronoun

Unit 10
Long u: u-C-e, ue, oo, ew

blue
cute
few
food
grew
rule
school
soup
too
true
you
zoo

amuse
avenue
costume
dew
flute
foolish
mood
rescue
scoop
value
view
youth

Other Pattern Words
blueberry
contribute
cue
gloomy
intrude
nephew
pollute
proof
prune
rude

Math Pattern Words
acute angle
obtuse angle

Science Pattern Words
food web
nodule

Social Studies Pattern Words
fuel
monsoon

MORE WORDS FOR HUNGRY WORD HUNTERS *continued*

UNIT 11 RED LIST

1. The waitress asked if we needed **anything** else.
2. Do you feel **better** today?
3. The **cattle** were grazing in the pasture.
4. Wake me up **early** in the morning.
5. Dewayne showed me the trick **himself**.
6. What **lovely** flowers!
7. The **rocket** ship landed on the moon.
8. Some birds fly **south** for the winter.
9. What **sport** do you like best?
10. Pat **thought** she saw a rainbow after the storm.

UNIT 11 BLUE LIST

1. She looked **different** with her hair cut short.
2. Let's go for a walk this **evening**.
3. Spelling is my **favorite** subject.
4. Please help me move the bedroom **furniture**.
5. Don't forget to wear a mouth **guard** during the game.
6. I have an **interesting** idea for my science project.
7. Jason is **lying** on the couch watching television.
8. The weather is quite **pleasant** today.
9. Does this sentence make **sense** to you?
10. Jan let her pet parrot sit on her **shoulder**.

UNIT 12 BLUE LIST

1. Let's divide this pizza **equally**.
2. Ice turns to **liquid** when it melts.
3. I don't like to **quarrel** with my friend.
4. Please go to the store for a **quart** of milk.
5. Don't be afraid to ask a **question** in class.
6. There will be a science **quiz** today.
7. That is a **quote** from the principal.
8. We grow **squash** in our garden.
9. Don't **squeeze** the puppy too tightly.
10. **Squirt** some lemon juice in your iced tea.

Unit 11

Think of a Rhyming Word

anything
better
cattle
early
himself
lovely
rocket
south
sport
thought

different
evening
favorite
furniture
guard
interesting
lying
pleasant
sense
shoulder

Other Strategy Words

ancient
aware
champion
forever
imagine
jacket
market
repair
secretary
spoken

Math Strategy Words

facts	loop
fraction	measure
graph	risk
groups	stock

Science Strategy Words

airy	host
cause	itch
core	lungs
crust	mood
dense	polar
gas	

Social Studies Strategy Words

barn	print
dam	resource
ferry	station
map	surf
mind	trap
pelt	

Unit 12

qu, squ

equally
liquid
quarrel
quart
question
quiz
quote
squash
squeeze
squirt

Other Pattern Words

quaint
quake
quartz
quill
quilt
quiver
squad
squawk
squid
squint

Math Pattern Word
quotient

Science Pattern Word
earthquake

Social Studies Pattern Words
aqueduct
equator

UNIT 13 RED LIST

1. José **bought** the last copy of the book.
2. Our dog and cat never **fight**.
3. The balloon floated **high** in the sky.
4. There is a **knot** in my shoelace.
5. Sid did not **know** he had made the team.
6. This **lamb** was born in the spring.
7. We **might** go to the circus tomorrow.
8. I hit my **thumb** with the hammer.
9. Linda will **wrap** the present in blue paper.

UNIT 13 BLUE LIST

1. **Although** it's sunny, it's very cold.
2. The mouse didn't leave one bread **crumb**.
3. Did you **design** that book cover?
4. Beavers can **gnaw** through trees.
5. The **knight** rode his horse bravely into battle.
6. **Knock** on the door before you enter the room.
7. The squirrel jumped onto the **limb** of the tree.
8. Drive **through** the tunnel and turn right.
9. **Wring** out the wet towel when you finish.
10. How did you hurt your **wrist**?

UNIT 14 BLUE LIST

1. The **average** grade on the math test was B.
2. The **barge** carried scrap iron down the river.
3. Let's play **dodge** ball during recess.
4. We made chocolate **fudge** for the bake sale.
5. How many uses does this **gadget** have?
6. Please leave your **message** at the sound of the beep.
7. I'm always happy to **oblige** a friend's request.
8. We made a **pledge** to be friends forever.
9. Buffalo once roamed the **range** looking for food.
10. The cougar stood on the **ridge** of the mountain.
11. A person you don't know is a **stranger**.
12. What was your **wage** for today's work?

Unit 13

Silent [Co]nsonants

ght

[...]
at
[...]b

[...]ugh
[...]b
[...]gn
[...]v
[...]ht
[...]k

[...]ugh
[...]g
[...]t

Other Pattern Words
bomb
gnat
knack
kneel
knob
knuckle
numb
plumber
tomb
wreck

Science Pattern Word
height

Social Studies Pattern Word
freight

Unit 14

ge, dge

average
barge
dodge
fudge
gadget
message
oblige
pledge
range
ridge
stranger
wage

Other Pattern Words
arrange
college
damage
fidget
grudge
hedge
knowledge
ledger
lodge
wedge

Science Pattern Word
plumage

Social Studies Pattern Word
heritage

MORE WORDS FOR HUNGRY WORD HUNTERS *continued*

UNIT 15 RED LIST

1. I have caught **another** cold.
2. There was a name tag on **every** desk.
3. Leaves have fallen **everywhere** in our yard.
4. Tim **forgot** to make the sandwiches for our picnic.
5. Dinosaurs **once** roamed the earth.
6. Ann gets **paid** to mow the grass each week.
7. Carmen had a birthday **party** last Saturday.
8. Make a **right** turn after the first light.
9. You should learn water **safety** rules before going boating.
10. My birthday is in the **summer**.

UNIT 15 BLUE LIST

1. Alberto and I own a flower **business** in the city.
2. A person's name should begin with a **capital** letter.
3. Her **diamond** ring fell down the drain.
4. Rick runs every day for **exercise**.
5. I think our new teacher is very **handsome**.
6. Did you get a **piece** of my apple pie?
7. My mom is a school **principal**.
8. Did you **receive** a letter in the mail?
9. My grandfather was a **soldier**.
10. We enjoy the plays at the community **theater**.

UNIT 16 RED LIST

1. The **baby's** bottle is empty.
2. Did you meet that **boy's** mother?
3. The neighborhood **boys'** club is on Elm Street.
4. Do not put candy in the **dog's** dish.
5. That **girl's** horse is named Frisky.
6. The **girls'** restroom is down the hall.
7. We cleaned the **horses'** stalls.
8. Who found the three **kittens'** mittens?
9. The **man's** hat was blown away by the strong wind.
10. Akeo won the **men's** race.

UNIT 16 BLUE LIST

1. The **author's** name was on the cover of the book.
2. I sat in the **dentist's** chair while she checked my teeth.
3. Wheat and corn grew in the **farmer's** fields.
4. The three **judges'** decision was final.
5. Our class visited the **mayor's** office.
6. You can buy all kinds of **runners'** shoes at this sports store.
7. Let's compare all these **scientists'** research notes.
8. Put your homework on the **teacher's** desk.
9. There is a **teachers'** meeting after school today.
10. The bus driver punched all the **travelers'** tickets.

Unit 15 Use Spelling Clues

Math Strategy Words: duet, fiftieth, sphere, subtraction, trio

Science Strategy Words: density, height, lizard, pulse, smog, solar, spinach, stomach, strength

Social Studies Strategy Words: colony, depot, diagram, freight, fuel, inlet, island, kayak, lava, oboe, prairie, scene, tornado

another, every, everywhere, forgot, once, paid, party, right, safety, summer

business, capital, diamond, exercise, handsome, piece, principal, receive, soldier, theater

Unit 16 Possessives

Other Pattern Words: couples', daughter's, fathers', fish's, friend's, nephew's, parents', poets', sons', umpires'

baby's, boy's, boys', dog's, girl's, girls', horses', kittens', man's, men's

author's, dentist's, farmer's, judges', mayor's, runners', scientists', teacher's, teachers', travelers'

1. The **child** fell asleep in the car.
2. The **children** sang four songs during the talent show.
3. I saw a **deer** run across the field and into the woods.
4. Those shoes are too small for your **feet**.
5. You have mud on your left **foot**.
6. That **man** is a police officer.
7. The **men** were playing horseshoes in the park.
8. The **mice** got out of their cages.
9. A small **mouse** ran across the kitchen floor.
10. There are fifty **sheep** in that flock.

1. We can hear the **echoes** of footsteps in the hall.
2. Who are your **heroes**?
3. The swarm of **mosquitoes** buzzed around my ears.
4. The **scissors** are in the top drawer.
5. Who do you think will win this **series** of games?
6. Peg and Oki are my **sisters-in-law**.
7. What **species** of plant is that?
8. How many **spoonfuls** of sugar did you put on your cereal?
9. How many movie **studios** did you visit in Hollywood?
10. We saw steam and lava coming from the two **volcanoes**.

1. I could see my **breath** in the cold air.
2. Nan **fed** lettuce to her pet rabbit.
3. We **felt** happy when the test was over.
4. Bella **kept** her hat on to hide her new haircut.
5. The trombones **led** the marching band in the parade.
6. Jim **left** the theater before the show was finished.
7. I **met** my best friend at softball camp.

Unit 17

...sual Plurals

...ren

...se
...p

Other Pattern Words
gentlemen
oboes
radios

Science Pattern Words
antenna
antennae
cactus
cacti
stimulus
stimuli

Social Studies Pattern Words
oasis
oases

Unit 18

Patterns That Show Meaning

breath
fed
felt
kept
led
left
met

...es
...es
...quitoes
...ors
...s
...rs-in-law
...ies
...nfuls
...ios
...anoes

UNIT 19 RED LIST

1. Your help is **badly** needed at home.
2. The stars shone **brightly** in the sky.
3. My grandpa is a **friendly** and outgoing person.
4. My spelling has improved **greatly**.
5. Would you **kindly** put the bread in a bag?
6. Ginny plays her music too **loudly**.
7. The heavy rainfall drenched **mainly** the coast.
8. Our jar of coins contained **mostly** pennies.
9. The new building is only **partly** finished.
10. The contented kitten purred **softly** as he napped.

UNIT 20 BLUE LIST

1. I won't **argue** with you about completing your homework.
2. Many **buffalo** once roamed the prairie.
3. Can you **describe** the purse you lost?
4. Do you like **foggy** gray November days?
5. At what temperature does water **freeze**?
6. Most of the town's cotton **industry** is gone.
7. Dan asked Karen to **marry** him.
8. The treasure is hidden in that **panel** in the wall.
9. We all had to **plod** through the mud.
10. Use a ruler to draw a **straight** line.

UNIT 19 BLUE LIST

1. The two countries made an **agreement** to stop the fighting.
2. He had a guide dog because of his **blindness**.
3. The **cloudless** sky was bright blue.
4. Many families have a **cordless** phone in their homes.
5. My sister Isabel works for the **government**.
6. Some plants are **harmful** to people.
7. Juan **proudly** raised the flag.
8. Her **sickness** kept her in bed for a week.
9. Maria left the room **suddenly**.
10. Nate is a kind and **thoughtful** person.

UNIT 20 RED LIST

1. You may **begin** the test as soon as you are seated.
2. It's hard to be **brave** when you are scared.
3. The stores are very **busy** during the holiday season.
4. You should **carry** an umbrella when it rains.
5. Ask the **lady** at the desk for the key.
6. Kim decided to **lie** on the bed and take a nap.
7. The flowers in Terri's garden are very **pretty**.
8. Try to **think** of a name for the class frog.
9. Penny lost her first **tooth** this morning.
10. **Write** your name on the top line of this paper.

Unit 19

Suffixes: -ful, -less, -ly, -ment, -ness

badly
brightly
friendly
greatly
kindly
loudly
mainly
mostly
partly
softly

Other Pattern Words

directly
endless
especially
fitness
powerful
skillful
thankless
thickness
treatment
wonderment

Math Pattern Words

equally
measurement

Science Pattern Word

hardness

Social Studies Pattern Word

amendment

agreement
blindness
cloudless
cordless
government
harmful
proudly
sickness
suddenly
thoughtful

Unit 20

Using a Dictionary

begin
brave
busy
carry
lady
lie
pretty
think
tooth
write

Science Strategy Words

behavior
digestion
hardness
prospector

Social Studies Strategy Words

boundary
crafts
tourist

argue
buffalo
describe
foggy
freeze
industry
marry
panel
plod
straight

UNIT 21 RED LIST

1. She tied a big red **bow** around the surprise package.
2. Please **close** the door softly.
3. April always **does** her homework.
4. The **dove** is usually smaller than the pigeon.
5. I got to **lead** the march.
6. Do you **live** in that stone house near the school?
7. We will **sow** the sunflower seeds tomorrow.
8. A **tear** slid down his cheek.
9. I didn't **use** all the paper.
10. The **wind** is very strong today.

UNIT 21 BLUE LIST

1. What will your new **address** be?
2. I always **associate** names with faces.
3. Sam won the pie-eating **contest** at the fair.
4. The **entrance** is on the south side of the building.
5. Can you **estimate** how long the job will take?
6. Use a **primer** before you paint.
7. I am making good **progress** in spelling.
8. My science **project** will be finished next week.
9. The strict new school rules caused some students to **rebel**.
10. My favorite **subject** is math.

UNIT 22 RED LIST

1. We rented a **cabin** by the lake.
2. The choir sang a song about a magic **dragon**.
3. We should have an **even** number of shoes.
4. Has the teacher **given** us too much to do?
5. My parents said I could have a **kitten**.
6. Lisa **often** helps me with my homework.
7. Only one **person** can ride in that small boat.
8. There was one **raisin** left in the box.
9. Winter will soon be over when you see the first **robin** in the spring.
10. I have **seven** brothers and sisters in my family.
11. Elena has **taken** three art classes this year.
12. The **wagon** wheels were made of wood.

UNIT 22 BLUE LIST

1. My uncle became a United States **citizen** last year.
2. Dandelions are **common** weeds in many places.
3. The children skated on the **frozen** pond.
4. Who made this strawberry **gelatin**?
5. The tablecloth is made of **linen**.
6. When you edit my report, please write notes in the **margin** of the paper.
7. Raul baked the chicken in the **oven**.
8. **Oxygen** is present in both air and water.
9. **Poison** ivy grows in our backyard.
10. Bees carry **pollen** from flower to flower.
11. Each school club has a **slogan**.
12. Susan has played the **violin** for three years.

Unit 21	Other Pattern Words
...mographs	buffet
	compact
	conduct
	console
	contract
	convert
	convict
	extract
	invalid
	wound
	Science Pattern Word
	bass

Unit 22	Other Pattern Words
en, in, on, on, an Words	American
	cinnamon
	fasten
cabin	Indian
dragon	Mexican
even	onion
given	origin
kitten	prison
often	satin
person	specimen
raisin	
robin	**Social Studies Pattern Word**
seven	swollen
taken	
wagon	

...ess	citizen
...iate	common
...est	frozen
...nce	gelatin
...ate	linen
...er	margin
...ess	oven
...ct	oxygen
	poison
...ct	pollen
	slogan
	violin

UNIT 23 RED LIST

1. Who is your favorite **actor**?
2. Mr. Highwater is a careful bus **driver**.
3. The **farmer** was busy planting corn.
4. The president is the **leader** of the country.
5. We need another **player** for our team.
6. Cory is an excellent **reader**.
7. Beth became a good horseback **rider**.
8. A good **sailor** does not get seasick.
9. My mother is a **teacher** at Lincoln Elementary School.
10. A construction **worker** must wear a hard hat.

UNIT 23 BLUE LIST

1. The movie **director** shouted at the camera crew to begin shooting.
2. I want to be a **drummer** in the band.
3. The **gardener** was proud of his roses.
4. The **governor** was elected to her second term.
5. The **juggler** used five balls in her act.
6. Our softball **pitcher** threw the ball to the catcher.
7. Marco's dad is a history **professor** at the university.
8. The **settler** claimed land in Ohio.
9. The weary **traveler** walked a thousand miles.
10. The **treasurer** of our club will write the check.

UNIT 24 RED LIST

1. A **bird** was singing outside my bedroom window.
2. How old will you be on your next **birthday**?
3. We could not get the wet logs to **burn**.
4. My little brother likes to play in the **dirt**.
5. An animal's **fur** helps keep it warm.
6. Many illnesses are caused by **germs**.
7. The **herd** of horses will follow the leader.
8. I bought a new **perch** for my parrot's cage.
9. Last year I was in the **third** grade.
10. Is it my **turn** to jump yet?

UNIT 24 BLUE LIST

1. The **burglar** fled when he heard the barking dog.
2. The stream's **current** is too strong for swimming.
3. Take that sharp **curve** slowly on your bike.
4. How did the puppy get so **dirty**?
5. Let me know if you need **further** help.
6. Did you get good **service** at the store?
7. My **stern** great-grandmother never seems to smile.
8. What are the **terms** of your agreement?
9. Water takes care of your **thirst** better than any other drink.
10. Yvonne can really **twirl** that baton!

Unit 23 — Suffixes: -er, -or	Other Pattern Words
actor	creditor
driver	dancer
farmer	dreamer
leader	hiker
player	instructor
reader	jeweler
rider	jogger
sailor	operator
teacher	senator
worker	skater

Social Studies Pattern Words
explorer
prospector
reaper
trawler

director	
drummer	
gardener	
governor	
juggler	
pitcher	
professor	
settler	
traveler	
treasurer	

Unit 24 — r-Controlled Vowels	Other Pattern Words
bird	alert
birthday	burnt
burn	disturb
dirt	external
fur	fern
germs	internal
herd	murmur
perch	squirm
third	squirrel
turn	turkey

Science Pattern Words
circuit
exert

Social Studies Pattern Words
cursive
govern
jury
permafrost

burglar	
current	
curve	
dirty	
further	
service	
stern	
terms	
thirst	
twirl	

UNIT 25 RED LIST

1. My favorite **animal** at the zoo is an elephant.
2. I would like to explore that old **castle** someday.
3. Our music teacher told us to form a **circle** around the piano.
4. My **uncle** lives in New York City.

UNIT 25 BLUE LIST

1. There is **ample** room on the bus for everyone.
2. Who is the president of the student **council**?
3. This is my **final** lap around the track.
4. I seem to get a new **freckle** every day.
5. The soldiers respected their **general**.
6. Is this smooth tabletop made of **marble**?
7. Anything is **possible** in a storybook.
8. The black part of your eye is the **pupil**.
9. Do you know how to **scramble** an egg?
10. Our hen laid **several** eggs today.

UNIT 26 RED LIST

1. Were you **able** to finish your homework last night?
2. The worm enjoyed the juicy **apple**.
3. Recycle that plastic **bottle** so it can be used again.
4. Ben has a **couple** of extra pencils for the math test.
5. My **little** sister got lost in the store.
6. The leaves on some **maple** trees turn red in the fall.
7. The crowd of **people** waved at the movie star.
8. I rode my bike through the large **puddle** of water.
9. Do not **scribble** in a library book.
10. This broken **table** has only three legs.

UNIT 26 BLUE LIST

1. I cannot get this **bridle** on the horse.
2. Adam is learning to play the **bugle**.
3. Amy likes to **doodle** while she talks on the phone.
4. We made a **double** batch of cookies.
5. Funny jokes make people **giggle**.
6. How many balls can you **juggle** at one time?
7. Twelve is a **multiple** of six.
8. Sometimes it is hard to thread a **needle**.
9. It takes strength to **paddle** a boat.
10. There is a **pebble** in my shoe.
11. Can you help **settle** our argument?
12. Tiaca ate a **waffle** for breakfast.

Unit 25

ds Ending th al, il, le

al

Other Pattern Words
ankle
evil
festival
loyal
normal
peril
rural
sparkle
stencil
wrinkle

Math Pattern Words
equal
numeral
ordinal

Science Pattern Words
fossil
petal
pistil
wobble

Social Studies Pattern Words
chuckle
civil
coastal
local
natural

e
il

e
al
le
ble

able
al

Unit 26

More Words Ending With le

able
apple
bottle
couple
little
maple
people
puddle
scribble
table

bridle
bugle
doodle
double
giggle
juggle
multiple
needle
paddle
pebble
settle
waffle

Other Pattern Words
brittle
idle
meddle
snuggle
wriggle

Social Studies Pattern Word
recycle

MORE WORDS FOR HUNGRY WORD HUNTERS *continued*

UNIT 27 RED LIST

1. Keisha is **almost** finished with her book.
2. The city planted trees **along** our street.
3. Gwen put the flowers in the **basket**.
4. Never stand **behind** a horse.
5. I counted a **hundred** signs on our trip.
6. Grandpa and I will go fishing early in the **morning**.
7. Count the **number** of beans in the jar.
8. Lincoln's picture is on a **penny**.
9. My **sister** is older than I am.
10. Did you sleep late **yesterday**?

UNIT 27 BLUE LIST

1. An **alligator** has very powerful jaws.
2. Let's stop at the rest **area**.
3. Al will **deposit** his money in the bank.
4. Today is an **important** holiday.
5. She bought enough **material** to make a dress.
6. I would like to be **president** someday.
7. That story **problem** was a challenge.
8. Norma would like to go **skiing** in Colorado.
9. The wind ruined my **umbrella**.
10. This is a **western** hat.

UNIT 28 RED LIST

1. We'll go outside for recess this **afternoon**.
2. Erin built that model **airplane**.
3. I like to go shopping **downtown**.
4. Stacy passed the **football** to Joe.
5. I helped my **grandfather** paint his boat.
6. My **grandmother** lives with us.
7. We played tag in the **moonlight**.
8. I think I hear **something** outside the tent.
9. Plants need water and **sunshine** to grow.
10. Kyle left his shoes **upstairs**.

UNIT 28 BLUE LIST

1. We had **applesauce** with our lunch.
2. The **cheerleader** yelled loudly.
3. I can't think with this **headache**.
4. Cecile hit her first **home run** today.
5. The dog ate my **homework**.
6. I rode every horse on the **merry-go-round**.
7. I like **peanut butter** cookies the best.
8. She went to the **post office** to mail the package.
9. The **skyscraper** has thirty stories.
10. I grew this **watermelon** in my garden.

Unit 27 — Look for the Vowels: almost, along, basket, behind, hundred, morning, number, penny, sister, yesterday

alligator, area, deposit, important, material, president, problem, skiing, umbrella, western

Other Strategy Words: apology, credit, dinosaur, discuss, enormous, mention, passenger, reward, silent, supply

Math Strategy Words: arithmetic, century, product, zero

Science Strategy Words: acid, atom, battery, chemical, clinic, formula, hospital, level, planet, solid

Social Studies Strategy Words: altitude, cargo, hogan, laughter, monument, pilgrim

Unit 28 — Compound Words: afternoon, airplane, downtown, football, grandfather, grandmother, moonlight, something, sunshine, upstairs

applesauce, cheerleader, headache, home run, homework, merry-go-round, peanut butter, post office, skyscraper, watermelon

Other Pattern Words: background, hindsight, outline, sister-in-law, throughout, typewriter, videotape, waterproof, wholesome, withdrawal

Science Pattern Words: cardboard, earthquake, grasshopper, sunspot, waterfall

Social Studies Pattern Words: aftershock, airport, freeway, handmade, handwriting, highway, landscape, outback, paperback, railroad, sailboat, skyline, sugarcane, taxicab, timberline, tugboat

UNIT 29 BLUE LIST

1. She is **actively** seeking a job.
2. My favorite ride at the **amusement** park is the roller coaster.
3. There were tulips in the flower **arrangement**.
4. Treat your pets with **gentleness**.
5. A dancer must learn to be **graceful**.
6. The game seemed **hopeless** at first.
7. It was calm and **peaceful** in the country.
8. I **sincerely** hope you had fun.
9. Lee will **surely** win the spelling bee.
10. Throwing away all that paper is **wasteful**.

UNIT 30 RED LIST

1. Jason spoke **angrily** to his sister.
2. The squirrel **busily** gathered nuts for winter.
3. Maria **buys** food for the homeless.
4. A kangaroo **carries** her baby in her pouch.
5. Dan **cried** when he heard the sad news.
6. Do you think math is **easier** than science?
7. This commuter plane **flies** to Washington, D.C., twice a day.
8. That's the **funniest** joke I've ever heard!
9. Sue is **happiest** riding her horse.
10. The rabbit **hurried** into its hole.
11. My uncle **pays** someone to mow his grass.
12. I **stayed** with my grandma this summer.

UNIT 30 BLUE LIST

1. Trish **denied** seeing anyone in the room.
2. Grasshoppers **destroyed** the farmer's crops.
3. That's the **dirtiest** dog I've ever seen!
4. Duke's **laziness** caused his room to be messy.
5. Amy is much **naughtier** than her twin sister.
6. The lion **obeyed** the command to jump through the hoop.
7. Is April the **rainiest** month of the year?
8. Connie **relies** on a road map when she travels.
9. My new neighbor **shyly** shook hands with me.
10. The water dripped **steadily** from the leaky pipe.
11. The swing **sways** in the breeze.
12. A germ is **tinier** than anything the eye can see.

Unit 29

ixes: -ful, ss, -ly, nt, -ness

ly
ment
gement
ness
ul
ess
ul
ely

ul

Other Pattern Words
advancement
barely
blameless
completely
loosely
politely
priceless
puzzlement
scarcely
tireless

Math Pattern Word
measurement

Social Studies Pattern Word
agreement

Unit 30

Changing y to i

angrily
busily
buys
carries
cried
easier
flies
funniest
happiest
hurried
pays
stayed

denied
destroyed
dirtiest
laziness
naughtier
obeyed
rainiest
relies
shyly
steadily
sways
tinier

Other Pattern Words
armies
driest
easiest
factories
funnier
happier
healthiest
heavier
heaviest
strawberries

Social Studies Pattern Words
hurried
pities
silliest
wittiest

UNIT 31 RED LIST

1. The firefighter **bravely** entered the burning building.
2. I am wearing a **colorful** shirt.
3. Thank you for your **kindness** when I was sick.
4. Your **payment** will be ten dollars a month.
5. You will save money if you **prepay** your bill.
6. Many children go to **preschool** before kindergarten.
7. We have a spelling **pretest** at the start of each week.
8. We can **reheat** this soup for lunch.
9. The **restless** tiger walked back and forth in its cage.
10. Your shoelaces are **untied**.

UNIT 32 BLUE LIST

1. The **argument** did not last long.
2. It was **awfully** cold this morning.
3. Everyone suffers from **loneliness** sometimes.
4. We'll **probably** see you at the concert.
5. I am happy with the **rearrangement** of the desks.
6. She pledged her **undying** support for the homeless.
7. It is hard to tell shyness from **unfriendliness**.
8. His pet's illness caused his **unhappiness**.
9. Although she was already late, Rudine packed her lunch in an **unhurried** manner.
10. **Unluckily**, I was not home when the package arrived.

UNIT 31 BLUE LIST

1. Having just finished the race, José spoke **breathlessly**.
2. We received a check for your **prepayment** on the car.
3. Most TV shows are **prerecorded**.
4. Ms. Berg was **previewing** a film for her science class.
5. I need a **replacement** part for this toy.
6. **Sleeplessness** can cause illness.
7. Her mother's **unemployment** was hard on the family.
8. Because of its **unfitness**, the horse was removed from the race.
9. The weather person said it is **unlikely** to rain today.
10. This dish cloth has outlived its **usefulness**.

UNIT 32 RED LIST

1. You are **becoming** a good speller.
2. Tad **changed** his clothes before he went out to play.
3. Gloria **divided** the pizza into eight equal parts.
4. Have you ever eaten **dried** apples?
5. I was **drying** the dishes when the phone rang.
6. I can solve this problem **easily**.
7. I have never seen a **lovelier** sunset.
8. Cinderella was wearing the **loveliest** gown at the ball.
9. We will be **moving** to Kansas City in June.
10. The flowers in the garden were **simply** beautiful.

Unit 31

Word Building

bravely
colorful
kindness
payment
prepay
preschool
pretest
reheat
restless
untied

breathlessly
prepayment
prerecorded
previewing
replacement
sleeplessness
unemployment
unfitness
unlikely
usefulness

Unit 32

Word Building

becoming
changed
divided
dried
drying
easily
lovelier
loveliest
moving
simply

argument
awfully
loneliness
probably
rearrangement
undying
unfriendliness
unhappiness
unhurried
unluckily

Each week students turn to **Graph Your Progress** to graph their score on their unit test. Maintaining this record helps students monitor their spelling progress.

Hardbound users may wish to duplicate **Teacher Resource Book** page 123 for students' use in graphing their progress.

NOTE: Since the number of words on students' lists may vary, the graph provides an empty square at the top of each column. Students who study more than 20 words should write the number of words spelled correctly in the empty box and then color the graph all the way to the top.

Graph Your Progress

Color one box for each word you spelled correctly on your unit test. If you spelled more than 20 words correctly, color the graph all the way to the top. Then, at the top of the column, write the number of words you spelled correctly.

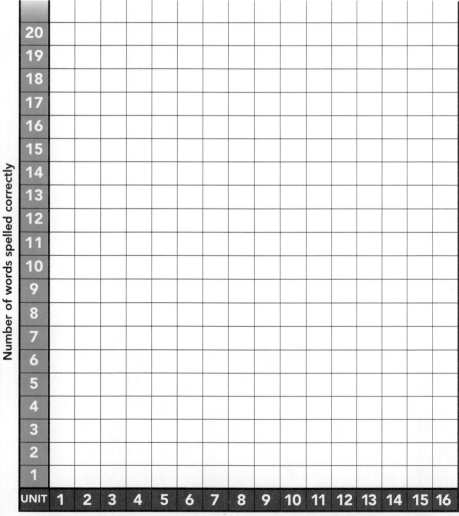

Remember to write misspelled words in **Words I Need to Know How to Spell**.

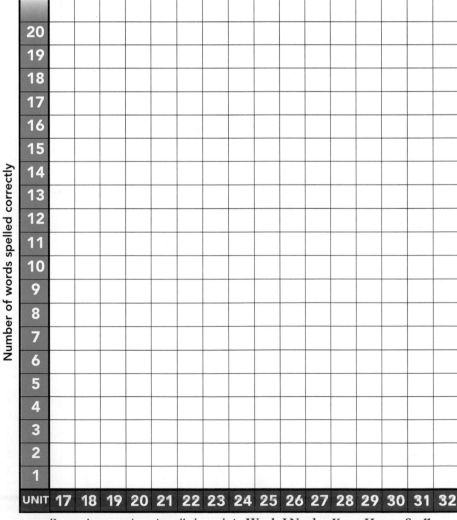

Graph Your Progress

Color one box for each word you spelled correctly on your unit test. If you spelled more than 20 words correctly, color the graph all the way to the top. Then, at the top of the column, write the number of words you spelled correctly.

Number of words spelled correctly

20 19 18 17 16 15 14 13 12 11 10 9 8 7 6 5 4 3 2 1

UNIT 17 18 19 20 21 22 23 24 25 26 27 28 29 30 31 32

Remember to write misspelled words in **Words I Need to Know How to Spell**.

Words I Need to Know How to Spell facilitates individual spelling progress by providing space for students to record:

• words misspelled on unit tests. Words recorded in **Words I Need to Know How to Spell** can be added to future weekly word lists until they are mastered. To help students monitor the length of time a word missed on a unit test has been in the word journal, teachers can remind students to also write the number of the unit during which that word was misspelled.

• words the student has "hunted" and wants to learn to spell, including words from the environment, words misspelled in writing, and words the student has encountered in reading.

Remind students to check the spelling of each word in **Words I Need to Know How to Spell** letter-for-letter. (This strategy is described on page 21 in the student edition.)

Page 6 in the **Teacher Resource Book** may be duplicated to supplement **Words I Need to Know How to Spell**. Students may also be asked to create their own **Words I Need to Know How to Spell** in a three-ring binder or a spiral notebook.

Words I Need to Know How to Spell

Use **Words I Need to Know How to Spell** to collect words you do not know how to spell. It is the place to write words you have misspelled in your writing or on a unit spelling test. **Words I Need to Know How to Spell** is also a good place to write new words you want to learn to spell.

Words From Other Languages

Students whose first language is not English may want to add words from their first language to **Words I Need to Know How to Spell**. These additions may be especially helpful if students are new to English. Observing students' literacy levels in their first language may help you provide instruction in English spelling.

If students want to add words from their first language to **Words I Need to Know How to Spell**, encourage them to:

• write the word under the appropriate letter.

• distinguish the word from their English entries. They can distinguish these words by writing them in a different color of ink or underlining them.

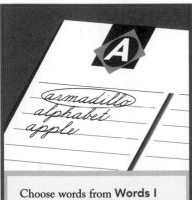

Choose words from **Words I Need to Know How to Spell** to add to your weekly spelling lists. When you add a word to your weekly list, draw a circle around it in **Words I Need to Know How to Spell**.

When you spell the word correctly on your unit test, cross it out in **Words I Need to Know How to Spell**. If you misspell the word on your unit test, add it to another weekly list later and study the word again.

Strategies for Checking Your Spelling

Strategies for Checking Your Spelling provides information on the various steps students may take to verify spellings they are not certain they have mastered. These three strategies are highlighted:

• Ask an "expert"

• Check your environment

• Use a dictionary

Strategies for Checking Your Spelling also provides information on how to use a dictionary to verify spellings.

Strategies for Checking Your Spelling

Strategy: **Ask an "expert"**

An expert, in this case, is anyone who is a good speller, or anyone who is interested in finding out how to spell a word. An expert can be an adult or a classmate. But try not to ask your teacher. If you ask your teacher, you are not doing the thinking, or the hunting, yourself.

Strategy: **Check your environment**

When you are writing and cannot think of how to spell a word, look around you! Your surroundings contain many resources that may have the answer you want. A map on the wall might be a quick way to check the spelling of a country name. Atlases, globes, and road maps might be helpful, too. You can also check encyclopedias, illustrated reference books, travel guides, signs on the walls, word walls, and posters hanging in your classroom.

When you add words to your **Words I Need to Know How to Spell,** you are building a personal spelling dictionary for the words you need when you write.

Strategy: **Use a dictionary**

Ask your teacher what kind of dictionary is best for you. A picture dictionary might not have all the words you need for your writing. An adult dictionary might not be the quickest way to find the words you need.

How to Use a Dictionary

Guide Words

The **guide words** at the top of each dictionary page can help you find the word you want quickly. The first guide word tells you the first word on that page. The second guide word tells you the last word on that page. The entries on the page will fall in alphabetical order between these two guide words.

> For example, a dictionary page with these guide words
>
> > barn | between
>
> would contain the words **basket** and **below**. The words **babble** and **cable** would not be on this page.

Entries

Words you want to check in the dictionary are called **entries**. Entries have a lot of information besides the correct spelling. Look at the sample entry below:

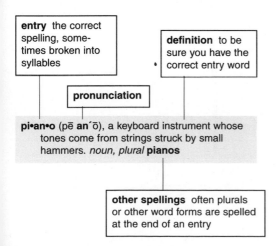

entry the correct spelling, sometimes broken into syllables

definition to be sure you have the correct entry word

pronunciation

pi•an•o (pē an´ō), a keyboard instrument whose tones come from strings struck by small hammers. *noun, plural* **pianos**

other spellings often plurals or other word forms are spelled at the end of an entry

Tips for Finding a Word in a Dictionary

- Practice using guide words in a dictionary. Think of words to spell. Then use the guide words to find each word's entry. Do this again and again until you can use guide words easily.

- If you do not know how to spell a word, guess the spelling before looking it up. Try to find the first three letters of the word. (If you just use the first letter, you will probably take too long.)

- If you can't find a word, think of how else it might be spelled. For example, if a word starts with the **k sound,** the spelling might begin with **k** or **c.**

- Some spellings are listed with the base word. To find **brightest,** you would look up **bright**. To find **walked,** you would look up **walk**. To find **tomatoes,** you would look up **tomato.**

WORDS I NEED TO KNOW HOW TO SPELL *continued*

T180-T192 Words I Need to Know How to Spell

GRADES 1–6 WORD LIST

Note: Each word is accompanied by its grade level, its unit number, and its list designation. All words not designated as "grade-level words in student edition" appear in **More Words for Hungry Word Hunters**.

G   grade-level word in student edition
R   word on Red List (below grade level)
B   word on Blue List (above grade level)
O   word on the list of Other Pattern Words
    or Other Strategy Words

S   science content word
SS   social studies content word
M   math content word

Words may be featured more than once per grade level, or in more than one grade level.

a 2-9-R
abdicate 6-5-SS
ability 6-15-O
able 2-6-B; 3-1-G;
    4-26-R
abolition 6-10-SS;
    6-22-SS
abolitionist
    5-25-SS
about 3-23-G;
    4-9-R
above 2-9-B;
    3-29-G
absence 5-11-B;
    6-8-G; 6-24-O
absolute 6-3-B
absorbent 6-19-B
abstract 6-20-G
accent 6-14-G
accept 3-20-B;
    4-8-G; 6-7-R
acceptable 6-8-G;
    6-14-O; 6-28-O
access 6-30-B
accessible 6-28-B;
    6-30-O
accessory 6-30-O
accident 5-13-B;
    6-14-G
accompany 6-14-B
accomplish 6-14-B
accord 6-14-G

accordance 6-3-B
account 6-14-B
accountant 6-19-B
accurate 6-5-O;
    6-14-G
accuse 6-14-O
accustomed 6-14-B
achieve 5-7-B;
    6-32-O
acid 3-30-B;
    4-27-S; 6-32-S
acorn 2-19-O
acquire 6-14-R
across 2-28-B;
    3-22-O; 3-29-G
act 3-8-B
action 5-18-G;
    6-10-R
active 5-6-R
actively 4-29-B
activities 5-5-O
activity 6-15-R
actor 4-23-R;
    5-25-O
actual 5-30-G
acute 6-3-O
acute angle
    4-10-M
A.D. 5-32-SS
ad 2-32-M
adapt 6-7-B
adaptation 6-14-S;
    6-16-S
adaption 5-18-S

add 1-12-B;
    2-5-G; 2-32-M;
    3-4-R
added 2-29-B
addend 5-16-M
addition 5-18-R
additional 5-30-B
additionally 6-6-O
address 4-21-B;
    5-13-G; 6-14-R
adequate 6-14-G
adjective 6-11-B
adjust 6-14-B
admiration 6-14-B
admissible 6-28-B
admission 6-14-B
admit 6-14-O
admitted 4-5-B;
    5-12-G
admitting 6-14-G
adobe 3-9-SS
adolescence 6-24-S
adopt 6-7-B
adorable 6-14-G
adore 6-14-O
adults 6-14-R
advance 6-14-G
advancement
    4-29-O; 5-19-O;
    6-14-O
advantage 5-6-B;
    6-3-G; 6-13-O
advantageous
    6-14-B

adventure 6-30-R
adventuresome
    6-30-G
adventurous 5-9-O;
    5-30-SS; 6-14-R;
    6-30-O
adverb 6-14-R
advertise 5-23-B
advertisement
    6-17-B
advice 6-7-G
advise 6-7-G
advisory 6-12-O
affect 6-26-B
affectionate 6-5-G
afraid 2-6-B;
    3-8-G; 4-4-R
Africa 3-16-O
after 2-15-G
afternoon 2-31-B;
    3-28-G; 4-28-R
aftershock
    4-28-SS
again 2-15-B
against 3-11-B;
    5-4-R
age 3-31-G
agency 6-17-B
agent 6-19-O
ago 2-13-G
agree 4-4-G;
    6-14-R
agreement 4-19-B;
    4-29-SS

agriculture 5-1-SS
ahead 3-7-B
air 3-26-G
airplane 2-31-B;
    3-28-G; 4-28-R
airport 3-26-B;
    4-28-SS; 6-11-G
airy 4-11-S
aisle 5-15-B;
    6-26-G
alert 4-24-O;
    5-8-O
alike 2-21-B; 4-3-R
alive 4-3-R
all 2-28-R
all ready 4-8-R
all right 6-2-O
all together
    5-28-B
all-star 5-20-B
alley 6-7-G
alliance 6-24-B
allied 5-12-SS
allies 5-5-SS
alligator 4-27-B;
    5-16-O
allow 4-9-B
allowance 6-13-G
allowed 4-7-B;
    5-15-G; 6-26-R
ally 6-7-G;
    6-17-SS; 6-22-SS
almanac 5-10-B;
    6-13-SS

almost 2-9-B; 3-17-G; 4-27-R
alone 3-4-G; 4-1-R
along 2-9-B; 3-1-G; 4-27-R
aloud 4-7-B; 5-15-G; 6-26-R
alphabetize 6-5-B
already 3-7-G; 4-8-R
also 2-13-B; 3-30-G; 4-6-R
although 4-13-B; 5-16-G; 6-17-R
altiplano 6-31-SS
altitude 4-3-G; 4-27-SS; 5-3-R; 6-3-SS
altogether 5-28-B
always 2-27-B; 3-29-G; 4-6-R
a.m. 5-32-B
am 2-1-R
amateur 6-8-O
amaze 5-3-B
ambulance 6-24-O
amendment 4-19-SS; 5-19-SS
America 5-13-G; 6-13-R
American 4-22-O
among 4-1-B; 5-11-G; 6-8-R
ampere 5-9-S
amphibian 5-4-S
amphitheater 6-8-SS
ample 4-25-B
amplifier 5-19-S
amplitude 6-3-S
amt. (amount) 5-32-O
amuse 4-10-B
amusement 4-29-B
amusing 6-22-R
an 2-15-R
analyze 6-32-B
ancestor 6-30-G
anchor 5-14-G

ancient 4-11-O
and 1-12-B; 2-27-R
anecdote 6-22-B
angel 4-8-B; 5-28-G; 6-7-R
angle 3-29-M; 4-8-B; 5-1-M; 5-28-G; 6-7-R
angrily 4-30-R
angry 2-8-B; 3-6-SS
animal 3-4-G; 4-25-R
animals' 4-16-G
ankle 4-25-O
anniversary 5-23-O
announce 5-6-B; 6-3-G
announcement 6-1-B
annoy 4-9-O
annual 4-1-O; 5-30-O
annually 6-8-B
another 2-23-B; 3-24-G; 4-15-R
answer 3-1-B; 4-6-G; 5-11-R
answered 5-12-R
ant 4-8-R
Antarctica 3-16-O
antelope 4-3-G
antenna 4-17-S
antennae 4-17-S
anthem 5-9-SS
antibiotic 6-1-S
antisocial 6-25-O
anxious 5-13-B; 6-13-G
any 2-8-G; 2-14-O; 3-6-R
anybody 2-31-O
anyone 2-31-O
anything 2-23-B; 4-11-R
anyway 3-8-B; 4-4-G; 5-3-R
anywhere 3-28-O
apartment 4-27-G

aphid 5-4-S
apologize 6-5-B
apology 4-27-O
apparent 6-14-B
appeal 5-3-B
appear 3-27-B; 6-14-R
appearance 6-14-O; 6-24-G
apple 2-2-SS; 4-26-R
apples 2-26-O
applesauce 4-28-B; 5-20-G
appliance 6-24-B
applicant 5-24-O; 6-14-O; 6-19-G
applied 5-12-B
apply 6-14-G
appoint 6-14-R
appointment 6-14-O
appreciate 6-8-O; 6-32-G
appreciation 6-10-B
apprentice 6-3-SS
approach 6-14-G
approachable 6-28-O
approval 6-14-B
approve 5-6-B; 6-3-G; 6-14-O
approximate 6-1-B; 6-5-O
April 3-16-B; 4-25-G
apron 5-9-R
aqueduct 4-12-SS; 6-32-SS
arable 6-28-SS
archery 6-15-G
architecture 6-17-SS
arctic 5-10-R
are 2-32-G; 3-20-R
area 4-27-B; 5-16-M
aren't 3-21-B; 4-2-B
argue 4-20-B; 5-6-O

argument 4-32-B; 6-22-G
arid 6-13-SS
arithmetic 4-27-M; 5-10-R
arm 2-19-O
armadillo 6-31-B
armchair 3-26-O
armies 4-30-O
armistice 6-3-SS
around 2-15-B; 3-29-O; 4-9-G
arrange 4-14-O
arrangement 4-29-B
array 4-1-M
arrival 5-30-G
arrive 4-3-B; 5-3-G
arriving 4-5-B
art 2-19-B
arteries 5-5-S
article 4-6-O
artifact 6-1-SS
artisan 6-32-SS
artist 5-25-R
as 2-2-O
ascent 6-26-B
Asia 3-16-O
aside 4-3-R
ask 1-12-B; 2-5-G; 3-5-R
asked 2-25-G
asking 1-27-B
asleep 2-7-B; 3-1-O; 4-4-R
aspect 6-29-G
assassination 6-10-SS
assent 6-26-B
assignment 6-6-O
assistant 5-24-G; 6-19-O
associate 4-21-B
assumed 5-12-B
aster 6-21-G
asterisk 6-21-B
asteroid 4-9-S; 6-21-G
astrolabe 6-21-SS
astrology 6-21-B

astronaut 6-21-R
astronomer 6-21-B
astronomical 6-21-B
astronomy 6-21-G
at 1-12-G; 2-1-R
ate 1-17-B; 2-5-G; 3-24-R
athlete 5-3-B; 6-32-G
atlas 6-17-SS
atoll 6-13-SS
atom 4-27-S; 5-4-B; 5-4-S
attack 5-10-G
attendance 5-13-B; 6-24-O; 6-26-G
attendant 5-24-B; 6-19-G
attendants 6-26-G
attention 3-11-B; 5-13-G; 5-18-O; 6-10-O; 6-13-R
attic 5-10-B; 6-22-O
attract 6-20-G
attraction 6-20-G
attractive 6-20-G
auction 5-18-R
audible 6-12-G
audience 6-12-G
audio 6-12-R
audiovisual 6-12-B
audition 6-12-B
auditorium 6-12-G
auditory 6-12-B
August 3-16-O; 3-22-B
aunt 2-5-B; 2-24-G; 4-8-R
Australia 3-16-O
author 4-6-O
authority 6-15-G
author's 4-16-B; 5-2-G
autobiographer 6-6-O
automobile 5-16-G; 6-30-R
autonomic 6-7-S

autumn 5-16-B;
6-17-G
available 6-1-B;
6-28-O
Ave. 5-32-G
avenue 4-10-B;
5-6-G; 6-3-R
average 4-14-B;
5-9-M
avocado 6-31-B
avoid 4-9-B
awake 2-21-B;
3-1-O; 4-3-R
award 3-29-O
aware 3-26-O;
4-11-O
away 2-6-G;
3-8-R
awful 6-32-R
awfully 4-32-B
awhile 3-13-B;
4-3-G; 5-6-R
ax 2-2-SS
axis 5-16-S; 6-1-SS

B

babies 5-5-R
baby 2-6-G; 3-4-R
baby's 4-16-R
back 2-21-G
backbone 5-3-S;
5-20-S
background 4-28-O;
6-2-O
badge 4-14-G
badly 4-19-R
baggage 3-31-O
bake 2-4-R
bakery 6-15-R
baking 2-30-O
balance 3-30-S
ball 2-28-R
ballet 5-14-G
balloon 3-14-B;
4-10-G; 5-3-R
balls 1-26-G
banana 3-1-O
band 2-1-B

bang 3-29-S
bank 2-9-O
bar graph 2-18-M;
2-20-M
barbarian 6-32-SS
barbecue 5-6-O;
6-3-O
bare 2-32-B; 3-26-G
barefoot 3-26-O
barely 4-29-O
bargain 5-4-G;
6-32-O
barge 4-14-B
bark 2-4-B; 3-20-G
barn 4-11-SS
barometer 5-23-G
barrel 3-4-O
barrette 5-14-G
barrio 6-31-SS
barter 5-9-SS;
6-17-SS
base 2-6-G; 3-8-R;
3-30-R; 4-7-S
baseball 2-31-G;
3-28-R
basic 5-10-G
basin 4-22-G;
6-13-SS
basket 4-27-R
basketball 3-28-B;
4-28-G; 5-20-R
bass 4-7-S; 4-21-S
bat 2-2-G
bath 2-5-G; 2-23-R
bathe 5-6-R
bathroom 2-31-O
batted 2-29-B;
3-18-G
batteries 5-5-B
battery 4-27-S
battle 4-26-G
bauxite 4-3-SS;
6-3-SS
bay 2-6-B; 3-8-SS
B.C. 5-32-SS
be 1-28-G; 2-32-R
beach 2-22-B;
3-12-G
beaches 3-2-SS

bean 2-8-SS
bear 2-32-B; 3-26-G
beard 2-20-B;
3-27-O
beast 3-6-O
beat 3-25-S
beautician 5-18-B
beautiful 4-32-G;
6-32-R
beauty 4-1-O
beaver 3-6-S;
4-4-R
became 3-8-B;
4-3-R
because 2-27-B;
3-22-G; 5-13-R
become 3-1-G;
3-11-O
becoming 2-30-B;
4-32-R
bed 1-13-G; 2-7-R
bedroom 2-31-O
bee 1-28-G; 2-7-R;
2-32-R; 3-20-R
beef 2-8-O
been 2-9-G; 3-24-R
beep 3-20-SS
bees 3-6-S
beeswax 3-28-S
beet 3-25-S
beetle 4-4-S;
4-26-G
before 2-19-M;
3-29-R
began 3-5-O
begin 2-14-B;
3-29-G; 4-20-R
beginning 2-30-B;
4-5-B; 6-9-G
begun 6-9-R
behave 5-6-B;
6-3-G; 6-9-O
behaved 5-12-B
behavior 4-20-S
behind 3-17-G;
4-27-R
beige 6-31-R
being 1-27-B;
3-6-G

beliefs 5-22-G;
6-9-O
believable 6-9-O;
6-28-B
believe 2-27-B;
3-24-B; 5-7-G
bell 2-2-O
belong 3-22-O
below 2-13-B;
3-4-G
belt 2-2-B; 3-7-G
bench 2-22-O
benches 2-26-O
benchmark 5-20-M
beneath 4-4-B;
5-3-G; 6-9-R
beneficial 6-17-B
benign 6-9-O
bent 2-25-G
bequeath 6-9-B
bequest 6-9-B
beret 5-14-G
berries 5-5-G
berry 3-20-O
beside 6-9-R
besides 6-9-G
best 2-4-G; 3-5-R
better 2-9-O;
3-11-G; 4-11-R
between 3-6-B;
4-4-G; 5-3-R
beverage 3-31-O
beware 3-26-O
beyond 6-9-G
biannual 5-21-B
bicuspid 5-21-S
bicycle 5-1-O;
5-21-G
biennial 5-21-O
bifocals 5-21-G
big 2-1-O
bigger 3-19-R
biggest 3-19-R
bike 2-21-G;
3-10-R
bilaterally 5-31-B
bilingual 5-21-B;
6-6-SS
bill 2-2-O

billboard 5-20-SS
billion 5-4-M
bimonthly 5-19-O;
5-21-O; 5-31-G;
6-6-R
biographer 5-25-SS
biomass 5-13-S
birch 3-12-S
bird 2-20-O; 3-1-S;
4-24-R
birds 1-26-B;
2-26-G; 3-2-R
birth 2-23-O
birthday 2-31-B;
3-8-G; 4-24-R
birthdays 5-5-R
birthmark 5-10-G
biscuit 4-1-0
bisect 5-21-O
bit 2-10-G
bite 1-19-B;
2-10-G; 5-15-S
biweekly 5-21-G;
5-31-O
black 1-22-G;
2-17-G; 3-3-R
blame 3-8-O
blamed 3-18-B
blameless 4-29-O
blew 3-14-R
blind 3-10-B
blindness 4-19-B
blink 2-4-O
blizzard 4-6-SS;
4-8-S
block 2-17-B;
3-9-G
blockade 5-11-SS
blood 3-20-S
bloom 3-14-S
blouse 4-9-O
blow 2-4-B
blue 1-22-G;
3-14-R; 4-10-R
blue-eyed 6-2-R
blueberries 5-5-B
blueberry 4-10-O
bluebird 2-31-G;
3-28-R

bluish 5-16-O;
5-24-O
blur 3-29-O
board 3-20-B;
4-7-G; 5-15-R
boast 3-9-O
boat 2-13-G
boats 1-26-B;
2-26-G; 3-2-R
bodies 5-5-R
boil 3-23-O
bomb 4-13-O
bone 2-13-B
bones 2-12-S;
2-26-S
bonus 3-9-O
book 2-21-R;
3-15-R
bookbag 2-31-R
bookcase 3-28-B
bookkeeper 6-2-B
bookmark 5-20-B
boomerang 5-14-O;
6-8-SS
boot 3-14-B
border 3-11-SS;
5-13-SS
bore 3-20-O
bored 4-7-G;
5-15-R
born 2-20-G
borough 4-8-O
borrow 3-11-M
boss 2-28-B
both 1-25-B;
2-23-G; 3-17-R
bottle 4-26-R
bottom 3-4-B;
4-27-G
bought 3-22-G;
4-13-R
bounce 2-9-S
boundaries 5-5-O
boundary 4-9-SS;
4-20-SS; 5-24-B
bouquet 5-14-B
boutique 6-31-O
bow 2-13-B; 4-21-R
box 1-15-G; 2-3-R

boxcar 2-31-R;
5-20-SS
boxes 2-26-G; 3-2-R
boy 2-9-R; 3-23-R
boy's 4-16-R
boys 2-26-O
boys' 4-16-R
brace 3-30-O
brag 3-5-O
braid 2-18-O
brain 2-18-S; 3-8-B
brake 4-7-G; 5-15-R
branch 3-12-S
branches 2-26-B;
3-2-G
brave 2-6-B; 4-20-R
bravely 4-31-R
braver 3-19-B
bravest 3-19-B
bread 2-20-B; 3-7-G
break 4-7-G; 5-15-R
breakable 6-28-R
breakfast 3-7-B;
4-28-G; 5-20-R
breath 3-7-G;
3-7-S; 4-18-R
breathe 5-6-B;
6-3-G
breathlessly 4-31-B
breed 3-6-O
breeze 3-6-B
brick 3-5-B
bridal 4-8-O
bridge 4-14-G
bridle 4-8-O; 4-26-B
brief 5-7-R
bright 2-11-B;
3-10-G
brightly 4-19-R
bring 2-18-G; 3-3-R
brittle 4-26-O
broad jump 6-2-G
broaden 6-5-G
brochure 5-14-B;
6-31-G
broke 2-21-B
broken 3-1-B;
4-22-G
brook 2-18-O

brother 2-24-G;
3-11-R; 3-24-SS
brother-in-law
5-20-B
brother's 4-16-G
brothers' 4-16-G;
5-2-R
brought 2-18-B;
3-22-G; 5-13-R
brown 1-22-B;
3-23-R
browse 6-13-O
brush 2-18-G
brushes 2-26-O
bubble 4-26-G
buccaneer 6-1-SS
budget 3-31-SS
buffalo 4-20-B
buffet 4-21-O;
5-14-B; 6-22-O
bug 2-4-R
bugle 4-26-B
build 4-1-G;
5-1-R
building 3-11-B;
5-4-R
built 3-20-B;
4-6-G; 5-11-R
bulb 2-3-S
bull 3-15-B
bulletin 5-11-B;
6-8-G
bunny 3-11-O
bureau 6-8-O
burglar 4-24-B;
5-4-G
burn 3-20-S; 4-24-R
burnt 4-24-O
burrito 6-31-B
burro 5-14-O;
6-31-R
burrow 4-8-O
burst 4-24-G
bus 2-3-G; 3-30-R
buses 3-2-R
bush 3-15-G
bushes 2-26-B;
3-2-G
busily 4-30-R

business 4-15-B;
5-13-G; 5-19-O;
6-13-R
busy 2-15-O;
3-6-G; 4-20-R
but 1-16-G; 2-3-R;
2-9-R
butcher 3-12-O
butter 3-4-O
butterflies 5-5-B
butterfly 2-11-S;
2-31-S
button 3-5-O
buy 2-9-G; 3-25-R
buys 4-30-R
by 3-10-R; 3-25-R
bystander 5-20-B
byte 5-15-S

c. 5-32-B
cabbage 3-11-B
cabin 3-5-SS; 4-22-R
cabinet 6-32-SS
cacti 4-17-S
cactus 4-6-SS; 4-17-S
cafeteria 5-9-B
cage 2-5-B; 3-31-G
cages 2-26-B;
3-2-G
cake 2-6-G; 2-21-O;
3-4-R
calcium 5-9-S
calculated 5-12-M
calculator 5-19-M
calendar 5-4-R
call 2-4-G
called 2-25-G;
3-18-R
calves 5-22-G
came 1-17-G
camel 3-20-S
camouflage 6-31-G
camp 2-2-B; 3-5-G;
3-5-SS
campesino 6-31-SS
can 1-12 G; 2-1-R
Canada 3-16-B

canal 4-1-SS;
5-16-SS
canaries 5-5-B
candle 4-25-G
candy 3-11-R
cane 2-5-O
cannot 3-28-R
can't 3-21-G; 4-2-R
canyon 5-16-SS
cap 2-5-B
capable 6-28-O
capacities 5-5-M
cape 2-5-B
capillaries 5-5-S
capital 4-15-B;
5-15-G; 6-26-R
capitalism 6-17-SS
capitalist 5-25-SS
capitalize 6-5-R
capitol 5-15-G;
6-26-R
captain 3-29-B;
4-15-G; 6-8-O
captain's 5-2-G
car 2-4-R
caravan 6-8-SS
card 2-19-O
cardboard 3-28-B;
4-28-S
care 3-26-G
career 3-27-B
careful 3-26-B;
4-29-G
carefully 5-19-G;
6-16-O
careless 4-29-G
carelessness 5-19-R
cargo 4-27-SS;
6-31-R
carnivore 5-16-S;
6-8-S
carousel 6-31-O
carpet 4-11-G;
5-16-R
carriage 5-6-B;
6-3-G
carried 4-1-G;
5-12-R
carries 4-30-R

carrot 3-4-O
carry 2-27-B;
   3-1-G; 4-20-R
carrying 4-5-B
cars 1-26-G
cartilage 5-6-S
carve 5-6-R
case 3-8-B
cashier 5-7-G
cassette 5-14-G
cast 6-26-SS
caste 6-26-SS
castle 3-24-SS;
   4-25-R
casual 6-22-O
cat 1-12-G
cataract 6-13-S
catch 3-12-G
catcher 3-12-O;
   5-25-G
category 6-32-B
caterpillar 3-11-S;
   5-9-R
catfish 3-5-O
cattail 6-2-R
cattle 3-11-G;
   4-11-R
caught 3-22-B;
   4-15-G; 5-11-R
cause 3-22-B;
   4-11-S; 5-1-SS
causeway 5-20-SS
caution 5-18-O
cavalry 5-9-SS
cave 3-8-G
cease 4-8-B; 5-28-G
cedar 3-30-O
cede 6-30-SS
ceiling 5-7-B; 6-1-G
celebrate 3-30-O;
   4-3-O
cell 3-25-B; 3-30-S;
   5-15-S; 6-26-S
cellar 3-25-O;
   3-30-B
Celsius 5-11-M
cement 3-30-SS
censor 6-26-SS
census 5-4-SS

cent 3-25-G; 4-7-R
center 3-30-O;
   5-9-M
centimeter 5-23-G
centipede 5-3-S
century 4-27-M
cereal 4-8-B;
   5-28-G; 6-7-R
cerebellum 6-13-S
cerebrum 6-32-S
certain 4-8-G;
   5-4-O; 5-28-R
certainly 5-1-G;
   6-1-R
chair 2-22-B;
   3-26-G
chalk 2-4-O
challenge 6-3-B
champion 4-11-O
chance 2-22-B
chandelier 6-31-B
change 3-12-R;
   3-12-S; 3-31-R;
   3-31-S
changeable 6-13-O;
   6-28-G
changed 4-32-R
changing 2-30-B
chaperon 6-31-B
character 5-14-G
charade 6-31-B
charcoal 4-4-O
charge 3-17-B;
   4-14-G; 5-6-R
charitable 6-28-B
chart 3-12-B
chase 2-22-O;
   3-12-O
chasing 3-18-B
chat 2-22-O
chatter 2-22-O
check 2-21-B; 3-6-B
checkbook 5-10-B;
   6-2-O
checkup 3-28-S
cheek 2-8-G;
   2-22-R; 3-12-R
cheer 3-27-G
cheerful 4-19-G

cheerfully 4-31-G
cheerleader 4-28-B;
   5-20-G
cheese 2-8-O
chef 5-14-B;
   6-31-R
chefs 5-22-B
chemical 4-27-S
chemist 5-25-S
cherry 3-11-O
chew 3-14-B
chic 6-26-SS
chicken 3-12-B;
   4-22-G
chief 5-7-R
chiefs 5-22-G
child 2-22-G;
   3-10-R; 4-17-R
childish 5-24-G
children 2-20-B;
   3-12-G; 4-17-R
children's 4-16-G;
   5-2-R
child's 4-16-G; 5-2-R
chill 2-28-S
chilly 3-6-S
chimneys 5-5-B
chin 2-22-R; 3-12-R
chipmunk 5-10-G
chirp 2-20-S
chloroplast 6-1-S
chocolate 5-11-G;
   5-16-O; 6-8-R
choice 3-23-B
choir 5-9-O; 6-32-G
choose 3-20-B;
   4-10-G
choosing 2-30-O
chop 2-22-O
chord 6-7-G
chores 3-12-SS
chorus 5-14-G
chose 3-12-B
chosen 6-5-R
chromosomes 6-17-S
chuckle 4-25-SS
church 3-12-O
chute 3-25-B;
   6-31-R

cider 3-30-O
cinnamon 4-22-O
circle 3-30-G;
   4-25-R; 5-8-M
circuit 4-24-S;
   5-8-S
circular 5-4-O; 5-8-B
circulate 5-8-O
circulatory 5-8-S
circumstance 5-27-O
circumvent 6-30-O
circus 3-30-B;
   4-24-G; 5-8-R
cities 3-30-SS;
   5-5-G
citizen 3-30-SS;
   4-22-B
citizenry 6-15-B
city 3-30-G
civil 4-25-SS
civilize 5-6-O; 6-5-G
claim 6-1-R
clam 2-17-S
clamor 6-22-G
clan 6-22-SS
clap 2-17-G
class 2-17-B
classes 2-26-B;
   3-2-G
classics 6-1-SS
classified 5-12-B
classify 6-22-G
classroom 3-14-SS
claw 3-22-O
clay 3-8-G
clean 1-24-B; 2-8-G;
   3-6-R
cleaning 3-18-R
cleanse 4-18-G
clear 3-27-G
clearance 6-24-G
clearing 3-27-O
clerk 3-4-SS;
   3-20-SS; 4-24-G
click 3-11-SS
cliff 3-20-SS
cliffs 5-22-R
climb 3-10-B;
   4-13-G

climbing 4-5-SS
clinic 4-27-S; 5-10-R
clock 2-3-O; 3-5-G
clockwise 5-3-M;
   5-20-M
close 2-12-B;
   3-20-G; 4-21-R
closed 2-29-B;
   3-4-SS; 3-18-G;
   4-5-R
closed figure 3-18-M
closer 3-19-O
closest 3-19-O
closing 4-5-R
cloth 2-17-O;
   2-23-O; 3-22-B
clothe 5-6-G; 6-3-R
clothes 3-1-B;
   4-15-G; 5-1-R
clothing 4-11-G;
   5-16-R
cloud 2-17-B
cloudless 4-19-B
cloudy 3-23-S
clover 3-9-S
clown 3-23-G; 4-9-R
clowns' 5-2-G
club 1-16-B; 2-17-G
clue 3-14-B;
   4-10-G; 5-6-R
clustering 5-13-M
coach 2-13-O; 3-9-B
coaches 3-2-O
coal 2-13-B; 3-9-G
coarse 4-7-B;
   5-15-G; 5-28-O;
   6-26-R
coast 3-9-SS
coastal 4-25-SS
coat 2-13-G; 3-9-R
cocoon 2-9-S
coffee 4-4-B
coin 2-9-M; 3-23-R
cold 2-13-G; 3-4-R
cold-blooded 5-20-S
collage 6-31-G
collapse 6-18-B
collar 3-5-O; 5-4-O
collect 6-18-G

collection 6-10-R
collective 6-18-SS
college 4-14-O;
  6-3-O; 6-18-G
collegiate 6-5-B
collide 6-18-B
collision 6-10-B
colonel 4-8-O;
  5-28-O
colonies 5-5-B
colonist 3-29-SS;
  5-25-G
colonize 6-5-R
colony 4-15-SS
color 3-29-G
colorful 4-31-R
colossal 6-22-B
columnist 5-25-B
comb 4-13-G
come 2-14-R; 3-1-R
comedies 5-5-SS
comet 5-4-S; 5-9-R
comfortable 6-28-G
comic 5-10-O
coming 2-30-G;
  3-18-R
command 6-18-R
commanded 5-12-SS
commander 5-25-B
commentary 5-24-B
commerce 5-8-SS
commercial 6-18-B;
  6-25-SS
commodity 6-15-O
common 4-22-B;
  6-18-R
commotion 6-30-G
communication
  6-18-B
communism 6-18-SS
communist 6-18-SS
communities 5-5-S;
  6-18-B
community 6-15-S;
  6-18-G
commuter 6-18-G
compact 4-21-O;
  6-18-G
companies 5-5-G

company 3-6-B;
  4-20-G
compare 3-26-O;
  6-18-R
compass 6-18-SS
compassionate 6-5-B
compelled 5-12-O
competition 6-10-B
complain 5-3-B;
  6-18-O
complained 5-12-O
complement 6-26-B
complete 4-3-G;
  4-6-B; 6-22-R
completed 5-12-G
completely 4-29-O
completion 5-18-O;
  6-10-O
complicate 6-18-B
compliment 6-26-B
compose 4-3-B;
  6-18-R
composer 5-25-B
composition 5-18-G;
  6-10-R
compound 3-23-S;
  4-9-S; 5-11-S;
  6-18-S
compromise
  5-13-SS
compute 5-3-M;
  6-18-R
computer 6-18-G
concave 6-18-S
concede 6-32-B
conceit 5-7-B;
  6-18-O
conceive 6-17-B
concern 6-18-G
concert 5-8-SS
conclude 6-18-O;
  6-22-R
conclusion 6-10-G;
  6-18-O
concrete 6-18-B
condition 5-18-G;
  6-10-O; 6-18-R
conduct 4-21-O;
  6-18-O; 6-29-R

conduction 6-29-S
conductor 5-25-B;
  6-29-R
cone 2-13-G;
  3-9-M
conference 6-18-B
confide 6-18-O
confident 6-19-B
confirm 5-8-B
conflict 6-18-B
Congress 3-16-SS
connect 6-18-G
connection 5-18-B
conscience 6-7-B
conscientious 6-8-B
conscious 6-1-B
conservation
  5-18-SS; 5-27-B;
  6-10-S; 6-18-S;
  6-25-SS
conserve 5-8-SS;
  5-27-B
consider 6-18-G
considerable 6-28-B
considerate 6-5-G
consideration
  5-18-O; 6-10-O
consistent 6-19-B
console 4-21-O
constant 5-27-G
constitution 5-18-B;
  5-18-SS; 6-18-G
construct 6-18-B
consul 6-18-SS
consume 5-3-SS
consumed 5-12-SS
consumer 3-24-SS;
  5-25-S; 5-25-SS;
  6-18-S; 6-22-SS
contact 6-12-R
contain 4-4-B;
  6-18-R
content 4-21-G;
  6-18-R
contest 4-21-B
contestant 5-24-B;
  6-19-G
continent 6-18-R
continental 5-30-S

continue 4-4-B;
  5-1-O; 5-3-G;
  5-6-O; 6-18-R
continued 4-5-O
continuous 5-30-B;
  6-18-O
contour 6-18-SS
contract 4-21-O;
  6-20-G
contraction 6-20-G
contradict 6-29-B
contradiction 6-29-B
contribute 4-10-O;
  6-18-O
contribution 5-18-B
control 5-16-S
controversy 5-23-O;
  6-13-B
convent 6-18-SS
convention 6-30-B
conventional
  6-30-SS
conversation 5-23-B
converse 5-23-O
convert 4-21-O;
  5-23-B
convertible 5-23-B;
  6-28-G
convex 6-18-S
convict 4-21-O
coo 6-26-SS
cook 2-21-O; 3-15-R
cookery 6-15-B
cookies 3-15-G
cool 3-14-B; 4-10-G
cooperate 4-3-O
coordinates 5-16-M
copies 5-5-O
copyright 6-2-B
coral 5-28-B
cord 2-19-SS
cordless 4-19-B
core 4-11-S
corn 2-19-G
corner 2-19-B;
  3-4-G; 3-4-M
corral 5-28-B
correspondence
  6-7-B

corrosion 6-10-B
corruptible 6-28-B
corsage 6-31-B
cosmopolitan
  6-32-SS
cost 3-22-O
costume 4-10-B;
  6-7-R
cot 2-1-O
cottage 3-31-O
cotton 3-29-O;
  4-22-G
couch 4-9-B
could 2-15-O;
  3-15-G
couldn't 3-15-B;
  3-21-O; 4-1-G;
  5-1-R
council 3-23-SS;
  4-25-B; 6-26-G
counsel 6-26-G
count 2-27-M
countdown 5-20-M
counterclockwise
  5-20-M
countries 5-5-G
country 3-11-B;
  4-8-O; 4-20-G;
  4-20-G
county 4-8-O
coup 6-26-SS
couple 4-26-R
couples' 4-16-O
courageous 5-30-G
course 4-7-B;
  5-15-G; 5-28-O;
  6-26-R
cousin 2-24-B;
  4-22-G; 6-32-R
cousins' 5-2-B
covenant 6-30-SS
cover 3-17-O
cow 2-9-R; 3-23-R
coward 4-9-B
coyote 5-4-SS
crab 2-20-S
crack 2-18-G
crafts 4-20-SS
crash 2-5-B

crater 3-24-S; 5-9-G
crawl 3-22-B
crayon 3-8-O
cream 2-4-B
create 4-6-O
creation 5-18-SS
creativity 6-15-O
credit 4-27-O
creditor 4-23-O;
   5-25-O
crept 4-18-G
crew 3-14-O
cried 4-30-R
cries 3-29-SS
critic 5-10-B
criticize 6-5-G
crochet 5-13-O;
   5-14-G; 6-31-R
crooked 3-15-B
croquet 5-14-G
cross 2-18-B
cross-country 6-2-O
cross section 6-2-B
crossing 3-18-B
crosswalk 3-28-SS
crow 3-9-S
crowd 3-23-B;
   4-9-G
crown 3-23-SS
cruel 5-16-B;
   6-17-G
crumb 4-13-B;
   5-13-G; 6-13-R
crush 2-22-B
crust 3-5-B; 3-20-S;
   4-11-S
cry 2-11-O; 3-10-G
cube 3-14-M
cubic 5-10-M
cue 4-10-O
cuffs 5-22-R
cultivate 6-5-SS
culture 3-20-SS
cup 1-16-B; 2-3-G;
   3-5-R; 3-5-M
cupboard 5-11-B;
   6-8-G
curiosity 6-15-B
curious 5-1-B; 6-1-G

current 4-24-B;
   5-9-S; 6-19-SS
cursive 4-24-SS
curtain 4-8-G;
   5-4-O; 5-28-R
curve 4-24-B
cushion 5-4-B
custom 5-4-SS
customary 5-24-G
cut 1-16-B; 2-3-G
cute 3-14-G; 4-10-R
cuter 3-19-G
cutest 3-19-G
cycle 4-26-G
cyclist 5-25-O
cylinder 5-16-M
cymbal 6-26-B
cytoplasm 6-32-S

dad 2-2-R; 2-24-R
daddy 2-24-G;
   3-11-R
daily 4-4-G; 5-3-O
dairy 3-26-SS;
   4-8-G; 5-28-R
daisies 5-5-G
daisy 2-6-O
dam 3-29-SS;
   4-11-SS
damage 4-14-O
dance 3-30-G
dancer 4-23-O
dandelion 5-9-G
danger 4-14-G
dangerous 4-6-B;
   5-30-G
dare 3-26-O
dark 2-19-O
darkness 4-19-G
data 5-4-M
dateline 5-3-SS;
   6-2-SS
daughter 2-24-B;
   3-22-O
daughter's 4-16-O
dawdle 3-22-SS
dawn 3-22-B

day 1-17-G; 2-4-R
daydream 6-2-G
days 1-26-B
deactivate 6-16-B
dead 3-7-G
deaf 3-7-O
deal 3-6-O
dealt 4-18-G
dear 2-27-G; 3-29-R
death 3-7-O
debrief 5-29-B
decade 4-3-M
decay 4-4-B; 6-9-R
decayed 5-12-S
December 3-16-B
decent 6-7-G
decentralize 6-16-B
decide 4-3-B; 5-3-G;
   6-9-R
decided 4-5-B
deciding 4-5-B
decimal 3-30-M;
   5-4-M
decision 6-9-G;
   6-10-O
declare 6-9-R
decode 5-29-G
decomposer 5-25-S;
   5-29-S; 6-6-S;
   6-9-S
decoy 6-9-O
decrease 4-4-O;
   6-9-O
deduct 6-9-G
deductive 6-29-O
deep 3-11-R
deer 4-17-R
defeat 5-3-SS
defendant 6-19-G
defense 6-9-G
defer 6-9-B
defiant 6-19-R
define 4-3-G
defined 5-12-R
definite 6-9-B
defrost 5-29-G
degree 4-4-G;
   5-11-M; 6-9-SS
degrees 3-2-M

dehumanize
   6-16-G
dejected 6-11-B
delay 4-4-R
deliberate 6-9-B
delicate 6-5-O
delicious 5-16-O;
   5-30-O; 6-9-O
delightful 6-9-O;
   6-16-G
deliver 6-9-B
demand 6-9-R
democracies 5-5-SS
demonstrate 6-9-G
demonstration 6-8-B
denied 4-30-B;
   5-12-G
dense 4-11-S
density 4-15-S
dental 2-9-S
dentist 2-2-SS
dentistry 6-15-B
dentist's 4-16-B
departure 6-9-G
depend 6-9-G
deposit 4-27-B;
   6-9-R
deposition 5-18-S
depositor 6-9-B
depot 4-15-SS
deprogram 5-29-B
depth 2-23-O;
   4-18-G
derrick 5-10-B
descendant 6-32-B
descent 6-7-B
describe 4-20-B;
   5-3-O; 6-9-G
description 6-32-B
desert 3-20-SS;
   4-21-G; 5-28-R
deserve 5-8-O;
   6-9-R
design 4-13-B
desirable 6-28-B
desire 4-3-B; 5-6-G;
   6-3-R
desired 5-12-G
desist 6-9-B

desk 2-2-O; 3-6-G
desperate 6-5-O
dessert 5-28-R
destroy 4-9-B;
   5-9-O; 6-9-R
destroyed 4-30-B
detailed 5-12-S
detain 4-4-O; 6-9-O
detective 5-6-O
detergent 6-9-B
determine 6-9-B
detract 6-20-G
develop 6-9-O
device 6-7-G
devise 6-7-G
devote 5-3-B
dew 4-10-B
diagram 4-15-SS
diameter 5-23-G
diamond 4-15-B;
   5-11-G; 6-8-R
diaries 5-5-O
diary 4-8-G; 5-28-R
dictate 6-29-B
dictator 5-25-SS;
   6-6-SS; 6-29-B
diction 6-29-B
dictionary 6-25-SS;
   6-29-B
did 1-14-G; 2-2-R
didn't 3-21-G; 4-2-R
died 3-25-O
diesel 5-9-B
differed 5-12-O
difference 5-6-B;
   6-3-G
different 4-11-B;
   5-11-G; 6-19-R;
   6-32-O
difficult 5-1-B;
   6-1-G; 6-22-O
digest 4-8-S
digestion 4-20-S
digging 2-30-O;
   3-18-O
digit 3-31-M
digits 5-4-M
dilemma 6-13-B
dim 2-10-B

dime 2-10-B; 2-11-M; 3-10-M
dinette 5-14-B
dinner 3-4-G; 4-1-R
dinosaur 4-27-O
directed 5-12-O
direction 5-18-G
directly 4-19-O
director 4-23-B; 5-25-G
dirt 4-24-R
dirtiest 4-30-B
dirty 4-24-B; 5-8-G
disadvantageous 5-31-B
disagree 4-4-O; 5-29-O
disagreeable 6-16-O; 6-25-G
disagreement 5-29-B; 6-22-G
disappear 3-27-O; 5-29-G
disappoint 5-29-B
disappointed 5-12-SS
disappointment 5-29-O
disaster 6-21-G
disastrous 6-21-B
discoloration 6-6-G
discontinue 5-29-B
discover 3-29-B; 4-27-G
discrimination 6-25-SS
discuss 4-27-O
discussion 6-10-G; 6-16-O
disease 4-4-S
disguise 6-13-O
dish 2-22-R
dishes 2-26-B; 3-2-G
dishonest 5-29-G
dishonorable 6-25-B
disinfectant 5-31-G
disintegration 6-6-B
disinterested 5-29-O

diskette 5-14-B
dislike 5-29-O
dislocate 6-20-B
disloyalty 6-16-G
disobey 5-29-G
display 6-22-G
disposition 6-10-G
disproportionate 6-16-B
dispute 6-3-O
disqualification 6-6-B
dissatisfied 6-8-B
distance 5-27-G
distant 5-27-G
distortion 6-25-SS
distract 6-20-G
disturb 4-24-O
diversity 6-17-SS; 6-22-SS
divide 3-10-M; 4-3-R
divided 4-5-M; 4-32-R
divisible 6-28-R
division 6-10-R
do 1-21-G; 2-15-R; 3-14-R
dock 2-21-O
doctor 2-12-SS; 3-29-B; 4-15-G; 5-13-R
doctor's 4-16-G; 5-2-R
doctors 3-2-B
dodge 4-14-B
does 2-27-B; 3-1-G; 4-21-R
doesn't 3-21-B; 4-2-G
dog 2-27-R; 3-22-R
doghouse 2-31-G; 3-28-R
dogs 1-26-B
dog's 4-16-R
doing 1-27-G; 2-30-G
doll 1-15-B; 2-3-G; 3-9-R

dollar 2-1-M; 3-24-B; 5-4-R
dollars 3-2-M
domesticate 6-5-SS; 6-22-SS
dominant 6-19-B
dominion 6-25-SS
done 3-17-G; 4-1-R
don't 3-21-G; 4-2-R
doodle 3-14-SS; 4-26-B
door 3-4-R
double 4-26-B
dove 4-21-R
down 2-1-G; 3-29-R
downstairs 5-20-O
downtown 3-28-G; 4-28-R
doz. (dozen) 5-32-O
dozen 4-22-G
Dr. 5-32-G
drag 3-5-O
dragon 3-11-G; 4-22-R
dramatic 5-1-O; 5-10-O
drank 2-18-S
draw 2-18-B; 3-22-G
drawer 3-1-O
dread 3-7-O
dreadful 6-22-G
dream 2-18-B; 3-6-G
dreamer 4-23-O
dress 2-18-G
dresses 2-26-G; 3-2-R
drew 4-10-G
dried 4-32-R
driest 4-30-O
drifted 2-25-O
drink 2-2-B; 3-10-G
drip 1-24-G
drive 2-18-G; 3-10-R
drive-in 6-2-R
driven 4-6-G
driver 4-23-R

driveway 3-28-O
driving 2-30-B
drop 1-15-B; 2-3-G
dropped 2-29-B
drought 5-11-SS
drove 5-6-R
drown 4-9-O
drugstore 3-28-SS
drum 2-3-O
drummer 4-23-B
dry 2-11-O; 3-10-G
drying 4-32-R
duck 2-21-G; 3-5-R
duct 6-29-R
due 3-14-B; 4-10-G
duet 4-15-M
dull 2-28-B
dune 4-1-SS
during 3-4-B; 4-27-G
dust 2-3-O
duties 5-5-G
duty 3-24-SS
dyed 3-25-O
dynamite 5-3-O

E

each 2-22-G; 3-12-R
eager 4-4-G
eagle 4-26-G
ear 3-27-G
eardrum 3-27-S; 3-28-S
earlier 5-8-G
earliest 5-8-B
early 3-11-G; 4-11-R
earn 5-8-R
earnest 5-8-B
earrings 3-27-B; 6-2-R
earth 3-11-G; 5-8-R
earthquake 3-28-S; 4-3-S; 4-12-S; 4-28-S; 5-8-SS; 5-20-SS; 6-2-S
earthworm 3-28-S
easier 4-30-R

easiest 4-30-O
easily 4-32-R
east 2-8-B; 3-6-G
eastern 4-4-O
easy 2-8-R; 3-6-R
eat 2-8-G
eating 1-27-B; 2-30-G
echo 5-14-G
echoes 4-17-B
eclipse 5-11-S
economic 6-1-B
economies 5-5-SS
economy 6-13-SS
ecosystem 5-16-S; 6-8-S
edge 3-31-M; 4-14-G; 5-11-M
edible 6-28-O; 6-28-SS
editor 4-23-G; 5-25-R
editorial 5-30-SS; 6-1-SS
educate 6-29-R
education 6-10-B
eerie 3-27-O
effect 5-11-SS; 6-26-B; 6-32-SS
effective 6-3-B
effort 6-13-G
egg 1-13-B; 2-7-G; 3-5-R
eggs 2-26-O
eight 1-23-B; 2-14-B
eighteen 3-6-O
eighteenth 5-7-M
eighth 3-24-B; 4-15-G; 5-7-R
eighty 5-7-G; 5-13-O
either 4-6-O
eject 6-11-B
elastic 5-10-B
elect 3-11-SS
election 5-18-R
electric 3-20-SS; 5-10-R
electrician 5-18-G

electricity 6-15-R
electromagnetic
   6-13-S
electron 5-9-S
element 5-13-S
elephant 3-24-S
elevation 5-13-SS
eleven 2-9-O
ellipse 5-11-S
elm 3-7-S
else 3-5-O; 3-30-B;
   4-6-G
elves 5-22-R
embargo 6-23-SS
embarrass 6-23-B
emblem 6-23-R
embroidery 6-23-B
emergency 5-8-B
emigrate 6-5-SS;
   6-23-SS
emotion 5-18-O;
   6-30-G
emotional 6-30-B
emperor 6-23-SS
empire 5-16-SS;
   6-3-O; 6-23-G
employ 6-23-R
employed 5-12-G
employee 5-3-B;
   6-23-G
employment 5-19-O
emptiness 4-32-G
empty 2-7-O
enclose 6-23-B
encyclopedia 6-23-SS
end 1-13-B; 2-7-G
endanger 6-23-G
endangered 6-23-S
ended 2-25-B
endless 4-19-O
endpoints 3-23-M
endurance 6-24-B
endure 6-23-B
enemy 3-20-S
energetic 5-10-O
energies 5-5-S
energy 4-6-B;
   6-23-R
engage 4-14-G

engine 3-31-O
engineer 5-16-B;
   6-17-G; 6-23-O
enjoy 3-23-G; 4-9-R
enjoyable 6-28-R
enjoyed 4-5-B;
   5-12-R
enjoyment 4-19-G
enjoys 4-30-G
enlist 6-23-G
enormous 4-27-O
enough 3-11-B;
   5-4-R
enroll 6-23-B
enthusiastic 6-23-B
entire 4-3-B
entrance 4-21-B;
   5-6-G; 6-3-R
entries 5-5-B
envelope 6-23-R
enviable 6-28-G
envious 5-30-G
environment 5-13-B;
   5-19-S; 6-23-G
envision 6-12-O
episode 5-4-SS
equal 4-12-G;
   4-25-M
equally 4-12-B;
   4-19-M
equation 5-18-M
equator 4-12-SS;
   5-13-SS
equatorial 6-25-SS
erase 3-29-O; 4-3-R
erode 6-3-SS
erosion 5-13-S;
   6-10-G; 6-16-SS
error 6-17-G;
   6-22-O
eruption 6-10-R
escape 5-9-B
especially 4-19-O;
   5-11-B; 5-19-O;
   6-1-O; 6-8-G
essays 5-5-B
estimate 4-21-B;
   5-6-M
estimation 5-18-M

estuary 6-25-SS
etiquette 5-14-B
Europe 3-16-O
evaporate 5-3-S
even 2-15-B; 3-1-G;
   3-24-M; 4-22-R
evening 4-11-B;
   5-16-G; 6-17-R
even numbers
   2-26-M
event 5-28-O;
   6-30-R
eventful 6-30-G
ever 2-7-B; 3-7-G
every 2-8-B; 2-14-O;
   3-6-G; 4-15-R
everybody 3-6-B;
   4-28-G; 5-11-R
everybody's 5-2-G
everyone 2-15-B;
   3-11-G; 3-28-O;
   4-6-R
everything 2-31-B;
   4-6-R
everywhere 4-15-R
evil 4-25-O
evolution 6-10-S;
   6-16-S
exact 4-1-0
exaggerate 6-23-B
example 3-17-B;
   4-25-G
exceed 6-30-B
excelled 5-12-O;
   6-23-O
excellence 6-24-G
excellent 5-11-B;
   6-23-G
except 3-30-B;
   4-8-G; 5-11-R
exception 5-18-B;
   6-10-G
excess 6-30-G
exchange 6-23-R
excite 4-3-B; 5-6-G;
   6-3-R
excited 5-12-G
excitement 5-1-B;
   6-23-G

exclaimed 5-12-B
excuse 3-17-B;
   4-21-G
exercise 4-15-B;
   5-6-O; 5-13-G;
   6-13-R
exert 4-24-S
exhibit 6-22-G;
   6-23-O
exile 6-23-SS
existence 6-24-G
expand 6-7-B
expanded 5-12-M
expansion 6-23-B
expatriate 6-23-SS
expect 6-7-R
expectation 6-10-B
expedition 6-23-B
expend 6-7-B
experience 5-1-B;
   6-23-G
experiment 6-23-G
expertise 6-31-O
explain 4-4-B;
   5-3-G; 6-23-R
explained 5-12-G
explanation 5-13-B;
   6-13-G
explode 4-3-G;
   4-3-S; 5-3-R
explore 3-20-SS
explorer 4-23-SS;
   5-25-SS; 6-23-SS
exploring 3-18-SS
exponent 5-9-M
export 5-13-SS;
   6-11-G
express 6-23-O
expression 6-10-O;
   6-23-G
extend 6-23-R
external 4-24-O;
   5-8-O
extract 4-21-O;
   6-20-G; 6-23-O
extracurricular
   6-27-G
extraordinary
   6-27-B

extrasensory 6-27-B
extraterrestrial
   6-27-G
extravagance 6-27-B
extravagant 6-27-G
extreme 6-23-B
extrovert 5-23-O
eye-opener 6-2-B
eyes 2-26-B; 3-29-G

face 3-8-M; 3-30-G
fact 3-5-B; 3-8-M;
   5-16-M
factor 4-1-M;
   5-1-M
factories 4-30-O
factors 5-16-M
factory 3-24-SS
facts 4-11-M
factual 5-30-B
fail 3-8-B
fair 3-26-G
fairy 3-26-B
fall 2-9-G
fame 3-8-O
familiarize 6-5-B
families 5-5-R
family 2-15-B;
   3-29-G; 4-6-R
famine 5-16-SS
famous 4-6-B;
   5-30-G
fanciful 6-1-O
fantastic 5-10-B
far 2-19-G
fare 3-26-G
farewell 3-26-O
farm 2-20-G; 3-17-R
farmer 4-23-R
farmer's 4-16-B
farming 4-5-SS
fascinate 6-32-B
fashion 5-4-G
fast 3-30-R
fasten 4-22-O
fat 2-2-O
father 2-24-G

father's 4-16-G; 5-2-R
fathers' 4-16-O
fatigue 6-31-O
fatter 3-19-R
fattest 3-19-R
fault 4-1-S; 6-1-S
favorable 6-28-O
favorite 4-11-B; 5-16-G; 6-17-R
fawn 2-1-S
fear 3-27-G
fearlessness 5-19-B
feather 3-7-B
feature 4-4-B; 5-3-O
February 3-16-B
fed 4-18-R
federation 6-10-SS; 6-16-SS
feeble 6-22-O
feed 3-11-R
feel 1-18-G
feeling 3-6-G; 4-4-R
feelings 3-2-S
feet 1-18-G; 4-17-R
fell 2-14-G; 3-17-R
felt 2-1-B; 3-5-G; 4-18-R
female 4-3-G; 5-3-R
fence 3-30-O
fern 4-24-O
ferry 4-11-SS
fertile 5-8-SS
fertilization 5-8-S; 5-18-S; 6-16-S; 6-25-S
fertilize 4-3-O; 6-5-O
festival 4-25-O
fever 3-6-B
few 3-14-G; 4-10-R
fibrous 5-30-S
fiction 3-17-SS
fictional 5-30-SS
fidget 4-14-O
field 3-17-B; 4-15-G; 5-7-R
fiendish 5-24-B

fierce 5-7-B; 6-8-G; 6-13-O
fiesta 6-31-SS
fifteen 3-17-M
fifth 3-4-B; 3-5-M; 4-11-G; 5-16-R
fiftieth 4-15-M
fifty 2-2-M
fifty-nine 3-17-M
fight 2-11-B; 3-10-G; 4-13-R
figures 3-2-M
fill 2-28-G
filled 2-25-O
final 4-25-B; 5-30-O
finally 4-8-G; 5-28-R
finance 6-24-SS
financial 5-30-B
find 3-10-O
fine 2-11-G; 3-20-R
finely 4-8-G; 5-28-R
finer 3-19-R
finest 3-19-R
fingernail 2-31-S
finish 3-4-B; 5-4-R
finished 4-5-B
fire 2-10-O; 3-10-G
fireplace 3-28-B; 4-28-G; 5-20-R
firm 4-24-G; 5-8-R
first 2-20-G; 3-17-R
first aid 3-29-S
fish 2-22-G; 3-5-R
fishery 6-15-R
fish's 4-16-O
fission 5-1-S
fit 2-2-O
fitness 4-19-O
five 1-23-G; 2-10-G
fix 1-14-B; 2-2-G
flag 2-17-G
flair 5-15-B
flame 2-6-B
flap 2-1-O
flare 5-15-B
flash 2-17-B

flashlight 3-28-B; 4-28-G; 5-20-R
flat 2-17-O
flatboat 5-3-SS; 5-20-SS
flatten 6-5-R
flatter 3-19-B
flattest 3-19-B
flavor 3-8-O
flew 4-7-S
flexible 6-28-G
flies 4-30-R
flight 3-10-B; 4-13-G
float 2-13-O; 3-9-B
flock 2-3-O; 3-5-B
flood 5-13-R
floor 2-17-B
floss 2-17-SS
flounder 4-9-SS
flour 3-23-O
flow 2-4-B
flowchart 5-20-M
flower 2-4-B; 2-17-S; 3-23-G
flu 4-7-S
fluffy 2-17-O
fluid 6-13-O
fluoride 5-4-S
flute 3-14-O; 4-10-B
fly 2-11-G; 3-10-R
flying 2-30-B; 4-5-R
foal 2-14-S
foam 2-13-O
focus 6-8-S
fog 3-22-R; 5-16-S
foggy 4-20-B
foghorn 3-22-SS
foil 3-23-B
fold 2-4-G
folk song 6-2-R
folktale 3-28-SS
follow 2-9-B; 3-1-G
followed 2-25-O; 3-18-B
following 3-1-B; 4-5-G
fond 2-12-B

food 1-21-B; 3-14-G; 4-10-R
food web 4-10-S
fool 3-14-O
foolish 4-10-B; 5-24-G
foot 2-14-M; 3-15-M; 4-17-R
football 3-28-G; 4-28-R
foothill 3-28-SS
footprint 3-28-B
footsteps 2-31-SS
for 2-15-R; 3-25-R
forbidden 6-5-B
force 3-30-S; 5-6-S
forcefulness 5-19-B
forcible 6-28-G
foreign 6-13-B
forest 3-29-G
forever 4-11-O
forgery 6-15-G
forget 2-20-O
forgetfulness 4-31-G; 5-19-R
forgot 3-24-G; 4-15-R
forgotten 4-6-B; 6-5-G
fork 2-19-O
form 2-20-G
formal 4-8-B; 5-28-G; 5-30-O; 6-7-R
former 4-8-B; 5-28-G; 6-7-R
formerly 6-17-B
formula 4-27-S
fortunate 6-5-G
forty 5-1-R
forum 6-17-SS
fossil 4-25-S; 5-11-S; 6-32-S
fought 3-22-B
foul 3-25-B
found 2-25-B; 3-23-G; 4-9-R
foundation 6-10-R

fountain 4-9-B; 5-4-O
four 1-23-G; 3-25-R
fourth 2-20-M; 2-23-B; 3-20-G; 4-1-R
fowl 3-25-B
fox 1-15-B; 2-3-G
foxes 3-2-G
fraction 3-20-M; 4-11-M; 5-18-R; 5-18-M
fractions 3-2-M
frame 2-5-O; 2-18-O
frantic 5-10-O
freckle 4-25-B
free 2-7-B; 3-6-G
freedom 4-4-B; 5-3-G
freeway 4-4-SS; 4-28-SS
freeze 4-20-B; 6-3-O
freight 4-13-SS; 4-15-SS; 5-1-O
fresh 2-22-B; 3-7-B
friction 5-18-S
Friday 3-16-G
friend 2-15-O; 2-18-B; 3-24-G; 5-7-R
friendly 3-1-O; 4-19-R
friend's 4-16-O; 5-2-R
friends 3-2-O
fries 4-30-G
fright 3-10-O
frighten 4-6-B; 6-5-G
frightened 5-11-B; 6-8-G
frisky 2-18-O
frog 1-24-G; 2-18-G
from 2-15-O; 2-20-G; 3-17-R
front 2-18-O; 3-4-G; 6-13-S

frontier 5-1-SS;
　5-7-G
frost 2-18-S
frostbite 5-3-S;
　5-20-S
frown 2-4-O;
　3-23-G; 4-9-R
frozen 4-22-B;
　6-5-R
fruit 3-14-B; 5-16-R
fry 2-11-B
ft. 5-32-B
fudge 4-14-B
fuel 3-4-S; 3-24-SS;
　4-10-SS; 4-15-SS;
　5-11-S
full 2-14-O; 2-28-G
fun 1-16-G; 2-27-R
fungi 6-17-S
funnier 4-30-O
funniest 4-30-R
funny 2-8-O
fur 4-24-R
furious 6-17-O
furniture 4-11-B;
　5-11-G; 6-8-R
furry 3-17-O
further 4-24-B
fusion 6-10-S;
　6-16-S
future 3-11-B;
　5-16-G; 6-17-R

gadget 4-14-B
gain 3-8-M
gal. 5-32-G
galaxy 5-9-B; 6-1-S
galleries 5-5-SS
gallon 3-4-M;
　5-11-M
gallop 3-29-O
game 2-5-G; 3-8-R
garage 6-31-R
garbage 5-6-O
garden 2-19-SS
gardener 4-23-B;
　5-25-O

gas 2-4-S; 3-30-R;
　4-11-S
gasoline 5-9-O
gaucho 6-31-SS
gauge 6-8-B
gave 1-17-B; 2-5-G
gear 3-27-B
geese 4-17-G
gelatin 4-22-B
gem 3-31-O
general 4-25-B
generalize 4-3-O;
　6-5-O
generator 5-25-S;
　6-6-S; 6-8-S
generous 5-30-O
genes 5-15-S; 6-7-S
genetics 6-13-S
genius 5-13-O
genre 6-31-G
gentle 3-31-B;
　4-20-G
gentlemen 4-17-O
gentleness 4-29-B
gently 4-32-G
geocentric 6-21-SS
geographer 6-21-G
geographic 6-21-B
geography 5-4-SS;
　6-21-R
geological 6-21-B
geologist 6-21-G
geology 6-21-G
geometric 6-21-B
geometry 5-23-G;
　6-21-R
geothermal 6-21-SS
germ 2-4-S; 2-20-S
germs 3-31-S;
　4-24-R
get 1-13-G; 2-7-R
getting 2-30-B;
　3-18-G; 4-5-R
giant 2-1-S; 3-31-G
gift 3-5-B
gigantic 3-31-B;
　5-10-R
giggle 4-26-B
gild 6-26-SS

ginger 3-31-B
giraffe 3-31-G
giraffes 5-22-G
girl 2-20-G; 3-17-R
girl's 4-16-R
girls 2-26-O
girls' 4-16-R
give 2-15-G
given 4-22-R
giving 2-30-G
glacier 5-9-SS;
　6-17-S
glad 1-24-G;
　2-17-G
gladiator 6-13-SS
glamorous 5-30-B
glare 3-26-O
glass 2-17-G
glasses 3-2-G
gleaming 6-22-R
glistening 6-22-R
globe 2-12-B;
　3-9-SS
gloomy 4-10-O
glossy 2-17-O
glove 2-12-G
glow 3-9-B
glue 3-14-O; 5-6-R
gnat 4-13-O
gnaw 4-13-B
go 1-20-G; 2-13-R
goal 3-9-O
goat 2-13-O
goes 2-27-G
going 1-27-G;
　2-27-G
gold 2-4-G; 3-11-R
golden 2-13-O
gone 3-24-R
good 2-27-R;
　3-15-R
good-bye 3-15-B;
　4-28-G; 5-20-R
good-natured
　6-2-G
goods 3-2-SS;
　3-15-SS
goose 4-17-G
gorgeous 6-1-O

gorilla 3-4-O
got 1-15-G
gourmet 6-31-O
govern 4-24-SS
government 4-19-B;
　5-11-O; 5-19-SS;
　6-32-R
governor 4-23-B;
　5-25-G
grabbed 3-18-B;
　4-5-G
graceful 4-29-B
gracious 5-30-G
grade 1-17-B;
　2-5-G; 2-20-O;
　3-1-R
gradual 5-30-G
grain 2-6-SS
grains 3-2-SS
gram 2-2-M;
　2-18-S; 3-8-M
grammar 5-4-B;
　6-32-G
grand 3-8-B
grandfather 2-24-B;
　3-28-G; 4-28-R
grandmother
　2-24-B; 3-28-G;
　4-28-R
grape 2-5-SS
graph 3-8-M;
　3-24-M; 4-11-M;
　5-9-M
grass 1-12-B;
　2-2-G
grasshopper 4-28-S
grassland 3-28-SS;
　5-20-S
grate 2-32-B
gravity 6-15-G
gray 1-22-B; 2-6-B
graze 2-5-O; 2-18-O
grease 2-18-O
great 2-32-B;
　3-29-G
greater 3-17-M
greatly 4-19-R
green 1-22-G;
　2-18-G

greenhouse 3-4-S;
　3-28-S
greet 2-7-O
grew 1-21-B;
　2-18-B; 3-14-G;
　4-10-R
grid 5-13-M
grief 5-7-O
grip 2-9-O
groceries 5-5-O
grocery 3-30-O;
　5-16-O; 6-15-O
ground 3-23-G;
　4-9-R
groundwater 6-2-SS
group 2-18-M;
　3-29-B; 4-10-G
groups 4-11-M
grow 1-24-B;
　2-13-G; 3-9-R
growl 3-23-O
grown 3-9-B
grudge 4-14-O
grumpy 2-18-O
guarantee 6-13-B
guard 4-11-B;
　5-16-G; 6-17-R
guess 2-14-M;
　2-28-B; 3-29-G
guessed 4-7-O;
　5-15-R
guesses 3-2-B
guest 3-6-B; 4-7-O;
　5-15-R
guidance 5-16-B;
　6-24-G
guild 6-26-SS
guitar 5-14-O
gulfs 5-22-R
gums 2-3-S
guppy 5-9-R
gym 5-9-R

habit 5-4-G
had 1-12-G; 2-27-R
haddock 5-10-R
hadn't 4-2-B

haiku 5-14-O
hail 3-20-S
hair 3-26-G; 5-15-S
haircut 3-26-SS
hair-raising 6-2-B
half 2-4-M; 3-17-G;
    4-1-R
halves 5-22-R
ham 2-1-O
hammer 2-14-SS
hammock 5-10-G
hand 2-5-G; 3-8-R
handkerchief
    5-16-B; 6-13-O;
    6-17-G
handkerchiefs
    5-22-B
handle 4-25-G
handmade 4-28-SS
hand-me-down
    6-2-G
hands 3-2-R
handsome 4-15-B;
    5-13-G; 6-13-R
handwriting
    4-28-SS
hangar 5-15-B
hanger 5-15-B
happen 3-1-O
happened 3-1-B;
    4-5-G; 5-12-R
happier 4-30-O
happiest 4-30-R
happily 4-30-G
happiness 4-30-G
happy 2-8-G
harbor 3-20-SS;
    5-11-SS
hard 2-19-G
harden 4-22-G
hardness 4-19-S;
    4-20-S
hare 3-26-G;
    5-15-S
harm 2-19-SS
harmful 4-19-B
harvest 3-11-SS
has 2-27-G; 3-1-R;
    3-5-R

hasn't 3-21-B;
    4-2-B
hasten 6-5-B
hat 2-1-R
hatch 3-12-G
hate 2-6-O
hats 1-26-G
haul 3-22-O
have 2-5-G; 3-29-R
haven't 3-21-B;
    4-2-G
having 2-30-B;
    3-18-G; 4-5-R
hawk 3-22-S
hay 2-6-SS; 2-32-SS
hay fever 6-2-G
he 1-18-G
head 2-9-O; 3-7-R
headache 4-28-B;
    5-20-G
headline 5-6-SS;
    5-20-SS; 6-2-SS
health 2-23-O;
    4-18-G
healthier 4-30-G
healthiest 4-30-O
healthy 3-7-G;
    3-24-S
hear 1-28-B;
    2-32-G
heard 3-11-G
heart 2-27-S; 3-24-S
heartthrob 6-2-B
heat 2-8-S
heavier 4-30-O
heaviest 4-30-O
heavy 3-7-B; 4-6-G;
    5-1-R
he'd 4-2-O
hedge 4-14-O
heel 2-7-S
height 3-24-B;
    4-13-S; 4-15-S
held 3-5-B
hello 3-1-G
he'll 4-2-O
help 2-1-G; 3-7-R
helped 2-25-G
helpers 2-26-SS

helpful 3-15-B
helpless 4-19-G
hen 1-13-G; 2-7-R
hens 1-26-G
her 2-27-R
herbivore 5-8-S;
    6-17-S
herd 4-24-R
here 1-28-B;
    2-32-G; 3-29-R
here's 3-21-O; 4-2-B
heritage 4-14-SS;
    6-3-SS
hero 3-9-O
heroes 4-17-B
heroic 6-22-B
herself 2-31-O
he's 3-21-O; 4-2-G
hesitant 6-19-G
hey 2-32-SS
hiccup 3-4-O
hiccupped 4-5-O
hiccupping 4-5-O
hid 2-10-G
hidden 3-11-SS
hide 1-19-B; 2-10-G
hieroglyphics 6-8-SS
high 2-11-B;
    3-10-G; 4-13-R
higher 3-10-O
highland 3-10-SS
high school 5-20-R
highway 3-28-B;
    4-28-SS
hiker 4-23-O
hill 2-4-G; 3-10-R
hillside 3-10-SS
him 1-14-G; 2-1-R
himself 2-31-B;
    3-11-G; 4-11-R
hindsight 4-28-O
hire 3-10-O
his 2-14-R
hiss 2-28-B
hisses 3-2-S
historic 5-10-SS
historical 5-30-SS
histories 5-5-SS
hit 1-14-B

hoarse 3-20-O
hobbies 5-5-G
hobby 2-12-B
hoe 2-1-SS
hog 3-22-R
hogan 4-27-SS
hold 2-4-G
hole 3-20-R
holiday 3-8-O
holidays 5-5-G
homeless 4-29-G;
    5-19-SS
homemade 6-2-R
homemaker 5-25-O;
    6-2-G
home run 4-28-B;
    5-20-R
homestead 5-20-SS
homesteader 5-25-SS
homework 4-28-B;
    5-20-G
homogeneous
    6-6-SS
honest 4-1-O
honesty 6-15-G
honey 3-24-S
honorary 5-24-G;
    6-17-O
hook 3-15-R
hooves 5-22-G
hop 1-15-B; 2-12-G
hope 2-12-G; 3-9-R
hoped 2-29-G;
    3-18-R
hopeful 4-29-G
hopeless 4-29-B
hopelessness 5-19-G
hoping 2-30-G;
    3-18-R
hopped 2-29-G;
    3-18-R
hopping 2-30-G;
    3-18-R
horizontal 5-4-M
hormone 6-3-S
horn 2-19-O
horrible 6-22-G

horse 2-19-G;
    3-20-R
horseback 3-28-B
horses 2-26-G;
    3-2-R
horses' 4-16-R
hose 2-13-G
hospital 3-29-B;
    4-25-G; 4-27-S
host 4-11-S
hostage 6-3-SS
hostility 6-15-B
hotel 3-9-O
hotter 3-19-G
hottest 3-19-G
hour 2-4-M;
    2-32-G; 3-23-M;
    3-25-R; 3-29-R
house 2-15-G;
    3-23-R
housefly 3-23-S
houses 2-26-G;
    3-2-R
how 2-14-G; 3-23-R
however 4-9-O
hr. 5-32-B
hug 1-16-B; 2-4-R
huge 3-14-B;
    4-10-G
hugged 2-29-G
human 5-28-B
humane 5-28-B
humanity 6-15-O
humidity 6-15-R;
    6-25-S
hummed 2-29-G
humorous 5-16-O;
    5-30-G; 6-22-R
hundred 2-20-B;
    3-17-G; 4-27-R
hundreds 3-5-M
hundredths 5-4-M
hung 2-4-SS
hunt 2-3-O
hurricane 5-3-S
hurried 4-30-R;
    4-30-SS
hurry 2-9-O; 3-1-O
hurt 4-24-G

husband 2-24-B
hybrid 6-1-S
hydrant 3-10-O
hydroelectricity
  6-16-SS
hypothesis 5-16-S

I 1-19-G; 2-27-R
ice 2-11-G; 3-30-R
icicle 3-30-B
I'd 3-21-B
idea 3-4-B; 4-27-G
identifiable 6-28-B
idle 4-26-O;
  5-16-B; 6-17-G
if 1-14-G; 2-15-R
ignorant 5-24-B;
  6-19-G
ill 2-28-S
I'll 3-21-G; 4-2-R
illegal 5-26-G
illegible 5-26-B;
  6-25-O
illegibly 5-31-B
illiterate 5-26-B;
  6-6-SS; 6-16-O
illness 4-19-G
illogical 5-26-G
illustrate 6-3-B
I'm 3-21-G; 4-2-R
image 5-6-S
imaginary 5-24-G
imagination 5-26-G
imaginative 5-26-B
imagine 4-11-O
imitate 5-26-G
imitation 5-26-B
immature 5-26-G
immaturity 6-16-G
immediate 6-5-O
immemorial 6-6-B
immense 6-22-B
immigrant 5-26-SS;
  6-19-B; 6-25-SS
immigration 6-6-B
immobile 5-26-G
immodest 5-26-B

immortal 5-26-B
impartial 5-26-O
impatience 5-26-B
impeach 5-3-SS
imperfect 5-26-O
imperfection 6-6-R
impersonate 6-16-G
impolite 5-26-G
import 5-26-SS;
  6-11-G
importance 6-11-G;
  6-24-O
important 4-27-B;
  5-1-G; 6-1-R;
  6-11-O
impossible 5-26-O
impression 6-10-B
improperly 5-31-G
impurity 6-16-G
in 1-14-G; 2-1-R;
  2-14-R; 5-32-O
inability 5-26-O;
  6-16-O
inaccurate 5-26-B
inactive 5-26-O
inadequate 5-26-B
inanimate 5-26-O
inattention 6-6-G
inch 2-2-G; 3-12-M
inches 2-26-G; 3-2-R
include 4-3-O;
  5-6-G; 6-3-R
income 2-9-SS
incomplete 5-26-G
inconsistent 6-25-B
incorrect 5-26-G
increase 4-4-O
incredible 6-32-B
incurable 6-25-G
independence
  5-26-SS
independent 6-19-R
Indian 4-22-O
indicator 6-6-S
indifference 6-24-G
indifferent 6-19-G
indigestible 6-25-G
indivisible 5-26-B
induct 6-29-O

induction 6-29-O
industrial 5-30-SS
industrialization
  6-16-B
industries 5-5-SS
industry 4-20-B
ineligible 5-26-O
inequality 6-16-B
inertia 5-8-S
inexcusable 6-25-B
inference 6-24-B
inflammation 6-6-B
inflation 6-25-SS
inform 4-6-O
informal 5-26-G
information 5-18-O;
  6-10-R
inhabitant 5-24-G
inheritance 6-24-G
inhumanity 6-16-B
inject 6-11-B
injection 6-11-B
injuries 5-5-S
ink 2-1-O
inlet 4-15-SS
innocence 6-24-O
insect 3-11-S
insert 5-8-B
inside 2-31-G;
  3-28-R
insincerity 6-16-B
insistence 6-24-B
insistent 6-19-B
inspect 6-29-G
inspection 6-29-G
inspector 6-29-O
instance 5-27-G;
  6-24-O
instant 5-27-G
instead 3-7-B;
  4-11-G
instinctual 5-30-S
instructor 4-23-O;
  5-25-O
insulator 5-25-S
insurance 6-24-O
intact 6-12-B
intensity 6-6-S;
  6-15-S

interact 6-27-O
intercede 6-27-O
intercept 6-27-B
interchange 6-27-O
interchangeable
  6-27-O
interdependence
  6-24-SS; 6-27-SS
interest 4-1-B;
  5-11-G; 6-8-R
interested 5-12-O
interesting 4-11-B;
  5-16-G; 6-17-R
interface 6-27-O
interfere 6-27-G
interference 6-24-G
interlude 6-27-O
intermediate 6-27-G
intermission 6-27-B
internal 4-24-O;
  5-8-O
international 6-27-B
interplanetary
  6-27-B
interrupt 6-27-B
intersect 5-1-M;
  6-27-O
interstate 4-3-SS;
  6-27-G; 6-27-SS
interval 6-27-G
intervention
  6-30-SS
interview 6-27-G
into 1-21-G;
  2-31-R
intracellular 6-27-B
intramural 6-27-G
intrastate 6-27-G
intravenous 6-27-B
introduce 5-3-B;
  6-29-R
introduction 5-18-B;
  5-31-O; 6-10-G;
  6-25-O
introductory 6-29-O
introvert 5-23-O
intrude 4-10-O
invalid 4-21-O;
  5-26-O

invent 5-28-O;
  6-30-R
invention 5-18-O;
  6-10-O; 6-30-G
inventiveness
  6-30-B
inventor 4-23-G;
  5-25-O; 6-30-O
invertebrate 5-26-S
invest 6-1-SS
invisible 5-26-O;
  6-12-O; 6-28-O
invite 4-3-G
invited 5-12-R
involuntary 5-26-S
involve 6-3-B
iodine 5-3-S
ion 6-8-S
irrational 5-26-B;
  6-25-O
irregular 5-26-G
irregularity 6-16-B
irreplaceable
  5-26-B
irresistible 5-26-O;
  6-1-O
irresponsible 5-26-G
irrigation 5-18-SS
is 1-14-B; 2-15-R
island 3-24-SS;
  4-15-SS
isle 5-15-B; 6-26-G
isn't 3-21-G; 4-2-R
isolate 6-5-SS
issue 5-6-B; 6-3-G
it 1-14-G; 2-1-R;
  2-14-R
itch 3-12-B; 4-11-S
it'll 4-2-O
its 3-25-O
it's 3-21-G; 3-25-O;
  4-2-R
I've 3-21-G; 4-2-R

jacket 4-11-O
janitor's 5-2-B
January 3-16-B

jar 3-31-G
jaw 2-4-S
jealous 5-1-B;
    6-1-G; 6-22-O
jeans 5-15-S
jelly 3-31-B
jellyfish 3-28-S
jewel 3-31-B
jeweler 4-23-O
jewelry 5-16-B;
    6-15-G; 6-32-O
jigsaw 3-22-O
job 3-5-R; 3-31-R
jogger 4-23-O
jogging 4-5-SS
join 3-31-G
joke 1-20-B;
    2-12-G; 3-31-R
journeys 5-5-SS
joy 3-23-G; 4-9-R
joyous 5-30-O
joys 5-5-R
judge 3-31-B;
    4-14-G
judges' 4-16-B
judgment 5-11-O
jug 3-31-R
juggle 4-26-B
juggler 4-23-B
juice 3-14-O; 3-31-B
July 3-10-B; 3-16-O
jump 1-16-B;
    2-3-G; 3-31-R
jumped 2-25-B
jumping 1-27-B;
    3-31-G
June 3-16-G
jungle 3-31-B
junk 2-21-SS
jurisdiction 6-29-SS
jury 4-24-SS
just 3-31-R

kangaroo 4-4-R
karate 5-14-O
kayak 4-15-SS;
    6-22-SS

keenly 3-6-O
keep 1-18-B;
    2-4-G; 3-6-R
kept 2-7-B; 3-5-G;
    4-18-R
kernel 4-8-O;
    5-28-O
kettle 4-26-G
keyboard 6-2-O
keys 5-5-R
kick 2-21-O
kids 4-6-R
kilogram 5-1-M
kilometer 5-23-G
kilowatt 5-4-S; 5-9-S
kind 3-10-G
kindly 4-19-R
kindness 4-31-R
king 1-14-B; 2-2-G
kingdom 3-29-SS;
    5-9-S
kiss 2-28-G
kitchen 3-12-B;
    4-22-G; 5-13-O
kite 1-19-G
kitten 4-22-R
kittens' 4-16-R
knack 4-13-O
kneads 3-25-SS
knee 4-13-G
kneel 4-13-O
knelt 4-18-G
knew 3-25-G; 4-7-R
knife 2-10-B; 4-13-G
knight 2-11-O;
    4-13-B; 6-26-SS
knives 5-22-G
knob 4-13-O;
    6-17-O
knock 4-13-B
knot 3-9-B; 4-13-R
know 2-13-O;
    2-27-G; 3-24-R;
    4-13-R
knowledge 4-14-O;
    6-13-G
known 3-29-B;
    4-6-G; 5-13-R
knuckle 4-13-O

L

ladder 4-8-G;
    5-28-R
ladies 5-5-R
lady 3-17-G;
    4-20-R
laid 2-6-O
lake 3-8-SS; 3-11-R
lamb 4-13-R
lamp 2-4-B
land 1-12-B; 2-2-G
landform 6-2-SS
landlocked 5-20-SS
landscape 4-3-SS;
    4-28-SS
language 4-1-B;
    5-6-G; 5-11-O;
    6-3-R
large 2-19-B; 3-31-G
larger 3-19-G
largest 3-19-G
laser 3-20-S
last 3-5-R
late 2-6-G; 3-24-R
lately 4-29-G
later 3-19-G
latest 3-19-G
latitude 5-16-SS;
    6-3-S; 6-13-S
latter 4-8-G; 5-28-R
laugh 2-5-B; 4-6-G;
    5-13-R
laughed 4-5-O
laughing 4-5-O
laughter 4-27-SS
lava 4-15-SS
law 3-11-SS; 3-22-R
lawn 3-22-G
lawn mower 5-20-B
lawyer 5-25-G
lay 2-6-G
laziness 4-30-B
lazy 4-6-G
lb. 5-32-G
lead 4-21-R
leader 2-8-SS;
    4-23-R
leaf 3-4-O

leap 2-14-S
leapt 4-18-G
learn 3-11-G; 5-8-R
least 3-6-O
leave 2-8-B; 3-6-G
leaves 5-22-R
leaving 2-30-B
led 4-18-R
ledge 3-31-SS
ledger 4-14-O;
    5-16-O
left 2-7-O; 4-18-R
legacy 6-32-SS
legend 5-13-SS
legible 6-28-O
legislate 5-9-SS
legs 3-2-G
leisure 5-7-O;
    6-17-O
lemon 2-7-O; 5-4-O
length 3-7-M
lens 3-5-S; 3-7-S
leopard 5-4-B
leotard 5-9-B
less 2-2-B
lesson 3-20-O
let 2-7-R
let's 4-2-G
letter 2-14-B;
    3-4-G; 4-1-R
level 4-27-S; 5-4-O
lever 3-5-S; 3-7-S
liberty 6-15-O
librarian's 5-2-B
libraries 5-5-B
license 6-13-O;
    6-32-G
lie 4-20-R
lieutenant 5-9-O;
    6-19-O; 6-32-G
life jacket 6-2-R
lift 2-1-B
liftoff 5-20-S
light 2-11-G; 3-10-R
like 1-19-G; 2-14-R
liked 2-29-G;
    3-18-R
lilac 5-10-G
limb 4-13-B

lime 2-11-O
limit 5-4-B
line 1-19-B; 2-10-G;
    3-29-M
lined 2-29-B
linen 4-22-B
lines 3-10-M
lion 2-9-S
lip 2-16-R
lips 2-26-B; 3-2-G
liquid 4-12-B
list 2-2-B; 3-5-G
listed 2-25-B
listen 4-6-O
listener 4-23-G;
    5-25-R
liter 2-27-M;
    3-11-M; 4-8-M;
    5-13-M
literacy 6-17-SS
litter 2-27-SS
little 2-15-G;
    3-11-R; 4-26-R
littler 3-19-R
littlest 3-19-R
live 3-20-R; 4-21-R
lived 2-29-B;
    3-18-G
lives 3-4-R; 5-22-R
living 3-18-G;
    3-20-SS; 4-5-R
lizard 4-15-S
load 2-13-B; 3-9-S
loaf 3-20-O
loam 3-9-S
loan 4-7-B
loaves 5-22-G
lobster 2-12-S
local 4-25-SS;
    6-20-B
locale 6-20-B
locality 6-20-B
locate 4-3-B;
    5-3-O; 6-20-B
location 6-20-B
lock 2-3-B;
    2-21-O
locomotion 5-6-SS;
    6-20-B; 6-30-O

locomotive 5-6-SS;
   6-20-B
lodge 4-14-O
log 3-22-R
logging 3-22-SS
logic 5-10-B
loiter 4-9-O
lone 4-7-B
loneliness 4-32-B
long 3-22-G
longhouse 6-2-SS
longitude 5-1-SS
look 2-21-R;
   3-15-R
looked 2-25-G;
   3-17-R
looking 1-27-G;
   3-11-R
loom 2-14-SS
loop 4-11-M
loose 3-20-B; 4-8-R
loosely 4-29-O
loosen 4-4-O
lose 3-14-G; 4-8-R
lost 3-22-G
lot 1-15-B; 2-3-G;
   3-5-R
lotion 5-18-R
lots 3-29-R
loud 3-23-O
loudly 4-19-R
lovable 6-28-R
love 2-12-G
loved 2-29-G;
   3-18-R
lovelier 4-32-R
loveliest 4-32-R
lovely 3-11-G;
   4-11-R
low 2-13-R; 2-16-G
lowland 3-28-SS
loyal 4-25-O
loyalty 6-15-R
luck 2-21-B
luckiest 4-30-G
lunar 5-11-S
lunch 2-22-B;
   3-5-G
lunches 3-2-O

lungs 2-3-S; 2-26-S;
   4-11-S
lying 4-11-B;
   5-16-G; 6-17-R

macaroni 5-14-O
machine 6-31-R
machinery 6-15-G
mad 2-5-G; 3-8-R
made 2-5-G; 3-29-R
magazine 5-11-B;
   6-8-G
magic 5-10-G
magician 5-18-G
magician's 5-2-B
magma 6-8-S
magnetic 5-10-S
magnificent 6-17-B
mail 2-6-B; 3-20-G
main 2-6-B
mainland 6-2-SS
mainly 4-19-R
majority 6-15-O
make 1-17-G;
   2-21-G; 3-1-R
make-believe 4-6-O
making 2-30-G
malignant 6-19-B
mall 2-28-O
malnutrition
   6-16-SS
mama 2-24-R
man 1-12-G; 2-2-R;
   4-17-R
maneuver 6-32-B
manner 5-15-B
manor 5-15-B
man's 4-16-R
mantle 5-1-S
many 2-15-G;
   3-17-R
map 3-5-SS; 3-8-G;
   4-11-SS
maple 3-20-S;
   4-26-R
marble 4-25-B
march 3-12-B

March 3-16-G
marched 4-5-SS
mare 4-7-B
margin 4-22-B
market 4-11-O
marriage 5-16-B;
   6-3-O; 6-17-G
married 5-12-G
marrow 5-9-S
marry 4-20-B
marshal 6-26-SS
martial 6-26-SS
marvelous 5-30-O
mask 2-5-O
masquerade 6-31-O
mass 3-4-S
match 2-27-SS;
   3-12-R
matches 3-12-B
material 4-27-B
mathematician
   5-18-M
mathematics 6-13-B
matter 3-29-S
maverick 5-10-O
may 1-17-G; 2-9-R
May 3-16-G
maybe 2-6-O; 3-8-G
mayor 3-8-SS; 4-7-B
mayor's 4-16-B;
   5-2-G
maze 2-6-S
me 1-18-G
meadow 6-22-O
meal 2-8-O
meals 3-6-S
mean 2-8-O
meant 3-7-O;
   4-18-G
measles 4-4-S;
   5-3-O
measure 3-7-B;
   3-7-M; 3-11-M;
   4-11-M
measurement
   4-19-M; 4-29-M
meat 2-32-O; 3-25-R
mechanical 5-30-S
mechanize 6-5-SS

medal 5-15-B;
   6-26-G
meddle 4-26-O;
   5-15-B; 6-26-G
median 5-11-M
medicine 5-13-B
meet 2-32-O; 3-25-R
meeting 3-18-SS
meiosis 6-32-S
melody 5-9-O
melt 2-2-S
members 3-2-O
members' 5-2-B
membrane 5-3-S;
   5-6-S
memorize 6-5-R
men 1-13-B; 2-2-G;
   3-6-R; 4-17-R
men's 4-16-R
menagerie 6-31-O
mention 4-27-O;
   5-18-O
menus 3-2-O
mercenary 5-8-SS
merchant 5-8-B;
   6-19-O
merry 2-9-B
merry-go-round
   4-28-B; 5-20-G
mesa 4-1-SS;
   6-31-SS
mess 2-28-R
message 4-14-B
met 1-13-B; 2-7-G;
   4-18-R
metal 4-25-G;
   5-15-S; 5-28-S
metamorphic 5-10-S
meteor 5-11-S
meteorite 5-6-S
meteorologist
   5-25-S; 6-6-S
meter 2-9-S; 3-1-M
metric 3-7-M;
   5-10-R
mettle 5-15-S
Mexican 4-22-O
Mexico 3-16-B
mi. 5-32-B

mice 2-11-B;
   4-17-R
midafternoon
   5-21-G
midair 5-21-O;
   5-31-G
midday 5-21-O;
   5-31-B
middle 3-20-B;
   4-26-G
midland 5-21-O
midnight 5-21-G
midstream 5-21-G
midsummer 5-21-B
midterm 5-21-O
midway 5-21-B
might 2-11-B;
   3-24-G; 4-13-R
migrant 6-19-G
migration 5-18-SS
mild 3-10-B
mile 2-10-G
mileage 6-17-O
militia 5-4-SS
milk 2-21-G
mill 3-4-SS; 3-11-SS
milliliter 5-9-M
millimeter 5-23-G
million 4-1-0
mimicry 6-15-B
min. 5-32-B
minaret 6-13-SS
mind 3-10-G;
   4-11-SS
mine 1-19-B;
   3-10-R
mineral 6-32-SS
miniature 6-32-B
mining 3-18-SS
minor 5-16-B
minus 2-9-M;
   3-10-M
minute 3-17-B;
   4-21-G; 5-11-R
mirage 6-31-B
mirror 5-16-B;
   6-17-G
misadventure
   5-29-SS

misbehave 5-29-G
miscalculate 5-29-M
miscalculation
    6-6-G
mischief 5-7-B;
    6-1-G
misconnection 6-6-G
misdirection 6-6-R
misfortune 5-29-B
misinform 5-29-B;
    6-6-O
misinformation
    6-6-G
misjudge 5-29-G
mislead 5-29-O
mismanagement
    5-31-G
misplace 5-29-O
misrepresent 5-29-SS
miss 2-1-G
Miss 3-16-SS
missed 4-7-O
mission 3-11-SS;
    5-11-SS
missionary 6-6-SS
misspell 5-29-G
mist 4-7-O
mistaken 6-5-B
mistrust 5-29-O
misunderstand
    5-29-B
misuse 5-29-O;
    6-1-O
mitosis 6-1-S
mitten 3-11-O
mixes 3-2-B
moan 3-9-O
mobilization
    6-30-SS
moderate 6-5-O
modern 2-20-O;
    5-4-G
modernize 5-1-O;
    6-5-R; 6-5-SS
moist 3-23-B
mold 5-16-S; 6-17-S
mole 2-13-B
molecule 5-13-S;
    6-3-S

molt 5-16-S
mom 1-15-G;
    2-3-R; 2-24-R
moment 4-6-G
momentary 5-24-B
mommy 2-24-G
Monday 3-16-G
money 2-9-B;
    3-17-G
monitored 5-12-S
monkey 2-27-SS
monkeys 5-5-G
monsoon 4-10-SS;
    5-9-SS
month 3-4-G
monument 4-27-SS
moo 2-27-S
mood 4-10-B;
    4-11-S
moon 3-14-G;
    3-14-S
moonlight 3-10-SS;
    3-28-G; 4-28-R
mop 2-12-G
moral 6-17-B
more 2-9-G
mores 6-22-SS
morning 2-19-B;
    4-27-R
mortality 6-15-SS
mosque 6-8-SS
mosquito 6-31-G
mosquitoes
    4-17-B
moss 2-28-G
most 2-13-G;
    3-9-R
mostly 3-17-O;
    4-19-R
motel 5-9-R
moth 2-23-O
mother 2-24-G;
    3-11-R
mother's 4-16-G;
    5-2-R
motion 5-18-G;
    6-30-R
motionless 6-30-G
motivate 6-30-B

motor 6-30-R
motorist 5-25-O;
    6-30-B
mountain 3-4-B;
    4-1-G; 4-9-SS;
    5-1-R
mountainous
    5-30-B; 5-31-O;
    6-17-O
mouse 4-17-R
mouth 3-23-B;
    4-9-G; 4-9-SS
move 2-15-O;
    3-14-G
moved 2-29-B;
    3-18-G; 4-5-R
movement 4-29-G;
    6-30-R
movies 4-6-O
moving 4-32-R
mph 5-32-G
Mr. 3-16-SS;
    5-32-G
Mrs. 3-16-SS;
    5-32-G
Ms. 3-16-SS
much 2-22-G;
    3-12-R
mud 2-3-O
mug 2-1-O
multiple 4-26-B;
    5-16-M
multiplication
    5-18-R
multiply 3-24-M
mumps 2-3-S
municipal 5-4-SS
murmur 4-24-O
muscle 5-9-B;
    6-8-O; 6-13-G
music 5-10-R
musical 5-30-G
musician 5-18-G
mustache 6-31-G
my 2-9-R
myself 2-14-G;
    3-24-R
mysterious 5-13-O;
    5-30-O

nail 2-6-G; 3-8-R
name 3-1-R
named 2-29-G
nap 2-1-O
narrative 6-22-B
nation 5-18-R
nationalize 6-5-SS
natural 3-17-SS;
    4-25-SS
naughtier 4-30-B
naval 4-8-O
navel 4-8-O
navigable 5-4-SS
navigation 5-18-SS
near 3-27-G
nearby 3-27-B;
    3-28-O
nearly 3-27-G
neat 2-8-O
nebula 6-17-S
necessary 5-11-B;
    5-24-O; 6-8-G;
    6-30-O
neck 2-21-R
necklace 2-7-O
necktie 5-20-B
need 1-18-B; 2-8-G;
    3-6-R
needed 2-25-G
needle 4-26-B
needlework 5-20-B
needn't 4-2-O
needs 3-2-SS;
    3-25-SS
neighbor 4-6-B;
    5-7-G
neighborhood 6-2-O
neighbors' 5-2-B
neither 4-1-0
nephew 4-10-O
nephew's 4-16-O
nerves 2-14-S;
    2-26-S; 3-17-S
nervous 5-8-B
nest 2-1-B
neutral 5-13-SS
neutrality 6-15-SS

neutralization
    6-16-S
neutron 5-1-S;
    6-32-S
never 2-27-B; 4-6-R
new 1-21-B;
    3-25-G; 4-7-R
news 4-10-G
newspaper 3-14-B;
    3-28-O
newsstand 6-2-B
next 2-2-G; 3-7-R
nice 1-19-B;
    2-10-G; 3-30-R
nicer 3-19-R
nicest 3-19-R
nickel 2-10-M;
    2-21-M
nickels 3-20-M
niece 5-7-B; 6-1-G
night 2-11-G;
    3-10-R; 6-26-SS
nine 1-23-B
ninety 3-24-B;
    5-13-R
ninth 3-17-B;
    4-1-G; 5-1-R
no 1-20-G; 2-13-R
no. (number) 5-32-O
nobody 2-31-O
nod 2-3-O
nodule 4-10-S
noise 4-9-G; 4-9-S
noises 2-26-B
noisy 4-9-B
nomad 5-1-SS
nonchalant 5-14-B
noncombatant
    6-25-B
nonconductor
    5-31-B
nonconformist
    5-31-B
nondeductible
    6-25-B
none 3-20-O
nonfiction 5-18-O;
    5-29-G
nonmetal 5-29-S

nonpoisonous
5-29-B
nonprofit 5-29-B;
6-25-O
nonrenewable
5-29-SS; 6-6-S;
6-28-S
nonreturnable
5-31-O; 6-25-G
nonsense 5-29-G
nonsmoking 5-31-G
nonspecialist 6-6-R
nonstop 5-29-O
nontaxable 6-25-G
nonviolent 5-29-O
noon 3-14-B
normal 4-25-O;
5-30-O
north 2-19-G
North Pole 3-16-SS
nose 1-20-B;
2-12-G
not 2-12-G
notable 6-28-O
note 1-20-B;
2-12-G
notebook 2-31-O
nothing 2-23-B
noticeable 6-28-B
notion 5-18-R
noun 4-9-B
November 3-16-B
now 2-27-G;
3-23-R
nucleus 5-9-S; 6-1-S
numb 4-13-O
number 2-3-M;
3-17-M; 4-27-R
numbers 3-2-M
numeral 4-25-M
numerator 5-1-M
numerous 6-13-B
nurse 2-20-S
nursery 6-15-G
nurses' 4-16-G;
5-2-R
nutrient 5-7-S
nutritious 6-13-O
nylon 2-11-O

o'clock 2-14-O;
2-21-B; 4-2-G
oak 2-21-B; 3-9-S
oases 4-17-S
oasis 4-17-S
obedience 6-24-O
obey 3-9-O
obeyed 4-30-B;
5-12-R
object 4-21-G;
6-11-O; 6-22-R
objection 6-11-B
objective 6-11-O
oblige 4-14-B
oboe 4-15-SS
oboes 4-17-O
observance 5-27-O
observant 6-19-B
observation 5-27-B
observatory 5-27-B
observe 5-27-B
obtain 4-4-O
obtained 5-12-O
obtuse angle 4-10-M
obvious 6-1-O
occasion 5-1-B;
6-1-G; 6-17-O
occurred 5-12-B
occurrence 6-24-B
ocean 3-9-B;
4-1-SS; 5-4-R
October 2-12-O;
3-16-B
octopus 2-12-O;
3-29-S
odd 2-3-B; 3-17-M
odds 3-5-M
odor 3-29-O
of 2-15-R
off 2-14-G; 3-17-R
office 3-1-B; 4-1-G;
5-1-R
officer 4-23-G
offices 3-2-B
official 5-30-G
often 3-24-G;
4-22-R

oh 2-32-O
oil 3-23-G; 4-9-R;
4-9-SS
ointment 3-23-O
old 1-20-G; 2-13-R
older 3-19-O
oligarchy 6-1-SS
olive 2-12-O
omission 6-10-B
omitted 5-12-B
omnivore 5-11-S
on 1-15-G; 2-14-R
once 2-15-B;
3-24-G; 4-15-R
one 1-23-G;
2-27-R; 2-32-M
ones 2-26-M
onion 4-22-O;
5-16-O
only 2-13-B
opaque 6-31-S
open 3-17-R
opera 2-12-O
operate 4-3-O;
5-3-O
operation 5-18-B;
6-10-G
operator 4-23-O;
5-25-B
opinion 5-11-B;
5-16-SS; 6-8-G
opponent 6-17-O;
6-19-G
opportunities 5-5-O
opportunity 6-11-G;
6-15-O
opposite 5-1-B;
6-1-G
opposition 6-10-B
oppression 6-10-SS
or 3-20-R; 4-7-SS
orange 2-9-O;
3-31-G
orbit 4-1-S; 3-24-S
orchestra 5-14-G
ordered 5-12-M
ordinal 4-25-M
ordinary 5-24-O
ore 4-7-SS

organ 3-17-S;
4-22-G; 5-1-S
organism 5-13-S
organization 6-10-B
organize 6-22-G
origin 4-22-O
oriole 4-3-B
other 2-15-O;
2-23-G
otherwise 3-10-O
ought 3-22-B
ounce 3-23-M;
3-30-M; 4-9-M;
5-13-M
our 2-32-G;
3-23-R; 3-25-R
ourselves 3-28-B;
5-22-G
out 2-15-R
outback 4-28-SS;
6-2-SS
outcome 5-20-M
outdoors 3-28-O
outline 4-28-O;
5-20-O
outrageous 5-30-B
outside 2-31-G;
3-23-R
oval 2-12-O
oven 4-22-B
over 3-4-R
overachiever 6-6-G
overboard 6-4-B
overcast 6-4-G;
6-6-O
overcharge 6-4-R
overconfidently
6-25-G
overdue 6-4-R
overextension 6-6-B
overglamorize
6-16-B
overhead 6-4-G
overproduction
6-6-R
overrated 6-4-B
overreaction 6-6-B
overrule 6-2-G
oversight 6-4-R

overtighten 6-16-G
overture 6-4-O
overwhelm 6-4-B
owe 2-32-O
owl 3-23-S
own 2-13-B; 3-9-G
owner 4-23-G;
5-25-R
ox 4-17-G
oxen 4-17-G
oxygen 3-31-S;
4-22-B; 5-11-S
oyster 4-9-O;
5-13-O
oz. 5-32-G
ozone 5-3-S

P

paced 3-18-SS
pack 2-21-R
package 3-31-O;
4-14-G
paddle 4-26-B
paddock 5-10-B
page 3-31-G
paid 2-6-G; 4-15-R
pail 2-6-O
pain 3-25-B
painful 4-19-G
painless 4-19-G
paint 2-6-B; 3-8-G
painted 2-25-B
pair 2-32-B;
3-26-G
palette 5-14-B
pan 2-4-R
pane 3-25-B
panel 4-20-B
panic 5-4-O
panther 2-23-O
papa 2-24-R
paper 2-9-B
paperback 4-28-SS;
5-10-R
parable 6-28-SS
parachute 5-14-B;
6-31-G
parade 2-5-SS; 4-3-R

parallel 5-13-B;
  6-13-G
parasite 5-6-S
parcel post 5-20-O
pardon 6-1-R
parent 3-4-B;
  4-27-G
parents 2-24-B
parents' 4-16-O;
  5-2-G
park 2-19-G
parka 2-19-O
parliament 5-11-SS
part 2-19-G
participant 5-24-O;
  6-19-O
particular 5-13-B;
  6-13-G
parties 5-5-R
partly 2-19-B;
  4-19-R
party 2-19-B;
  3-24-G; 4-15-R
pass 2-2-B;
  3-30-G
passage 6-3-O
passed 4-7-O
passenger 4-27-O
passionate 6-5-B
past 3-5-G; 4-7-O
patch 3-12-G
patches 3-2-O
path 2-23-R
patience 5-28-B;
  6-7-G; 6-24-O
patient 5-7-G;
  6-32-R
patients 5-28-B
patio 6-31-G
patriot 5-13-SS
patted 2-29-G;
  3-18-R
paw 3-22-R
pay 2-6-G; 3-8-R
payment 4-31-R
pays 4-30-R
pea 2-8-R
peaceful 4-29-B
peacefully 5-19-G

peacefulness 4-31-G
peach 3-12-B
peaches 3-2-B
peak 3-25-SS
peanut 3-6-B;
  4-28-G
peanut butter
  4-28-B; 5-20-G
pear 2-32-B;
  3-26-G
pearl 5-8-R
peasant 6-19-SS
pebble 4-26-B
peek 3-25-SS
peeled 4-18-G
peer 3-27-B
pelt 4-11-SS
penalty 6-15-R
pencil 3-30-B;
  4-25-G
peninsula 5-4-S
pennies 5-5-R
penny 2-2-M;
  2-14-B; 4-27-R
people 2-15-O;
  2-27-B; 3-24-G;
  4-26-R
percent 5-17-M
perch 4-24-R
perfect 5-17-R
perfectly 5-17-G
perform 5-17-G
performance
  5-17-B; 6-24-G
perfume 5-8-G;
  5-17-O
perhaps 5-17-R
peril 4-25-O
perimeter 5-17-M;
  5-23-G
permafrost 4-24-SS
permissible 6-28-B
permission 5-17-B;
  6-10-G
permit 5-17-G
permitted 5-12-G
perpendicular
  5-17-M
persecute 6-7-B

persist 5-17-O
persistent 6-19-B
person 3-30-G;
  4-22-R
personal 6-1-B
personalize 6-16-G
personnel 6-17-B
perspire 5-17-B;
  6-22-O; 6-32-G
pesticide 6-32-SS
pet 1-13-G; 2-2-R
petal 3-1-S; 4-25-S
petroleum 5-9-SS;
  6-17-SS
pheasant 3-7-O
phrase 5-6-B;
  6-3-G
physician 5-18-G;
  6-17-O
pianist 5-25-B
pianos 4-17-G
picked 2-25-B
picnic 3-4-B;
  4-20-G; 5-10-R
pictograph 5-4-M;
  6-13-M
picture 3-20-G
picturesque 6-31-O
piece 3-24-B;
  4-15-B; 5-7-G
pier 5-9-O
pierce 5-1-O; 5-7-G
pies 2-26-O
pigs 1-26-G
pigeon 5-9-B;
  6-32-G
piglet 2-2-S
pigpen 2-31-R
pike 2-21-O
Pilgrim 3-16-SS
pilgrim 4-27-SS;
  5-4-SS
pilgrimage 6-13-SS
pill 2-2-O
pillow 3-9-O
pilot 3-10-SS
pin 1-22-G; 2-16-R
pink 1-22-G
pint 3-10-M

pioneer 3-27-B;
  5-4-SS
pipe 2-10-B
pistil 4-25-S;
  6-17-S
pitch 3-12-G
pitcher 3-12-O;
  4-23-B; 5-25-G;
  6-32-R
pitied 5-12-R
pities 4-30-SS
pkg. 5-32-O
place 2-5-B; 3-30-G
placid 6-22-B
plain 3-8-SS;
  3-25-G; 4-7-R
plains 5-15-SS
plan 2-5-B; 3-8-G
plane 2-5-B;
  3-25-G; 4-7-R;
  5-6-M
planes 5-15-SS
planet 3-11-S;
  4-27-S; 5-4-G;
  5-13-S
planned 2-29-O;
  4-5-G
planning 4-5-G
plant 2-17-G; 3-3-R
plantation 5-18-SS
planted 2-25-G
plastic 5-10-G
plate 2-6-O
play 1-17-G; 2-17-G
played 2-25-G;
  3-24-R
player 4-23-R
playing 1-27-G
playground 3-8-SS
playpen 2-31-G;
  3-28-R
plaza 3-4-SS; 5-14-O
pleasant 4-11-B;
  5-24-G; 6-19-R
please 2-17-B;
  3-1-G
pleasure 5-16-G;
  6-17-R
pleat 2-17-O

pledge 3-31-SS;
  4-14-B
plod 4-20-B
plumage 4-14-S
plumber 4-13-O
plumbers' 5-2-B
plus 3-5-M
p.m. 5-32-B
pocket 2-3-O;
  3-5-B
pocketbook 5-10-R
poetry 6-15-R
poets' 4-16-O
point 3-23-G;
  4-9-R; 5-1-M
poise 4-9-O
poison 4-22-B;
  5-11-O; 6-1-R
polar 4-11-S
pole 2-13-G;
  3-9-SS
pole vault 6-2-B
police 3-29-B;
  4-1-G; 5-6-R
polite 4-3-O
politely 4-29-O
politician 5-18-B
poll 6-7-B
pollen 4-22-B; 5-1-S
pollination 5-18-S;
  6-10-S
pollute 4-10-O
pollution 5-18-B;
  5-18-S; 6-32-S
poncho 6-31-G
pond 2-3-B
ponies 5-5-R
pony 3-9-G
pool 4-10-G
poor 2-14-O;
  3-15-B
pop 2-3-R; 2-24-R
popular 5-4-B
populate 4-3-O;
  5-3-O
population 5-18-SS;
  6-10-R; 6-16-S
porch 2-19-O
porches 3-2-G

porcupine 5-9-G
portable 6-11-O
porter 6-11-G
portion 6-22-R
position 5-18-G;
  6-10-R
positive 5-6-B;
  6-3-G
possession 6-13-B
possible 4-25-B;
  6-8-R
possibly 5-1-B;
  6-1-G
post 3-9-G
post office 4-28-B;
  5-20-G; 6-2-O
posttest 6-2-R
pot 2-16-G
potato 3-1-O
potatoes 4-17-G
pounce 3-30-O
pound 3-23-M;
  4-9-M; 5-13-M
pour 3-20-B
powder 3-23-B;
  4-9-G
power 4-9-O
powerful 4-19-O
practical 6-17-G
practically 6-1-B
practice 4-1-B;
  5-6-G; 6-3-R
prairie 3-26-B;
  4-15-SS; 5-13-SS
prance 2-27-SS
prancing 2-30-S
pray 3-25-S; 5-15-S
precaution 5-17-G
precautionary
  5-31-G
precious 6-1-O
precipitation 5-17-S
predict 5-17-B;
  6-29-B
predictable 6-29-B
prediction 6-29-B
prefer 5-17-B
preference 6-24-B
preferred 6-1-B

prefix 5-17-O
prehistoric 5-10-O;
  5-17-O
prehistory 6-16-SS
prejudice 5-6-SS;
  5-17-SS
premier 6-26-SS
premiere 6-26-SS
prepaid 5-17-O
prepare 4-1-B;
  5-17-G; 6-32-R
prepay 4-31-R
prepaying 4-31-G
prepayment 4-31-B
prerecorded 4-31-B;
  5-12-O; 5-17-O;
  5-19-G
preregistered 5-19-B
prerevolutionary
  5-31-B
preschool 4-31-R
preschooler 4-31-G;
  5-19-R
presence 6-26-G
present 4-21-G;
  5-17-R
presents 6-26-G
preservation 5-27-B
preservative 5-27-B
preserve 5-27-B
President 3-16-SS
president 4-27-B;
  5-1-G; 5-17-SS;
  6-1-R
presidential 5-30-B
president's 5-2-B
press 2-2-O
pressed 2-25-O
pretest 4-31-R
pretested 4-31-G;
  5-19-R
prettiest 4-30-G
pretty 3-6-B;
  3-17-G; 4-20-R
prevent 5-17-G
prevention 6-30-S
preview 5-17-R
previewing 4-31-B;
  5-19-G

previous 5-17-B
prey 3-17-S;
  3-25-S; 5-15-S
price 2-18-B
priceless 4-29-O
prime 5-9-M
primer 4-21-B
prince 3-30-SS
princess 3-30-SS
principal 4-15-B;
  5-15-G; 6-26-R
principle 5-15-G;
  6-26-R
print 3-5-B;
  4-11-SS
prism 5-11-M
prison 4-22-O;
  5-4-G
privilege 6-3-B
prize 2-10-O;
  3-10-B; 4-1-G;
  5-1-R
prizes 3-2-B
probable 6-28-O
probably 4-32-B;
  5-9-G; 6-32-R
problem 4-1-M;
  4-27-B; 5-9-G
procedure 5-17-M
proceed 6-13-B
process 5-17-O;
  6-30-R
procession 5-17-B;
  6-30-O
proclaim 5-3-SS;
  5-17-SS
proclamation
  5-17-SS
produce 4-21-G;
  5-17-R
producer 5-17-B;
  5-25-S; 6-6-S;
  6-29-R
product 4-27-M;
  5-17-M; 6-29-R
production 5-17-SS;
  6-29-O; 6-29-SS
profession 5-17-O;
  6-10-G

professor 4-23-B;
  5-25-G
professor's 5-2-B
profit 5-17-O;
  6-26-SS
profitable 6-25-O;
  6-28-G
program 5-17-M
progress 4-21-B
project 4-21-B;
  5-17-G; 6-11-O
projection 6-6-SS;
  6-11-B
projector 6-11-B
promise 4-6-B;
  5-17-G
promote 6-30-O
pronoun 4-9-SS
pronounce 5-17-G
proof 4-10-O
proofs 5-22-B
propel 5-17-B
propeller 6-32-G
proper 5-4-B
property 3-24-SS;
  6-15-S
prophet 6-26-SS
propose 5-17-B
proprietor 5-17-SS
prosecute 6-7-B
prospect 6-29-G
prospector 4-20-S;
  4-23-SS; 6-29-SS
protect 5-17-G
protection 6-10-R
protein 5-4-S;
  5-7-S; 5-17-S
protist 5-17-S;
  5-25-S
proton 5-17-S
protractor 5-17-M
proud 3-23-O
proudly 4-19-B
prove 2-12-B
proved 4-5-B
provide 5-17-R
provided 5-12-R
province 5-1-SS
provision 6-12-G

prune 4-10-O
pry 2-11-O
pt. (pint) 5-32-O
public 3-17-SS;
  5-10-G
publication 6-10-G
publicity 6-15-B
publisher 5-25-B
puddle 4-26-R
pueblo 3-9-SS;
  6-31-R
pull 2-28-G
pulled 2-25-B
pulley 3-11-S
pulse 4-15-S
pumpkin 4-22-G
punctuated 5-12-SS
pupil 3-24-S;
  4-25-B; 5-9-G
puppet 3-4-O
puppies' 5-2-R
puppy 2-8-O
purple 1-22-B
purpose 6-22-R
purse 3-17-O
pursue 6-3-B
push 2-22-R
put 2-15-G; 3-15-R
putting 2-30-G
puzzle 2-1-M
puzzlement 4-29-O
pyramid 5-9-M;
  6-8-SS

qt. 5-32-B
quaint 4-12-O
quake 4-12-O
quarrel 4-12-B
quart 4-12-B; 5-1-M
quarter 4-12-G;
  5-13-R
quarterback 6-2-B
quartet 4-8-M
quartz 4-12-O
queen 4-12-G
question 4-12-B
questionable 6-28-B

questions 3-2-O
quick 3-10-B;
    4-12-G
quiet 4-12-G;
    5-7-R
quill 4-12-O
quilt 4-12-O
quit 4-12-G
quite 3-1-B;
    4-12-G; 5-11-R
quitting 3-18-B;
    4-5-B
quiver 4-12-O
quiz 4-12-B
quotation 6-10-G
quote 4-12-B
quotient 4-12-M;
    5-7-M

rabbit 3-4-S
raccoon 3-14-S;
    4-4-R
race 2-5-B; 2-5-SS;
    3-30-G
radiant 5-24-O;
    6-19-R
radiation 5-18-S
radio 3-4-B; 4-27-G
radios 4-17-O
radishes 3-2-B
radius 5-16-M
raft 3-5-B
rage 4-14-G
railroad 2-31-B;
    4-28-SS; 5-3-SS;
    5-20-SS
rain 2-6-G; 3-8-R;
    5-15-S
rainbow 2-31-O;
    3-28-R
raincoat 2-31-G;
    3-28-R
rained 2-25-G
rainiest 4-30-B
rainy 3-8-O
raise 3-8-B; 3-8-S;
    4-11-G; 5-16-R

raised 3-18-B
raisin 2-6-S; 4-22-R
raising 3-18-B
rang 2-4-SS
range 4-14-B;
    5-13-M
rapid 5-4-B
rare 3-26-B
rash 2-22-S
rather 4-6-O
rating 4-5-M
ratio 5-11-M
ration 5-11-SS
rattle 4-26-G
raw 3-22-O
ray 2-6-B
rays 5-5-G
Rd. 5-32-G
reach 2-22-G
reached 2-25-B
reaction 6-25-S
read 2-8-G; 3-7-R
reader 4-23-R
reading 3-18-G
ready 3-7-G
real 2-8-B; 3-20-G;
    4-1-R
reality 6-15-B
realize 6-5-G
really 3-6-B; 4-19-G
reaper 4-23-SS;
    5-25-SS
reappearance 6-24-B
rear 3-27-G
rearrangement
    4-32-B
rearranging 5-19-G
reason 3-6-B;
    4-4-G; 5-3-R
reassignment
    5-19-B
rebel 4-21-B
rebuild 3-32-O
rebuilding 4-32-G
receipt 4-8-B;
    5-7-O; 5-28-G
receive 4-15-B;
    5-7-G
received 6-8-B

recent 5-28-B
receptionist 5-25-B
recess 6-30-R
recession 6-30-G
recessive trait 6-30-S
rechargeable 6-25-B
recheck 3-32-G;
    5-10-R
recipe 4-8-B; 5-28-G
recite 3-30-O; 4-3-O
reclaim 4-4-O
reclassifying 5-19-B
recognize 6-3-B;
    6-16-O
record 4-21-G
recorder 5-25-B
recover 3-32-O
rectangle 5-1-M
rectangular 5-4-G
recycle 3-32-S;
    4-26-SS; 5-19-S
red 1-22-G; 3-7-R
redder 3-19-G
reddest 3-19-G
redesigned 5-19-B
reduce 4-3-B;
    5-3-G; 5-6-M;
    6-29-R
reduction 6-29-R
reefs 5-22-B
reference 6-24-B
referring 6-8-B
refill 3-32-G
reforestation 6-8-SS
reform 5-19-SS
refraction 6-16-S
refuel 3-32-O
refunded 5-12-SS
refuse 4-21-G
regain 3-32-M
regime 6-31-B
region 5-1-SS
regroup 3-32-M
regular 5-4-B
rehearse 5-1-O;
    5-8-G
reheat 3-32-G;
    4-31-R
reign 5-7-B; 5-15-S

reindeer 3-27-B;
    5-7-R
reject 6-11-B
rejection 6-11-B
rejoin 3-32-B
related 5-12-S
relative 5-16-G;
    6-17-R
relay 3-8-O
release 4-4-O
released 5-12-B
relief 5-7-B
relies 4-30-B
relocate 6-20-B
relocation 6-20-B
remain 4-4-G; 5-3-R
remainder 4-4-M;
    5-3-M; 6-1-M
remake 3-32-R
remarkable 6-28-G
remember 3-29-B;
    4-27-G
removal 6-30-B
remove 6-30-R
removed 3-18-O;
    4-5-O; 5-12-O
removing 4-32-G;
    5-19-O
rename 3-32-M
renewable 6-28-S
renewal 5-30-B
rent 2-1-O
rented 3-18-G
reorder 3-32-O
repaint 3-32-G
repair 4-11-O
repay 3-32-R
repayment 4-31-G;
    5-19-R
repeat 4-4-G
repetition 6-17-B
replacement 4-31-B;
    5-19-G
replay 3-32-G
replied 5-12-R
replies 5-5-B
reply 3-10-B;
    4-20-G
report 6-11-G

reporter 6-11-G
representative
    6-16-SS
reproduce 6-29-R
reproduction
    6-25-S; 6-29-S
reptile 4-3-S;
    5-9-R
republic 5-10-SS
require 4-3-O;
    5-3-B
reread 3-32-R
rerun 3-32-B
rescue 4-10-B;
    5-6-O
research 5-8-B
resell 3-32-B
resent 5-28-B;
    6-7-G
reservation 5-27-B
reserve 5-27-B;
    6-3-SS
reservoir 5-27-O
residence 6-24-G
resident 6-19-G
residential 5-30-G
residue 5-6-B;
    6-3-G
resistance 6-24-B
resource 4-11-SS;
    5-19-S; 6-3-S
resources 3-30-SS
respect 6-29-G
respectfully 6-29-O
respectively 6-29-O
responsible 6-28-B
rest 2-1-G; 3-6-R
restaurant 6-8-B
restless 4-31-R
restlessly 4-31-G;
    5-19-R
retell 3-32-R
return 3-1-B;
    4-24-G
reuse 3-32-R
revenue 6-3-B;
    6-30-SS
reversal 5-30-S
reverse 5-23-B

reversible 5-23-B; 6-28-G
review 3-32-O
revise 6-12-R
revised 5-12-SS
revision 6-12-B
revitalize 6-16-B
revolt 6-22-SS
revolution 5-18-S; 6-1-B
revolve 6-22-B
reward 4-27-O
rewind 3-32-B
rework 3-32-SS
rewrite 3-32-B
rewriting 4-32-G; 5-19-R
rhythm 5-13-B; 6-8-O; 6-13-G
ribbon 3-17-O
rich 2-1-B; 3-12-G
riddle 2-10-SS
ride 1-19-G
rider 4-23-R
ridge 4-14-B
riding 2-30-G
right 2-32-B; 3-24-G; 4-15-R
rigid 3-31-O
ring 2-2-O
rip 2-10-B
ripe 2-10-B
rise 3-10-B
risk 4-11-M
river 3-29-SS
road 2-13-G; 3-9-R; 3-25-R
roar 2-4-S
roast 2-13-O
rob 2-12-B
robbery 6-15-R
robe 2-12-B
robin 3-24-S; 4-22-R
robot 5-9-G
rock 2-21-G; 3-9-R
rocket 4-11-R
rod 2-12-B

rode 2-12-B; 3-9-G; 3-25-R
rodeos 4-17-G
role 4-7-G
roll 4-7-G
roller coaster 5-20-B
romped 2-25-S
roof 3-14-O
roofs 5-22-R
room 1-21-B; 3-14-G
roommate 6-2-G
rooster 5-3-B
roots 3-14-S
rope 2-13-R
rose 1-20-B; 2-12-G
rotate 3-17-S; 6-22-B
rotation 5-18-S; 6-25-M
rough 3-11-B; 4-20-G
round 3-23-B
rounding 5-16-M
route 3-20-B; 4-1-B; 5-1-G; 6-1-R
row 2-13-G
rowed 2-29-B
royal 3-23-B; 4-9-G
rub 2-3-O
rubbed 2-29-O; 4-5-R
rude 4-10-O
rug 2-4-R
rule 1-21-B; 2-9-SS; 3-14-G; 4-10-R
ruler 4-23-G; 5-25-R
rummage 3-31-O
run 1-16-G; 2-3-R
runners' 4-16-B; 5-2-G
running 2-30-G; 3-18-R
rural 4-25-O; 5-16-O

S

sack 2-5-O; 2-21-O
sad 2-2-O
sadder 3-19-O
saddest 3-19-O
saddle 4-26-G
safe 2-6-O
safely 3-17-O
safer 3-19-B
safes 5-22-R
safest 3-19-B
safety 4-15-R
said 2-27-G; 3-1-R
sail 2-32-O
sailboat 2-31-G; 3-28-R; 4-4-SS; 4-28-SS
sailor 4-23-R
sale 2-32-O
salmon 6-17-O
salt 3-30-G
salt water 2-14-S
sample 5-13-M
sanction 6-1-SS
sand 2-5-O
sandwich 5-9-R
sandwiches 3-2-O
sang 3-1-SS
sank 2-4-S
sat 2-2-R; 2-4-R
satellite 5-3-S
satin 4-22-O; 5-4-O
satisfaction 5-18-B; 6-10-O
satisfied 5-12-B
Saturday 3-16-G
sauce 6-32-O
save 2-6-O
saved 2-29-G
saving 2-30-O; 3-18-O
savings 3-2-SS
saw 2-14-G; 3-22-R
say 2-16-G
says 2-15-B; 3-1-G
scale 3-8-B
scar 4-20-G
scarce 4-1-O

scarcely 4-29-O
scare 3-26-B; 4-20-G
scared 3-18-B
scarf 2-16-O; 2-19-O
scarves 5-22-B
scary 4-1-O
scavenger 5-25-S
scene 3-20-B; 4-15-SS
scent 3-25-G
schedule 6-17-B
school 3-14-G; 4-10-R
science 3-30-B; 5-1-G; 6-1-R
scientific 5-10-B
scientist 5-25-G
scientists' 4-16-B
scissors 4-17-B
scoop 4-10-B
scooter 2-16-O
scout 3-23-O
scowl 3-23-O
scramble 4-25-B
scrape 3-3-O
scratch 3-3-G; 3-12-O
scratches 3-3-B
scrawl 3-3-O
scream 3-3-G
screen 3-3-O; 5-3-O
screw 3-14-SS
scribble 3-3-O; 4-26-R
scrub 2-3-S; 6-22-SS
scrubbing 2-30-O; 3-3-O; 3-18-O
sea 1-28-G; 2-8-R; 2-32-R
seahorse 3-28-S
search 5-8-G
seas 4-7-SS
season 4-4-G
seat 3-6-R
secede 5-3-SS

secession 6-30-SS
second 2-27-M; 3-17-B; 5-4-R
secondary 5-24-B
secret 2-14-O; 3-6-B
secretary 4-11-O
section 5-18-G; 6-22-R
security 6-15-G
see 1-28-G; 2-7-R; 2-32-R; 3-30-R
seed 2-7-R; 3-6-S
seeing 1-27-G
seek 2-8-O
seem 2-7-G; 3-6-R
seen 1-18-B; 2-7-G; 3-4-R
seep 3-6-O
sees 4-7-SS
seesaw 2-31-R
segments 3-2-M
seismograph 6-8-S
seize 4-8-B; 5-7-O; 5-28-G
selection 6-10-B
self-addressed 6-2-O
selfish 5-24-G
sell 3-25-B; 5-15-S; 6-26-S
seller 3-25-O
semiannual 5-21-B
semicircle 5-21-G
semicolon 5-21-O
semifictional 5-31-G
semifinal 5-21-B
semiformal 5-21-B; 5-31-O
semiofficially 5-31-B
semiprivate 5-21-B
semisweet 5-21-G
senate 6-13-SS
senator 4-23-O; 5-25-B
send 3-29-R
sense 4-11-B
sensible 6-28-G
sensor 6-26-SS

sent 2-16-B;
   3-25-G; 4-7-R
sentence 4-1-B;
   4-8-M; 5-11-G;
   6-8-R
separate 4-21-G;
   5-11-O
September 3-16-B
sequence 6-24-O
serene 6-22-B
serial 4-8-B;
   5-28-G; 6-7-R
series 4-17-B
serious 4-6-O
servant 5-24-G;
   6-19-R
serve 4-24-G; 5-8-R
service 3-30-SS;
   4-24-B; 5-8-G
services 3-2-SS
set 3-7-R
settle 4-26-B
settler 4-23-B;
   5-25-G
settlers' 5-2-B
seven 1-23-B;
   3-30-G; 4-22-R
seventh 3-7-M
several 3-17-O;
   4-25-B; 5-1-G
sew 3-25-SS
sewing 4-7-SS
shack 2-21-O
shade 2-22-O
shaken 6-5-R
shall 2-22-B
shampoo 4-4-B;
   5-3-G
shape 2-22-O
share 3-26-B
sharecropping
   5-16-SS
shark 3-17-S
sharp 2-22-O
sharpen 6-5-R
sharper 3-19-O
she 1-25-G; 3-6-R
she'd 4-2-O
sheep 2-7-O; 4-17-R

sheepishly 5-31-G
sheer 3-27-B
sheet 1-25-B; 2-8-G
sheikh 6-26-SS
shell 3-5-B
she'll 4-2-O
shelves 5-22-B
sherbet 5-9-B
sheriffs 5-22-B
she's 3-21-O; 4-2-B
shield 5-7-B
shift 2-22-O
shin 2-22-S
shine 2-10-B
shiny 2-22-O
ship 1-25-G;
   2-22-G
shipment 4-19-G
shipping 3-18-SS
shipwreck 2-21-O;
   5-10-G
shirt 3-1-O; 4-24-G
shock 3-5-G
shoe 1-25-B;
   2-22-G; 3-24-R
shoelace 2-31-O
shone 2-13-O
shook 2-21-B
shoot 3-25-B
shop 2-22-R
shopping 2-30-O;
   3-18-O
shoreline 3-28-SS
short 2-19-B
shortstop 6-2-G
shot 2-3-B; 3-9-G
should 2-14-O;
   2-22-B; 3-15-G
shoulder 4-11-B;
   5-13-G; 6-13-R
shouldn't 3-15-B
shove 2-12-B
shoving 4-5-G
show 1-25-B;
   2-13-G; 3-9-R
showed 2-25-B
shown 3-9-O
shriek 5-7-O
shrimp 2-22-S

shut 2-22-R
shutter 3-20-O
shy 3-10-O
shyly 4-30-B
sick 2-21-G; 3-5-R
sickness 4-19-B
side 2-10-M
sides 3-10-M
sidewalk 3-22-B
siege 5-7-O
sigh 2-11-O;
   3-10-B
sight 2-11-O;
   4-13-G
sign 4-13-G
signal 3-11-SS;
   5-16-R
significant 6-19-B
silent 4-27-O
silhouette 5-14-B;
   6-31-O
silk 2-1-O
silliest 4-30-SS
silo 2-9-SS
similar 5-4-O;
   6-8-B; 6-32-O
simple 4-25-G
simply 4-32-R
since 3-30-B;
   4-1-G; 5-6-R
sincere 3-27-O
sincerely 4-29-B;
   5-1-G; 5-11-O;
   6-1-R
sing 3-10-R
single 4-25-G
sink 2-10-O
sip 2-16-R
sis 2-24-R
sister 2-24-G;
   4-27-R
sister-in-law
   4-28-O; 6-2-O
sisters' 4-16-G;
   5-2-R
sisters-in-law 4-17-B
sit 2-2-R
sitting 2-30-G;
   3-18-R

six 1-23-B; 2-2-R
sixteen 2-8-B
sixth 3-10-M
sixty 2-2-M
sixty-one 3-17-M
size 3-10-O
skate 2-5-O
skater 4-23-O
skating 2-30-O;
   3-18-O
sketch 3-12-B;
   3-12-SS
skiffs 5-22-B
skiing 4-27-B;
   5-11-O
skill 3-10-B
skillful 4-19-O
skin 2-16-S
skip 1-24-G;
   2-16-R
skirt 3-17-O
skull 3-5-O
skunk 3-5-S
sky 2-11-G; 3-10-R
skyline 4-3-SS;
   4-28-SS
skyscraper 4-28-B;
   5-20-G; 6-2-O
slammed 3-18-B
slavery 6-15-R
sled 2-7-B; 3-6-G
sledding 2-30-O;
   3-18-O
sleep 1-18-B; 2-7-G
sleeping 2-7-O;
   4-5-R
sleeplessness 4-31-B
sleeve 2-16-O
sleigh 5-7-O
slept 2-17-B; 3-7-S;
   4-18-G
slice 3-30-O
slid 3-17-SS
slide 2-10-O;
   2-17-B; 5-6-M
sliding 2-30-O
slight 3-10-O
slim 2-10-O
slip 2-16-R

slippers 3-2-O
slogan 4-22-B
slow 1-24-B; 2-16-G
slowly 4-19-G
sly 2-11-O; 2-17-O
slyly 4-30-G
small 2-16-O;
   2-28-O
smell 3-7-B
smile 2-10-O;
   3-10-G
smiling 3-18-O;
   4-5-G
smock 2-3-O
smog 4-15-S
smoke 2-16-B
smooth 4-10-G
smoother 3-19-O
snack 2-21-S
snail 2-6-S; 2-16-S
snake 2-21-B; 3-8-S
snare 3-26-O
sneakers 2-16-O
sneeze 2-8-O
snore 3-4-O
snow 1-24-B;
   2-16-G
snowed 4-5-R
snuggle 4-26-O
so 1-20-G; 2-13-R;
   3-25-SS
soak 2-13-O
soap 2-13-B; 3-9-G
soar 3-25-O
society 5-7-SS;
   6-1-SS
sock 2-21-R
socket 4-8-S
soft 3-22-O
softly 4-19-R
software 5-20-S
soil 3-23-O
solar 4-15-S
sold 2-13-B
soldier 4-15-B;
   5-13-G; 6-13-R
sole 2-12-S
solemn 5-9-O
solid 2-10-S; 4-27-S

solitary 5-24-O
solution 5-18-B
solve 5-6-G; 6-3-R
solvent 5-16-S
sombrero 6-31-B
some 2-15-G;
2-32-M; 3-1-R;
3-25-M; 3-30-R;
4-7-M; 5-15-M
someone 2-31-O
something 2-31-B;
3-28-G; 4-28-R
sometime 3-17-G;
4-1-R
sometimes 3-28-O
somewhere 3-13-B
son 2-24-B; 2-32-S
sonar 6-13-S
song 3-22-B
sons' 4-16-O
soon 1-21-G;
3-14-G
soothe 6-3-B
sophomore 6-32-G
sore 3-25-O
sorry 2-8-O;
3-17-O
sort 2-16-B
sound 2-4-B;
3-23-B; 4-9-G
soup 4-10-R
sour 4-9-O
source 3-30-S
south 3-23-SS;
4-11-R
South Pole 3-16-SS
southerner 5-25-SS
souvenir 6-31-O
sovereignty
6-16-SS
sow 4-21-R
sowing 4-5-SS;
4-7-SS
space 2-5-B
spacecraft 5-20-S
spacious 5-30-B
spare 3-26-B
sparkle 4-25-O
speak 4-20-G

speaker 4-23-G;
5-25-R
special 3-11-B;
4-1-B; 5-1-G;
6-1-R
specialization 6-8-SS
specialize 6-5-R;
6-5-SS
specialty 6-15-G
species 4-17-B;
6-13-S
specimen 4-22-O
spectacle 6-29-G
spectacular 6-29-G
spectator 6-29-G
spectroscope 6-3-S
spectrum 6-29-G
speech 2-16-O
speed 3-6-O
speedometer 5-23-G
spell 3-3-R
spelling 2-16-O
spend 2-2-B
spent 2-16-B; 3-7-G
sperm 5-8-S
sphere 3-24-M;
4-15-M; 5-11-M
spice 2-11-O
spider 2-1-S; 2-16-S
spied 4-30-G
spill 2-28-B
spin 2-16-R
spinach 4-15-S
spinal 5-30-S
spine 5-6-S
spinning 2-30-O
splatter 5-9-G
spoil 4-9-G
spoke 3-9-O
spoken 4-11-O
spoonfuls 4-17-B
sport 2-16-B; 4-11-R
spot 2-16-G
spotted 2-29-O;
3-18-O
sprain 3-3-G
spray 2-6-B; 3-3-G
sprayed 4-30-G
spread 3-3-B; 3-7-O

spreadsheet 5-3-M;
5-20-M
spring 3-3-R
sprout 2-16-SS
spy 2-11-B
sq. (square) 5-32-O
squad 4-12-O
squall 2-28-O
square 3-26-B;
4-12-G; 5-9-M
squash 4-12-B
squawk 4-12-O
squeak 2-8-S;
4-12-G
squeal 4-12-G
squeeze 4-12-B
squid 4-12-O
squint 4-12-O
squirm 4-24-O;
5-8-R
squirrel 4-24-O;
5-1-O; 5-8-G
squirt 4-12-B
St. 5-32-G
stable 5-27-G
stadium 3-8-O
staffs 5-22-G
stage 3-31-B;
4-14-G
stain 2-6-O
stair 3-26-O
stairs 3-26-G;
3-26-SS
stake 3-25-O
stalk 3-22-B
stall 2-28-B
stamen 5-13-S
stamp 2-5-O
stand 3-8-G
standard 5-9-M;
5-27-G
star 1-24-G
stare 3-26-B
starfish 3-28-S
stars 2-19-S
start 2-16-G; 3-3-R
started 2-29-G
state 2-5-B; 3-8-G;
3-8-SS

statement 4-29-G
static 5-10-S
station 4-8-SS;
4-11-SS; 5-27-G;
6-8-SS
stationary 6-26-B
stationery 6-26-B
statue 4-4-B;
5-6-SS; 5-27-G
stay 1-17-B; 2-16-G
stayed 2-29-G;
4-30-R
steadily 4-30-B
steady 3-7-B
steak 3-25-O
steal 4-7-G; 5-15-R
steam 3-6-O
steel 4-7-G; 5-15-R
steep 2-8-B; 3-6-S
steer 3-27-G
stem 3-5-S; 3-7-B
stencil 4-25-O
step 4-7-SS
steppe 4-7-SS
stepped 2-29-B
steppes 6-26-SS
stepping 2-30-B
steps 6-26-SS
stern 4-24-B; 5-8-G
stew 3-14-O
stick 2-16-B
still 2-28-G
stimuli 4-17-S
stimulus 4-17-S
sting 3-17-S
stitch 3-12-B
stitchery 6-15-B
stock 3-9-B; 4-11-M
stockade 5-3-SS
stomach 4-6-S;
4-15-S; 5-13-O;
5-14-G
stone 2-12-B
stood 2-4-O;
3-15-G
stop 1-15-G;
2-16-R
stopped 2-14-B;
3-18-G; 4-5-R

stopping 3-18-G;
4-5-R
store 2-9-G; 3-20-R
stories 5-5-G
stork 2-16-O
storm 2-19-B
story 2-19-G
stove 2-12-B;
3-9-G
straight 3-3-O;
4-20-B; 5-15-SS
straighten 5-11-G;
6-8-R
strain 3-3-O
strait 5-15-SS
strange 3-3-B;
4-14-G
strangeness 4-29-G
stranger 4-14-B;
4-23-G; 5-25-R
straw 3-22-G
strawberries 3-3-O;
4-30-O
stray 3-3-B
stream 3-3-O
street 2-7-O;
2-16-B; 3-3-G
strength 3-3-B;
4-15-S
stretch 3-3-G;
3-12-O
string 3-3-G
strings 3-3-B
stripe 3-3-O
stripes 2-10-SS
stroke 3-3-B
strong 3-3-G
student 3-1-B;
4-11-G; 5-16-R
students' 5-2-G
studies 4-30-G
studios 4-17-B
studious 5-31-O;
6-8-O
study 2-16-B;
3-24-G
studying 6-13-R
stump 2-9-O;
2-16-O

stylish 5-9-O;
 5-24-B
subbasement 6-6-R
subconsciously
 6-6-B
subdivision 6-6-G
subhead 6-4-R
subject 4-21-B;
 6-4-R
subjected 5-12-SS
submarine 6-4-G
submerge 6-4-B
submitted 6-4-O
suborbital 6-6-G
subscribe 6-4-O
subsistence 6-16-SS;
 6-24-SS
substance 6-3-B
substandard 6-4-G
substantial 5-27-O;
 6-4-B
subtotal 6-4-O
subtract 3-24-M
subtraction 4-15-M;
 5-18-R
subtropical 6-6-R
suburb 3-20-SS;
 5-11-SS; 6-4-SS
suburban 6-4-O
subway 6-4-G
succeed 6-13-B
success 5-1-B;
 6-30-G
successfully
 5-19-B
succession 5-1-S
successive 6-30-B
successor 6-30-O
such 2-3-B; 3-5-G
sudden 3-30-B;
 4-22-G
suddenly 3-29-O;
 4-19-B
sufficient 6-19-B
suffrage 5-6-SS
sugar 2-14-O;
 3-15-G
sugarcane 4-3-SS;
 4-28-SS

suggestion 5-18-B;
 6-10-G
suit 3-30-B; 4-11-G
suitcase 6-2-R
suits 3-2-B
sum 2-3-M;
 2-32-M; 3-17-M;
 3-25-M; 4-7-M;
 5-15-M
summarize 6-5-G
summarized 5-12-SS
summary 6-17-SS
summer 3-4-G;
 4-15-R
sun 2-3-R; 2-9-R;
 2-32-S
Sunday 3-16-G
sung 2-1-O
sunniest 5-9-O
sunshine 3-28-G;
 4-28-R
sunspot 4-28-S
suntan 2-31-R
superconductor
 6-6-G
superficial 6-4-B
superintendent
 6-6-O; 6-19-G
superluxurious
 6-6-B
supermarket 6-4-R
supernova 6-4-S
superpower 6-4-G
supersonic 6-4-G;
 6-6-O
superstar 6-4-R
superstitious 6-4-B
superthriller 6-6-R
supervise 6-4-O;
 6-12-G
supervision 6-4-O;
 6-12-B
supervisor 6-12-O
supper 3-30-G
supplied 5-12-G
supply 4-27-O
support 6-11-G
suppose 4-3-B;
 5-3-G; 6-17-R

sure 2-15-O;
 3-15-G
surely 4-29-B;
 5-11-G; 6-8-R
surf 4-11-SS
surface 5-6-O
surprise 4-3-G;
 5-3-R
surrounded 6-13-B
survey 5-1-M; 6-1-O
surveyed 5-12-B
suspect 6-29-G
swallow 3-20-O
swam 2-1-B
swamp 2-9-S;
 4-1-SS
sways 4-30-B
sweater 3-7-O
sweatshirt 5-20-O
sweet 2-7-B
swept 2-25-B;
 4-18-G
swim 2-10-O
swimming 3-18-B;
 4-5-G
swing 2-4-O;
 2-16-O
swirl 5-8-B
switch 3-12-G
swollen 4-22-SS
syllable 5-16-O
symbol 3-24-SS;
 5-16-SS; 6-26-B
symmetric 5-10-M
symmetrical 5-23-G
synthetic 6-13-SS
system 5-9-S

table 4-26-R
tablespoon 5-20-M
tacks 3-25-SS;
 5-15-SS
taco 6-31-R
tact 6-12-G
tactful 6-12-G
tactile 6-12-B
tactless 6-12-G

tadpole 3-9-S
tagged 2-29-B
tail 2-32-O; 4-7-R
take 1-17-B; 2-5-G
taken 4-22-R
taking 2-30-B;
 3-18-G
tale 2-32-O; 4-7-R
talk 2-21-G; 3-22-R
talking 2-30-B;
 3-22-G
talks 3-2-SS
tall 2-28-G
tall tale 2-28-SS
tank 2-9-O
tape 2-5-O
tapped 2-29-G
tardiness 5-13-O
tariffs 5-22-B
taste 3-8-O
taught 3-22-G
tax 3-5-SS;
 3-25-SS; 5-15-SS
taxicab 4-28-SS
tbsp. 5-32-B
tea 2-8-R
teach 3-12-G
teacher 2-27-B;
 4-23-R
teacher's 4-16-B;
 5-2-G
teachers' 4-16-B
team 2-8-B; 2-8-SS;
 3-20-G
teams 3-2-O
tear(v.) 3-26-B;
 4-21-R
tear(n.) 3-27-G;
 4-21-R
technician 5-18-S
technology 5-11-SS
teeth 2-23-B; 3-6-G
telephone 5-9-B
telescope 5-3-S;
 5-11-S; 6-8-SS
televise 6-12-B
television 6-12-G
tell 2-4-G; 3-7-R
temporary 5-24-O

ten 1-23-B; 2-2-R
tenant 5-24-O;
 6-19-O
tendon 5-13-S
tens 2-2-M;
 2-26-M
tension 6-10-O
tent 2-1-B; 3-6-G
tentacle 5-13-S
tepee 5-1-SS
term 4-24-G; 5-8-R
termite 5-8-S
terms 4-24-B;
 5-8-G
terrace 5-6-SS;
 6-21-B
terrain 6-21-G
terrestrial 6-21-B
terrible 5-1-G;
 6-28-R
terrier 6-21-G
terrific 5-10-G
territorial 6-21-G
territories 5-5-SS
territory 6-21-R
test 2-1-B
textile 5-6-SS
than 1-25-B;
 2-23-G; 3-29-R;
 4-8-R
thank 2-23-G
thankless 4-19-O
Thanksgiving
 4-28-G; 5-20-R
that 1-25-G;
 2-23-G
that's 3-21-O;
 4-2-G
thaw 2-23-S
the 1-25-G; 2-23-R
theater 4-15-B;
 5-13-G; 6-13-R
their 2-23-B;
 3-25-G; 4-8-R
them 2-23-G;
 3-1-R
theme 6-3-O
themselves 4-6-B;
 5-20-O; 5-22-G

then 2-23-R; 3-7-R;
4-8-R
theory 6-1-B
there 2-20-G;
3-25-G; 4-8-R
there's 3-21-O;
4-2-B
thermometer
5-23-G; 6-17-S;
6-32-R
these 2-23-G
they 2-23-G; 3-1-R
they'd 4-2-O
they'll 3-21-B
they're 3-21-O;
3-25-G
they've 3-21-O
thick 2-21-B
thickness 4-19-O
thief 5-7-O; 6-13-O
thieves 5-22-B
thimble 2-23-O
thin 2-23-R
thing 2-10-O;
2-23-R
things 2-26-O
think 2-23-B;
4-20-R
thinner 3-19-B
thinnest 3-19-B
third 2-20-M;
4-24-R
thirst 4-24-B
thirty 2-8-M;
2-23-M
thirty-two 3-17-M
this 1-25-G;
2-23-R
thorax 5-16-S
thorn 2-20-B;
3-17-S
thorough 5-11-O;
6-7-R
those 2-23-O
though 4-15-G;
5-11-R
thought 3-22-G;
4-11-R
thoughtful 4-19-B

thoughtfulness
5-19-G
thousand 4-9-G;
4-9-M
thread 2-23-O;
3-3-G
threat 3-3-B; 3-7-O
three 1-23-G;
2-20-G; 3-3-R
threw 3-3-B;
4-11-G; 5-16-R
throat 2-23-S; 3-3-B
throne 2-20-B
through 4-13-B;
5-11-G; 6-8-R
throughout 4-28-O
throw 2-4-B; 3-3-G
thumb 2-3-B;
3-24-S; 4-13-R
Thursday 3-16-G
ticket 3-5-O
ticklish 5-24-B
tide 2-11-B; 5-15-S
tied 5-15-S
tiger 2-9-S
tight 3-10-B
timberline 4-3-SS;
4-28-SS; 6-2-SS
time 1-19-G; 3-1-R
timid 5-4-G
tinier 4-30-B
tiny 3-10-O
tired 3-17-B; 4-5-G
tireless 4-29-O
tires 2-20-B
tissue 5-1-S; 5-3-B;
6-1-S; 6-3-O
title 4-26-G
to 1-28-B; 2-32-G;
3-14-R
toad 2-13-S
toast 3-11-O
today 2-6-G; 3-8-R
toe 2-14-SS
toenail 2-31-S
together 3-1-B;
4-27-G
told 2-25-G; 3-9-R
tomato 3-29-O

tomatoes 4-17-G
tomb 4-13-O
tomorrow 3-4-B;
3-24-SS; 4-11-G;
5-16-R
ton 3-4-O
tone 5-3-O
tongue 3-24-S
tonight 3-10-S
too 1-28-B; 2-32-G;
3-14-R; 4-10-R
took 2-21-G;
3-15-R
tool 2-4-SS
tooth 2-23-O;
4-20-R
toothbrush 5-20-S
toothpaste 3-14-SS
top 2-16-R
topic 5-10-G
torn 2-19-O
tornado 4-15-SS;
6-31-G
toss 2-28-O
total 4-25-G
totalitarian 6-1-SS
touch 4-1-O
touchdown 5-20-B;
6-2-R
tough 3-11-B
tourist 4-20-SS;
5-25-O
toward 3-24-B;
4-1-G; 5-1-R
tower 4-9-B
town 4-9-R
towns 3-23-SS
toy 2-9-R; 3-23-R
toys 1-26-B
trace 3-30-S
track 2-21-B
tractor 6-20-G
trade 3-8-SS
trading 5-16-M
traffic 5-10-B
trail 3-8-SS
trailer 3-8-O
train 2-18-G; 3-8-R
trains 2-26-O

trait 6-7-S
traitor 5-25-SS
transmission
6-10-B
transparent 6-19-S
transport 6-11-O
transportation
5-18-SS; 6-11-G
trap 4-11-SS
trapeze 5-3-G
trash 2-22-SS
travel 5-4-R
traveler 4-23-B;
5-25-G
travelers' 4-16-B
trawler 4-23-SS
tray 2-6-O
trays 5-5-B
treason 3-6-O
treasurer 4-23-B
treaties 5-5-SS
treatment 4-19-O
tree 1-18-B; 2-7-G;
2-8-R; 3-3-R
tremendous 5-9-B;
6-1-G
triangle 5-21-G
triangular 5-21-B
trick 2-21-B;
3-10-G
tricycle 5-21-G
tried 3-17-B;
4-15-G; 5-7-R
tries 2-20-B
trimmed 4-5-O;
5-12-O
trimming 4-5-O
trio 4-15-M
trip 2-18-B; 3-5-G
triple 4-26-G
tripod 5-21-B
tripped 2-29-O;
3-18-O
trisect 5-21-O
triumph 6-32-O
tropics 4-6-SS
trot 2-12-G
trouble 3-29-B;
4-26-G

trough 5-13-S
trousers 4-9-O
truck 2-21-G
trucks 2-26-O
true 2-20-O;
3-14-G; 4-10-R
truly 3-29-B;
4-32-G; 5-11-R
trust 3-5-B
truth 3-14-B
try 1-24-B; 2-11-G;
3-10-R
trying 1-27-B;
2-14-B
T-shirt 4-28-G;
5-20-R
tsp. 5-32-B
tube 3-14-O
Tuesday 3-16-G;
4-4-R
tugboat 4-28-SS
tulip 3-14-O
tundra 5-9-SS
tune 3-14-B;
4-10-G
turbulent 6-22-O
turkey 4-24-O
turkeys 5-5-G
turn 3-17-G;
4-24-R
turned 2-25-B
turnpike 5-20-SS
turtle 3-17-B;
4-24-G
twenty 2-8-M
twenty-one
5-20-G
twice 3-30-B
twig 3-10-S
twine 2-10-O
twirl 4-24-B
twist 2-9-O
twitch 3-12-O
two 1-23-G;
2-32-G; 3-14-R
typewriter 4-28-O
typical 6-8-O
typist 5-1-O;
5-25-O

U

ugly 3-4-O
ultimate 6-5-O
umbrella 4-27-B;
    5-9-G; 5-11-O;
    5-13-O
umpire 4-3-G
umpires' 4-16-O
unable 3-32-G
unacceptable 6-25-B
unadventurous
    5-31-G; 6-6-R
unbelievable 6-25-B
unbutton 3-32-B
uncertainty 6-16-G
uncle 2-3-B;
    2-24-G; 4-25-R
uncommon 3-32-O
uncover 3-32-G
undeniable 6-25-G
under 2-3-B
undercover 6-4-O
underdeveloped
    6-4-B
underestimate 6-4-B
underground 6-4-G
underline 3-28-B;
    5-20-O; 6-4-R
underneath 6-4-G
undernourished
    6-6-B
underpass 6-4-R
underpayment
    6-6-R
underpopulated
    6-4-SS
underrated 6-2-B
understand 5-27-G
understandable
    6-28-R
understatement
    6-6-G
understood 6-4-O
underwater 6-4-G
underwear 6-4-R
underweight 6-4-B
undivided 4-32-G
undo 3-32-R

undoubtedly 5-19-B
undying 4-32-B
uneasily 4-32-G
unemotional 5-31-B
unemployment
    4-31-B; 5-19-G
unequal 3-32-O
unexplainable
    6-25-B
unfair 3-32-G
unfaithful 5-19-B
unfitness 4-31-B
unfortunate 5-19-O;
    6-5-O; 6-16-G
unfriendliness
    4-32-B
unfriendly 3-32-B;
    4-31-G; 5-19-R
unhappily 4-32-G;
    5-19-R
unhappiness 4-32-B
unhappy 3-32-G
unhealthy 3-32-S
unhurried 4-32-B
unification 6-10-SS
unique 5-10-B
United States
    3-16-B; 3-29-SS
university 6-15-B
unkind 3-32-B
unkindness 4-31-G
unknown 3-32-O
unlikely 3-32-O;
    4-31-B
unlisted 3-32-O
unload 3-32-B
unlock 3-32-R
unlocked 5-19-R
unluckily 4-32-B;
    5-19-G
unlucky 3-32-G
unobservant 5-31-B
unpack 3-32-R
unpleasant 5-31-O;
    6-16-O; 6-25-G
unpredictable
    6-29-O
unreasonable
    6-25-G

unrecognizable
    6-25-B
unsafe 3-32-R
unsuitable 6-25-G
unsure 3-32-B
untie 3-32-R
untied 4-31-R
until 4-27-G
unusually 5-19-B
up 1-16-G; 2-3-R
uproar 6-22-G
upstairs 3-28-G;
    4-28-R
urban 3-24-SS;
    5-9-SS
urbanization
    6-32-SS
urge 3-31-O
urgent 6-19-G
us 1-16-G; 2-3-R
use 1-21-G;
    3-14-R; 4-21-R
used 2-29-B; 4-5-G
useful 4-29-G
usefulness 4-31-B
useless 4-29-G
using 4-5-G
usually 4-1-B;
    5-1-G

V

vacant 5-24-O;
    6-19-R
vacation 4-1-B;
    5-18-G; 6-32-R
vaccine 3-1-SS;
    5-9-R
vacuole 6-8-S
vacuum 6-8-B
vain 4-7-O; 5-28-O
valiant 6-22-B
valley 5-11-SS
valleys 5-5-B
valuable 5-11-B;
    6-28-G
value 4-10-B;
    5-6-G; 6-3-G
valve 5-6-G; 6-3-R

vane 4-7-O; 5-15-S;
    5-28-O
vanish 5-4-G
vanity 6-15-O
variable 5-9-M
variety 6-32-B
various 5-30-B;
    6-8-O
vegetables 3-31-S
vein 4-7-O; 5-7-S;
    5-15-S; 5-28-O
venture 6-30-B
verb 5-8-R
verdict 6-29-B
verse 5-8-G
version 5-23-B
versus 5-23-B
vertebrae 5-4-S
vertebrate 5-23-B
vertex 5-8-M
vertical 5-8-M;
    5-23-B
very 2-15-G; 3-6-R
veto 5-9-SS
vibrant 6-19-R
vibrate 4-3-SS
vibration 6-10-S
victory 5-13-B;
    6-13-G; 6-32-O
videotape 4-28-O
view 4-10-B; 5-7-R
viewpoint 5-7-SS
vigorous 5-30-O
village 3-31-B;
    4-14-G; 5-6-R
villain 5-4-B;
    6-8-O; 6-17-G
vinegar 5-9-G
violin 4-22-B
virus 6-13-S
visibility 6-12-O
visible 5-1-B;
    6-12-O; 6-28-G
vision 6-12-G
visit 4-6-G; 5-4-R
visitor 4-23-G;
    5-25-R
visor 6-12-B
visual 6-12-O

visualize 6-5-B
visually 6-12-B
vocational 5-30-B
voice 3-23-O
volcano 5-9-R;
    5-13-SS
volcanoes 4-17-B
volleyball 5-20-B
volt 5-9-S
volume 5-6-B;
    5-6-S; 6-3-G
volunteer 6-1-O
vote 3-9-SS
vowel 3-23-B;
    4-9-G
voyage 4-9-B;
    5-6-G; 6-3-R

W

waffle 4-26-B;
    5-13-O; 5-14-O
wage 3-31-O;
    4-14-B
wagon 4-22-R
waist 4-7-B;
    5-15-G; 6-26-R
wait 2-6-B; 3-13-G;
    5-15-S
wake 2-21-G
walk 2-27-G;
    3-22-R
walked 2-25-G
walking 3-22-G
wall 2-28-G
walruses 3-2-B
want 2-14-G;
    3-24-R
wanted 2-25-G
wants 3-2-SS;
    3-13-SS
war 3-25-B
warlord 6-2-SS
warm 3-13-G
warm-blooded
    5-20-S
warn 3-20-O
was 2-14-R
wash 2-22-G; 3-4-R

washable 6-28-R
wasn't 3-21-B;
   4-2-G
wasp 3-13-S
waste 4-7-B;
   5-15-G; 6-26-R
wasteful 4-29-R
watch 3-12-G
watches 3-2-B
water 3-13-G;
   3-13-S
waterfall 4-28-S
Watergate 5-3-SS
watermelon 4-28-B
waterproof 4-28-O;
   5-20-O
wave 2-5-O
wavelength 5-20-S;
   6-2-S
waving 2-30-G
way 2-6-G; 3-13-R;
   3-20-R
we 1-18-G; 3-6-R
weak 4-7-R
wealth 3-7-O
wear 3-26-B;
   5-16-R
weary 3-27-B
weather 2-23-B;
   3-7-G; 3-25-S;
   5-15-S
weave 2-8-SS
web 2-2-S
wedge 3-13-S;
   3-31-S; 4-14-O
Wednesday 3-16-G
week 2-7-O; 4-7-R
weekend 3-28-O;
   4-28-G; 5-20-R
weigh 5-7-R
weight 4-6-B;
   5-7-G; 5-15-S;
   6-8-M
weird 5-7-O;
   6-32-O
welcome 2-7-O
well 3-13-R
we'll 3-21-B; 4-2-G
went 2-1-G; 3-7-R

wept 4-18-G
were 2-9-G;
   2-14-O; 3-13-R
we're 4-2-G
weren't 3-21-G;
   4-2-R
west 2-7-B; 3-5-G
western 4-27-B
wet 2-1-G; 3-7-R
we've 3-21-B; 4-2-B
whale 3-13-G
wharves 5-22-B
what 2-14-G;
   3-13-R
what's 3-21-O;
   4-2-B
wheat 2-8-SS
wheel 3-6-SS;
   3-13-G
wheels 2-7-B
when 1-13-B;
   2-7-G; 3-13-R
whenever 3-13-B;
   3-28-O
where 2-14-B;
   3-13-G; 4-6-R
wherever 5-20-G
whether 3-13-B;
   3-25-S; 5-15-S
which 3-13-G
while 3-13-G
whisper 3-13-B
whistle 3-13-B
white 1-22-B;
   3-13-G
who 2-14-G;
   3-13-R
whole 3-9-B;
   4-15-G; 5-13-R
wholesome 4-28-O
who'll 4-2-O
who's 3-21-O;
   4-7-G; 5-15-R
whose 3-14-O;
   3-24-B; 4-7-G;
   5-15-R
why 2-11-G;
   3-13-R
wide 2-10-B

wider 3-19-B
widest 3-19-B
width 3-13-B
wife 2-24-B
wild 3-10-G
will 1-14-B; 2-28-R
win 2-2-B; 3-5-G
wind 2-9-G; 3-5-S;
   3-13-S; 4-21-R
window 2-13-O
wing 2-10-O
winner 2-1-SS
winning 2-30-B
winter 4-1-R
wire 3-13-B
wise 3-13-B
wish 2-1-G; 3-13-R
wished 2-25-B
wishes 2-26-G;
   3-2-R
with 2-23-R;
   3-24-R
withdrawal 4-28-O
withhold 6-2-G
without 2-31-B
wittiest 4-30-SS
wives 5-22-G
wobble 4-25-S
woke 1-20-B;
   2-12-G; 3-9-R
wolves 5-22-G
woman 3-17-O;
   4-17-G
women 3-20-B;
   4-17-G
women's 5-2-G
won 2-32-M;
   3-20-G
wonder 3-13-B
wonderment
   4-19-O
wondrous 6-32-O
won't 3-21-G;
   4-2-R
wood 3-15-G
wooden 3-15-B;
   4-22-G
woodpecker 3-15-B
wool 3-15-G

word 2-9-B; 3-13-G
wore 3-25-B
work 2-21-G;
   3-4-R; 3-13-S
worker 3-13-SS;
   4-23-R
world 2-15-B;
   3-20-G; 4-1-R
worm 3-29-O
worried 4-30-G
worry 3-1-O
worst 5-1-O
would 2-14-B;
   3-15-G; 4-6-R
wouldn't 3-15-B;
   4-11-G
wound 4-21-O
wrap 3-20-O;
   4-13-R
wrapped 2-29-O;
   4-5-B
wrapping 4-5-B
wreath 3-6-O
wreck 4-13-O
wriggle 4-26-O
wring 4-13-B
wrinkle 4-25-O
wrist 3-10-S;
   4-13-B
write 2-32-B;
   3-4-G; 4-20-R
writer 4-23-G;
   5-25-R
writing 3-18-B;
   4-5-G; 5-11-R
written 3-24-B;
   4-13-G
wrong 3-22-B;
   4-13-G
wrote 3-9-B;
   4-13-G; 5-6-R
wt. (weight) 5-32-O

yard 2-19-B;
   2-20-M; 3-20-G;
   3-29-M
yarn 2-20-SS

yawning 3-22-O
yd. (yard) 5-32-O
year 2-15-B;
   3-27-G; 4-6-R
yell 2-28-B; 3-5-B
yellow 1-22-B;
   3-9-G
yes 1-13-G; 2-1-R;
   2-7-R
yesterday 3-8-B;
   4-27-R
yet 3-5-R
yield 5-7-B; 6-1-O
yodel 5-14-O
yogurt 5-14-O
yoke 2-32-O
yolk 2-32-O
you 1-21-G;
   2-14-R; 4-10-R
you'd 4-2-B
you'll 3-21-B
young 3-24-B;
   4-15-G; 5-13-R
your 2-9-G;
   2-14-O; 3-20-R
you're 4-2-G
yourself 2-15-O;
   3-28-R
yourselves 5-22-B
you've 4-2-B
youth 4-10-B
yr. (year) 5-32-O

zebra 3-20-S
zero 3-9-B;
   4-20-G; 4-27-M
zipped 2-29-B
zipper 3-5-O
zone 2-13-B
zoo 2-1-G; 3-14-R;
   4-10-R
zygote 6-3-S

	GRADE 3	GRADE 4	GRADE 5
...ing	page 36		Unit 16
Associate, Try, Check, Ask			Unit 16
Be a Word Hunter	Unit 1	Unit 1	Unit 1
Easily Confused Words			Unit 28
Look for the Vowels		Unit 27	
Relating Known and Unknown Words			Unit 16
Rhyme for **ie** and **ei**			Unit 7
Rhyming Spelling Strategy	Unit 11		
Same Sound	Unit 11		
Same Spelling Pattern	Unit 11	Units 11, 18	
See, Say, Spell			Unit 11
Similar Meaning		Unit 11	
Similar Words		Unit 11	
Sorting Words	pages 27, 31, 39, 43, 47, 51, 57, 61, 69, 73, 77, 81, 95, 99, 111, 115, 129, 133, 145, 149, 153	pages 31, 35, 39, 57, 61, 69, 73, 77, 95, 99, 111, 115, 119, 125, 129, 141, 145	pages 31, 39, 43, 47, 51, 61, 69, 77, 91, 95, 103, 107, 111, 119, 125, 129, 141, 145
Spelling Is Important	Unit 1	Unit 1	Unit 1
Think of a Rhyming Word	Unit 11	Unit 11	
Unexpected Spellings			Unit 4
Using a Dictionary	Units 4, 20	Units 8, 20	Units 9, 16
Using Spelling Clues/Sayings (mnemonics)	Unit 24	Unit 15	Unit 13
Word Building		Units 31, 32	Units 19, 31
Words Writers Use		Unit 6	
Write, Try, Check	Unit 29		

SPELLING PATTERNS

	GRADE 3	GRADE 4	GRADE 5
Short Vowel Patterns			
short a	Units 5, 8		
short e	Units 5, 6, 7		
short i	Units 5, 10		
short o	Units 5, 9		
short u	Units 5, 15		
Word Beginnings			
per-, pre-, pro-			Unit 17
Word Endings			
-tion, -cian			Unit 18

	GRADE 3	GRADE 4	GRADE 5
Long Vowel Patterns			
long a	Unit 8	Units 3, 4	
long e	Unit 6	Units 3, 4	
long i	Unit 10	Unit 3	
long o	Unit 9	Unit 3	
long u	Unit 14	Units 3, 10	
long vowel pairs		Unit 4	Unit 3
vowel-consonant-**silent e**	Units 8, 9, 10, 14	Unit 3	Unit 3
r-Controlled Vowels			
air, ear, are	Unit 26		
ear, eer	Unit 27		
er, ir, ear			Unit 8
er, ir, ur		Unit 24	
Diphthongs			
ou, ow, oi, oy	Unit 23	Unit 9	
Other Vowels			
u, oo, ou	Unit 15		
o, ou, aw, au, al	Unit 22		
Consonants			
j, gi, ge	Unit 31		
s, ci, ce	Unit 30		
w, wh	Unit 13		
ge, dge		Unit 14	
k sound: **c, k, ck**			Unit 10
Final **Silent e**	Units 8, 9, 10, 14	Unit 3	Units 3, 6
Consonant Blends			
scr, spr, str, thr	Unit 3		
qu, squ		Unit 12	
Consonant Digraphs			
ch, tch	Unit 12		
wh	Unit 13		
Silent Consonants		Unit 13	
Commonly Misspelled Words		Unit 6	Unit 11
WORD STRUCTURE			
Base Words	Units 18, 19, 32, page 96	Units 5, 19, 29, 31, 32	Units 12, 19, 25, 26, 31
Changing **y** to **i**		Units 30, 32	Units 5, 12
Compound Words	Unit 28	Unit 28	Unit 20
Contractions	Unit 21	Unit 2	
Doubling Final Consonants	Units 18, 19	Unit 5	Unit 12
Dropping Final **e**	Units 18, 19	Units 5, 32	Unit 12

	GRADE 3	GRADE 4	GRADE 5
Endings			
an, en, in, on		Unit 22	
al, il		Unit 25	
le		Units 25, 26	
Inflected Forms			
-ed	Unit 18	Units 5, 30, 31, 32	Units 12, 19
-er	Unit 19	Unit 30	
-est	Unit 19	Unit 30	
-ing	Unit 18	Units 5, 31, 32	Units 19, 31
Plurals			
-s, -es	Unit 2		
Changing **y** to **i**		Unit 30	Unit 5
Changing **f** to **v**			Unit 22
Unusual	page 43	Unit 17	
Possessives		Unit 16	Unit 2
Prefixes			
bi–			Units 21, 31
de–			Unit 29
dis–			Units 29, 31
il–			Unit 26
im–			Units 26, 31
in–			Unit 26
ir–			Unit 26
mid–			Units 21, 31
mis–			Units 29, 31
non–			Units 29, 31
pre–		Unit 31	Units 19, 31
re–	Unit 32	Units 31, 32	Units 19, 31
semi–			Units 21, 31
tri–			Unit 21
un–	Unit 32	Units 31, 32	Units 19, 31
Suffixes			
-al			Units 30, 31
-ant			Units 24, 31
-ary			Units 24, 31
-cian			Unit 18
-er		Units 23, 31	Unit 25
-ful		Units 19, 29, 31, 32	Unit 19
-ish			Units 24, 31
-ist			Unit 25

	GRADE 3	GRADE 4	GRADE 5
-less		Units 19, 29, 31	Unit 19
-ly		Units 19, 29, 30, 31, 32	Units 19, 31
-ment		Units 19, 29, 31	Units 19, 31
-ness		Units 19, 29, 30, 31, 32	Unit 19
-or		Unit 23	Unit 25
-ous			Units 30, 31
-tion, -cian			Unit 18
Word Roots			
cent			page 115
meter			Unit 23
serv			page T133
sta			Unit 27
vers, vert			page T115

<h2>BUILDING VOCABULARY and WORD STUDY</h2>

	GRADE 3	GRADE 4	GRADE 5
Abbreviations			Unit 32
Antonyms	page 153		
Borrowed English Words		page 137	
British and American English		page 145	page 73
Building Words		Units 31, 32	Units 19, 23, 27, 31
Changes in Meaning	pages 27, 65, 115	pages 51, 65, 99, 153	pages 91, 137
Changes in Pronunciation	pages 73, 111	page 73	page 129
Changes in Spelling	pages 47, 115, 129	pages 57, 65, 69, 85, 153	page 129
Clipped Words	page 39		
Eponyms/Words From Names	page 85		page 145
Exact Words	page 35		page 43
Homographs		Unit 21	
Homophones	Unit 25	page 27, Unit 7	Unit 15
Idioms	page 141	page 111	pages 51, 111, 141
Invented Words/Coined Words		page 107	page 103
Meanings of Prefixes			pages 99, 107
Multiple Meanings	pages 61, 104, 115, 149	Units 10, 21, page 115	pages 39, 133
Native American Words			page 61
Near Synonyms		page 129	
Portmanteau Words			page 57
Related Words	pages 51, 91		pages 95, 119
Root Words			page 115
Spelling Rhyme	page 40		page 47
Suffix **-er**	page 99		
Suffixes **-er, -or**		page 23	

	GRADE 3	GRADE 4	GRADE 5
BUILDING VOCABULARY and WORD STUDY continued			
Unexpected Spellings		page 43	Unit 4
Unusual Plurals	page 43		
Word Histories	pages 27, 31, 65, 69, 81, 95, 103, 107, 119, 125, 137, 145	pages 31, 35, 39, 43, 47, 51, 57, 65, 69, 73, 77, 81, 85, 91, 95, 99, 119, 125, 133, 141, 149, 153	pages 35, 65, 69, 81, 85, 107, 115, 119, 125, 137, 149, 153
Word Hunting	page 23	page 23	page 23
Words From Greek	pages 77, 137		pages 35, 77, 85, 145
Words From Latin	pages 137, 145	pages 95, 133	pages 27, 35, 69, 81, 85, 91, 95, 149
Words From Other Languages	pages 57, 133	pages 91, 103	page 31, Unit 14
PROOFREADING			
Proofread your writing and the writing of others for:			
-al, -ous endings			page 147
-ant, -ary, -ish			page 121
bi-, tri-, mid-, semi-			page 109
capital letters	page 87		
compound words		page 139	page 105
-de, -dis, -mis, -non			page 143
en, in, on, an		page 113	
er, est endings	page 101		
ge, dge		page 79	
homographs		page 109	
homophones			page 83
-il, -im, -in, -ir			page 131
j, gi, ge	page 151		
-le endings		page 131	
long vowel pairs		page 37	
misspelled contractions		page 29	
misspelled homophones		page 49	
misspelled possessives		page 87	
misspelled words	pages 23, 37, 41, 45, 59, 67, 82, 83, 87, Unit 17, pages 91, 92, 101, 105, 117, 121, 131, 143	Unit 1, pages 25, 45, 53, 67, 83, 97, 105, 135	pages 25, 37, 59, 67, 75, 79, 87, 139, 155
o, ou, aw, au, al	page 113		
ou, ow, oi, oy	page 117	page 59	

	GRADE 3	GRADE 4	GRADE 5
per, pre, pro			page 93
possessives			page 29
prefixes, suffixes		pages 151, 155	pages 101, 131
qu, squ		page 71	
r-controlled vowels	pages 131, 135	page 131	
s, ci, ce	page 147		
scr, spr, str, thr	page 33		
short a, long a	page 53		
short e, long e	page 45		
short i, long i	page 63		
short o, long o	page 59		
short vowel sounds	page 41		
silent e			page 45
suffixes **-ful, -less, -ly, -ment, -ness**		page 143	
un-, re-	page 155		
unusual plurals		page 93	
w, wh	page 75		
word root **meter**			page 1
word root **sta**			page 135
y changing to **i** (plurals)			page 41

WORD HUNTING is an essential part of the spelling process that happens in every

WRITING IDEAS

	GRADE 3	GRADE 4	GRADE 5
Ads	page 83	pages 67, 151	
Advice Column			
Book Review	page 97		
Business Letter			
Cartoon		page 105	
Common Phrases			
Compare/Contrast	pages 101,		
Descriptions	pages 135, 155	page	
Dialogue			
Draw a Map	page 53		
Draw Pictures	pages 29, 105	page 97	
E-mail Messages		page 45	
Essay			
Explanation			
Expressive Paragraphs	pages 41, 87, 93, 139, 155	pages 63, 71,	
Expressive Stories	pages 45, 147, 151	pages 25, 53, 87, 113	page 59
Flier			

	GRADE 3	GRADE 4	GRADE 5
WRITING IDEAS continued			
Friendly Letters	pages 25, 37, 121	page 127	
Health Tips	page 49		pages 49, 113
How to/Directions	pages 53, 113	pages 49, 59, 75	pages 33, 139, 155
Informative Paragraphs	pages 29, 33, 67	page 29	page 101
Interviews	page 75		
Invitation			page 29
Job Descriptions			page 97
Joke			page 83
Journal Entries	page 117	page 41	page 71
Letters	pages 25, 37, 79, 121	pages 33, 127, 135	pages 29, 151
Lists	pages 33, 109, 113, 147	pages 29, 49, 121	pages 37, 49, 75, 105, 115, 139, 155
Math Problem	page 143		
Newspaper Notice			page 25
News Story			page 67
Personal Narrative	page 87		
Personal Travel Guide			page 105
Persuasive Paragraphs	page 97	page 109	pages 25, 71
Picture Captions	page 127		
Play			page 135
Poems	pages 63, 131	pages 37, 131	page 79
Postcards	page 105	page 97	
Poster			page 143
Report	page 71		
Reviews		page 83	page 147
Riddles	page 59		
Science Fiction Story			page 131
Slogans		page 139	
Speech		page 155	
Tongue Twisters		page 93	
TV Commercial	page 83		
ABBREVIATIONS			Unit 32
CAPITAL LETTERS	Unit 16		Unit 32
DICTIONARY SKILLS			
Easily Confused Words		Unit 8	
Finding Other Forms of Entry Words		Unit 20	
Guide Words	Unit 4		

	GRADE 3	GRADE 4	GRADE 5
How to Use a Dictionary	page 176 (hardbound) page 179 (softbound)	page 176 (hardbound) page 179 (softbound)	page 176 (hardbound) page 179 (softbound)
Multiple Meanings	Unit 20		
Spellings, Word Meanings, Word History			
Syllabication		Unit 27	Unit 4
STANDARDIZED TEST-TAKING SKILLS	pages 33, 53, 63, 75, 93, 105, 113, 135, 143, 155	pages 25, 37, 49, 59, 67, 83, 97, 113, 135, 151	pages 37, 53, 67, 83, 93, 121, 131, 147
SPELLING AND HANDWRITING	page 158	page 158	page 158